Contents

PART TWO

What Christianity Still Can Give

Acknowledgements

My thanks are due to those members of the clergy and others involved with the churches and the practice of faith in England who were willing to speak to me in the course of my research.

The parish, congregation and volunteers of my home church of St Michael's, Shute, in Devon, and its daughter chapel, St Mary-at-the-Cross, Whitford, have been a constant inspiration with their quiet dedication.

I would also particularly like to thank for their help and offers of help Joe and Clem Watson, Celia Pilkington, James Breen, Julie Lomas, John Lees, Peter Lea Cox, Norman Doe, Malcolm Brown, Alison Milbank, Charles Vyvyan, Rose Van Orden, Kate Hayward, Andrew Heavens, Paul Avis, Gareth Mann, Ayla Lepine, James Mumford, Mark Vernon, Ginnie Luckett, Joshua Bennett, Rakib Ehsan, Sebastian Jones, John Hawke, Mark Hatcher, Robin Griffith-Jones, Nico Stone, Alex Chula, Susan Owens, Stephen Calloway, Carley Franke and especially George Owers.

I am particularly grateful to the team at Forum for their hard work in the publication of this book: Julie Gunz, Lucie Ewin, Robin Baird-Smith, Mark Richards, and Matthew Burne for the cover. My thanks also to my publicist, Ruth Killick, and my agent, Kelly Falconer, without whose unstinting support and vision this book would never have been completed.

My thanks also to my family for their enduring love and support, again without which I would never have finished this work: Jane, Jason, Danesh, Prim, Michael, Judy, Cassian and Beatrix (seek, and ye shall find), and Sam, who has borne very patiently the chaos of books and a writer in the house. And thanks also to Clovis, who has made sure I don't spend too much time in front of the computer screen.

Introduction

Debt to a Dying God

Christianity is dying in England. In this generation, the religion that has defined the spiritual life, identity and culture of the country since its origins as a unified state in the tenth century has come into its death agony. The statistics tell a stark and unambiguous story. The 2017 Social Attitudes Survey found that 53 per cent of British adults had no religious affiliation, up from 48 per cent in 2015, and 31 per cent in 1983. Of 18–24-year-olds, almost three in four said they had no religion, and only 3 per cent described themselves as Anglican.[1] The 2021 census found that only 46.2 per cent of people in England and Wales identified themselves as Christians, down from 59.3 per cent ten years previously.[2] Regular Sunday church attendance has fallen from 1.2 million in 1987 to 685,000 in 2023. Between 2000 and 2024, 641 churches were closed and between 2016 and 2021, 278 parishes were amalgamated.[3] Recent projections suggest that, at current rates, Christian church congregations will vanish by the 2060s.[4]

The death of Christianity in England represents a change far more profound than anything like Brexit. The British membership of the European Union and its predecessors lasted for a little short of 50 years, and its practical effect for the most part was confined to trade, commerce and the movement of people. The presence of Christianity, by contrast, reaches back to before the emergence of England as a country, and has been a lodestar in the development of nearly every facet of English life – its language, law, literature, calendar, spirituality, the very existence of the nation itself.

Despite this, Christianity's disappearance is being accepted with little consideration or debate. The ebbing away of the faith is greeted with barely a fraction of the passion which accompanied Brexit. Many treat the end of Christian observance as an unremarkable inevitability in an age of technology, diversity and democratic emancipation. When the trend does receive attention, it is often seen as a good thing. Christianity, so say the commentators who discuss it, was a disaster. They blame it for a host of crimes, from the destruction of Classical and pagan heritage, to the stifling of free speech and scientific investigation, a series of religious wars, the Inquisition, the burning of witches, the repression of women, the support of slavery and endemic sexual abuse. 'Christianity is so closely tied up with issues of nationalism, whiteness and privilege in England that it's impossible to separate them', said an article in the *Independent* following the publication of the 2021 census figures. The decline in Christianity 'doesn't mean a decline in morality but could reflect a more critical approach to "traditional" knowledge that's previously gone unquestioned. That's something to celebrate, not to lament.'[5]

Given its fundamental role in England's past, the future of Christianity in England deserves a far more engaged and informed debate. Such a debate, to consider the future, needs to be based on a more measured assessment of the way in which Christianity has contributed to the formation of so much of English life up to the present. It also needs to be more open to the possibility, contrary to the tendency of present discourse, that Christianity's influence has not been entirely malign.

This book is intended to encourage and contribute to the debate, first by laying out as clearly as possible the multifarious and fundamental ways in which Christianity has contributed to English life and culture. Tom Holland, in his seminal work *Dominion: The Making of the Western Mind* (2019), powerfully made the case that many European ideas now thought non-religious and universal, for example secularism, liberalism, feminism and even Marxist ideologies and revolution, were ultimately derived from Christian thinking. I hope to take this approach further by applying it to English ideas and institutions, making clear how many of them owe their genesis or character specifically to Christianity. The origins of English kingship, the very idea of English nationhood, the rule of law,

English law generally, education, spirituality, notions of ethics, charity, tolerance and public duty all have their roots in Christian doctrine, and English culture – the arts, landscape, language, literature, music, social life – would be unrecognisable without the Christian leaven.

The second part of this book begins by examining how Christianity, in the twentieth century and the 1960s in particular, started to decline in a way that was entirely without precedent. It then asks if, despite this decline, Christianity in the twenty-first century has anything left to give. Can it, and should it, play any role in a modern notion of English national identity? Is its decline a matter for concern, or even a danger? Does it offer any benefit in terms of cohesion as an established religion, particularly given England's contemporary multifaith and multicultural situation? Is there any merit in it as a moral guide for the modern age? And does it have a valid spiritual offering in a time where science, technology and a restless media culture have fostered a climate of scepticism?

In a work with such wide-ranging ambitions, there will inevitably be omissions. The greatest is that the work is only able to deal with England rather than the whole United Kingdom. This is, if anything, out of respect for the different nations in the Union. Whilst there is much in common between England, Scotland, Wales and Northern Ireland (and Ireland before it) in terms of the impact of Christianity upon them, in each case there are also considerable and intricate differences in its influence and development on their respective cultures and institutions, and I felt unable to do justice to the distinctiveness of each nation in one book alone.[6] There is, however, merit in looking at England alone, given the increased level of devolution since the 1990s and the impact this has had on English national consciousness. I would also hope, whilst the experience of every nation in the UK is different, that there is enough in the way of shared experience to make the book of interest to those beyond England itself – and, indeed, such shared experience extends beyond the shores of the UK to wherever there was an English imperial or cultural presence, whether the USA or the English-speaking Commonwealth with the shared inheritance of the Common Law, education and literature.

Another omission is that, as I have chosen to focus on England itself, I have not been able to cover the work of missionaries sent from Britain around the world and the inestimable contribution they made to humanitarian development. I have covered the domestic campaign motivated by evangelical Christianity for the abolition of slavery, but not the extraordinary self-sacrifice made on the ground in Africa and elsewhere by nineteenth-century missionaries and sailors to root out the trade.[7] My focus on England has also meant leaving aside global responses to English Christian culture, particularly the King James Bible and its associated literature;[8] indeed, such is the debt of domestic English literature and art to the Bible and Christian thought that it has been only possible to scratch the surface on these points. These grand subjects deserve their own books, but at least here is a start.

Shakespeare's Mark Antony said of the dead Caesar: 'The evil that men do lives after them; The good is oft interred with their bones.'[9] I hope here not just to disinter some of that now-forgotten good, but also to suggest, with the Prophet Ezekiel,* that these dry bones might just still live.

* See Ezekiel 37.

PART ONE

What England Owes Christianity

I

The Land of Angels

This royal throne of kings, this sceptered isle . . .
This earth, this realm, this England[1]

AD 597

Forty men in a boat are crossing the English Channel. They are heading for the Isle of Thanet, the easternmost tip of the Anglo-Saxon kingdom of Kent. Their boat is laden with treasures, but the men are simply dressed, in rough, drab woollen tunics. Never before have they been this far north, and they are all, to a man, terrified.

Their journey had begun in Rome, as a mission instigated by Pope Gregory, the Bishop of Rome. The idea for it, so they heard, had come to Gregory one day in the city's marketplace. It had been a busy day there, and some new merchants had arrived with a particularly fine cargo of slaves. These had caught Gregory's eye: a group of boys, fair-skinned, with beautiful faces and hair.

He asked where they were from. Britain, he was told. Were they Christians? No, they were not. Gregory sighed at the news. 'How can the Author of Darkness possess those with such fair faces?' he exclaimed. 'What', he then asked, 'is the name of their people?' They were Angles. 'Not *Angles*, but *Angels*', he replied in a flash. Pope Gregory could never resist a bad pun. 'They have angels' faces, and they ought to have a share with the angels in heaven. Which part of Britain are they from?' A northern province, they said, called Deira. 'A good name', said Gregory, warming to his theme. 'They will be saved from the *ire* of God. What,' he went on, 'is the name of their king?' It was Aella. This clinched it for Gregory. 'Alleluia! The praise of God the Creator must be sounded in those parts.'[2]

This exchange of bad jokes had taken place before Gregory became pope. It had put in his mind the idea that Britain, that distant island beyond the sea, should be won for Roman Christianity. As an ordinary monk, he had asked to be allowed to undertake this challenge but was not given permission to do so. Now he had obtained the papacy, he was finally determined to make it happen. So it was that the 40 men now found themselves on the boat sailing to Thanet. Gregory had rounded them up in Rome and ordered them to make the journey to convert the island of Britain. He himself would not be travelling but would be supporting them with his prayers and devotions.[3]

Many of these 40 men were monks, plucked from a monastery that Gregory had founded in the heart of Rome. It was a pleasant place. It had been converted from a grand house which had once belonged to Gregory's family, and which overlooked the city from the heights of the Caelian Hill. Now they had been forced to leave this agreeable spot to make a perilous journey across Europe, from which many of them knew they would never return. The further they went from Rome, the greater their fear and discontent. By the time that they had reached Provence, they rebelled. It was a ridiculous enterprise. The people in Britain were savages, barbarians, unbelievers. What good could a mission such as theirs possibly achieve? They didn't even speak the language there. Much better that they just turn around and go home.

They sent Augustine, the leader of the mission, back to Rome to beg that they be allowed to return. Pope Gregory gave him short shrift.

> It would have been much better not to begin something, than to start it and let whatever is going on in your mind turn you back ... You must complete the work you have started, with the help of God. Do not let the exhausting journey or whatever the backbiters say deter you ... After your great labour, the greater glory of an eternal reward will follow ...[4]

If the lure of the reward in heaven was not enough, Gregory also wrote to his colleague in Provence, the Bishop of Arles, with a veiled request to keep a close eye on the members of the mission.[5]

And so, without any choice, the 40 men made their way northwards across France towards the Channel coast, picking up a few interpreters en route. Yet, by the time the coast of Thanet had finally come into view, perhaps their fears began gently to subside. When they had started their journey, they may well have heard stories of Britain being a miserable and perilous wreck. It was once, they knew, a prosperous province of the Roman Empire. Now it was in ruins, torn apart by a vicious horde of barbaric and squabbling warlords who proudly claimed descent from a rabble of Germanic mercenaries, not to mention the occasional pagan god. However, as they sighted the chalk cliffs of Kent, things might well have taken on a different complexion. Instead of poverty and wretched desolation, they could see that Thanet, at least, was a bustling, energetic place, full of noise and activity.[6] Smoke rose from the fires of kilns, and bales of wool were hauled along the streets. There was the clatter of loom weights, the cry of hunting dogs, the shouting and chatter of sailors and merchants. Other boats, laden with merchandise, were also making for land. On the shoreline, little rows of neat wooden houses clustered near docks, where traders were waiting to inspect the new goods that had arrived, to make deals, and to hear news from the continent. They pass from hand to hand a selection of wares that may well have astonished the visitors from Rome: amphorae, Byzantine pottery, jewellery and glassware from the Mediterranean south. What could these barbarians possibly want with the luxury goods of high European living?

The interpreters would also doubtless have told the Roman missionaries that their old stereotypes of Britain were a little wide of the mark, at least in the south-east. Aethelbert, the ruler of Kent, to whose kingdom they were travelling, was not to be treated as insignificant. He had pushed the frontiers of his power far north across the island so that he now controlled around a third of it, up to the River Humber. The kingdom of Kent also faced the Merovingian kingdom of the Franks. Here, the old Roman traditions of civic life and trade had, to an extent, persisted, and some of that continental sophistication had rubbed off on the British side. It was not just in trade that Britain was connected to the continent. Aethelbert had married a Merovingian princess, Bertha. She was a Christian, like any other member of the Merovingian royal family, and Aethelbert had allowed her to continue practising her faith after their marriage, even allowing a Merovingian bishop to take up residence as her personal chaplain.[7]

When Augustine and his companions arrived on the island, their reception was mixed. Augustine immediately sent a message to Aethelbert to announce that he had arrived from Rome with very good news: that anyone who obeyed him would have everlasting joy in heaven, and a kingdom without end with the true and living God. Aethelbert's response to this offer was not one of unalloyed warmth. He ordered that the 40 travellers should be provided with food and lodging, but that they should not be allowed to come onto the mainland. They would have to wait on Thanet for Aethelbert to visit and decide what to do with them.[8]

The king kept them waiting several days. As they waited, perhaps they began to reflect again on how quixotic this entire mission was. Aethelbert already knew about Christianity through Bertha and her chaplain. And yet he had shown no desire to take up his wife's religion, nor to allow it to be spread amongst his people. What good would their mission do, when Aethelbert already knew about Christianity but had shown no interest in it? Augustine may have believed that the king could be won over by God's grace. Yet, Augustine might also have had serious doubts about what benefits – in terms of this life on earth – he could offer Aethelbert to convert him. Aethelbert was already a powerful ruler, at least in British terms, who claimed descent from a pagan god. Why, in his right mind, would he want to do away with his native traditions from this apparent position of strength?

When Aethelbert finally turned up, his suspicion of the delegation was obvious. He refused to meet them indoors. He feared that they might have some powers of sorcery which they would use to overcome him, and believed that these could be counteracted by remaining outside.

Whether because of this precaution or not, they were unable to win him over. They brought out their treasures before him – a cross of silver and a painted icon of Christ. They then sang prayers in Latin in the plainsong style they knew from Rome, beseeching God for their salvation, and the salvation of Aethelbert. When, finally, they had explained the message of their faith to the king and his household, his response was aloof: 'The words and promises you bring are attractive. But they are also new and uncertain. And so, I cannot just sign up to them, and leave behind all of those customs and beliefs which I have kept for such a long time with the whole of the people of the Angles.'[9]

There was, however, a ray of light. The king acknowledged that the travellers had come a long way, and that they were sincere in wishing to share knowledge of a religion which they believed to be true. He therefore gave them permission to remain, and offered them board and lodging in Canterbury, his capital. He would also not stand in their way if they wished to preach to the ordinary people.

If the travellers had hoped that their lack of success in converting the king would have been rewarded with a return to their pleasant monastery on the hills overlooking Rome in its Mediterranean warmth, they were to be sorely disappointed. Canterbury, to be sure, was an old Roman city, but its monumental buildings from the age of empire – the theatre, temples and fine houses – were all in ruins, and must have presented Augustine and his companions with a forbidding prospect. As they approached the remains of the city which was to become their new home, it is recorded that they sang a verse from the Book of Daniel that was reserved for times of distress: 'We beseech Thee, Lord, in all Thy mercy, that Thy fury and anger may be taken from this city and from Thy holy house, because we have sinned.'[10] And as they sang and prepared to take up residence in the wreckage of an ancient city so far from their homeland, surrounded by a people whose goodwill was far from assured, they must have asked themselves again: 'What earthly gift can we possibly offer the king of this place that will make him heed our message? What worldly benefit can we give to a king who already seems to be pre-eminent in power?'

The answer was more than Augustine or his companions could possibly imagine. It lies in the very nature of English kingship.

* * *

Aethelbert was a king. Although we rightfully call him King Aethelbert, the word 'king' has here an extraordinary delusional power. In the 1400 years since his time, the form of the word in the English language has hardly changed. Aethelbert would have used the Old English word *cyning*. Yet, over the centuries since then, the word has accrued a host of associations which it is almost impossible to escape.

Say the word 'king', and what comes to mind? First, perhaps the king on a throne, wearing a crown, surrounded by lords, knights and churchmen. It is an image that is easy to evoke, whether from news reports of the latest State Opening of Parliament, Pathé footage of twentieth-century coronations at Westminster Abbey, or Holbein's paintings of the Tudor court. In these tableaux, there is an order which seems completely self-evident. The king is the centre of attention. Power and authority radiate from his person. It is his to command, and his to make laws. He is the dispenser of gifts and the demander of tribute. All others around him are dependent, and wait on his pleasure. He is a protector, the father of his people. His robes, his sceptre and crown (surmounted by a cross) speak of not just his temporal authority, but something of his holiness. He is an anointed one, and his power comes not just through wealth or military might, but because he is sacred. The king is a nexus between the earth and the divine, and sanctity emanates from him. It is this holiness, if anything, which generates the cosmic order of which he is at the heart.

Such is the power of the word 'king', that when we call Aethelbert or his other early Anglo-Saxon contemporaries by that title, it is difficult to escape the assumption that this was also their experience of kingship. One automatically imagines that they, being kings, enjoyed the authority, prestige and sanctity that much later monarchs possessed. One also imagines that the people around them had the same understanding of kingship, and that they would offer the same deference to these early kings on the grounds that they were not just powerful, but also sacred. A further assumption is that those around the king believed themselves to be one people, unified in identity under his rule.

All of these assumptions have to be forgotten. If we want to understand what extraordinary earthly gifts Augustine was able to offer to Aethelbert and his English successors, we have to grasp how scanty a thing kingship was at this time. It was not just that they had a 'hollow crown'; there was simply no crown at all.

* * *

What did it mean to be an Anglo-Saxon king in the time of Aethelbert? To understand this, we should briefly trace, as best we can, the history of the British isles from the end of Roman power up to Aethelbert's own reign.

It is not an easy task to unravel this history. The written sources are meagre and unreliable. The archaeological evidence, moreover, can only take us so far, and, like the written evidence, is open to various interpretations. To a certain extent, scholars have to rely on conjecture to fill out the picture. Discussions about the period can often be heated, especially since recent scholarship has challenged and overturned long-held ideas about this foundational time in English history. With all these caveats, it is still possible to give a not-too-contentious account of this era that will allow us to approach the question of the rise of English kingship.

In the first half of the fourth century AD, Britain was a prosperous part of the Roman Empire. The Empire had managed to recover from a host of problems in the middle of the previous century, and in Britain a whole slew of opulent new country villas built by the Romano-British aristocratic class was a result of the province's restored wealth and stability.

One sign of Britain's prosperity, aside from the villas which date to this period, was the interest that pirates and raiders had in attacking the coastline. It was well known beyond the Empire's frontiers that Britain was a rich place and thus a ready source of plunder. At around this time, a whole series of imposing forts were constructed at strategic coastal locations, including Richborough, Pevensey and Portchester, to ward off the menace of Germanic ship-borne attack. Similarly, the fortifications of Hadrian's Wall were also strengthened against an increase in forays made by the Picts.[11]

These attacks meant that a strong military garrison had to be maintained in Britain. Paradoxically, although the attacks caused disruption, the fact that they ensured the continuing presence of a not insubstantial army contributed greatly to the province's prosperity. Aside from agricultural wealth, it appears that much of Britain's commerce was dependent on the service of the Roman armed forces. Another important factor in British prosperity was the close proximity of supreme Roman power. The western emperor, for long periods, was resident in the city of Trier (on the modern-day border of Germany and Luxembourg) and it was easy for Romano-British aristocrats to approach him to seek favours, offices and lucrative patronage.[12]

In the last quarter of the fourth century, this order began to collapse. In 376, the Roman Empire suffered a disastrous defeat at the Battle of Adrianople (in modern-day Turkey), caused by the mishandling of an influx of Gothic migrants into the Empire. The Roman Emperor Valens was killed, and around 20,000 Roman soldiers – two-thirds of the army on the battlefield – also fell. In the aftermath, Roman garrisons further west on the Rhine frontier were run down to provide extra manpower in the east. As the Rhine frontier grew less stable, the western emperors moved their seat to the Italian heartland, firstly Milan, and later Ravenna.

These changes hit Britain hard. The running down of the Rhine frontier garrison curtailed British exports of grain, and perhaps other commodities, to the continent. The withdrawal of the western emperor further into Italy also made it difficult for British aristocrats to benefit from imperial patronage and favour. This absence of imperial power provoked usurpers to revolt. Such revolts were not designed to throw off the Roman yoke, but to ensure that an executive imperial presence, with all the economic benefits it brought, remained near the British periphery.

However, they were ultimately futile and self-defeating. The first revolt by a British-based commander, Magnus Maximus in 383, led to large portions of the British garrison being shipped to the continent to fight in the resulting civil war. These soldiers, it seems, were never replaced. Their disappearance went hand in hand with an economic decline. Aristocrats started to abandon their villas, and there are also signs that the towns began to empty. This may have been down to a lack of military protection, making raids against these targets easier. It might also be the case that the decline in the number of soldiers led to the evaporation of most commercial activity.[13]

The economic chaos in Britain can particularly be seen in the coinage record. After Maximus's departure, coins were no longer minted in London, and the province relied on shipments of coin from the continent for the payment of the remaining soldiers. However, after the western imperial capital moved from Milan to Ravenna in 402, these shipments also ceased. Nearly all of the Roman coinage recovered from this period shows signs of clipping, where the edges of existing coins are shaved off and the silver recovered from this is turned into new coins.[14]

This scarcity of coinage is likely to have been a primary reason behind further revolts in Britain after 407. Soldiers had likely been unpaid for several years, or paid with inadequate clipped coinage. Their frustration led to uprisings where they again attempted to have their own candidates established as emperor in the local vicinity, in order to restart the economic flows and connections on which the military and economic infrastructure of the province was based. However, these actions further aggravated the effects of the earlier revolts. British usurpers by around 410 had stripped the province of the final remaining Roman detachments, who were used to fight in civil conflicts on the continent, as well as against incursions of migrants from beyond the frontier.

The final withdrawal of Roman troops from Britain had an immediate impact. Around 408, there was a substantial attack by Germanic seaborne raiders. Shortly afterwards, according to the Greek-speaking historian Zosimus who wrote in Constantinople in the sixth century, the British 'revolted from Roman rule' to 'live on their own, no longer obedient to Roman laws'. The British, he says, 'armed themselves and ran many risks to ensure their own safety, and freed their cities from attacking barbarians'.[15]

Zosimus's characterisation of this situation as a British 'revolt' needs to be carefully understood. It is not that there was any desire to secede from the Roman Empire. Rather, it was a fundamental principle of the Empire that civilians should not bear arms. Yet, in this case, with the army absent and unwilling to assist against the Germanic and Pictish attacks, the British civilians had no choice but to flout these rules and take up arms to defend themselves. However, their decision to do so made them rebels and secessionists in the eyes of the Roman authorities. In the circumstances, there was no benefit for the province in even attempting to show obedience to the Roman state or collect taxes, when it could not fulfil the most basic function of upholding security. As a result, says Zosimus, the British 'expelled the Roman magistrates and established the government they wanted'.[16]

Zosimus's statement that the British had set up a government of their own choosing sounds like a positive and confident step. The reality was very different. The years after 410, with Britain's final disconnection from the Roman Empire, saw a precipitous economic and social collapse. Towns and villas were abandoned. Money and valuables were buried. Long-established industries producing the necessaries of life evaporated. Good-quality pottery was no longer to be found. Common metal goods, even nails, also disappeared. The rapid desertion of the towns and villas, along with the breakdown of industries and trade networks, must have meant that food and basic goods were in short supply. Many people within the province would have been displaced, on the move in the search for food and shelter. It is inevitable that this economic collapse would have been marked by famine and violence, leading to widespread early mortality.[17]

This chaos was mercilessly exploited by pirates and raiders. A small number of fifth-century sources written on the continent shine a light on the situation. Around 429, a bishop, St Germanus of Auxerre, visited Britain to investigate a charge of heresy amongst Romano-British Christians, but upon arriving found himself having to lead a defence of one of the communities against an attack of seaborne marauders and Picts. The British community, reveals the biographer of Germanus writing in about 480, 'judged their resources to be utterly unequal to the contest.' Another writer, Sidonius Apollinaris, Bishop of Clermont-Ferrand, alluded several times in his letters to 'the Saxon pirate, who deems it sport to furrow in British waters with his hides, cleaving the blue sea in a stitched boat.' They were, he said, 'the most ferocious of all foes,' who 'come down on you without warning. When you expect his attack he slips away. Resistance only moves him to contempt. A rash opponent is soon down.' Movable wealth was seized and locals captured to be taken into slavery. According to Sidonius, the greatest horror was that these pagan raiders, whilst sailing homeward, would perform human sacrifice at sea: 'it is their practice . . . to abandon every tenth captive to a watery end . . . .'[18]

In the face of these dangers, the remaining authorities in Britain took the only action they could. They knew that after the departure of the Roman army the remaining population, no matter their willingness, did not have the training and leisure to fight or maintain order. They therefore invited war-bands from amongst the barbarian raiders to act as mercenaries and protect them from further attacks by sea or across the Pictish border.

The first written evidence of this comes from a sixth-century monk named Gildas, who was born somewhere in the Celtic fringes of the British isles, and who wrote an account of the period after moving to Brittany later in life – well over 100 years after these events. His description, even despite the relatively short time he was from the actual events, had accrued much in the way of legend. For example, he claims that the first leaders of the war-bands were called Hengst and Horsa (meaning 'mare' and 'horse') and that they came to Britain in three ships; yet, similar details are found in many other ethnic foundation legends (for example, Romulus and Remus were the two brothers involved in the foundation of Rome).

If one discounts the legendary accretions, and does one's best to assign a credible chronology to events, Gildas offers the following account. The first Germanic war-bands (generally called Saxons) arrived sometime in the second quarter of the fifth century. The deal that the Romano-British had made with them for protection was not unusual at that period. The Western Roman Empire itself in its decline had made similar pacts with war-bands (also led by barbarian commanders) to fight for it and offer protection in the absence of regular troops. In the case of Britain, after a short period the arrangement broke down. The Saxons demanded ever more money and privileges from the Romano-British to carry on protecting them. When these increases were not forthcoming, the Saxons turned against their hosts. Piece by piece, they began to take over Romano-British territory in the southern and eastern parts of Britain.[19]

Further Germanic migrants arrived from the continent throughout the fifth and sixth centuries, adding impetus to this process. Although the Romano-British attempted to resist, occasionally with some success – for example, they won a notable victory at an unknown spot called Mons Badonicus around 500, under the leadership of a noble called Ambrosius Aurelianus, who later became a character in Arthurian legend – by the mid-sixth century they only retained their freedom in the western fringes of the British isles.[20]

In the lands where the Germanic peoples settled, there was general devastation. The traces of four centuries of Roman government had been obliterated. In the words of a later, eighth-century Anglo-Saxon poem, 'The Ruin', which described the crumbling remains of an unknown Roman settlement, 'the work of giants is in decay'. The imperial structures of administration had vanished.* The cities lay in

* Some have argued that (aside from the not infrequent and perhaps surprising persistence of Roman field boundaries), in a small number of cases, there may have been survivals of small post-Roman (i.e. British) territorial entities which were taken over by Germanic mercenaries and migrants, preserving something of the earlier political character of the entity. Such has been suggested for Canterbury, Winchester and York amongst others. However, the evidence is unclear, and even if there were some sort of continuity it would be significant neither in itself, in terms of the extent of political ideas and institutions preserved from earlier times, nor in terms of the wider territorial extent of Anglo-Saxon England where the depth of discontinuity is clear.[21]

ruins. The country villas were abandoned, and their wide estates had fallen to pieces. Traditional education and literacy were nowhere to be found; the books narrating the history of Britain, in Gildas's words, had been burned or carried away. The Christian faith, which had been introduced in Roman times, but perhaps not deeply, only survived in scattered pockets as a folk religion. As for the Romano-British population itself, many would have died, a number would have retreated into the unconquered western regions, but the others who remained appear to have been reduced to the status of slaves.

In this situation, the Germanic incomers did not attempt to base their own ways and society on the remnants of the past. There was either nothing of it left, or nothing that they considered worth saving. Across the Channel, the cities, churches and bishoprics in Roman Gaul and Spain continued in operation, holding wealth and carrying out administrative functions. Partly as a result of this, the barbarian elites who took over these regions adopted the use of Latin and other ideas of government which these institutions preserved. In Britain, there was next to none of this. Latin, and the Celtic languages otherwise spoken by the Romano-British, was supplanted by the use of Germanic languages, as these latter were spoken by the incoming military elite who took control of the land, although these incomers probably made up no more than a quarter of the population. Moreover, the Church and all structures of government having disappeared, there was no attempt by the incomers to base their own ideas of rule on Roman or any other local precedent.[22]

Did these early Germanic migrants to Britain have any kings amongst them? In earlier periods along the Rhine frontier, powerful chieftains certainly emerged whom the Romans described as kings (*reges*). The Romano-British who had been driven back into Wales and the south-west also had a number of powerful rulers in Gildas's time, although Gildas preferred to call them 'tyrants' rather than kings. Despite this, it seems that the newcomers to Britain, certainly until well into the sixth century, had no kings amongst themselves, and little idea of kingship as it later came to be.

The Germanic peoples who migrated to – or invaded – Britain, it appears, did not come in coherent ethnic or tribal groupings, over which a king could rule. Later authors, such as the Venerable Bede, writing in the eighth century, give the impression that large and cohesive groups did enter Britain from defined areas on the continent, and settle together in particular regions. Bede's famous claim was that the Jutes came from the area to the west of Saxony and settled in the Isle of Wight and Kent; the Saxons from 'Old Saxony' gave rise to the kingdoms of the South, East and West Saxons; and the Angles, from an area between the Jutes and Old Saxony, came to populate East Anglia, Mercia and Northumberland. However, Bede's own account is contradictory, and it is not borne out by archaeological evidence. This latter suggests that the Germanic migration was piecemeal. The newcomers came over a long stretch of time, in small and fragmented bands, settling in no particular place. The identities which Bede describes seem to have developed amongst these settlers a considerable time after they arrived.[23]

Not only were there no coherent tribal groupings for kings to rule over before the second quarter of the sixth century; there is simply no sign that anyone before this time bore anything like kingly power amongst the Germanic migrants. The society that they developed was flat. Hierarchy was minimal. There is no evidence of any particular disparity of wealth amongst its members. There are no traces of grand residences, pockets of abundance or overwhelming displays of power which belong to this period. Each incoming family group appears to have procured a small parcel of land (called in Old English a *hiwisc*, or 'hide') sufficient to its needs. These hides appear to have been worked by a combination of Germanic newcomers and slaves or unfree dependants, who may have been descended from the earlier Romano-British population. Around half of the burials excavated from this time contain weapons, and half are without, but none contains any conspicuously rich grave goods which might have signified a royal or commanding status. That half of the population which bore weapons, and were buried with them, would have enjoyed the status of free men, whilst the rest would have been of servile rank. The free men on their hides would likely have been undifferentiated in their power, confining their attentions to their own small plots, rather than one ruling over the other.[24]

By around 570, the situation had started to change. The number of burials furnished with weapons declined suddenly and sharply. However, a fraction of interments became very grand. They included ostentatious grave goods, and were even made under tumuli or barrows – a custom which had not been followed in the British isles since the Bronze Age. Besides this, buildings on a much more substantial scale began to appear. These things are signs that an elite class had started to emerge who were attempting to assert their power over others.[25]

If the Germanic migrants in Britain had lived without kings or an elite class for around a century, what had happened in the sixth century to change their relatively egalitarian society? The best explanation attributes the transformation to a series of climatic disasters. In 536, a huge volcanic eruption in Iceland spewed an enormous amount of dust into the atmosphere, so that for the whole year, as the Byzantine chronicler Procopius recorded, the sun appeared to be 'in eclipse'.[26] The volcano erupted again in 540 and 547. In the ten years after the first eruption, global temperatures plummeted to their lowest since the birth of Christ. The immediate result was widespread crop failures. Shortly afterwards, plague spread across Europe, followed by smallpox. These pandemics are recorded both by Procopius in the Greek east as well as by Irish chroniclers in the far west, so it is practically certain that they also afflicted Britain.

The result of these disasters can only have been famine, along with widespread death and dislocation. Shortages of food are likely to have compelled the hungry and displaced to submit themselves to whichever of their neighbours were faring well enough to guarantee them sustenance. It may be to this time that we owe the origin of the English word 'lord' – from the Old English *hlāf-weard*: 'bread-warder' – the one who keeps the bread.[27]

The earliest English place names come from this period, and they also attest to the way that local strongmen were beginning to project their power over wider groups of dependants. Particularly telling are the place names which end in -ing, -ingham and -tun. For example, Lancing means 'the people of Wlanc'; Birmingham signifies 'the settlement of Beorma's people'; and Islington 'the homestead of Elesa's people'. The appearance of these place names in the latter part of the sixth century points to the rise in influential local leaders as an emerging elite during this time of disorder and upheaval.[28]

Thus, the rise of the early elites was not down to an inherent ideology amongst the Germanic migrants which inclined them to the idea of lordship or hierarchy. It emerged later on through the force of chance, where a series of natural cataclysms compelled society to develop in an unexpected way, giving the opportunity for the strong to dominate the adjacent weak. It was a question of the survival of the fittest. The more prosperous would have compelled their less fortunate neighbours to submit themselves for protection. With this added strength, they could then coerce other rivals to offer tribute and accept a subordinate status. Conflicts would have arisen between neighbouring landholders in the struggle for possessions and influence. In this way, local strongmen began to accumulate land, wealth and followers. And this process of accretion of land, tribute and power was the origin of the earliest kingdoms amongst the Germanic migrants.[29]

The earliest kings rose not thanks to their pedigree or any notion of royal blood. Nor did they owe their position to any concept of the sanctity of kingship or the duty owed to a monarch. They gained their position by personal strength, vigour and daring. Indeed, anyone with the right character and skills of leadership could advance from the lowest status to a position of power. The epitome of this can be seen in the character of Scyld at the very beginning of *Beowulf*, which although written after the eighth century may provide an idea about the early nature and origins of English kingship. Scyld is the founder of a legendary royal family, the Scyldings, but he starts life as an orphan. His rise to eminence is through a trail of violence and charisma. Although at first a waif, who 'Puny and frail ... was found on the shore', says the poet, 'he grew to be great'. He attracted a crowd of loyal followers and led them on forays for plunder, and 'From raiders a-many their mead-halls wrested'. In the end, '... the border-tribes all obeyed his rule, / And sea-folk hardy that sit by the whale-path / Gave him tribute, a good king was he . . .'. Scyld's career of raiding and extracting obedience and tribute from his neighbours as a path to eminence is likely to have been the same route followed by the petty strongmen descended from the Germanic migrants. On such foundations did kingship emerge amongst them.[30]

* * *

This overview of Britain in the fifth and sixth centuries shows the weakness of kingship when it first arose amongst the Germanic migrants. Kingship could be claimed through power and charisma. But beyond these qualities, there was little else to help. The earliest kings had next to nothing of those tools and tricks which later kings took for granted.[31] They were without any indigenous traditions of kingship on which they could model their conduct, or depend upon to demand awe and obedience from their followers. They had no established administration, and no bureaucratic class. They were not accustomed to making laws.[32] Even though later stories about the Anglo-Saxon kings recount a belief that they were descended from the gods, there is no clear evidence that they were seen as sacred, such that their persons were accorded religious awe.[33] On top of this, there was no concept of an enduring ethnic shared identity to which the kings could appeal. Identities would have been fluid and dependent on the local leader, shifting easily when another challenger was able to gain control.

The one thing on which the kings could rely was the power of gift-giving. The loyalty of retainers could be bought with presents, the more showy and opulent the better. For the kings who had access to the greatest abundance of treasures to dispense to prospective followers, the greater was their power likely to grow. As a result, the mere possession of such treasures bestowed power, as much as the giving of them. *Beowulf* again bears witness to the importance of gift-giving and the possession of treasure in the conduct of the early kings. After Beowulf kills the monster Grendel, King Hrothgar rewards him with a 'gold-wove banner, guerdon of triumph,

/ broidered battle-flag, breastplate and helmet; / and a splendid sword was seen of many / borne to the brave one.' With these gifts, Beowulf drank proudly in Hrothgar's mead hall before other warriors, 'for such costly gifts / he suffered no shame in that soldier throng.' In receiving these presents, his own honour and authority were enhanced.[34]

This brings us back to Aethelbert and the early Saxon kings, and the question of what the Christianity brought by Augustine and his fellow missionaries could offer them. In fact, whatever their thoughts of its spiritual merit, in terms of enhancing their rule as kings, Christianity was a gift as potent and ostentatious as any golden breastplate or helmet. As a doctrine, it was a magical artefact that could bring to these petty and transitory warlords on the cold north-western edge of the European continent the authority and prestige of emperors, and which could resurrect the shattered order and civilisation that had been lost with the collapse of Roman society over two centuries previously. It was something that they could offer in their turn to those around them as a gift, which would also give these retainers and subjects access to its glamour and esteem, and garner their loyalty more securely.[35] Thanks to this gift from Pope Gregory and Augustine, Aethelbert and his successors were finally in a position to lay the foundations for the idea of English kingship and the idea of English nationhood.

* * *

It was not that the new presence of Christianity amongst the Germanic peoples was without physical treasures or splendour. Soon after Augustine's arrival, there are records of a string of gifts made from the pope to kings in England. In 601, Pope Gregory wrote to Aethelbert sending what he modestly called 'small presents.'[36] These appear to have included wood from Christ's Cross, a piece of Christ's seamless garment, hair of the Blessed Virgin Mary, and part of the rod of Aaron.[37] Shortly afterwards in 625, there is a record of Pope Boniface sending a cloak made in Ankara and a shirt ornamented with gold to Aethelbert's son-in-law, King Edwin of Northumbria, and to his wife Ethelburga, the daughter of Aethelbert, a silver mirror and a gilded ivory comb, all of which had received a papal blessing.[38] There was also a stream of fine religious paraphernalia – for example illuminated scriptures, paintings, crosses and other relics – that would have been used to adorn the new Christian sites that were constructed at this time.[39]

Yet, these physical treasures were not the greatest assets to the first kings. In Pope Gregory's letter to Aethelbert, as Gregory exhorted the king to spread the Christian message, he reminded him that it was not only by Christ in heaven that he would be blessed for his good deeds and his fame made known to posterity. There was also an important temporal connection that Aethelbert would make in his zeal for the faith: 'For even so the most pious emperor, Constantine, of old, recovering the Roman empire from the false worship of idols, brought it with himself into subjection to Almighty God, our Lord Jesus Christ . . . Whence it followed, that his praises transcended the fame of former princes; and he excelled his predecessors in renown as much as in good works.'[40]

Likewise, in 601 Pope Gregory wrote to Aethelbert's wife, Bertha. He urged her to uphold her husband's fervour for spreading Christianity and, again, he called to mind the example of one of the most famous past members of the Roman imperial family: 'For just as God had inflamed the hearts of Romans to the Christian faith through Helena, mother of the most pious emperor Constantine, to be preserved in memory, so also we trust that His mercy will work for the race of Angles through the zeal of your glory.' It was not just that Bertha's ardour for Christianity would make her similar to Helena. If she were able to inflame Aethelbert's heart for the fullest conversion of his subjects, said Gregory, it would prove the good reputation she had in the very highest imperial circles: 'your good deeds have become known not only to the Romans, who have prayed fervently for your life, but also in various places and up to the most serene prince of Constantinople.'[41] Thus, he claimed, Bertha was well known for her piety even by the emperor of the Eastern Roman Empire, which had survived the collapse of the Roman Empire in the west.

Pope Gregory's letters start to give a new definition to kingship in the British isles. Before, it had been little more than warlordism. Now, Gregory offered new ideas. It was the first duty of a king to be pious. Before anything, his piety was to be expressed in the propagation and protection of the Christian faith. The reward for piety was not just a heavenly treasure, but also glory on earth. That glory came not just in the material treasures which were sent from Rome, but in reputation. No longer were the kings in England who accepted Christianity from the hands of Gregory and Augustine petty warriors with no heritage or standing beyond their passing strength. The mantle of the Christian faith connected them to the past glory of imperial Rome, and made them fit to be spoken of in the same breath as the emperors themselves. Aethelbert was now as the Emperor Constantine the Great, who started the process of Christianising the Roman Empire. Bertha was as Constantine's mother, Helena, a saint who was hailed for her discovery of the relics of the True Cross. The Christianity received from Rome in 597 bridged the gap caused by the collapse of Roman authority in 409. The credit accorded by this connection to Rome and the emperors was powerful. It would be used by the kings to develop their authority, define their role and, in the fullness of time, forge the idea of a unified English people.[42]

Aethelbert and his Christian successors were eager to proclaim their new-found Roman nature as a sign of their growing authority. The missionaries and emissaries who came from Rome after Augustine assisted them in this desire. It was no accident that the churches they built for their mission were distinctively Roman in style. What they created in their churches reflected on the kings, who were their patrons and protectors. The first Anglo-Saxon cathedral in Canterbury was built in the style of the Constantinian basilicas in Rome, with apses at both the eastern and western ends. Its crypt, according to a monk, Eadmer, was made 'in the likeness of St Peter's'.[43] The cathedral itself, like the papal cathedral at the Lateran, was dedicated to Christ the Saviour. Other new churches and monasteries were dedicated to saints closely associated with Rome – St Peter and St Paul, St Pancras, and the Quattuor Coronati (the Four

Crowned Martyrs). Even their placement was used to evoke the geography of Rome and Roman ideas. St Peter and St Paul was intended to include royal and episcopal burials. As Roman custom did not permit burials within the city walls, this foundation was placed outside the walls of Canterbury. Canterbury's St Pancras, like that of Rome, was also placed outside the city walls, but the Church of the Quattuor Coronati, in imitation of Rome, was built within the walls. Similar Roman-style dedications were made in the seventh century in other cities associated with the Roman mission, including London and York.[44]

These Roman connections were enhanced by the gift of Roman relics. Pope Gregory sent relics of the martyred Pope Sixtus II (257–8). Later, in 668, Pope Vitalian sent similar treasures to King Oswiu of Northumbria, who had been brought up as a Christian from an early age, and who had ensured that the Christian rites practised in Northumbria would be carried out in conformity with Roman rather than Irish custom. Amongst other things, Oswiu received relics of St Peter, including a cross and a golden key containing filings from St Peter's chains (to be passed to his queen), and relics of St Laurence, whose martyrdom was said to have led to the conversion of Rome. The Northumbrian nobleman and bishop, St Wilfrid, who visited Rome in the 650s and brought back his own selection of Roman relics, built crypts at his foundations in Hexham and Ripon, which were designed either in imitation of Roman crypts, or else the Roman catacombs.[45]

These churches also zealously maintained a Roman style of liturgy. Canterbury became famous for its chant being done 'according to the Roman manner'. The chanters, trained as they had been by 'the successors of the disciples of St Gregory', were highly sought after for many years after Augustine's mission. Surviving psalters from Canterbury up to the time of the Norman Conquest show a strict adherence to Roman custom, as opposed to other practices that sprung up in France or elsewhere. The personal connection between the Archbishop of Canterbury and the pope in Rome was also emphasised by Gregory's desire that the archbishop should wear a traditional Roman scarf-like garment, the pallium, and that new archbishops should come to Rome to receive it in person from him or his successors.[46]

It was not only the dress of the missionaries or clergy that was Roman in style. Over the seventh century, fashions changed markedly throughout all the Anglo-Saxon kingdoms. Excavations of Anglo-Saxon burials show that the old double brooches that had been used to fasten garments at the shoulders were abandoned. Instead, people had begun to wear a style of dress that was inspired by Christian Rome, often marked by the use of necklaces with a cross at their centre. It is the same style that can be seen worn by Empress Theodora (wife of the Emperor Justinian) and her attendants in the mosaics of San Vitale in Ravenna. It appears that the change in style started from the time of Augustine's mission. Those around Aethelbert and the other Anglo-Saxon kings began to proclaim their Roman tastes. This newly reimported Roman culture was something around which the disparate peoples – Germanic migrants and indigenous British remnants in the territories conquered by the migrants – could unite. Although this culture was seen as Roman, its unifying role was vital and became one of the foundations for the development of a single English identity.[47]

The Anglo-Saxon kings began to follow customs which appeared to be Roman. For example, King Edwin started to process with a banner before him when travelling, in a manner like that of the Roman emperors.[48] However, the presence of Roman Christianity changed the idea of kingship in ways that were more than superficial. Clerical writers, drawing from biblical examples, began to develop concepts of kingship that were fundamentally to shape the behaviour and ideals of the English kings for centuries to come, even if those kings did not always live up to the aspirations that these writers expressed.

One of the most influential authors to write on kingship was the Venerable Bede, who has been briefly mentioned above. He was born around 672, a couple of generations after the death of Aethelbert, and lived until 735. He spent most of his time in the twin monasteries of St Peter and St Paul at Monkwearmouth-Jarrow in the kingdom of Northumbria. He was a monk, scholar and teacher, and had access to one of the most extensive libraries in Europe of the period. His work included not only the *Ecclesiastical History of the English People*, a fundamental source for this period, for which he is regarded as the father of English history, but also various works of biblical scholarship and commentary. Throughout these texts, which were read by contemporary and later kings – and, in the case of the *History*, even translated into English by King Alfred – he scatters his ideas and beliefs as to the essential nature of kingship.

In the mind of Bede, the office of kingship is the same throughout history, no matter whenever or wherever in the world it should be held. Even though he might be commenting on the kings of the Old Testament, for example Saul or David, the qualities expected of them are also those which should be expected of the newly Christian kings in his own age. He even sometimes makes direct comparisons between contemporary kings and biblical texts. The pagan King Aethelfrith of Northumbria, who was a great warrior but 'ignorant of God's religion', calls to Bede's mind the text in Genesis: 'Benjamin is a ravening wolf: in the morning he shall devour his prey, and at night he shall divide the spoil.'[49]

For Bede, kingship was no longer just a matter of brute force and the expression of power, as it had earlier been amongst the Germanic migrants. Morality and sanctity were now to be seen as the foundation of kingship amongst the Anglo-Saxons. The perfect example of a king is Christ, a 'moderate and just ruler'. A good king has the attributes of prudence, fortitude, justice and temperance. Bede's thoughts about kingship were moulded by Pope Gregory's own writings on how a bishop, following the example of Christ, should take care of his flock; for Bede, the relationship between kings and their peoples was similar.[50] Like bishops, kings needed moral qualities, but they also needed to treat kingship as a professional calling. Kings needed to have a special aptitude and training for their position. They also needed to subject themselves to constant self-examination.[51]

In his biblical commentaries, Bede repeatedly praises King Saul for exhibiting humility, for example when he declined to wear regal costume at the beginning of his reign. Such praise is also given to the kings of his own time when they demonstrate this virtue. Oswald, the Christian king of Northumbria, before fighting a battle against a tyrannical British ruler, Caedwalla, helped to put up a wooden cross with his own hands on the battlefield, kneeling in the mud to do so.[52] At another time, on Easter Sunday, he was about to feast off a silver platter when he was told that a large crowd of poor people were in the streets begging. The king immediately not only sent his food to the poor, but also ordered the silver dish to be hacked into pieces and divided amongst them.[53]

King Edwin of Northumbria, in Bede's telling, similarly had consideration for the ordinary people. He kept the peace, so that 'even if a woman should have wished to walk along with a newborn baby over all the island from sea to sea, she might have done so without injury from any'. By the roadside, where there were springs, he ordered posts to be set up and copper drinking vessels hung from them, so that travellers could refresh themselves.[54] With all of these stories, Bede defines how kings should behave and appear to their people.[55] Oswald, 'though raised to the height of regal power ... was always humble, kind, and generous to the poor and to strangers'.[56] Edwin also exemplified another necessary characteristic of kings: the ability to inspire both fear and love amongst his subjects.

Beyond their care for ordinary people, the primary duty of kings had to be the advancement and protection of the Christian faith.[57] Some of the ways in which they were expected to do this were little more than a continuation of their pre-Christian behaviour, for example the violent subjugation of neighbouring rivals in battle. This expectation is seen in the generations even before Bede was writing. An earlier cleric, Aeddi,* writing in the mid-to-late seventh century, saw the success of the Northumbrian King Ecgfrith in the light of biblical examples: 'trusting in God like Judas Maccabeus, he attacked with his little band of God's people an enemy host (the bestial Picts) which was vast ... He slew an enormous number of the people, filling two rivers with corpses ... the tribes were reduced to slavery.' Ecgfrith was 'strong like David in crushing his enemies yet lowly in the sight of God, breaking the necks of tumultuous tribes and their warlike

* Also known as Stephen of Ripon or Eddius Stephanus.

kings'. It was this piety and zeal for God that allowed him to triumph over his neighbouring rival, Wulfhere of Mercia: 'countless numbers were slain, the king was put to flight, and his kingdom laid under tribute'.[58]

Yet, there were ways beyond success in battle that the newly Christian kings were encouraged to follow. Over the course of the seventh century, a host of monasteries were either established by the kings, or else given large endowments of land, money and slaves. This early generation of establishments that enjoyed such royal patronage included Whitby, Lindisfarne, Selsey, Hartlepool and Bede's own houses of Monkwearmouth-Jarrow. Monasteries kept close relationships with the kings and families who established them. They reflected the prestige of these families in their localities and proclaimed the extent of royal power. They also offered practical benefits. They offered women in the royal families who did not wish to be married the chance of a distinct career as nuns or abbesses, thus allowing them to govern large tracts of land in their own right.*

The kings were expected to protect these properties and cooperate with the clergy. Ecgfrith, who was praised for his martial exploits against the Picts and Wulfhere, was said to have lost his way when he tried to claw back the extensive endowments he had given to monasteries.[60] One of the instruments used to protect the rights of the Church was imported by the new Christian clergy in the company of Augustine, and again laid the foundations for a fundamental change in the role of the kings: written law. Within a few years of Augustine's arrival in Kent, King Aethelbert, with the assistance of the new clergy, issued the first written law code to be known in the islands since Roman times. Its first section guaranteed the inviolability of the property of the Church. Anyone who stole 'the property of God and the Church' had to pay 'twelvefold compensation'; the property of a bishop, 'elevenfold compensation'; a priest, 'ninefold'; down to an ordinary clergyman, 'threefold'. Anyone who disturbed 'the peace of the Church' had to pay 'double compensation'.[61]

* Bede was, however, critical of the new foundations whenever they seemed to fall short on proper monastic discipline and pastoral care.[59]

The work of Bede and other early Christian writers did not just offer a template for the development of kingship. It also laid the very foundations for national identity itself. The origins of Englishness, a single identity bringing together the many disparate peoples – whether indigenous British or Germanic migrants – living under the Germanic kings, appear as a vision amongst these writers as something derived from biblical concepts mixed with Roman imperial culture.

The idea that the adherents of Roman Christianity under the rule of Germanic kings in the British isles should be seen as a single people does not seem to have originated with Bede. Earlier, the Devon-born missionary St Boniface made what was perhaps the first expression of national shame when he claimed that the 'English' disgraced themselves through their propensity to sodomy, adultery and drunkenness, as well as subjecting monks to forced labour.[62] However, in the hands of Bede, the concept of English national identity was altogether more lofty.

At the beginning of Bede's history, Britain is described as a wealthy paradise. It abounds in 'grains and trees ... cattle and beasts of burden', vines, game birds, fish, rivers, hot springs, precious metals and even jet, which, 'when heated, drives away serpents'. It is, in essence, like ancient Israel, a promised land, running with milk and honey.[63] From an early moment, Bede frames his portrayal of Britain's history in the context of the Old Testament. He observes that five languages were spoken in the British isles – English, British, Scottish, Pictish and Latin – and that this was equivalent to the number of books in the Pentateuch at the beginning of the Old Testament.[64]

The first inhabitants of the islands were the Britons. For Bede, their history and civilised life began when the islands were first connected to Rome through the initial Roman conquest under Caesar and Claudius. In Roman times, Christianity first came to Britain. However, by the time of the Roman Empire's collapse, the Britons had fallen into wickedness. They had been attacked by the Irish, Scots and Picts after the Roman departure but, managing to hold these back for a time in the second quarter of the fifth century, 'the island began to abound with such plenty of grain as had never been known in any age before; with plenty, luxury increased, and this was immediately attended with all sorts of crimes; in particular, cruelty, hatred of truth, and love of falsehood'. Even the priests, claimed Bede, addicted 'themselves to drunkenness, animosity, litigiousness, contention, envy, and other such like crimes'.[65] A new plague hit the Britons, and the attacks of the Scots, Picts and Irish were redoubled. Because of these attacks, the British first invited the Germanic peoples to come to Britain and act as mercenaries.

These pagan Germanic peoples soon turned against their hosts, however, according to Bede, because of the Britons' continuing wickedness. Although pagan, they were acting as an instrument of God, who was using them as a scourge for the Britons' continuing sinfulness. One of the leading crimes of the Britons, says Bede, was their failure to share the message of Christianity with the Germanic migrants.[66]

In the earlier part of his narrative, Bede calls the Germanic migrants 'Saxons', and then 'Saxons, or Angles'. However, after Pope Gregory sees the slaves in Rome and decides that they must be converted to Christianity as they are not 'Angles but angels', Bede's terminology changes. Thereafter, the people under the various Germanic kings are collectively called the Angles, or English. Gregory's pun was more than a simple enjoyment of wordplay. In pragmatic terms, it showed that he probably did not understand that Britain was a fragmented place in terms of rulers and identities. Yet, for Bede, the pun had a spiritual significance. It was a sign that, like the Israelites, the English were a single and chosen people, who had been led to a promised land under divine guidance. They were one nation before God, the *gens Anglorum*. They would have a role to play in history. Taking their Christianity afresh from Rome, they would in time be called upon to bring the other errant Christians in the British isles back into line with Roman practice (particularly over the date at which Easter was celebrated), and later to be missionaries to introduce Christianity to the Germanic peoples on the continent.[67]

This English identity conjured by Bede was flexible, and not bound by tribal or ethnic origin. Its main marker was the adherence to a single

Roman Christian Church. Indeed, Bede seems to disregard ideas of tribe and ethnicity in the face of Roman Christianity. In his account, one British saint who was still revered in his time, St Alban, when being interrogated about his family and tribal background, said 'What does it matter to you what my parentage is? But if you want to know the truth about my religion, know that I am a Christian and am ready to do a Christian's duty.'[68] Bede's elevation of St Alban is a demonstration that an English identity is not confined to those who came with the Germanic migrations, but is open to any adherent of Roman Christianity in the region. It was perhaps this openness that allowed not just the Britons remaining under Germanic rule to assimilate. It also allowed foreigners like the Italian Augustine to be seen as English, and even his successor as Archbishop of Canterbury, Theodore, who was Greek.[69]

Bede conjured up the idea of a single people who adhered to a single Church. His biblical vision also tied together the idea of a people with the notion of kingship. There were, of course, a number of Germanic kings in Bede's time. However, in parts of biblical history the Jewish people were likewise ruled by different kings. For Bede, the fortunes of the English people under particular kings, as in biblical history, were intimately tied to the goodness and piety of those kings. The people prospered under kings who adhered faithfully to Roman Christianity, and suffered when they did not. A pious king, such as Oswald, was able to extend the bounds of his empire and bring different peoples together in unity. Wicked kings, such as Ecgfrith of Northumbria, who launched unjust attacks on the wealth of churches and monasteries in Ireland, not only came to a bad end, but their people and kingdoms also went into decline, in Northumbria's case being worsted by the Picts.

* * *

Bede's idea of a *gens Anglorum* did not remain as an abstract notion in the pages of his history. Subsequent generations recognised the power of Bede's concept of a unified people, and used it not only as the basis of a national identity, but also to develop a unified English kingdom. Such unity was elusive in Bede's own time and for over a century afterwards but, towards the end of the ninth century, Bede's ideas became a vital political tool in the struggle for domination of the English kingdoms. Their most adept user was arguably the best known of pre-Conquest rulers, King Alfred.

In 871, King Alfred came to the throne of the kingdom of Wessex. It was a desperate time. In 865, a pagan horde from Denmark had attacked the British isles. They were able to conquer Northumbria and East Anglia by 867, and launched assaults on Wessex, which, for the time being, were repelled. In 872, they were also able to capture the northern kingdom of Mercia, leaving Wessex isolated. By 878, the pressure on Wessex had become so great that the Danish horde were able to occupy the kingdom. In response, Alfred and his followers retreated to fortified outposts on the Somerset levels, from where they were able to plan a guerrilla campaign. In this, Alfred had a stunning success, managing to inflict a heavy defeat on the Danes at the Battle of Edington in May 878.

Part of the settlement after the Battle of Edington was the partition of the kingdom of Mercia between Wessex and the Danes. Following this, Alfred faced the challenge of making the northern kingdom accept his rule. The main part of his strategy for enforcing his hegemony over Mercia and annexing it to the control of Wessex was to resort to Bede's ideas of a national identity amongst the kingdoms of Germanic migrants, marked by a unity of religion as well as language. Alfred promoted the ideals of Bede through political declarations. He began to refer to himself not as a king of the Saxons (*rex Saxonum*) but as a king of the Angles and Saxons (*rex Anglorum et Saxonum*, or *rex Angulsaxonum*), thus moving towards Bede's and Gregory's terminology of 'Angles' as designating the whole of the people.[70] Like Bede, he also used the idea that the Angles speak one language as a mark of ethnic communion. He not only urged all of the 'free-born young men amongst the *Angelcynn*' or English-kind to learn to read English, but he also oversaw the translation of a select number of books 'which are the most necessary for all men to know'. His selection of texts was designed to promote a combination of Christianity and English identity. These included Bede's history and also works by Pope Gregory. In his preface to the translation of Pope Gregory's work, he conjures up a nostalgic, though manufactured, view of an earlier age of English Christian unity:

> It has very often come to my mind what wise men there were formerly throughout the *Angelcynn*, both in sacred and secular orders; and how there were happy times then throughout England the *Angelcynn*; and how the kings who had rule over the people in those days were obedient to God and his messengers, and both maintained their peace and their morality and their authority at home, and also enlarged their territory abroad; and how they prospered both in warfare and in wisdom.[71]

There was a time, said Alfred, in the generations after Augustine, where Christianity was properly observed in England. This brought peace, strength and unity to the land. In his own time, however, the English had sunk from proper Christian observance as the Britons had done soon after the fall of the Roman Empire. To avoid the same divine judgement that the Britons had faced, the English had to come together, and adhere properly to the Christian faith. The English had a shared history, argued Alfred; thanks to him, they also had shared laws. Collecting together various parts of law codes issued 'in the time of my kinsman King Ine, or of Offa, king of the Mercians, or of Aethelbert (who first among the *Angelcynn* received baptism)', he reminded his readers that these laws stood in a succession to those issued in the Old Testament. Following the vision of Bede, the *Angelcynn* were a chosen people, a new Israel, whose king was like a biblical law-giver.[72]

Alfred was never able to rule over all England, but his pursuit of Bede's vision – using religion to generate an ethnic unity which could then be spun into a political unity – set a precedent which would be followed by his grandson Aethelstan and his later successors for centuries to come and lead to the unification of England under a single royal house with developed ideas of kingship.[73] Without the gifts brought by Augustine and Pope Gregory's love of a pun, it is a result which would likely never have come to pass.

2

Teach Me Thy Laws

One could start the story of the deep relationship between Christianity and English law back in the time of Aethelbert and the Anglo-Saxons, but an easier place to begin is in the twentieth century, with a strange tale of some ginger beer and a dead snail.

On a Sunday evening in August 1928 a Glasgow shop assistant, May Donoghue, took a tram to the western suburb of Paisley to see a friend. It was, no doubt, a welcome excursion. Her life, at that time, had been difficult. That year, she had separated from her husband, and had earlier lost her daughter, Mabel, at the age of just 11 days. She was living in a poor tenement with her young son; thus, the prospect of a few hours away from her cares was almost certain to be pleasing.

Mrs Donoghue went with her friend along the cobbled streets to the Wellmeadow Cafe, not far from the Thomas Coates Memorial Church. It was nearly 9 p.m. when they arrived. Her friend ordered a Scotsman's ice-cream float for Mrs Donoghue, and a pear and ice for herself. The ice-cream float would have been a refreshing treat at the end of a warm day – a scoop of ice cream floating in a bowl of ginger beer. The cafe's proprietor, an Italian migrant called Francis Minchella, brought the ice cream in a tumbler and the ginger beer in a dark bottle to their table. He poured some of the beer into the tumbler, and Mrs Donoghue fell on the concoction with relish. After a moment, she poured the rest of the ginger beer into her tumbler. But immediately her pleasure in the languid evening turned to horror. Out of the bottle, from the dregs of the beer, came the decayed remains of a snail.

It was an unpleasant end to the day. Mrs Donoghue suffered not only acute distress at finding herself inadvertently consuming the fragments of a decomposing gastropod, but also lingering gastric problems from the material she had ingested. Her illness required not only treatment from her doctor, but also a stay in the Glasgow Royal Infirmary.[1]

Should Mrs Donoghue be compensated for her injury and distress? And if so, how? Who was responsible? The beer bottle had been brown and opaque; she could not have known that the snail was inside, nor could Mr Minchella. The person obviously responsible was the manufacturer, a man called David Stevenson, who ran a ginger beer and lemonade production plant in Glen Lane, less than a mile from the cafe.

And that is who was sued. The plant was, according to legal papers presented at the trial, a place where 'snails and the slimy trails of snails were frequently found'.

Despite what might have appeared an open-and-shut case, there was a serious legal problem. As the law stood, it would have been impossible for Mrs Donoghue to sue Mr Stevenson. For a start, there was no contract between them; therefore, she could not sue him for breach of contract on the grounds that he had supplied defective goods. In fact, the contract was between her friend and Mr Minchella, for the sale of the ginger beer, but her friend could not sue because she herself had not suffered any loss. Mrs Donoghue would therefore have to sue Mr Stevenson for negligence; however, the circumstances in which negligence claims could be brought stretched only to when there were already contractual relationships between the parties, or where the defendant had behaved fraudulently, or had been making something dangerous. This did not include ginger beer. The law at that time held that manufacturers had no general duty of care to consumers further down the line who might be harmed by their defective products. Thus, Mr Stevenson might allow all manner of snails to infest his beer with impunity.

This seemed an outrage to Mrs Donoghue and her determined solicitor, Walter Leechman. Together, they pursued her claim for £500 compensation all the way to the UK's highest court (then the House of Lords) in London. Mrs Donoghue's barristers worked for free, and to protect herself from the costs of the case she declared before the House that: 'I am very poor . . . and am not worth in all the world the sum of Five Pounds.'[2] Regardless of her financial circumstances, some of the generation's foremost legal minds were involved in the case, including the Solicitor General for Scotland, and other King's Counsel who would go on to become leading judges. Mrs Donoghue's representatives argued that manufacturers who marketed products must be liable for any defects that could not be checked by the ultimate consumers before use. Mr Stevenson's defence argued that there was no relationship in law between the manufacturer and the ultimate consumer that would make the manufacturer liable.

Finally, in May 1932, nearly four years after the appearance of the unfortunate snail, Lord Atkin of Aberdovey rose in the splendour of the upper chamber to deliver his determination of the case. His speech marked a fundamental change in the law which is the basis of a host of protections enjoyed by everyone in the UK to this day:

> The rule that you are to love your neighbour becomes in law, you must not injure your neighbour; and the lawyer's question, Who is my neighbour? receives a restricted reply. You must take reasonable care to avoid acts or omissions which you can reasonably foresee would be likely to injure your neighbour. Who, then, in law, is my neighbour? The answer seems to be – persons who are so closely and directly affected by my act that I ought reasonably to have them in contemplation as being so affected when I am directing my mind to the acts or omissions which are called in question.[3]

Lord Atkin's speech established in law a general duty of care in almost any relationship, and in almost any circumstance. Not just when there might be a snail in a bottle, but also if a doctor harms a patient through a careless diagnosis, or when a dangerous production line causes injury to a worker, or even when a lawyer impoverishes a client through misguided legal advice. Direct physical contact was no longer necessary. It became a question of whether there was a fault that created an injury or loss. Lord Atkin thus laid the foundation for the modern approach to compensation for personal injury, product liability and professional negligence.

Though Lord Atkin drew from scattered remarks by judges in earlier cases to show a precedent for his approach, the overriding influence on his judgment was not legal precedent but Christianity. The passage he had in mind was the story of the Good Samaritan. In Luke's Gospel (10.25–37), a lawyer asks Christ what he should do to inherit eternal life. Christ replies by asking the lawyer what the law said. The lawyer responds by quoting the 'Golden Maxim': to love God and 'thy neighbour as thyself'. When Christ approves of this answer, the lawyer then asks: 'And who is my neighbour?', a question that prompts Christ to tell the parable of the Good Samaritan. Lord Atkin relied on this passage to derive an imperative not to injure one's neighbour, but also to widen the idea in English law of who, in these circumstances, might be considered one's neighbour.

Lord Atkin's reference to the Good Samaritan was not a one-off rhetorical trope. His reasoning about the case had been profoundly influenced by the text of the gospel.[4] Two months before his speech in the House of Lords he had delivered a lecture at King's College London on the idea of neighbourliness in law, where he again repeated the Golden Maxim: 'I doubt whether the whole of the law of tort could not be comprised in the Golden Maxim to do unto your neighbour as you would that he should do unto you.'[5]

Lord Atkin's grandson, the Member of Parliament Toby Low, also recalled that, in the summer of 1931, as Lord Atkin carved the joint at lunch on Sundays, he would talk to the family about the snail-in-the-bottle case. The idea of 'who is my neighbour?', said Low, 'was an easily understandable theme immediately after church'.[6]

The snail-in-the-bottle case, *Donoghue v Stevenson*, is one of the first studied by students at English law schools; however, few tutors allude to the influence of Christianity on the ruling. Lord Atkin's findings are instead presented as a matter of pure reasoning and precedent. The idea that Christianity, despite its place in English life and history, has played, or may play, a fundamental role in developing the laws of England and its guiding principles is one that would likely make many contemporary judges and barristers uncomfortable. Indeed, in a 2011 judgment, Lord

Justice Munby and Mr Justice Beatson put it bluntly: 'the laws and usages of the realm do not include Christianity, in whatever form'.[7]

This statement would have deeply surprised not only Lord Atkin, but also his predecessors such as Lord Blackstone, who in the eighteenth century wrote the leading treatise on the Common Law with the statement that 'the Christian religion . . . is a part of the law of the land'.[8] His contemporary the Lord Chancellor, Lord Hardwicke, agreed, using exactly the same words as Blackstone.[9] In 1729 Chief Justice Raymond stated that 'Christianity in general is parcel of the common law of England',[10] repeating the dictum of the Chief Justice Lord Hale, in 1676, that 'Christianity is parcel of the laws of England'.[11] In 1651, another judge, Lord Keble, expressed the same proposition as strongly as he could:

> Whatsoever is not consonant to the law of God in Scripture, or to right reason, which is maintained in Scripture, whatsoever is in England, be it acts of Parliament, customs, or any judicial acts of the Court, it is not the laws of England, but the error of the party which did pronounce it; and you or any man else at the bar, may so plead it.[12]

Such views are not only of earlier centuries. In 1965, Lord Devlin wrote that the Common Law rested on basic principles of Christian morality.[13]* In 1989, the renowned judge Lord Denning said in a lecture that 'The common law of England has been moulded for centuries by Judges who have been brought up in the Christian faith. The precepts of religion, consciously or unconsciously, have been their guide in the administration of justice.'[14]

In 2011 Lord Justice Munby and Mr Justice Beatson would have been aware of these statements but gave them short shrift, writing in their

* In 2021, Lord Devlin's daughter, Clare Devlin, at the age of 81 testified to the Independent Inquiry into Child Sexual Abuse that her father had abused her from the age of seven until her teens. Devlin's statements on the history of the common law remain part of the scholarly record, but they cannot be repeated without an acknowledgment of this context.

judgment that: 'The aphorism that "Christianity is part of the common law of England" is mere rhetoric.'[15]

If this contradiction between earlier and modern authorities is confusing, a return to the history of English law may redeem us. Which of the learned judges above erred in their judgment?

The Roots of the Law: Aethelbert and the Saxon Beginnings

Nearly two centuries after the end of the Roman Empire in Britain, Christianity and written law returned to the islands hand in hand. Literacy, which allowed codification of the laws, was one of the treasures brought by St Augustine to Aethelbert of Kent after his arrival in 597. It is also likely that Augustine brought the impetus for laws to be codified.[16]

Aethelbert published his law code around 600. It was remembered with reverence by Bede writing over a century later: 'Among other benefits which Aethelbert conferred upon his nation in his care for them, he established, with the help of his council of wise men, judicial decisions, after the Roman model; which are written in the language of the English, and are still kept and observed by them.'[17] Yet at first sight Bede's reverence is puzzling. Aethelbert's law code might be venerable on the grounds that it contained the first written laws in Britain since Roman times, and because it is the first known text written in Old English;[18] however, the laws hardly seem to be Roman in character. They also scarcely seem to have anything Christian about them. Although they begin with provisions to protect the nascent Church – anyone who steals from 'God's property or the Church' is to make a twelve-fold compensation to them, whilst the king himself is only to receive a nine-fold compensation for a similar wrong – the Christian note soon ebbs away. Much of the code is concerned instead with detailed compensation payments for deaths and injuries caused by an endemically violent society. For example, 50 shillings are to be paid to a victim if his eye is gouged out, 20 shillings for a broken jawbone, down to 6 shillings for a gashed nose.

Indeed, Aethelbert's laws, aside from those new provisions connected with the protection of the Church, are likely to be a written version of customary folk laws already in oral circulation, offering alternative means of dispute resolution to revenge attacks and long-lasting vendettas. Justice was personal, the organs of the state weak, and the responsibility for obtaining redress for wrongs was down to the individual who had been harmed, or their close relatives in the case of a death. Violence and injury inflicted against another was seen as a private matter and not, as now, a crime offensive to society as a whole.[19]

Although Aethelbert's code appears to be void of any deep Christian ethic, Bede and his contemporaries would have seen its mere publication as a profoundly Christian act. Up to that point in early Saxon society, law, custom and procedure were hardly distinguishable. Law was what the people did by custom to settle disputes. The king, therefore, had little part in making legislation. By publishing a written law code, Aethelbert followed precedents set by two other types of law-making rulers originally outside Saxon society: the late Roman emperors, who were Christian, and the biblical kings of the Old Testament. Aethelbert's publication of a written law code was an attempt to mimic their behaviour, and win for himself a similar prestige: the publication of a law code was the action of a biblically inspired ruler.[20]

This act also made a further political statement. The arrival of Christianity, as described in the previous chapter, provided not only for the development of kingship but also for a unified people. As in Bede's vision for England, to follow in the mould of biblical precedent required there to be one king and one people under God. The promulgation by a king of a written law code, in the manner of the Old Testament kings, also implied the unification of a people under such a code, with the king responsible before God for their conduct and morality; thus, the development of law, following Christian precedent, was crucial to the development of English nationhood.[21]

In the generations after Aethelbert the laws began to show greater influence of Christian ideas. In 685, King Wihtred of Kent issued a law code in consultation with his nobles and with the Archbishop of Canterbury and the Bishop of Rochester. Under these laws, the Church was exempted from taxation, but had to pray for the king. 'Illicit marriages' – concubinage and unions unblessed by the Church – were forbidden. Work on Sunday – the Lord's day – was prohibited for all social classes, as was eating during religious fasts. Sacrifices to devils could incur forfeiture of all goods if done by a freeman or his wife, or – if done by a slave – the choice between a 6-shilling fine or the lash.[22]

At around the same time, Wihtred's neighbour, King Ine of Wessex, issued his own code, even more forthright about maintaining the sanctity of Sundays: any slave ordered to work on a Sunday was to be made free, and his lord fined 30 shillings. Wihtred's laws also were some of the first to give churches the capacity to offer sanctuary. Anyone who had been sentenced to death but who then took refuge in a church would be spared and could pay compensation instead; anyone sentenced to the lash would be immune from scourging. English churches retained the legal right to offer sanctuary until 1623.[23]

King Alfred, who issued his law code – better known as the 'Doom Book' or Judgement Book – two centuries after Wihtred and Ine, went far beyond them in claiming Christian inspiration. Although, by his own confession, he drew much from the law codes of his predecessors, Alfred's leading source for his text was the Bible. His Doom Book begins with the Ten Commandments, continues with extensive quotations from Mosaic law in the Old Testament, and is followed by a summary of the Acts of the Apostles. It also restates the 'Golden Maxim' as later repeated by Lord Atkin. The text itself is made up of 120 chapters, echoing the age at which Moses is said to have died.[24]

There was much in the laws of Alfred and his later successors, including Aethelred and Cnut, that found its origins in Christian scripture and doctrine. Many of their provisions, whether concrete rules or broader guidance, sought to promote a biblical approach to morality. 'Judge very evenly', urged Alfred, following the injunctions of Exodus and Leviticus, 'judge not one judgement to the rich, another to the poor; nor one to your friend, another to your foe.'[25]

Aethelstan introduced some of the first laws requiring the state to look after the poor: 'you shall always provide', he directed his reeves (officials), 'a destitute Englishman with food … From two of my rents he shall be supplied with an amber of meal, a shank of bacon or a ram worth four pence every month, and clothes for twelve months annually.'[26] If the reeves failed to follow these orders, they would face a fine of 30 shillings, distributed to the local poor. In King Cnut's second law code, drafted by Wulfstan, Archbishop of York, the promises were of equality of access to justice: 'all men, both poor and rich shall be regarded as entitled to the benefit of the law, and just decisions shall be pronounced on their behalf'. His laws likewise offered more merciful treatment and greater dignity for Christian subjects: 'we forbid the practice of condemning Christian people to death for very trivial offenses. On the contrary, merciful punishments shall be determined upon for the public good, and the handiwork of God and the purchase which he made at a great price shall not be destroyed for trivial offenses.'[27]

Yet Christianity's impact was not just on the substance of the laws. Its influence altered a number of fundamental ideas and assumptions, without which the later development of English Common Law (the standardised law used by royal judges across England following reforms in the latter part of the twelfth century) could never have taken place.

Alfred and his successors explicitly placed their law codes in a grand tradition which swept back to the beginnings of history, its thread beginning with the Ten Commandments and the laws of the Old Testament – the 'Dooms which the Almighty God himself spoke unto Moses, and commanded him to keep', in the words of Alfred. This was followed by the coming of Christ, who 'came not to break nor to forbid these commandments' but to fulfil them in goodness, and mollify them with 'mercy and humility'. The later Church councils and synods were able to articulate to secular rulers some of the ways in which this mercy might be manifest in the development of the law according to the changing needs of the time; for example, as Alfred claims, in allowing compensation to be paid for first offences instead of the more severe punishments otherwise used.[28]

The grandeur of the pedigree of the law, reaching back almost to the dawn of biblical time, and drawing its origin from the Almighty Himself, gave to the royal law codes of the Anglo-Saxon kings, thus to the kings themselves, a prestige difficult to assail. Whereas formerly the source of law was folk custom that evolved independently of the will of kings, now the kings were staking a claim, in consultation with their bishops and other advisors, to be a new source of law by publishing their own codes based on biblical precedent. At the beginning, the Saxon kings did not presume to make law. But through Christian influence, the making of law and the administration of justice became one of their most elementary duties.[29]

Christian ideas may have mollified the law, but there was one instance in which – according to Alfred – the laws of Christ denied any mercy: treason against one's lord. 'God', according to Alfred, gave no mercy 'to those who despised Him', nor did Christ 'adjudge any mercy to him who sold him to death'. One should certainly love God and one's neighbour as one's self, as Christ said, but Alfred offered his own striking gloss on this injunction. Christ, he argued, also meant that 'a lord should be loved as one's self'. This increase in the king's prestige, tied to the law, changed the relationship of the king's subjects with the law. Formerly an act such as a killing, a wounding or a theft was simply a matter to be resolved between individuals. In the new dispensation, these acts changed from being understood as a private issue to being an act of rebellion not just against God, the ultimate origin of the laws, but also against the king, because they were in breach of the law codes he had published.[30]

From around the tenth century, if not earlier, subjects of the Anglo-Saxon kings began to take oaths of loyalty, which included commitments to avoid the serious misdeeds described in the royal law codes (a practice that persisted well into the Middle Ages). To commit such a misdeed thus made the miscreant not just treasonous to the king, but also a perjurer. The effect of failing to adhere to such oaths by disobedience to the law is summed up by Archbishop Wulfstan when discussing the disorder that accompanied Viking attacks at the beginning of the eleventh century:

> It is no wonder that things go wrong with us, for ... this people ... has

> become very corrupt through manifold sins and many misdeeds: through murders and mischiefs, grasping and greed, stealing and spoliation, kidnapping and heathen vices . . . kin-fights and killings, violations of holy orders and violations of marriage, lying with kin and lying with various illicit partners. And also . . . more than should be are in perdition and perjury through oath-breaches and pledge-breaches . . .[31]

Misdeeds including murder and theft were now the concern not just of those immediately harmed; they became an assault on all of society. The offence caused to God by the transgression of laws derived from religion called down divine retribution on society as a whole. The offence caused to the king was an attack on his authority, and against those other subjects who had pledged to obey the laws. It was therefore the duty of the king and society as a whole, not just the wronged parties, to seek redress. Since these misdeeds were so grave, they merited especially severe punishments, which might include the loss of life or limb, or condemnation as an outlaw. Such serious misdeeds, which wore the taint of treason and perjury, came to be known by the time of the rise of the Common Law in the twelfth century as 'felonies' – a term still used in many American states that follow the Common Law today.* It is from this line of development (supported by emerging Christian philosophical ideas about the nature of sin and atonement, including those of St Anselm, the early-twelfth-century Archbishop of Canterbury) that English Common Law makes a distinction between torts – wrongdoings for which individuals must seek redress privately by themselves through the courts or otherwise – and crimes, which are seen as being so malicious and such an affront to society that society as a whole must seek redress.[32]

Whilst Christian doctrine magnified the role and prestige of the king, it did not mean that he could act as he pleased. As much as it exalted the office of kingship, Christianity also served to restrain it. Bede, in the early eighth century, was one of the first to express the principle: '[he] who sees

* The use of the term 'felony' was abolished in the English legal system by the Criminal Law Act 1967.

himself as exalted to rule over the people must remember that he himself is to be ruled and subject to divine laws.'[33] Even though kings began to play an ever greater role in making the law, they had no right to break the law. To the contrary, as the law was drawn from biblical antecedents and Christian principles, the king, more than anyone in his kingdom, was under God and the law. Deuteronomy warned kings to 'write a copy of this law' and to 'read therein' throughout their lives, so that they would not 'turn aside from the commandment'.[34] In the same mode, the eighth-century scholar and churchman Alcuin of York admonished King Aethelred: 'Whether you will or not, you will have [God] as judge.'[35]

The principle that the king was under God and the law, which was well established in Saxon times, had a profound effect on not only the development of English law, but also government. At the beginning of the thirteenth century, during the tensions between the English barons and King John, it was the influence of this idea that proved vital to the emergence of the Magna Carta. Stephen Langton, who became Archbishop of Canterbury in 1207, followed a number of biblical ideas to insist that the fundamental laws of the kingdom should be written down. In the First Book of Samuel, God only allowed Israel to have a king with many reservations and misgivings. Thus, when Saul was hailed as king, the prophet Samuel proclaimed the law of the kingdom and had it written down. The purpose of this, as theologians who had influenced Langton argued, was to circumscribe the powers of the king. The biblical law made it absolutely clear what the duties of the people were to the king, but also the limits of what the king could demand from the people. To put this in writing prevented the king from going any further than the lawful limits of his power. Langton believed that the same was necessary in his own time. For Langton, the Magna Carta, which he helped to draft, was the same as an Old Testament covenant between God, king and people, ensuring that the king himself abided by the law. Clauses 39 and 40 of the 1215 Magna Carta (which still remain valid in English law), which state that 'No free man shall be seized, imprisoned, dispossessed, outlawed, exiled or ruined in any way, nor in any way proceeded against, except by the lawful judgement of his peers and the law of the land . . .' and

'To no one will we sell, to no one will we deny or delay right or justice . . .', are also born of this biblical influence. A part of the king's role in observing the law was his duty to ensure that the remedies of the law were available to all and administered fairly and openly.[36]

In later disputes over the way the Crown exercised its power, recourse was made to this principle. It was articulated as an essential point of English law in the generation after the Magna Carta in one of the most important early texts on the law, *De legibus et consuetudinibus Angliae* (*On the Laws and Customs of England*), attributed to the judge Henry de Bracton.[37] Bracton drew a connection between the submission of the king to the laws and the humility of Christ:

> that as a vicar of God the king ought to be under the law is clearly shown by the example of Jesus Christ . . . for although there lay open to God, for the salvation of the human race, many ways and means . . . He used, not the force of his power, but the counsel of His justice. Thus He was willing to be under the Law, 'that He might redeem those who were under the Law'. For He was unwilling to use power, but judgment.[38]

These ideas maintained their force undiminished in the seventeenth century. In 1608, Chief Justice Sir Edward Coke clashed with the increasingly absolutist King James I over the king's claim that he himself should be the final arbiter of the Common Law, and that he had a right to act arbitrarily above the law. To counter this behaviour, Coke quoted other lines of Bracton: 'the King is under no man, save God and the law, for the law makes the king . . . for where will and not law doth sway, there is no king'. Coke's stand, inspired by this principle, was vital in underpinning the constitutional rule that the king could not generate new laws by himself through proclamations, and could act only with the advice and consent of Parliament. It also articulated the notion that statute law, issued by Parliament, could limit the powers of the king, and that the courts had the right to determine not only the extent of the king's prerogative powers, but also whether the king had acted lawfully. These principles were essentially endorsed by Parliament in the 1688 Bill of Rights, and remain on the statute books in England and many other Commonwealth countries.[39]

Coke's approach also helped to lay the foundations for the development of judicial review, where anyone affected by the decision of a government official made wrongly or unlawfully can apply to a judge to review the decision and ask for it to be taken properly.[40] The most famous recent example was the Miller no.2 case challenging then Prime Minister Boris Johnson's attempt to seek the dissolution of Parliament during the Brexit controversy in 2019.[41] Judicial review has been a vital ingredient in protecting citizens against illegal or irrational decision-making in areas from police use of facial recognition cameras to unreasonable behaviour by parole boards, school-exam syndicates and universities, planning bodies, local councils and tax authorities. The warnings issued by Bede and Alcuin to the Saxon kings retain their ghostly force.

Canons and Conscience: High Medieval Changes

It was not only the pure injunctions of scripture that helped lay the foundations of English law. Profound changes in the Catholic Church in the tenth and eleventh centuries also exerted a deep gravitational pull on the development of English law.[42]

Until the beginning of the tenth century, the administration of the Catholic Church in Europe was essentially in the hands of local kings and potentates. Many Church properties, particularly monasteries, had been endowed by such royal and noble families, who expected to retain a measure of control over their management and revenue. Senior clergy, particularly thanks to their level of education, also played a significant role in the running of local affairs beyond the Church. This being so, kings and nobles expected to be able to choose who should become abbots and bishops. At this time, ordinary clergy (who had not taken monastic vows) could still marry, with the result that Church properties were often family affairs, and clerical offices inherited. The corporate identity of the

Church was therefore very different to the strictly hierarchical organisation that developed later. It was a decentralised institution. Decisions for the most part were taken locally, and the pope in Rome was a distant figure with spiritual authority but little practical power.

In the early tenth century, a reform movement emerged to purge the Church of these local, feudal strangleholds and the corruption that was said to accompany them. One of the first fruits of this movement in 910 was the foundation of a Benedictine monastery at Cluny in Burgundy. Cluny's constitution, unlike those of other monasteries controlled by local bishops, put it under direct protection of the pope, giving it autonomy from local entanglements. This, along with its efforts to promote reformed morals and improved liturgy, attracted many lucrative bequests. It soon became one of the richest monastic houses in Europe, and began to build 'daughter' houses across the continent. Cluny maintained control of these establishments, and as a result it generated a new type of institution: a transnational corporation managed by a central administration.

One of Cluny's greatest early achievements was to promote a peace movement, forbidding acts of war on certain days of the week – originally from Saturday noon until Monday morning, and later from Wednesday evening until Monday morning – as well as during Lent, Advent and on certain saints' days. It prohibited violence against clerics, pilgrims, merchants, Jews, women, peasants and against ecclesiastical and agricultural property. To secure support for these measures and enforce its authority, Cluny used the device of the oath. It would in some cases require whole populations to swear collectively to keep the peace, and even to join militias charged with supressing conflict.[43]

Cluny's success, due largely to its international reach and centralised government, was not lost on the papacy. In the second part of the eleventh century, Rome took up Cluny's ideas of centralisation and independence, not just for one monastic order but for the whole of the Catholic Church. Following the impetus of Hildebrand of Sovana, a papal official who had spent time at Cluny and who was then elected Pope Gregory VII in 1073, the Catholic Church began to propound a new and revolutionary set of principles. From being a first amongst equals with a certain spiritual dignity, the pope claimed for himself the ultimate primacy and universal jurisdiction. He insisted that he alone had the right to depose rulers, appoint bishops and absolve anyone from oaths of obedience to feudal lords. He claimed the authority to govern the Church and its property and the right to make laws; further, his own court became the forum for trying all important cases.

Gregory's reforms gave the Catholic Church the characteristics of a modern state, ahead of any other European nation. The Church was transformed from a spiritual community to a legally constituted entity. It was independent, hierarchical and acted as a public authority, enforcing law through its administrative officers. The conversion of the papal curia in Rome into Europe's leading court of law wrought one of the most significant changes to the Catholic Church. Before the tenth century the churches, being local and effectively independent, tended to follow their own local customs and laws under the authority of regional potentates. There were no broad compilations of Church law, no judges nor legal professionals, and little by way of formal procedure; however, with the centralisation of Church government, all of this had to change. The eleventh and twelfth centuries saw the rapid development of a legal profession for the Church with advocates, judges and the emergence of due process – the idea that legal matters had to be treated consistently using established rules which were fair to all parties. This brought in its train the foundation of law schools, academic specialists and an endeavour to systematise the law with compilations of past rules and statutes, and philosophical treatises on the nature and operation of legal principles. Efforts were made, primarily by the Italian scholar Gratian (*c.*1140), to assemble and reconcile a mass of contrary legal ideas expressed over centuries by the scriptures, by Church Fathers, councils, popes and other customs. The resulting Canon Law furnished not just the fundamental rules of the Catholic Church, but also the first modern legal system in the West.[44]

This rapid evolution of Church institutions and the Canon Law spurred the development of the laws and legal institutions of England.

In the first instance, the Church's claims of jurisdiction over its own affairs and the moral conduct of its flock led to a split in the legal system whose effects were to persist for centuries. Around 1072, William the Conqueror, who was a strong supporter of Pope Gregory's reforms, ordered that all cases to do with Church matters and the 'cure of souls' should be held not in ordinary courts, but in new separate courts presided over by bishops, and governed by Canon Law.[45] This was the origin of a division between Church courts and 'secular' courts which dealt with non-Church and non-religious matters. Such a split allowed for secular law to progress in its own way, but nevertheless still under the influence of ideas from Christianity and the Canon Law. The new legal establishment of the Church, with its professional advocates, judges, theorists and teachers, set an example for the national secular courts to follow in their development. It also offered notions of rights and due process, which over time found their way into English law and in some instances have become abiding and fundamental principles of the English legal system.*

One example of such a right is well known from TV dramas: 'you have the right to remain silent . . .' the suspect is told in US productions, or 'you do not have to say anything . . .' in British versions. This right, 'to remain silent', is another way of expressing the privilege against self-incrimination. In its traditional form, a criminal suspect is not compelled to say anything to assist the police or prosecution when they are investigating a crime that he or she might be involved in, or taking it to court. The defendant is not required to prove anything or justify themselves. It is for the prosecution to prove its case by its own efforts, and to avoid inferring anything from a defendant's silence. The right was well established in English case law by the seventeenth century (although it has recently been somewhat eroded in the UK, with juries given the right to make limited inferences from a defendant's silence).[46] Following a

* Despite the Reformation and the break with Rome, Canon Law remained operative in England. The Submission of the Clergy Act 1533 provided that the pre-1533 Roman Canon Law continued to apply in England as part of the law of the land, i.e. 'the king's ecclesiastical law'.

recommendation by James Madison, it was also enshrined in the USA by the Fifth Amendment to the US Constitution in 1791.

The earliest origin of this right is not found in the Enlightenment theories of the eighteenth century. Instead, it arises from scripture, and from a maxim of Canon Law, which reputedly first appeared in the writings of St John Chrysostom at the end of the fourth century, stating that: '*nemo tenetur prodere seipsum*' ('no one shall be compelled to betray themselves'). This maxim was closely associated with another, '*nemo tenetur detegere turpitudinem suam*' ('no one shall be compelled to reveal their own shame'). Chrysostom and his successors drew these ideas from a statement in St Paul's Letter to the Hebrews: 'Reveal your ways unto the Lord.' The injunction was seen as making a particular point in legal terms: one should confess one's sins to God, without obligation or compulsion to confess to anyone else. Some commentators took this idea further, with considerable insight into psychology and society. No one, they observed, was untainted by guilt for crime at some time or another. If the truth of everyone's actions were apparent, all would be liable to punishment: 'use every man after his desert, and who should 'scape whipping?' as Hamlet said.[47] If officers of the Church or state could compel people to confess their sins publicly, no one would be able to avoid prosecution. Anyone would be in danger, at any time. The results would be chaotic. The Canon Law therefore would overlook a number of sins if the attempts to root them out would lead to worse consequences. Christ tolerated Judas, observed the commentators, and so the Canon Law might be justified in the toleration of some sin.[48]

Canon Law, and its contribution to the privilege against self-incrimination, also influenced judicial independence. Judges do not initiate prosecutions, nor do they order investigations to take place by themselves. Cases can only be brought by a plaintiff or accuser with a particular interest in the matter in question, on the basis of evidence that is already established. Although some English tribunals historically did have the power to make their own investigations and 'go fishing' for evidence before levelling an accusation, this came to be seen as invidious, and was in decline by the seventeenth century. A doctrine of Canon Law states: '*nemo punitur sine accusatore*' ('no one shall be punished without an accuser'), an idea derived from scripture. In St John's Gospel, Christ disperses a mob about to kill an adulterous woman by commanding 'He that is without sin among you, let him first cast a stone at her.' He then asks the woman 'Where are those thine accusers? Hath no man condemned thee?' She replies: 'No man, Lord', to which Christ gives His final judgement: 'Neither do I condemn thee: go, and sin no more.' The legal idea drawn from this exchange is that prosecutions are not to be made on the basis of gossip, and that without a legitimate and specific accuser, prosecutions and punishments are strictly forbidden.[49]

What about 'innocent until proven guilty' – a line heard regularly on TV dramas? This, often described as the 'golden thread' running through English criminal law, again finds its origins in Canon Law and scripture. Medieval commentators argued that ideas of due process of law (which were certainly found in Roman law) were first seen in the Garden of Eden. After Adam and Eve ate the forbidden fruit, God came to them and asked: 'Where are you?' Although God was omniscient, and knew that Adam and Eve had disobeyed Him, He still took the trouble to question them about what had happened, allowing them to put their case to Him, before He judged them and cast them out of the Garden. The commentators drew from this that if God Himself summoned Adam and Eve to defend themselves, human judges were also bound to summon defendants, to allow them a right to a trial where their pleas and evidence could be heard, and for their innocence to be presumed until proven otherwise by substantive evidence shown and heard in court. The connection of this right with God Himself allowed the commentators to argue later in the Middle Ages that these rights were not something that could be changed or overridden by kings or popes – that they were inalienable, and should be allowed to all.[50]

And what about another phrase well known from courtroom dramas: 'It is better that ten guilty persons escape than that one innocent suffer'? It was put in this form by the great judge and legal writer Sir William

Blackstone in the 1760s,[51] but the idea is considerably older, underpinned by both Canon Law notions of due process as well as scripture. Chief Justice Sir John Fortescue's textbook on English law, written around 1470, remarks that it was better if 20 people escaped than one innocent person be condemned.[52] In around 1660, Chief Justice Sir Matthew Hale discussed the idea in a private diary, unfolding the religious origins of the point: 'the hand of divine justice in the way of [God's] providence may reach in after time a guilty person, or of evidence to convict him, he may hereafter repent and amend; but the loss of the life of an innocent is irrecoverable in this world'.[53] Hale bases this approach on a dictum from Exodus – 'the innocent and righteous slay thou not, for I will not justify the wicked' – as well as the requirement of Mosaic law that at least two witnesses give testimony in a capital case, which in Hale's view showed that full evidence is needed to exclude the conviction of the innocent.[54]

The early concern of the legal system to allow room for repentance has left its mark in many ways. Part of the sanctity that attaches to the wishes of the testator of a will is because many of the bequests from the early Middle Ages onwards were concerned with the salvation of the testator's soul: for example, bequests for a funeral with masses and prayers, gifts to churches and orders of friars, or other acts of charity. The making of a will, therefore, was seen in Canon Law as a religious act, falling under the jurisdiction of Church courts, and the Church aimed to protect bequests that might aid the testator's salvation. This interest affected the development of testamentary law.[55]

Related to this is the curious tradition that if someone was convicted of murder and sentenced to death, but subsequently became insane, his execution would be postponed until he recovered his sanity. The original reasoning behind this was that if the convict was insane, he would not have the opportunity freely to make confession of his sins and receive Holy Communion before his death, thus depriving him of his best chance of expiation.[56]

The question of conscience – of not just the parties in the courtroom, but even the judge himself – was of great moment to Canon Law, which from the twelfth century onwards was used to develop ideas of right conduct for judges. The *Leges Henrici Primi* (Laws of Henry I, written *c.*1116–18) set out that in all judicial proceedings, judges' disposition must be 'irreproachable, not open to suspicion', using the maxim '*affectus, non suspectus*' which the Canon Law originally applied to plaintiffs and witnesses. Judges, say the *Leges*, must make sure that they give all parties in court full and frequent chances to state and clarify their case and ensure that their understanding of the points at issue is not lost through trickery, for 'The danger is so much greater to the judge than to the person who is being judged to the extent that we know, from the words of the Lord [in Matthew's Gospel], that any judgment we pass on others is held in store for ourselves.'[57] Over five centuries later, Chief Justice Hale wrote that as 'in the administration of Justice, I am intrusted for God, the King and Country' and that he had to fulfil his function '. . . Uprightly . . . Deliberately . . . Resolutely . . . not biassed with Compassion to the Poor, or favour to the Rich . . . Not to be sollicitous what Men will say or think . . . to incline to Mercy . . . .'[58]

Christianity was not only instrumental in inculcating the idea amongst judges that justice had to be tempered with mercy. It also for centuries was a constant source of guidance, helping judges balance these often conflicting necessities. Indeed, the tension between these two impulses was at the base of a fundamental development in the English legal system: the emergence of the courts of Equity. In the medieval period, when the strict rules of the Common Law used in the royal courts produced results that seemed unnecessarily harsh or unreasonable, in particular because the rigidity of the system was unable to deal with the complex and individual circumstances of every single case, petitioners would apply directly to the Lord Chancellor for a remedy. The Chancellor's Court was different in character to the Common Law courts. Up to the Reformation in the 1530s, the Lord Chancellor was always a cleric, with a grounding in Canon Law, and though the court was secular, its character was religious. Petitions to it were often made 'For God and Charity'. The Chancellor, with his clerical and Canon Law training, would take a different approach to the Common

Law judges. As a cleric, his primary concern was not the strict restoration of what a plaintiff might have lost, or stood to gain, but rather the question of the parties' consciences. His understanding of what might be a 'conscionable' and reasonable solution to a case beyond the strict application of the Common Law was moulded by ideas from Canon Law, scripture and Christian philosophers including St Thomas Aquinas.

The idea of the Chancellor's Court applying this 'equitable jurisdiction' was succinctly set out by the Lord Chancellor Lord Ellesmere in a 1615 case: 'The Office of the Chancellor is to correct Men's consciences for Frauds, Breach of Trusts, Wrongs and oppressions, of what Nature soever they be, and to soften and mollify the Extremity of the Law', for 'when a Judgment is obtained by Oppression, Wrong and a hard Conscience, the Chancellor will frustrate and set it aside, not for any error or Defect in the Judgment, but for the hard Conscience of the Party'. Common Law and Equity, he said, may be different, and with different courts, 'yet they both aim at one and the same end, which is to do right; as Justice and Mercy differ in their effects and operations, yet both join in the manifestation of God's glory'.[59]

Although the courts of Equity and Common Law existed separately for centuries and were finally merged in the legal reforms of 1873–5, they remain distinct parts of the English legal system. Legal remedies such as injunctions or an order for the specific performance of a contract come from the equitable part of the court's powers, but cannot be used if the party claiming them has behaved improperly: 'He who comes into equity must come with clean hands' is one of the maxims used when determining whether an equitable remedy should be made available, and the courts still take an approach based on conscience, the foundations of which were laid by medieval theologians and Canon lawyers.[60]

These Christian ideas of conscience were also vital to the development of contract law. Early Common Law provided few practical avenues for the enforcement of day-to-day commercial agreements, save those which had been made with various formalities, in particular with sealed deeds. It put complex barriers in the way of recovering named sums of money for breaches, and it was impossible to enforce obligations against the heirs of a debtor after his death. Canon Law developed a way through these difficulties, in step with increased international trade. The principle behind its approach was simple: why should one keep a promise? Because to break a promise was a sin. This being so, it was the business of Canon Law to correct it. The Church would see to a suitable penance for the person who broke the promise and, in the public forum of the Church courts, the rights of the person who had been damaged by the breach of promise would be protected, only if the object of the contract was morally justified; the substance of the promise had to be reasonable and equitable. From this foundation, and drawing from both Christian theological texts as well as elements of Roman law, Canon Law developed a series of principles that eventually influenced English Common Law. These include that contracts should be legally enforceable even if they had been entered into 'on a handshake', and without formalities; that contracts might be void if they were entered into by fraud, duress or mistake; and that unconscionable contracts would not be enforced, for example contracts in restraint of trade that prevented people from exercising their right to work.[61]

Eminently Holy: Calvin and the Laws of Perfection

Despite the upheavals of the break with Rome in the 1530s and the Civil War in the 1640s, there remained a profound continuity in connection between Christianity and English law. Jurists, churchmen and thinkers from Sir Matthew Hale and John Selden to Richard Hooker and John Locke continued to develop notions from scripture and Christian thought about the origins of the law, the use of scripture in the making of the law, its relationship to reason and the capacity of kings and peoples to make law independently and in view of local circumstances.[62] Many thinkers into the seventeenth century followed earlier medieval Christian thought derived from Aquinas and others who argued that there was a universal natural law springing from the will of God and perceived by the correct operation of the divine gift of reason. This natural law, however, was not always clearly discerned because the Fall of Man depraved the human mind. It therefore needed supplemental guidance from scripture and the revelation of truth offered in Christianity. Thus, 'this law of nature is part of the laws of England', held a panel of 14 judges in the Exchequer Chamber in *Calvin's Case* (1608),* who deemed the law to be 'before any judicial or municipal law in the world . . . immutable, and cannot be changed'.[63]

However, the adoption in England of many of the ideas of the sixteenth-century Protestant reformer Jean Calvin could not fail to change the way that Christianity interacted with the law. This change had an inescapable impact on the nature of English life. A number of principles derived from Calvinist thought came to be generally accepted by English legal thinkers over the course of the seventeenth century: the emphasis on the innate sinfulness of fallen humanity, and the necessity to reform and better the world. This was a religious imperative according to Calvin, commanded by God Himself, and required puritan virtues such as hard work, austerity, frugality, reliability, discipline and vocational commitments. Such duties to pursue a perfect life fell on each Christian individually (and not, as in the pre-Reformation world, on a monastic or spiritual elite). These ideas resonated across the religious spectrum. In the words of the seventeenth-century Anglican bishop Jeremy Taylor, Christians had to be not just holy but 'eminently holy' – a view he held despite having much more liberal ideas than Calvin on Original Sin.[64] The justification of sinners in the eyes of God, proclaimed Calvin, was available through faith alone; hence came the imperative of spiritual self-improvement. Yet these duties were to be followed firmly within a social dimension. The call for reformation touched all society; thus, such virtues were to be expressed in a public-spirited way, and in support of civic virtue.[65]

Social cohesion, and indeed the cohesion between humanity and God, was expressed by means of covenants, or sacred agreements. As, in the

* This is unrelated to Jean Calvin, the religious reformer. The case was brought by one Robert Calvin over a dispute about land ownership in Shoreditch.

Calvinist view, there was a covenant between God and man established in the time of Adam which laid down the obligations of man to God and vice versa, including the promise of God for man's prosperity and salvation, so too there should be covenants to hold together nations, people and their governments, churches and even families. The covenant between God and man prohibiting idolatry, blasphemy, murder, incest and civil disobedience, in the view of the legal scholar John Selden, writing in 1640, was to be treated as the original source of moral and legal obligation. As a result, the most vital idea of natural law was the rule '*pacta sunt servanda*' ('agreements must be kept'), which applied to contracts not only between God and man, but between humans as well.[66]

One further consequence of this change was in the field of criminal law. It is, at first sight, counterintuitive. From the mid-seventeenth to late eighteenth centuries, the number of crimes punishable by death increased from approximately 50 to around 200, many relating to crimes against property. This, at first sight, seems hardly a Christian development. Indeed, some Marxist historians have attributed this development to the rise of a new class of landed gentry, eager to protect their wealth. Perhaps, but many of the prosecutions were brought not at the instigation of the wealthy, but by artisans, shopkeepers and petty tradesmen. The defendants were, for the most part, not from the destitute but rather a habitual class of somewhat successful criminals. Moreover, membership of the juries trying such cases was open to those on the lower rungs of the social spectrum – they had to be property owners, but the value of their property was set at a modest limit. These juries frequently acquitted, or the judges often found ways to convict on lesser charges with lesser punishments.

This availability of harsh punishments with a marked reluctance to use them is best accounted for by the prevailing Calvinist sentiments: as all are called to a holy life of moral and unblemished perfection, the distinction of mortal and venial sins falls away. All transgressions in themselves are of equal and severe gravity; hence, criminal law began to reflect a tendency towards the equal and heavy gravity of potential sentences. And because salvation is a matter of faith, the personal disposition of the spirit, distinctions were made in criminal law between crimes not on the basis of the gravity of the sinful act, but on the degree of depravity of the sinful will. If a defendant had been led astray by weakness of mind or spirit, every endeavour would have been made to treat them with lenience, with such faults pardonable. If, however, a defendant was proven to have acted from malice or a perversion of their will, the behaviour was deemed unpardonable and met with its due punishment according to law. If a defendant had been led astray, it was believed that society had a collective duty to help reform the criminal. Factors taken into account included the age of the defendant, their weakness, their previous good character, the poverty of their background and the prospects for reform. In the end, it was the character, rather than the crime, that often determined the sentence.[67]

One lasting consequence of this attempt to find lenient ways of treating reformable convicts was the emergence of prison sentences as a punishment for felonies. This was first made possible for Common Law courts by an act of Parliament in 1706. Before then, courts could only imprison suspects before trial, to compel payment of debts, or else to punish lesser misdemeanours; some other courts also used it to punish contempt (obstructing the process of justice and the work of the court). For some felonies, imprisonment of six months to two years would have been available, particularly for first offenders. The same impulse for relative leniency led to the establishment of transportation in 1716 as another alternative punishment. Both imprisonment and transportation were accompanied by hard labour. This was also seen by the Calvinist approach as being a means of reform and a duty which arose by covenant for all members of society.[68]

Mere Rhetoric?

Well into the nineteenth century judges, understanding that Christianity was parcel of the laws of England, developed fundamental points of law based on Christian doctrine or directed their judgments accordingly; for example, in 1825 Chief Justice Best held it to be illegal for spring guns to be set without warnings to poachers: 'there is no act', he held, 'which Christianity forbids, that the law will not reach: if it were otherwise, Christianity would not be, as it has always been held to be, part of the law of England. I am, therefore, clearly of opinion that he who sets spring guns, without giving notice, is guilty of an inhuman act . . .'.[69] And in 1867, the Exchequer Court held that a landlord could break a contract to hire a room to a man whose lectures were heretical, proposing that 'the character of Christ is defective, and his teaching misleading, and that the Bible is no more inspired than any other book'.[70] Because such material was blasphemous, the contract could be broken.

Despite this, and even as late as a 1917 case, the House of Lords was divided on whether Christianity was part of the Common Law.[71] The Lord Chancellor, Lord Finlay, maintained it as good law but his colleague, Lord Sumner, called the idea 'mere rhetoric' – with which Lord Justice Munby later agreed. In the 1917 case the House of Lords found that the purposes of the National Secular Society – propagating the ideas of secularism – were not illegal, but, in a series of conflicting opinions, the Law Lords did not concur that the maxim was 'mere rhetoric' or against current developments in public policy.

Over the course of the twentieth century, judges such as Lord Denning and Lord Devlin continued to draw upon Christianity, even though they acknowledged, as they had in the National Secular Society case, that its role as a source of authority in national life was no longer universally acknowledged. However, by the 1990s judges had clearly discarded any notion of following the idea of Christianity being a part of the Common Law, thanks in part to the increasingly multifaith and multi-ethnic nature of English society. Article 9 of the European Convention on Human Rights, which guaranteed everyone freedom of thought, conscience and religion, was another, as it implied to judges that the law took an 'essentially neutral view of religious beliefs' and had to maintain a 'benevolent tolerance of cultural and religious diversity', in the words of Lord Justice Munby, after he became president of the Family Division of the High

Court.[72] 'Religion is something to be encouraged', said Lord Hope in 2009, 'but it is not the business of government.'[73]

Yet how could it be mere rhetoric, when written and codified law made its first appearance in the British isles after the fall of Rome as part of a Christian impulse; when Christian scripture contributed much of the substance of many of the subsequent law codes, an ethical framework for the law, philosophical ideas for the sources of the law, ideas of procedure, oath-taking, the accountability of kings and governments before the law, a slew of fundamental rights including the right to a fair trial and to silence, the emergence of distinct branches of the law such as crime, tort and the court of Equity, essential ideas in contract and tort law, and other areas including wills, matrimony,[74] patents[75] and defamation?[76] Scriptural precepts were used in submissions,[77] and judges were reluctant to allow ideas that contravened what they understood to be biblical morality. Indeed, we are so indebted to Christian assumptions in our law and the moral foundations on which it is built that, although it may no longer be 'operative' in the same sense that it was, it will always remain part of the law. If, as the contemporary judges have said, Christianity is no longer a part of English law, it still remains, to a great extent, its parent.

3

Angel's Wit and Singular Learning

The Rise of English Education

There was a time when the greatest library in northern Europe was to be found not in London, nor in Paris, nor Berlin, neither in Oxford, Cambridge, Antwerp nor Wittenberg. Instead, it was to be found in a cluster of stone buildings on the cold, rainy banks of the estuary of the River Tyne.

The double monastery of Monkwearmouth-Jarrow, which sat on both sides of the Tyne, would have seemed a modest establishment to later eyes, each with its small church, chapel, hall and range of guesthouses and dormitories. However, when these were built towards the end of the seventh century, they were the first stone constructions in that region since the fall of the Roman Empire. Their founder was a rich Northumbrian noble called Benedict Biscop. He became a monk in mid-life, and put his considerable wealth at the service of his new monastery to adorn it in the best Roman style. He travelled several times to Gaul and Rome, and brought back not only a host of icons, relics, embroidered silks and even a specialist in Roman plainsong to lend sanctity to its altars, but also glassmakers to make windows and 'masons who could build a church for him according to the Roman manner which he always loved'.[1]

Far more costly than any of these, however, was his collection of books. His devotion to the gathering of new volumes was as obsessive as the age – where books were in desperate scarcity – would allow. He returned from every trip abroad laden with tomes. On his fourth trip to Rome, records the Venerable Bede, he 'brought back no small number of books covering every aspect of divine learning which he had either bought at a good price, or had been given by friends'. On the fifth trip, 'he came back weighed down with ... wares yet more plentiful than before ... [a] countless wealth of books of every kind'. On the sixth, 'there was indeed a great wealth of holy books'.[2]

Thanks to the endeavours of Benedict Biscop and his immediate successor, Ceolfrith, who shared Benedict's book-hoarding proclivities, by the first decade of the eighth century the monastery had been able to accumulate from mainland Europe, Canterbury, and perhaps even other monasteries in Ireland, a library of more than 300 volumes. It could boast copies of the scriptures, including a large copy of the Bible which had been made for the Roman statesman Cassiodorus, as well as biblical commentaries, the works of Augustine, St Jerome and Pope Gregory the Great, saints' lives, Eusebius on the history of the Church, the Jewish historian Josephus, St Isidore's *Etymologiae* (an encyclopaedia of universal knowledge), technical writings on the reckoning of time, medicine, the Roman army, sections of Pliny's natural history, handbooks of Latin grammar and verse, Christian Latin poets and also a copy of Virgil's Roman epic, the *Aeneid*.[3]

The cost of even one book at this time would have been the equivalent in the modern age of a supercar or helicopter. In the era before paper, the creation of a bible would have required the skins of at least 500 sheep, and a copy of the works of Pope Gregory the Great around 2100 skins. Just as difficult to obtain would have been the time of highly skilled workers required in the preparation of parchment or vellum, binding, manuscript illumination and copying. Those who had the ability to write were especially in short supply, and copying books in the elegant, clear calligraphy of the period was a slow business. To make a copy simply of the four gospels was reckoned to take up to eight months.[4]

In view of the difficulty and cost of obtaining books, it may seem surprising that the nascent Church in the British isles was so devoted to obtaining them. Although they were undoubtedly prestigious items, a very low value was generally placed on literary learning amongst the barbarian warlord elites who made up the nobility and royalty of the earliest English and European nations. With the decay of the papyrus-hungry western Roman imperial bureaucracy, the expensive decade-long education course in Latin grammar, logic and rhetoric which was considered a basic necessity for upper-class or aspirational youth across the continent came to be seen as an enervating white elephant. In the instability of post-imperial times, the elites preferred a training in arms to that in books. When Amalasuntha, the daughter of Theodoric, ruler of the Ostrogothic kingdom of Italy in the early sixth century, wished to give her son a traditional Roman literary education, she was warned by the Gothic nobility that 'Letters ... are far removed from manliness'. Even Theodoric, they cautioned her, 'would never allow any of the Goths to send their children to school; for he used to say ... that, if the fear of the [teacher's] strap once came over them, they would never withstand sword and spear'.[5]

In the face of this collapse of literacy and traditional learning amongst the worldly elites, the Church stood steadfast. Its work was the proclamation of doctrine and the offering of praise, both of which were grounded in scripture. Knowledge of the written word could never be severed from the Church's mission. Without a culture of teaching and education, the capacity of the Church to fulfil its most elementary duties would vanish. The Gothic nobles admonished Amalasuntha that 'The man who is to show daring ... and be great in renown ought to be freed from the timidity which teachers inspire',[6] but the Church's rigid insistence on the preservation, development and propagation of book learning, grammar and ancient texts through a chaotic age in a hostile and fragmented continent was in itself an extraordinary and determined act of courage. The Church, and none other, saw the value in preserving literary culture and education when all around held it close to contempt.

If anything, it was this insistence of the Church on the value of education and literary culture which succeeded in the vital work of restoring its prestige in the eyes of the royal elites. Bede was adamant that the wide flourishing of education went hand in hand with the flourishing of

England itself. 'Nor were there ever happier times since the English came into Britain', he said, speaking of the latter part of the seventh century when a number of eminent teachers came to prominence, 'for … the minds of all men were bent upon the joys of the heavenly kingdom of which they had but lately heard; and all who desired to be instructed in sacred studies had masters at hand to teach them'.[7] The great scholar Alcuin, who had been taught by Bede's pupil Ecgbert, Archbishop of York, and who was later poached by the Emperor Charlemagne to revive learning in his court, praised King Offa of Mercia for his interest in learning, calling him 'the glory of Britain, a trumpet of Christian proclamation', and sent him one of his pupils to act as a teacher for any students King Offa might put forward.[8] In the latter part of the ninth century, King Alfred, imbibing the ideas of Bede, lamented that slackness in learning and Christian education went hand in hand with Viking attacks: 'Consider what punishments befell us in this world when we neither loved wisdom at all ourselves, nor transmitted it to other men; we had the name alone that we were Christians, and very few had the practices'.[9] Such a belief prompted his extensive patronage of education with the translation of a number of essential educational texts into English – 'Books most needful for all men to know', in his words – the establishment of new monasteries and a school at his court, after the example of Charlemagne.[10]

The greatest churchmen of the age saw education as a fundamental part of their work. They were teachers as much as they were monks or priests. Their desire to seek out and impart knowledge was one of the signs of their saintliness. In this era, where the chain of transmission of learning and letters was so fragile, their eagerness to teach was fraught with urgency. 'I warn you not to lose the chance of learning from me, for death is upon me', said Boisil, Prior of Melrose, at the end of his life in 664 to his pupil St Cuthbert, later Bishop of Lindisfarne. '… By next week my body and voice will have lost its strength …'. Together they read St John's Gospel with a commentary, which Boisil said could be read and discussed in a week. Similarly, at the end of his life in 735, Bede is recorded as hurrying to complete his unfinished writings whilst still on the verge of death: 'I cannot have my children learning what is not true', he admonished his pupil Wilbert, '... take your pen and mend it fast ...' he commanded, only relaxing into his final contemplations of the everlasting when the final necessary sentence had been dictated.[11] Elsewhere, at the end of his *Ecclesiastical History of the English People*, Bede recorded that from the age of seven he had applied himself to the study of the scriptures, and that it had always 'been my delight to learn or to teach or to write'.[12]

Books Most Needful for All Men to Know

From the beginning, Christian scholars understood that a spiritual education required more than just a knowledge of the Bible. Aldhelm, Abbot of Malmesbury, who lived in the generation before Bede, and who is often hailed as the 'first English man of letters', once instructed his pupil Aethilward that there was an important reason to seek secular knowledge. Since the words of divine law and scripture were arranged in accordance with the rules of grammar, 'the more fully you have learned beforehand the most diverse rules of that art ... the more easily will you understand the deepest and holiest meanings of the same divine discourse in the course of your reading'.[13]

The Bible, as Aldhelm observed, could not be fully understood without a knowledge of language or wider culture. This being so, a secular component was an inescapable part of a higher Christian education. With Aldhelm, we have a clear sight of the breadth of this learning which formed a part of his clerical education. In 671, when he had the opportunity for an extensive period of study at Canterbury, he became so engrossed in this work that he had to write to his bishop, Eleutherius, to apologise for not returning to spend Christmas with his fellow monks at Malmesbury. His letter reveals the subjects he had been investigating. Roman law was at the forefront of his notice, but then the seven liberal arts – a course of education which emerged from the later Classical world – seized his attention. These were the three linguistic arts of grammar, logic and rhetoric, and the four scientific arts of arithmetic, geometry, music and astronomy. He mentions work on poetry, the 'hundred types of meters,' how its 'hidden ornaments . . . are grouped according to letters, words, feet, poetic figures, verses, accents, and rhythms,' the 'musical modulations of song,' the 'most difficult proofs of [mathematical computation] and the reckonings of calculations, which they call "fractions" through persistent study . . .' and finally the zodiac, 'the circle of the twelve signs that rotates at the peak of heaven . . . .'[14]

Aldhelm's mastery of these subjects and his dedication to the pursuit of knowledge was far more than a boast, or an excuse to escape from his monastic duties. Of this, his surviving literary work is a proof. The most striking is a collection of 100 riddles, written in Latin verse (Aldhelm is the first known Anglo-Saxon to write poetry in Latin):

> Long since, the holy power that made all things
> So made me that my master's dangerous foes
> I scatter. Bearing weapons in my jaws,
> I soon decide fierce combats; yet I flee
> Before the lashings of a little child.

This short riddle, a description of a dog, is joined by an extraordinary range of other items: anything from elements and natural phenomena – earth, wind, water, sparks, rainbows – to celestial bodies – sun and moon, the Pleiades, the Evening Star – flora and fauna both common and fantastical – the locust, gadfly, cat, palm tree, weasel, beaver, eagle, ram, flying fish, ostrich, serpent, ant-lion, water-spider, peacock, salamander and minotaur – to inanimate objects he might have seen in the monastery or further afield – bookcase, organ, weighing scales, trumpet, cauldron, mill, sieve, candle, shield, whetstone, wine-cask, lighthouse, diamond.[15]

Aldhelm's riddles were innovative, but based on the examples of other late-Latin authors, some Christian, others apparently pagan. Likewise, he drew his information about many of the items from both Christian and pagan works, whether the encyclopaedia of St Isidore of Seville, or the *Natural History* of Pliny, in addition to his own experience. The prologue to the riddles even mimicked the opening of Classical epic poems, but with the Christian God being invoked to aid his poetry instead of the Muses. His intentions in writing the riddles were manifold. They were tools to educate others about poetic metre to assist them in reading poetry and writing new verse: even if he used pagan verse forms, it was still a valid expression of piety for him and others to create new praises to God in 'measured hymns', divinely inspired like the psalmist. They also served to teach about the meaning and nature of words, language and figures of speech. But most of all, the wide range of items which he described – 'heavenly and earthly ... now of a grand, now of a simple nature' – were an encomium to the breadth and variety of God's creation, all of which, in a Christian education, was worth the student's acquaintance.[16]

If it seems a little frivolous for Aldhelm to have had such a breadth of interests, this idea is dispelled by looking at some of his near contemporaries. One of his teachers at Canterbury, Theodore of Tarsus – a Greek-speaker who had fled a Persian invasion of the Byzantine Empire as a child, had been educated in Constantinople, and who was later sent from Rome to become Archbishop of Canterbury – is not known to have written poetry like Aldhelm, but some of his biblical commentaries were rediscovered and published in the 1990s. They are rich with both recondite and practical knowledge that he owed to his eastern upbringing close to the biblical lands and his Greek education. There are explanations of Greek and Hebrew words, analyses of grammar and rhetoric, the location of settlements in the Holy Land, explanations of weights and measures, types of coins, eating utensils, Jewish sacrificial customs, the behaviour of oriental shepherds, information on pearl-fishers in the Red Sea and their behaviour during thunderstorms, the provenance of incense and spices. Theodore was concerned with teaching the literal meaning of scripture, but believed that it could not be understood without knowledge of the linguistic, cultural and historic context. His teaching of the Bible, which Aldhelm would have experienced, showed him the practical need for a wide education.[17]

Even Bede, in a later generation, who followed what was to become the more established fashion of looking for allegorical meaning in the Bible beyond the purely literal, still sought in the natural histories and encyclopaedias to illuminate the meanings of hard verses of scripture. What, for example, did the Song of Songs mean when the bride described her beloved as having a 'belly as of ivory, set with sapphires'? Bede turned to Isidore and Pliny as well as elsewhere in scripture, and with them pondered the anatomy of the groin, its lack of bones and vulnerability to wounds; the origins of ivory and the nature of elephants, with their reputed character of chastity and cold-bloodedness; and the purported connection between sapphires and heavenly sublimity. From these ingredients, he derived an interpretation of the passage. Whichever approach one chose – literal with Theodore, or allegorical with Bede – the Bible might lead, but it could not stand alone. In order to make it understood, it was necessary to bring a whole host of other books and knowledge into the classroom with it, even from the pre-Christian pagan writers.[18]

Rivers of Wholesome Knowledge

From almost the moment of Augustine's arrival in Kent, and for centuries afterwards, the Church and the clergy were pre-eminent as the educators of England. According to Bede, the second boat of missionaries to reach Kent after Augustine, in 601, contained 'many manuscripts.'[19] A later historian recorded that these included a complete Bible, copies of the gospels and psalter, hymns and scriptural commentaries. The work of school education at Augustine's base in Canterbury must have started promptly. Within half a century, several natives from the Anglo-Saxon kingdoms had taken Christian names – Ithamar, Damian, Thomas, Boniface and Deusdedit – and been appointed to bishoprics. This could not have happened unless they had become literate and had received sufficient education in the scriptures.[20]

Canterbury soon gained a strong reputation as a centre of learning. In 631, the devout convert Sigbert, king of the East Angles, who had spent some time in exile in Gaul, ordered a school to be established in his kingdom in imitation of the 'good institutions which he had seen in Gaul', where boys could be taught to read and write in Latin. This work was achieved by the local bishop, Felix, who 'furnished [the school] with masters and teachers after the manner of the people of Kent'.[21] Canterbury's renown was further burnished by the arrival in 669 of Theodore of Tarsus and his equally learned colleague Hadrian, a Berber from North Africa who was appointed abbot of the Canterbury monastery of St Peter and St Paul. Hadrian was, according to Bede, well versed in the scripture, monastic and ecclesiastical teaching, and 'excellently skilled both in the Greek and Latin tongues'. For Aldhelm, he was 'endowed with ineffably pure urbanity'. Together, in Bede's view, Theodore and Hadrian were responsible for a golden age in learning: 'they gathered a crowd of disciples, and rivers of wholesome knowledge daily flowed from them to water the hearts of their hearers'. Such knowledge was in not only the scriptures, but also 'the metrical art, astronomy, and ecclesiastical arithmetic'.* They would even have examined pagan Classical poetry, including the epic writers Virgil and Lucan, and the raucous satirist Juvenal, quotations of which were embedded in the Latin-language textbooks of Donatus and Priscian. Late in Bede's life, there were still students living who were 'as well versed in the Greek and Latin tongues' as in their native Anglo-Saxon.[22]

Canterbury, however, was not the only centre of learning. Lindisfarne and Bede's own Monkwearmouth-Jarrow had reputations just as grand. Malmesbury, where Aldhelm first began his studies, was also held in high regard. Other centres particularly esteemed for their educational traditions included Nursling in Hampshire, where the Devonian St Boniface taught Latin before leaving as a pioneering missionary to Germany, gaining a national reputation there similar to St Augustine's in England; Breedon-on-the-Hill enjoyed Tatwine as a teacher of Latin, who later

* Ecclesiastical arithmetic had the ultimate end of calculating the correct date of Easter and other moveable feasts.

became Archbishop of Canterbury; St Hilda of Hartlepool and later Whitby was known as a teacher of not only nuns but also male clergy, and another abbess, Leofgyth of Wimborne, taught Latin verse composition before joining her kinsman Boniface as a missionary in Germany where she was also recognised as a saint.[23]

The work of teaching was then of particular prestige. It was not a distinct profession in its own right, but was often one of the duties carried out by priests, monks, nuns and even bishops amongst their other work. This being so, practical questions of how best to teach pupils were a direct concern of senior members of the Church, and thus the clergy made their own substantial contribution to the development of pedagogy and classroom practice. St Boniface and Tatwine both wrote their own grammar textbooks for use in their classrooms – the *Ars Bonifatii* and the *Ars Tatuini*, whose use was known on the continent. The riddles and writings on poetic metre by Aldhelm have already been mentioned, and Bede himself also produced similar material for the purposes of teaching. The work on the craft of teaching was often highly innovative. Later in the tenth century, Aelfric, Abbot of Eynsham, wrote a new grammar book which explained Latin in terms of English, the first known grammar book anywhere in Europe where Latin was expounded by way of a vernacular language. He was also one of the first teachers in England known to write colloquies. These were parallel text dialogues in Latin and English about vivid everyday subjects – ploughing, hunting, types of fish, princes, abbots, pilgrimage to Rome, wars between Saxons and Britons – which schoolchildren could learn by heart in Latin and perform in class, thus allowing them to develop a quick conversational proficiency in the language.[24] One of his pupils, Aelfric Bata, developed the form further, with sometimes raucous or comic scenes of students arguing about the ownership of stationery or problems about going to the toilet.[25*]

* These methods are being rediscovered by Latin teachers today as being far more effective ways of learning Latin, rather than treating it as a language purely to be read and deciphered on the page.

The Church made its learning available in a wide variety of venues. This variety lay at the origin of the different types of schools and routes of education that later arose in England. In almost every case, the Church moved beyond the initial offer of learning just to its clergy and monks in training, so that education became ever more available to members of the broader laity. The knowledge brought by the Church thus became, over generations, a leaven for all of English society and culture.

At first, monasteries were the most significant outlets for education. Learning was a fundamental part of monastic life, and the early-sixth-century Rule of St Benedict (written as a guide for monks and monasteries) made explicit provision for the tutelage of boys (who were frequently placed in the monasteries at an early age as 'oblates') and young men who were to become monks. The rule required them to learn how to recite and sing the texts of the daily offices, and stipulated that a separate part of the monastery should be set aside for them to study, eat and sleep.[26] By the twelfth century, the practice of placing child oblates in monasteries fell into disuse, but the monasteries still continued to provide education to the young. Until the Reformation, abbots and priors often personally took the sons of gentry to board with them as private pupils to learn Latin, knowledge of religion and good manners. Similarly, most nunneries accepted girls and younger boys, again usually from upper-class families, as boarders for short periods to teach them reading, singing and again good manners.[27]

However, there was also more substantial provision for the disadvantaged. From about the end of the twelfth century, records survive of monastic houses taking in destitute children, to whom they gave not only food, but also teaching. Orphans and other poor boys came to be housed in the monastic almonry, a building usually on the periphery of the monastery where food and other items were distributed as charity to the needy. The first known examples of such schools are at Bury St Edmunds and Durham. At Norwich, a set of statutes for the almonry school exists from around 1288 giving a good picture of life there. The school had room for 13 poor boys, known as 'clerks', who were chosen by the monastic almoner and the subprior. Their lodgings were in the almonry itself, and they were provided with a daily ration of bread as well as a share of the leftovers from the monastery (the rest of which were distributed to the city's poor). They were taught Latin by a master who was appointed from outside the monastery, and also learned how to sing plainsong. However, on Sundays and feast days they were sent to help sing the services not in the monastery itself, but in one of the local parish churches. In the case of Norwich, the city and the boys enjoyed the benefit of the monastery's charity, rather than the monastery itself.[28]

In some cases, the boys who attended the almonry schools did assist with services or work in the monasteries, and indeed went on to become monks themselves. However, this was far from being universally the case. The alumni of the schools included bishops, ordinary clergy, members of the gentry (who occasionally sent their sons to the almonries as fee-paying students), merchants, tradesmen, down to yeoman and peasant farmers. One of the former pupils of the St Albans almonry school, William Grindecobbe, was even a leader of the Peasants' Revolt in 1381.[29]

The monasteries did not have a monopoly on education. In towns and cities, the large churches staffed by non-monastic clergy also offered teaching to local children. The extent of their work before the Norman Conquest cannot be known with any certainty, but their role as centres of learning becomes clear in the decades immediately after 1066. Many charters survive from this period showing that cathedrals and minster churches* were required to establish schools. The non-monastic foundations often had two types of school. The first was the song school. This offered a more elementary education, with knowledge of reading, writing,

* Minster churches are, strictly speaking, churches which were originally founded as monasteries, often in the Anglo-Saxon period, which lost their monastic component after some time, but continued to be staffed by a number of non-monastic clergy, often living in a collegiate fashion. It should also be remembered that some cathedrals until the Reformation were part of a monastic foundation, for example Winchester and Durham, and others were run by secular (or non-monastic) clergy, for example Exeter or St Paul's in London.

prayers and plainsong. Such schools were intended for members of the minster or cathedral choir, but also seem to have been open to the wider public. The second type of school was the grammar school. It was generally in these schools, which children might enter at around the age of eight or nine, that they would take up the weightier challenge of the Latin-language textbook. Although the boundaries between the two types of school were far from rigid, the statutes of the grammar school in Bruton,* founded by the Bishop of London Richard FitzJames in 1519, give an idea of the distinction. The scholars, by that level, should not be dealing with 'song nor other petty learning, [such] as the cross row [alphabet], reading of the matins, or of the psalter, or such other small things, neither reading of English, but such [things] as shall concern learning of grammar'. The teaching in such schools was generally conducted by an official of the cathedral. Nevertheless, they were also open to the general public, and their pupils were not tied to entering a career in the Church.[30]

By the end of the 1200s, it appears that many smaller towns throughout England, without cathedrals or large minster churches, could also boast of having schools. Nevertheless, their establishment was for the most part thanks to the patronage of the Church and clergy, and they were often connected to the Church or similar monastic institutions in their form. Their teachers were also very often members of the clergy. Winchester College, founded in 1377 by William of Wykeham, Bishop of Winchester, included ten fellows who were required to be priests, three chaplains and 16 choristers, whose primary duty was to maintain daily worship in the college chapel. Its grammar-school component was made up of two teachers and 70 'poor and needy' scholars, with Wykeham's intention being to give boys from humble backgrounds the opportunity to acquire the learning needed to fit them for the highest offices in the Church. Eton College, founded by Henry VI in 1440, had a similar number of chaplains and choristers also bound to sing the services in the

* This school still exists as the King's School Bruton, refounded around 1549 by King Edward VI.

college chapel – which, had it been fully completed, would have had one of the longest naves in Europe – and likewise a grammar-school component for the education of 70 poor boys in imitation of Winchester. However, schools did not need to be as grand as Eton or Winchester to be part of a church establishment with regular services. Towards the end of the Middle Ages, new grammar schools were frequently attached to church chantries, where a priest sang regular masses for the repose of the soul of the founder; this chantry priest was also endowed to teach grammar, and the school under his charge was known as a 'chantry school'. A considerable number of these medieval grammar and chantry schools still exist today, often refounded around the time of the Reformation.[31]

Changes in English society and Church organisation towards the end of the Anglo-Saxon period meant that another substantial channel for elementary and intermediate education emerged beside the more formal institutions of church schools. As great estates were carved up into smaller portions and an increasing number of villages emerged deeper in rural areas away from minsters and large churches, local lords tended to endow new, more humble churches to look after the souls in these emerging territorial units. This was the origin of the parish system, which endures in England to this day. Thousands of parishes had emerged by the eleventh century, and each parish church was generally overseen by a single priest, thus making the parish clergy more numerous than the monastic population. In addition to the ordained clergy, each parish also possessed a parish clerk. The services at parish churches were, in essence, dialogues, and therefore at least a second person in addition to the priest was needed who could read out or sing the Latin of the service books. This role came to be performed by the clerks, who also assisted with other duties such as ringing bells, serving at altar during mass and carrying the vessels of holy water, frequently used in medieval liturgies. For their assistance, they were paid a small remittance, but also possessed a none-too-demanding schedule of work.[32]

The development of parishes was a further spur to the spread of education and book learning. The increased number of clergy naturally increased the demand for education. The parish clerks themselves were often young men who were in training for the priesthood. Their position gave them the impetus to learn how to read and develop their knowledge of letters, and their relative leisure gave them the chance to seek an education either at a school in a nearby town if they happened to be within range of it, or from the parish priest himself if not. This prompting for the parish priest to act as a teacher to his clerk extended into an imperative to teach other parishioners. In France, where the parish system had developed somewhat in advance of England, such an ethic had emerged at least by the ninth century. In 821, Theodulf, Archbishop of Orléans, issued rules for his clergy which included provisions about education. Priests, said Theodulf, should hold schools, and not refuse to teach anyone who sent them their children to learn letters. Moreover, they should not charge fees for such teaching, but only accept whatever contributions the parents might voluntarily offer. At the beginning of the eleventh century, Archbishop Wulfstan of York, under the influence of Theodulf's rules, composed his own code for English clergy, which came to be known as the Canons of Edgar. 'Elders' should 'zealously love and teach their juniors' said Wulfstan. The priests should 'diligently teach youth and educate them in crafts' but never take the scholar of another priest without permission. The ethical imperative for the clergy to teach is perhaps best summed up in the twelfth canon: '... we enjoin, that no learned priest put to shame the half learned, but improve him, if he know better'. All of these trends helped to make learning more available to the lower classes and the rural districts.[33]

This growth in the clerical population not only increased the demand for elementary and middle education. Another effect was an impetus for the development of higher education. Beyond their knowledge of liturgy, song and scripture, and the liberal arts which assisted them with understanding and expounding the faith, many clergy were increasingly in need of knowledge of the complexities of theology and Canon Law. This was particularly on account of the increasing bureaucracy of the Church's administration which was a consequence of the rising power of the papacy after the eleventh century. The twelfth and thirteenth centuries saw the emergence of the universities of Oxford and Cambridge as part of the response to these needs, but they were certainly not the only venues that attempted to cater to the desire for higher learning. By the late 1100s, English non-monastic cathedrals were giving clerical posts such as canonries to leading experts to allow them an income to lecture to local priests and scholars. Echoing this trend, the Fourth Lateran Council, held in Rome in 1215, ordered that all metropolitan cathedrals (the seats of archbishops, which in England meant Canterbury and York) should formally appoint an official to give public lectures in theology. However, the English cathedrals went far beyond this order, so that by the middle of the century it appears that all non-monastic cathedrals had made their chancellors responsible for offering such public lectures; the chancellors were also generally responsible for oversight of the cathedral's library and grammar school.[34]

One witness to the vitality of higher education and intellectual life around the cathedrals at this time is the scholar Simon de Fresne, a canon of Hereford. Around the end of the twelfth century, he wrote a letter in the form of a Latin poem to his friend, the historian and traveller Gerald of Wales, urging him to pursue his studies in Hereford. The seven liberal arts, he wrote, 'have flourished and continue to flourish' especially in his city. There, grammarians teach correctness of speaking, the rhetoricians lend beauty to the language, the logicians sound forms of argument; mathematicians expound the forms of objects and geometry, musicians the proportions of tone and harmony, astronomers the movement of the sun and moon, and predictions of eclipses, and astrologers attempt to predict the future based on these movements. Whilst such learning, he says, might allow one a sight of the very foundations of the world, one could also come to a mastery of 'new law' and 'old law', by which one could plead cases and fittingly establish justice. In his city, declared Simon, the fine arts in the study of justice were refulgent in their excellence.[35]

Despite these claims of academic vitality, and also the fact that cathedrals never ceased to offer such higher education throughout the Middle Ages – indeed, Salisbury even established a university-like college to offer such an education in the mid-thirteenth century – Oxford and Cambridge by the end of the period had overtaken the cathedrals to become pre-eminent in the field. The emergence of these two non-cathedral towns as seats of learning may have owed somewhat to practical circumstances – geographically central and thus easier to reach from many other parts of the country, with good provisions for food and accommodation and enjoying (not to be forgotten in the early Middle Ages) a dialect of English that was more universally intelligible. However, a part of the reason for their development in these non-cathedral towns might have been the desire for the companies of scholars and teachers to become self-regulating without the oversight of a bishop or cathedral chancellor.

Nevertheless, the order of life and study at the universities was still thoroughly entwined with the needs and customs of the Church. The first known legal privileges of the University of Oxford, for example, were granted in 1214 by the legate of Pope Innocent III, Cardinal Pandolfo.[36*] The dress of students (from which modern academic dress is derived) was clerical, the students being regarded as clergy in minor orders. The Master of Arts degrees and higher doctorates were granted (as they still are in Oxford today at the degree ceremonies) in the name of the Holy Trinity, 'For the honour of our Lord Jesus Christ, and for the profit of our holy mother, the Church, and of learning . . . .'

The two universities became especially important to the new orders of friars, such as the Dominicans and Franciscans, which were founded in the thirteenth century. The friars said the daily offices and kept vows of poverty, chastity and obedience like the older orders of monks, but they did not live a cloistered life, and their orders were dedicated to pastoral work in the community, particularly in giving spiritual counsel, hearing confessions and especially preaching. In order to excel in this public ministry, they took

* These served to placate the Oxford students after three of their number, although innocent, had been lynched by the townspeople (with the connivance of King John) in revenge for the accidental killing of a young girl.

the view that they had to have the greatest possible facility in the liberal arts, philosophy and theology, and thus they became especially dedicated to education. 'Study is not the end of the order', said Humbert of Romans, the master general of the Dominicans in the mid-1200s, 'but it is exceedingly necessary to secure its ends, namely preaching and the salvation of souls, for without study we can do neither.'[37] The friars especially, but also in time the older monastic orders, sent many members for long periods of advanced study at the universities. Following such study, they were often required to return to their original friaries or monastic houses to lecture to their junior brethren, who might later come to the university in their place. This practice entrenched the idea of deep learning as an ideal of medieval English monastic culture, and re-enforced the earlier desire of monasteries to develop themselves as centres of education. Even if they did not always succeed, in the four decades before the Reformation the monasteries were responsible for more university graduates than in any period beforehand, and, before they were sold off or lost, their libraries began to fill with the newly rediscovered humanist texts and ideas which were then emerging with the onset of the Renaissance.[38]

What has Ingeld to do with Christ?

The fact that the monasteries after the 1500s were easily open to new humanist ideas – the teaching of Latin in a more correct Ciceronian rather than medieval style, the exposition of long-lost Classical texts, or new writing by Italian scholars – indicates a long trend in English education.[39] The notion, which belonged to so much schooling from the dawn of literate education in the seventh century until long beyond the Reformation, that study was to serve an understanding of the Christian faith, 'preaching and the salvation of souls', has over time been responsible for a high level of cultural openness, dynamism and creativity, the fruits of which we still enjoy today.

As a leading example, if we wish to read a stirring heroic tale, with accounts of combat with monsters and drunken revels in the mead hall, we can reach for our bookshelves and take down a copy of *Beowulf*. The poem, like other Anglo-Saxon literature, was born in the world of oral recitation amongst a pre-Christian Germanic warrior elite. Yet, despite these pagan roots, it could only have been written down and preserved during Saxon times by Christian scholars in a Christian institution, most likely a monastery. Indeed, the preservation of the entire surviving corpus of Old English text, even despite its pagan aesthetics and antecedents, is thanks to the painstaking work of Christian scholars in the Saxon age.

That Christian monks devoted extremely precious and scarce resources to copying out such material from a different and apparently hostile tradition and which they might easily have allowed to perish was not something that pleased every Christian scholar. 'What has Ingeld to do with Christ?' asked Alcuin in a letter written in 797 to Higbald, Bishop of Lindisfarne, evoking one of the heroes mentioned in *Beowulf*.* However, many Christian scholars of the age did see its value. For one thing, they would have taken the view, like Bede, that there was a providence in the return of Christianity to the lands under the Anglo-Saxon kings, and as a result there was some sort of providence in the pagan culture and circumstances which brought them to power, ready to receive the Christian message from Augustine and other missionaries. In the old stories and poems which sung of the heroes, kings and even their descent from the warrior god Woden, there was a sense of approval from the Christian God – provided that Woden and his kin were demoted from their original divine status.[40]

But in addition to this, the old forms of Anglo-Saxon literature became original and creative vehicles for Christian ideas.[41] It should be remembered that in the age after Augustine, many converts who entered monasteries were members of the warrior elite, for whom battle and heroic song in Anglo-Saxon – rather than Latin – were the most intrinsic

* Alcuin's question smacked a little of hypocrisy, given his own pleasure in reading Classical literature from the pagan age of Rome. One of his nicknames at the Carolingian court was 'Flaccus', after the Roman poet Horace (Quintus Horatius Flaccus).

parts of their culture. English expression became a vital part of their religious identity and the propagation of the faith. Their new literature melded strands from Anglo-Saxon song, the scriptures, as well as Roman tradition. *The Dream of the Rood*, for example, is a haunting nocturnal vision of Christ's crucifixion as the agonised, bloody death of a Saxon-like warrior chief, the 'young hero, who was almighty God' – but with his death contemplated in a particular Roman tradition of the veneration of the Cross. In other poems, Christ takes on further characteristics of the leader of a Saxon warband. He is 'Lord of Victory', 'Defender of those fighting the fight, Protector of all creatures', leader of 'His band of thanes' and 'their Dispenser of treasure'.[42] In a more contemplative vein, the poet Caedmon, who claimed to have received a visionary gift at the monastery of Whitby in the mid-seventh century, hailed God the Father with the word normally used for the leader of a warband – *Dryctin* – but conjured up a vision of Him in this guise at the very beginning of creation:

> Now we must laud the heaven-kingdom's Keeper, the Ordainer's might and his mind's intent, the work of the Father of glory: in that He, the Lord everlasting, appointed of each wondrous thing the beginning; He, holy Creator, at the first created heaven for a roof to the children of men; He, mankind's Keeper, Lord everlasting, almighty Ruler, afterwards fashioned for mortals the middle-earth, the world . . .[43]

In terms of English culture and education, the impact of Christianity is seen in areas far beyond the foundations it helped to establish for the development of the English language and its literature. If one happens to glance up from this book at a clock, for example, one might pause to think on the life of Richard of Wallingford. Richard was born in 1292, the son of a blacksmith. Orphaned at an early age, he was taken in by the monks of Wallingford priory, and subsequently sent to study and teach at Oxford. After a number of years there, he became Abbot of St Albans. However, his work went far beyond prayer and the exposition of scripture. His best-known achievement was his design and construction of an astronomical clock which was the most original and intricate of any such machine known to that date, and certainly up until the English Reformation. It was based on a knowledge of mathematics, astronomy and mechanics that was so acute, that its accuracy was honed to the order of around a millionth part.[44]

Richard was only one of a large number of scholars produced by Oxford and the English firmament of higher education in the fields of mathematics, astronomy, science and philosophy, as well as theology. Their work, whose legacy is legion, was impelled by the idea of science and philosophy being demanded as a means of understanding Christianity and scripture, rather than the two principles being at loggerheads. In his late-eleventh-century *Proslogion*, St Anselm, Archbishop of Canterbury, conceived the dictum '*fides quaerens intellectum*', 'faith seeking understanding', which articulated the belief that scientific and philosophical enquiry went hand in hand with religious belief, and that belief drove rather than stifled enquiry. In the 1260s, around a century and a half after Anselm, the Franciscan friar Roger Bacon, who spent a large part of his career at Oxford, declared that 'philosophy is nothing except the unfolding of divine wisdom by teaching and writing'. The seeker of divine wisdom is bound to reject flawed authority, prejudice and ignorance cloaked as understanding. One should not fear to deal with new ideas – such as those which arose from the recent rediscovery of the texts of Aristotle – and investigate how they might be reconciled with Christianity (as did other Franciscan philosophers at Oxford such as Duns Scotus and William of Ockham), rather than attempting to ignore or suppress them. Science, he argued, should be the handmaiden of scripture; but there is barely any field of human enquiry which does not assist with the understanding of scripture or the divine. For scriptural exegesis, knowledge of philosophy and languages is essential – Latin, Greek and Hebrew, but also Arabic, particularly for reference to philosophical texts from the Arab tradition. Indeed, a grasp of all languages should be sought for commerce, government, diplomacy, missionary work. Beyond this, mathematics, he argued, is also essential, preparing the mind and elevating it to 'sure knowledge of all things'. Mathematics goes with 'experimental science', based on direct testing of reality and reason. From this comes an understanding of the properties and possibilities of all material – flora, stones, unusual minerals, magnets, fireworks – indeed, Bacon was the first westerner to record the formula for the Chinese invention of gunpowder.[45]

Bacon is often remembered for a number of apocryphal stories that were told about him after his death. Some paint him as being a pioneering scientist far ahead of his time; others suggest that he was a devotee of the occult, obsessed with creating automated magical brazen heads. In fact, he was just one of the scholars generated by a system of education which cherished scientific as well as philosophical and literary creativity. Bacon had a particular interest in the science of optics, but he was building on the work of one of his Oxford predecessors, Robert Grosseteste, who was also Bishop of Lincoln. Grosseteste's surviving texts include books on astronomy, a cutting-edge work on the nature of light, and works on the rainbow and colour.[46] He was far from the only cleric or bishop to write on science. Abbot Richard of Wallingford, mentioned above, wrote on trigonometry and calculations of planetary movements. John Peckham, Archbishop of Canterbury (d.1292), who taught at Oxford, wrote on the nature of perspective. Shortly afterwards, a circle of thinkers at the new Merton College, known as the Oxford Calculators, worked particularly on mathematical problems of velocity and physical forms. Their leading member, Thomas Bradwardine (d.1349), who was fully engaged with this work, was also a theologian and later Archbishop of Canterbury. Recent scholarship has shown that Bradwardine and his colleagues were in fact responsible for many of the first discoveries about the physics of acceleration which, for a long time, have been attributed to Galileo. Indeed, Galileo is known to have had access to some of their writings, and these writings were also praised by the seventeenth-century German mathematician Gottfried Leibniz, one of the developers of the calculus. It was not in the creation of fantastical brazen heads that such a system of education had its culmination, but in foundational, and usually forgotten, contributions to every field of literary and scientific endeavour.[47]

4

Mirrors of the Blessed

One evening several months ago, on turning up to a weekly choir rehearsal in a local church, St Mary's Axminster, I was surprised to see the interior of the building unexpectedly swathed in scaffolding. The structure covered the entire whitewashed chancel arch facing into the nave, and reached almost to the ceiling, around 30 or 40 feet. I assumed that the roof was probably falling down, and thought little more of it.

The following week, as I was absent-mindedly gawping into the air over my shoulder whilst our patient choirmaster was explaining to us tenors exactly how he wanted us to sing a particular passage of Henry Purcell, I suddenly realised that the scaffolding had nothing to do with the state of the roof.

I knew that there once had been medieval paintings on the archway. Indeed, a few fragments still remained here and there amidst the whitewash: a hint of a pattern in one place, the suggestion of a little crenelated turret in another. Somehow, it had not occurred to me that the paintings as a whole had actually survived beneath the whitewash, which was now being painstakingly removed.

Over the next few months, the lost paintings little by little were revealed. They had been dimmed and scarred by the near 500 years they had spent beneath the whitewash, but these ravages had done little to detract from their presence. At each weekly rehearsal, more could be seen. Indeed, before long, not just one painting but a whole palimpsest began to emerge.*

* An unpublished research report on these paintings has recently been written by the conservator and art historian Ruth McNeilage, who worked on uncovering them. Copies are available in St Mary's Axminster itself.

Above the arch appeared a grand doom depicting the Last Judgement; a ghostly white crucifix loomed in the midst of it, flanked by angels and the Virgin Mary, her head bowed in weeping, all seen as if in mist. On top, the outlines of the castellated walls and gabled roofs of an opulent medieval city, an earthly metropolis transfigured into a vision of the heavenly Jerusalem as an eternal home for the souls of the righteous.

Lower down the arch were swirling and elaborate painted niches, a latticework in imitation of Gothic stone tracery boldly picked out with floral motifs and foliation. But rudely stamped on top of them and interrupting their sinuous curves were a later generation of paintings – harsh rectangular boxes of black-letter text on clean white backgrounds, quotations taken apparently at random from the King James Bible: 'He that shall believe and be baptised, shall be saved: but he that will not believe, shall be damned ... Is any among you afflicted? Let him pray. Is any merry? Let him sing. Is any sick among you? Let him call for the Elders of the Church, and let them pray for him ...'.

After the scaffolding, the ladders and tarpaulins had finally been packed away, it was possible to appreciate – even if still damaged and fragmentary – the overwhelming appeal to the senses offered by the church before the Reformation, and the calls it made on the creativity of artists and craftsmen over generations to find ways of making the faith available through the sight. One could also see, standing in this spot, the shock that would have been suffered as the old images were covered up in the mid-sixteenth century with verses of scripture, the move made from devotion through the senses to devotion through word and intellect – before these bare texts themselves were also concealed with thick coats of whitewash in favour of complete visual austerity.

There is an implicit difficulty in talking about the contribution that Christianity has made to the history of English arts and material creativity. For hundreds of years until the Reformation, Christianity was arguably the greatest spur to such creativity in England. Yet, as with the wall paintings here in Axminster, a vast amount of what the era had brought to birth was covered up, defaced, dispersed, buried, destroyed.

One can only apprehend the wealth of what there was either in fragments, or often out of context in museums, unsupported by the matrix of other material, music, rituals and liturgies, of which such artwork would have formed an intrinsic part.

Nonetheless, the fragments still remain. Again like the wall paintings, damaged and shorn of their context as they might be, they can still speak with eloquence of the generations of artistic and material flowering that radiated from earlier English Christian devotion. Their effect was felt not only in their own ages, but also by later epochs and even the present, haunted by the very absence of the old artwork, or inspired by its access to spirituality. Even the most austere and puritanical times could not completely escape from the idea that a painting, a sculpture, the craft of a building were a path to Christian devotion. Such a sense of sanctity left its mark not only by way of paintings, sculpture and stained glass, but – from before the Reformation up to the present day – on the arts of England more widely, and the very landscape of England itself.

How Should I Read in the Book of Painting and Imagery?

When St Augustine came to spread the gospel in Kent in 597, images were a part of his spiritual cargo. According to Bede, even before Augustine began to preach any of the Christian doctrines to King Aethelbert he first set up a silver cross and a painted picture of Christ in his presence, chanting a litany in front of it before attempting to expound the principles of the faith. The display of this image of Christ was a conspicuous part of his arrival. Not only was it exhibited in front of the king, but it was also carried, along with the silver cross, in front of Augustine and his retinue as they processed for the first time into Canterbury.[1]

There is no doubt, regardless of the spiritual worth Augustine considered his image of Christ to possess, that he knew in pragmatic terms it was a prestige item. As has been said in Chapter 1, the access to prestigious foreign goods was one of the ways in which the earliest English kings could add to their tenuous authority. The sheer lustre of the goods, with their exotic materials, craftsmanship, and suggestion of foreign empires and an ancient wisdom, added to the grandeur of their possessors and became objects of desire to their retinues. It is not for nothing that Pope Gregory made sure to send gifts to Aethelbert after Augustine's arrival, as did later popes to subsequent Anglo-Saxon kings. From the earliest, and for centuries afterwards, the splendour of Christian art was a means of evangelism.[2]

The need for splendour was a constant in English Christian art. From the first, it was open to influences, materials and motifs, no matter their source, which might add to its sense of majesty. Some of the earliest surviving works achieve this by evoking the inheritance of Rome. The stone crosses erected across the Anglo-Saxon kingdoms, and which can still be seen in country churchyards or in the churches themselves – for example Ruthwell, Bewcastle, Easby – are replete with naturalistic relief carvings in a Roman style of Christ narrating biblical scenes: Christ in the wilderness, Christ healing a blind man, Mary Magdalen anointing Christ's feet. Along with these, the stones luxuriate with intertwining vine scrolls, clustering with rich grapes, amongst which birds, hares and other beasts nestle and feed. This motif, of a vine inhabited with animals, is also taken from Roman art, but repurposed as a piece of Christian iconography: from John's Gospel, Christ Himself is the 'true vine' in which the disciples and all Christians are invited to dwell. The vine itself also drew from another motif popular in late Roman art, the Tree of Life which sheltered and fed the birds and beasts. This sinuous tree or vine motif mixed with animals became identified with Christ's Cross, and became common on jewellery, illuminated manuscripts and sacred vessels.[3]

Some of the early Anglo-Saxon churchmen took the desire to imitate Roman artistic styles to an extreme. Wilfrid, Archbishop of York from 669 to 678, built monastic churches in Ripon and Hexham designed to proclaim his *Romanitas*. The church at Hexham was built of stone robbed from Hadrian's Wall. Its surviving passageways and staircases leading into the crypt were laid out in close imitation of the catacombs and galleries beneath St Peter's Basilica in Rome. Wilfrid commissioned pictures of the apostles engraved on silver plaques in imitation of votive tablets used in earlier Roman temples. In the monastery at Ripon, he displayed an altar cloth in imperial purple cloth, and even commissioned a set of the gospels written in gold letters on purple parchment – a privilege which was reserved for the Roman emperors. A few years later in the nearby scriptorium of Monkwearmouth-Jarrow, Abbot Ceolfrith commissioned another copy of the scriptures, the Codex Amiatinus – the oldest extant copy of the entire single-volume Bible in any language, and one of the heaviest and largest manuscripts to survive from the Middle Ages – whose illustrations were so close in nature to late Roman originals that until the nineteenth century it was considered to be a product of the Italian peninsula, not England.[4]

Yet, in the monastery of Lindisfarne, itself not far from Monkwearmouth-Jarrow, the monks looked even further afield and more widely to add lustre to their creative work. The Lindisfarne Gospels, written around the same time as the Codex Amiatinus, draw from the Roman and Italian traditions in the portraits they contain of the four evangelists, being similar in spirit to the depiction of the prophet Ezra in the Amiatinus. But in addition to these conventional Italian-style portraits is something quite different: the so-called 'carpet pages' before each gospel, dizzyingly ornate and exuberant patterns derived from a central cross, winding and fretted together in an endless geometric dance of colour, whose whorls, knots and spindles suddenly come to a head as snakes or gyres of mysterious birds in a mutual chase. The initial capital letters of each gospel are similarly adorned, twisting into borders which writhe with cats consuming herons, or letters formed, almost impressionistically, with thousands of tiny red dots. Such illustrations seemingly weave together styles taken from the traditions of Celtic or continental Germanic art, particularly the intricate patterns of interlacing animals which would adorn the brooches and jewellery of the Irish elites or in the Sutton Hoo treasures, but mixed with ideas, such as the red dots, which appear to have been drawn from Coptic art in Egypt or the Near East.

This eclectic approach became a distinctive style of the Anglo-Saxon kingdoms and the British isles in their initial Christian centuries, and in turn influenced artists on the European mainland.[5]

These creations, like the finely wrought helmets and brooches of the pre-Christian warriors, were often thought to possess a magic power. Such early elites believed that their patterns of interlocking animals and foliage conferred a supernatural protection against injury in battle or other misfortune, or offered their bearers capacities of enchantment. It is through such a fear of enchantment that King Aethelbert would at first only meet Augustine with his cross and image of Christ outdoors. The idea that art and symbols could offer such powers did not ebb with the advent of Christianity, and in the first generations after the arrival of Augustine Christian motifs, including crosses, were displayed on armour mixed up with overtly pagan imagery in the hope that each would contribute to the safety of the wearer.[6]

However, the notion that such man-made items enjoyed a magical power, and the fear that reverence might be paid to them in themselves, contributed to an unease about art that came from a fundamental part of Christian doctrine. The second of the Ten Commandments was apparently clear in its injunctions: 'Thou shalt not make unto thee any graven image, or any likeness of any thing that is in heaven above, or that is in the earth beneath, or that is in the water under the earth. Thou shalt not bow down thyself to them, nor serve them . . .'. On a strict reading of the commandment, the use of art depicting Christ, the apostles or even the animal decorations of the Lindisfarne Gospels, was all a form of idolatry.

The fear of falling into this sin troubled the churchmen of Augustine's time. Nevertheless, Pope Gregory was able to lay out a middle way between the human desire and need for art and ornament on the one hand, and the prohibition of idolatry on the other. Around 600, he was concerned by a report that one of Augustine's brother bishops, Serenus of Marseilles, had smashed images being used by Christian worshippers. Gregory wrote to him temperately:

> we suggest that you should not have broken these images . . . For a picture is introduced into a church so that those who are ignorant of letters may at least read by looking at the walls what they cannot read in books . . . You, brother, therefore should have preserved the images and prohibited the people from worshipping them, so that those who are ignorant of letters might have the means of gathering a knowledge of past events and so that the people might in no way sin by worshipping a picture.[7]

Pope Gregory's formula, that images in worship were books for the layman, or books for the unlettered, became a canonical idea in England (despite dissent from the Lollards in the fourteenth century) until the Reformation. Even until the end of the reign of Henry VIII, the English bishops maintained in words similar to Gregory's that 'images may be had and set up in churches, so it be for none other purpose but only to the intent that we (beholding and looking upon them, as in certain books, and seeing represented in them the manifold examples of virtues) would be stirred to follow the example of the saints and holy living'.[8] It laid down one of the fundamental spurs and directions for Christian artistic creativity in England. Such art should be didactic, used as a teacher, in a way that everyone could comprehend.

Bede was one of the first to witness that art was having the effect that Pope Gregory had intended. In the 670s and 680s, when Bede was a child, Benedict Biscop, the founder of the monastery of Monkwearmouth-Jarrow, made several trips to Rome, and brought back with him, amongst many things, panel paintings to adorn the monastic churches. Bede described them with relish:

> there was an image of Mary, the blessed mother of God and virgin forever, together with the twelve apostles, with which he encircled the apse of [St Peter's Wearmouth]; the painted board stretched from one wall to the other. There were images of the gospel stories with which he adorned the south wall of the church, and images of the visions of the apocalypse of the blessed John with which he similarly decorated the north wall.

Bede relates how they were intended, before anything, to instruct.

> [Biscop's] aim was that all who came into the church, even those who did not know how to read, should always gaze on the lovely sight of Christ and his saints wherever they looked, albeit in a picture; they should either recall with a keener mind the grace of the Lord's Incarnation, or remember to examine themselves more closely, seeing the decisive nature of the Last Judgement as though they had it before their very eyes.

The paintings could even give subtle lessons about the nature of scripture. In the Jarrow church, Biscop had juxtaposed scenes from the Old and New Testaments, for example 'Isaac carrying the wood with which he was to be burned and the Lord likewise carrying the cross on which he was to suffer', or another placing Christ 'raised up on the cross to the serpent raised up by Moses in the desert' to show how the Old Testament, in Christian thought, prefigured the New.[9]

Later in the Middle Ages, the manner of reading these images was elucidated in a dialogue between a rich man and a poor man, *Dives and Pauper*, written around 1400. 'How should I read in the book of painting and imagery?' asks the rich man, to which the poor man replies:

> When you see the image of the Crucifixion, think about him who died on the cross for your sins and your sake, and thank him for his endless charity that he would suffer so much for you. Take heed by the image how his head was crowned with the garland of thorns till they went into his brain and the blood burst out on every side to destroy the high sin of pride that he saw most in man's head and woman's, and make an end of your pride.

It was necessary to look closely, observe details, use the art to recall the particulars of holy stories or morals, and then apply these to one's own experience.[10] Preachers elucidated the background and details of the images in churches to teach both prince and pauper in real life. 'Many thousands of people could not imagine in their hearts how Christ was done on the cross except that they learn it by the sight of images and paintings', said John Mirk, who was also active as a preacher around 1400.[11] St Hugh, Bishop of Lincoln at the end of the twelfth century, used the sculptures of a final judgement above a church porch to admonish King John about his behaviour before his accession to the English throne. Pointing to figures amongst the damned arrayed as kings about to be dragged off by demons into hell, St Hugh warned John: 'Fix your mind always on their howls and perpetual torment, and let your heart dwell on their unceasing punishment . . .'.[12]

The formal injunction that the religious arts of the pre-Reformation age should, before anything, be an aid in the instruction of the people had an impact on the character of the art. Although there were inevitably changes in artistic style over the centuries depending on fashions and the emergence of new trends – for example, a growth in Byzantine influence over the course of the tenth century, or the development of the Gothic following the French lead in the twelfth century – a number of fundamental ideas remained constant.

In general, the images of the age did not aspire towards realism. At times, they might tend towards greater naturalism, but – especially when they dealt with biblical or divine subjects – they did not particularly interest themselves in correct perspective or accurate representations of the human anatomy. For images to fulfil their didactic function, there was no need for the careful rendering of the facial expression or the sculptural weight of the body. Instead, the substance of their stories and ideas was conveyed through a clarity of gesture, and a vast array of symbols which became popular artistic currency. Christ may be portrayed as a lamb; His mother Mary as bearing a lily for a sign of purity and virginity; the four evangelists with their symbols of a man or angel, lion, ox and eagle (John, Mark, Luke and Matthew respectively); the biblical patriarchs holding wheels to signify their imperfect knowledge; the apostles holding open books to show that they had been taught by Christ; the martyrs with palms and the instruments of their torture – St Stephen, the first martyr, holding stones, St

Laurence with a gridiron. The list is long, but such symbols would have been common knowledge amongst the people.

It was not just on account of its didactic function that the art of this time was less concerned with realism, or that it laid a particular stress on beauty and opulence. The paintings in churches, scriptural manuscripts and the other associated arts had an even more important purpose, which was cogently summed up by a twelfth-century continental monastic author and artisan, Theophilus. Addressing artists and craftsmen in a treatise on the subject, he wrote: 'You have shown the beholders something of the likeness of the paradise of God . . .'. In the words of a modern scholar, Christian worship of the time liberally employed the visual arts 'to open doors between this world and the next.'[13] Yet, the artist could not, and indeed should not, hope to signify God or holy things exactly as they were in any painting or image. 'The images of the church cannot represent to the eyes of onlookers any semblance of divine nature in themselves,' cautioned the mystic writer Walter Hilton.[14] Such were in the spiritual world, and beyond exact representation in the physical. Nonetheless, works of art could still act as figures or signs for the divine. As such, they did not strive for similitude, but rather to evoke in a corporeal medium ideas which could only be understood spiritually. The arts of the Church were thus a channel for not just teaching, but devotion. They brought the ideas of heaven and spiritual stories closer to the sight and senses, imagination and memory. In their other-worldly stylisation, wealth of symbolism and richness, they offered a broad but intimate channel for the offer of reverence, not to the images themselves, but to the ineffable world behind them: 'worship God and not the image' counselled *Dives and Pauper*, 'worship him above all things, not the image, not the . . . tree, but him that died on the tree for thy sin . . . so that you kneel . . . before the image, but not to the image.'[15]

John Mirk's notion that Christian images had brought 'many thousands of people' to a closer connection with the divine was not misplaced.[16] The art and images that were to be seen in lavishly decorated churches engendered over centuries a deep-rooted and popular devotion. They offered an access to the realm of the spiritual and contemplative which was eagerly pursued not just by a wealthy elite, but by the multitudes. The scale of this engagement is most tangible in the fifteenth and early sixteenth centuries, up to the beginning of the Reformation. During this time, the veneration of saints was at its most popular, and churches were replete with images not only of Christ and the Virgin Mary, but hosts of saints. These were usually endowed by local patronage from people within the parish, and even the less well-off gave gifts and bequests to provide for paintings, statues, luxurious embroideries, carvings, their embellishment with jewels, rich coverings, and most of all the funds to keep candles perpetually burning in honour of the holy images. The very sensation of light created by the shimmering of lamps and candles reflected in the burnished gold backgrounds and trimming of the images made each church a place where anyone could perceive for a moment the essence of paradise, a sense of the very moment of creation when God brought the light into being. To stand in the presence of light, as Robert Grosseteste, the thirteenth-century Bishop of Lincoln wrote, was to stand before the first corporeal thing, but 'more exalted and of a nobler and more excellent essence than all corporeal things.' Indeed, in his theory of light and vision, the act of seeing created a physical bond between the seer and the seen, close to a communication not just of information, but even of power between the two. Seeing created not just believing, but also a deep and ineffable connection.[17]

Had in Houses, Set Up in Churches

Despite the destruction of paintings, sculptures and other ornaments in the monasteries and churches over the course of the Reformation in the sixteenth and seventeenth centuries, which swept away all but a fragment of the artistic heritage of England of a whole millennium, the Church and English Christianity ultimately found themselves unable to deny Pope Gregory's fundamental doctrine about the validity of art and images. For all the vigour of the puritanical assault on the 'idolatry' of previous generations, such as the cry of the Elizabethan preacher

William Fulke that 'it is to the great honour of God that [the images] should be despised, defaced, burned, and stamped to powder', the regret at their loss and the counter-reaction was felt throughout the period and beyond.[18] In 1536, Robert Aske, one of the leaders of the Pilgrimage of Grace which opposed the dissolution of the monasteries, lamented that the devastation was doing away with one of 'the beauties of this realm'. Another Elizabethan preacher, Francis Trigge, said that many people complained that it was 'never merry world' since the pulling down of the abbeys.[19]

By the end of Elizabeth's reign, some clergy were becoming more vocal in their defence of images. Those who had so raged against idolatry, they argued, had fallen into the equally bad or even worse sin of sacrilege, robbing the Church of its seemliness as well as its property. 'Was there any in Solomons time, of so cursed a stomach, that Consecrated Things must be his Morsels?' complained a young Lancelot Andrewes, later Bishop of Winchester, at a sermon in Cambridge in 1585. The iconoclasm of the mid-1500s, argued Richard Neile, a seventeenth-century Archbishop of York, should simply be treated as having been 'the forbearing of food for a time' over the period of Protestant reforms, but which had now become irrelevant. The idea that the English were in danger of actually worshipping images, maintained Henry Hammond, another theologian of the time, was quite out of date. Richard Montague, a contemporary Bishop of Chichester, put forward a view fully concordant with the original ideas of Pope Gregory. 'Unto Christians', he said, images:

> are not unlawful, for civil uses: nor utterly in all manner of religious employment. The pictures of Christ, the blessed Virgin, and Saints may be made, had in houses, set up in churches . . . Respect and honour may be given unto them: the Protestants do it: and use them for helps of piety, in rememoration, and more effectual representing of the prototype.[20]

Over the course of the seventeenth and eighteenth centuries, images were again 'set up in churches', albeit fitfully. In the 1620s, King James himself rejoiced in paintings of the apostles and a golden crucifix in the Chapel Royal. In the 1630s, William Laud, Archbishop of Canterbury, sought to re-embellish England's churches more widely after the earlier depredations of the Reformation, seeking that worship should be conducted in 'the beauty of holiness'. However, his policy met with frequent hostility from those who maintained that images were a sign of 'popery': 'many idle, ridiculous, vain, and absurd pictures, representations, and stories', thundered one observer, Sir William Brereton, of the interior of St Chad's Shrewsbury in 1635, 'of late gaudily painted' in a manner that Laud would have found congenial.[21] The Puritan ascendancy in the Civil War put a temporary halt to this embellishment of churches and prompted further despoilment and iconoclasm, but the Restoration again made such decoration a possibility. In 1684, a case before the ecclesiastical courts confirmed that it was lawful for images to be displayed in churches.[22] Yet for the next century and a half it was far from a widespread practice. Depictions of the apostles and some scenes from the life of Christ are known to have been displayed during this time, and paintings or statues of Moses and Aaron were sometimes placed by altars, symbolising amongst other things the authority of the Church of England, its priesthood and sacraments.[23] Nonetheless, the fear of being charged with popery and idolatry meant that churches generally well into the nineteenth century remained far removed from the exuberance of the medieval past.

Only tombs were exempt from such concerns if they were solely established 'to show a memory to the posterity of the persons there buried' and not 'for any religious honour'.[24] Thus, from the Elizabethan age onwards many parish churches and cathedrals still boast a remarkable legacy of flamboyant and ornate monuments often rich with painted heraldry, sculptures of the departed, and long, florid encomia. Such monuments offered an outlet for devotion to the dead which before the Reformation found expression in prayers to the saints to save the souls of the departed from Purgatory, but which afterwards was channelled into an exhalation of the faithful and their pious expectations of the life to come.

It was, however, where religious images were 'had in houses' that

Christianity pre-eminently left its mark on the artistic life of England in this age. As much as Puritan theologians denounced the use of images in churches and places of public prayer, they were far from being universal iconoclasts, utterly opposed to the display of any image at all. 'The arts of painting and graving are the ordinance of God', said the Elizabethan Puritan cleric William Perkins, 'and to be skilful in them is the gift of God.' It was not just portraits which found religious approval: 'the representation of men or women, whom for their authority or other good parts in them we reverence, or love, is not unlawful; or if they be made to garnish and beautify any place', said Perkins's contemporary, Francis Bunny, then there was no hint of breaking the Second Commandment. The very representation of biblical scenes and characters which, before the Reformation, would have been found in churches, was perfectly acceptable in the home. 'We hold the historical use of images to be good and lawful', said Perkins, '. . . whether they be human or divine; and thus we think the histories of the Bible may be painted in private places.' This view was echoed by the seventeenth-century cleric Simon Birckbek: 'we mislike not pictures or Images for historical use and ornament; for when the same was only made, and looked upon, it was a Medicine; when it was worshipped, it became a poison, and was destroyed'.[25]

With this endorsement, there was a wide flourishing of art inspired by Christian ideas and scripture within the English home. Every sort of dwelling, from the great country manors of the nobility and gentry, to the town house of the merchant, to the rustic cottage or farmhouse, might boast decoration and adornment based on biblical tales: fine plasterwork on the ceilings or fireplaces of the grand houses, down to cruder painted wooden panels or murals in the humbler dwellings. Popular images included the Old Testament stories of Adam and Eve, David and Goliath, or Abraham and the Sacrifice of Issaac, not to mention the Judgement of Solomon, and Daniel in the Lions' Den. At Lanhydrock House in Cornwall, the 100-foot-long intricate plaster barrel-vaulted ceiling in the Long Gallery displays as many as 24 biblical scenes, as overwhelming and elaborate as anything that might have been seen in a pre-Reformation church. Thousands of such ceilings, although generally smaller in scale, survive across the country.[26]

Such images were seen not only in paintings or plaster reliefs. Indeed, they made their way onto every sort of furniture and domestic accoutrement. Biblical scenes appeared on heavy woodwork – the panelling of linen chests and chair backs – to lighter tapestries and hangings, pillowcases, embroideries, lace mats and damask napkins. They are frequently to be seen on the household crockery and cutlery – grand English delftware chargers painted in vivid blues, yellows and greens, with the Temptation in the Garden of Eden being an especially popular subject, but also on smaller items such as jugs, mugs and posset pots. Even 'apostle spoons' ornamented at the top of the handle with little sculptures of the apostles – a pre-Reformation idea – remained popular long afterwards. Devotional books in the home also, whether Bibles or other religious tracts, were liberally illustrated with woodcuts and prints, going so far as to depict not just incidents of biblical history, but even God the Father enthroned in heavenly splendour.[27]

Well into the nineteenth century, religious art remained highly popular in the home, and even set the standard for national taste. The most revered paintings in England in this time were the Raphael Cartoons – New Testament scenes painted around 1515 as designs for tapestries to be hung in the Sistine Chapel. Seven of the Cartoons were bought by Charles I, who intended to have further tapestries made from them. Oliver Cromwell declined to sell them with the rest of the Royal Collection after Charles's execution, keeping them back for the nation. At the end of the seventeenth century, they were put on display at Hampton Court in a gallery specially designed by Sir Christopher Wren. Before long, there was a huge demand for copies, as both paintings and tapestries, which were hung in a multitude of the great country houses, and also woodcuts and engravings, a set of which could be had for anything between 5 guineas and the more moderate price of 1 shilling. They served to decorate even modest homes and editions of the Bible intended for children. Artists clamoured to study and copy them as peerless examples of technical and aesthetic virtuosity. They were referred to so frequently in poems, sermons and literature that they became known by the simple shorthand of 'The Cartoons'. Although the art was foreign, Catholic and commissioned by a pope, it found a home deep in English culture, and Raphael was treated almost as an honorary Englishman. Purged of any tendencies towards idolatry by the fires of the Reformation, as English commentators viewed themselves as being, they were best able to appreciate the sublimity and even religious merit of the art: 'Impossible ... to behold, without being warmed with the noblest sentiments that can be inspired by love, admiration, compassion, contempt of this world, and expectation of a better', wrote Richard Steele in *The Spectator* in 1711.[28]

Raphael's Cartoons were far from the only Catholic religious art which became popular during this period. The nobility and gentry, many of whom developed their tastes on the Grand Tour, imported art with religious subjects from the continent. Some was even hung in private chapels. The critics of the period maintained that, particularly when the art was of non-biblical matter which tended to support the claims of the Roman Catholic Church or papacy, the reformed English could, unlike others, appreciate the aesthetic 'perfection', as Horace Walpole wrote of Guido Reni's *The Doctors of the Church* in his collection at Houghton, of 'what seems to surpass the genius of human nature'. Yet, if the images depicted were more strictly of scripture, then one could certainly look at them with a devotional eye. For Walpole, meditation on such pictures in the gallery of a country house was as good as a retreat into the wilderness for contemplation of the divine: 'Here are stronger lectures of piety, more admonitions to repentance ... sights like these, must move, where the preacher fails; for each picture is but scripture realized ... The painter but executes pictures, which the Saviour himself designed.'[29]

Heaven in a Wild Flower

In the eighteenth and nineteenth centuries, responses to Christianity contributed to some of the most fundamental new ideas and developments in the world of English art. The authority of the Renaissance masters may have seemed unchallengeable when Sir Joshua Reynolds, first president of the Royal Academy of Arts, pointed to them in his *Discourses on Art* (1769–90) as timeless examples to be imitated. It was right, he argued, that Raphael represented the apostles as 'drawn ... with great nobleness [with] as much dignity as the human figure is capable of receiving [although] we are expressly told in scripture that they had no such respectable appearance'. Religious and historical painting should eschew simple naturalism and local specifics. Instead, it should convey the subject's dignity by giving it an 'external appearance of grandeur' based on idealised conventions which were unchanging and universal.[30]

Whilst Reynolds's approach set the standard for the Royal Academy and the artistic establishment until the mid-nineteenth century, resistance to it came ultimately from religious motivations. The poet and artist William Blake was early to express his opposition to Reynolds's orthodoxy, annotating his copy of Reynolds's writings with screeds of scathing marginalia: 'To Generalize is to be an Idiot. To Particularize is the Alone Distinction of Merit. General Knowledges are those Knowledges that Idiots possess ... All Sublimity is founded on Minute Discrimination.'[31] Blake's intellectual animus against Reynolds (aside from personal dislike) sprang from a disagreement over the idea of 'genius'. For Reynolds, it was 'the child of imitation' and sprang from practice, hard work and a respect for the unchanging conventions which he had articulated in his *Discourses*. For Blake, this was a mockery of 'inspiration and vision'. Genius, and the creation of art, was the act of an individual. It was not dependent on the adherence to a body of rules, but rather on the individual giving imagination and vision their freest rein.[32]

Blake's insistence on this idea of individual genius and the personal well-spring of art came from his strong but highly unconventional

Christian beliefs, moulded by his deep knowledge of the Bible and his reading of Christian mystical writers including the Swedish philosopher Emanuel Swedenborg and the German Lutheran theologian Jakob Böhme. Jesus Christ, for Blake, was the fullest embodiment of the living God, but He was not 'wide separated from the Human Soul'. 'All deities reside in the human breast', said Blake, and Christ Himself could be equated with the human imagination; individual human imaginations were 'those Worlds of Eternity in which we shall live for ever; in Jesus our Lord'. The exercise of the individual imagination was therefore the embrace and the apprehension of God: 'This World of Imagination is the World of Eternity. It is the Divine bosom into which we shall all go after the death of the Vegetated body.'[33]

Blake's notion of the presence of Christ in each individual imagination was the source of his abhorrence of Reynolds's disdain for the particular. As Christ did not dwell in another world, but in the present, each individual thing and place in the present took on a special significance. 'All that has existed', said Blake, is 'Permanent, & not lost [nor] vanished, & every little act, Word, work, & wish . . . not one sigh nor smile nor teach, One hair nor particle of dust, not one can pass away'. One could see 'a World in a Grain of Sand / And a Heaven in a Wild Flower'. Blake saw many visions in his everyday life – a tree filled with angels at Peckham Rye, angels walking amongst haymakers at work – which gave him access to the divine presence he found immanent in creation, and his art strove to convey not just the exercise of his individual imagination, but his visionary capacity to see the divine in the immediate and the local.[34]

Blake's challenge to the establishment views of Reynolds and the Royal Academy had few immediate followers. Around 1824, towards the end of his life, a small number of devotees inspired by his work and his personal charisma – they likened him to the prophet Isaiah, and one, Samuel Palmer, would kiss the bell-handle of his rooms before visiting – formed a group called the Ancients. Although they did not share Blake's political radicalism, hostility to the established Church or the exact tenets of his personal theology, they were deeply moved by his visionary capacity. For

Palmer, Blake's engravings had 'a mystic and dreamy glimmer as penetrates and kindles the inmost soul', and his work as a whole put aside the 'gaudy daylight of this world [and] the fleshly curtain', offering instead 'the glimpse which all the most holy, studious saints and sages have enjoyed, and . . . that rest which remains to the people of God'.[35]

Palmer himself moved to the Kent village of Shoreham in 1826, which became, in his words, his 'valley of vision', 'Inchanted ground' or 'the Countrey of Beluah'.* Here, he was frequently visited by other members of the group, including George Richmond and Edward Calvert, and for around ten years they created art which paid little regard to the academic conventions, but which cherished the individual imagination and the visionary sense of the divine in the immediate and local world. Their work tended towards the archaic, and evoked what they knew of early Renaissance art. Palmer even wore an antique-style pleated smock, which, together with his long hair and beard, gave him a slightly Christ-like appearance, prompting George Richmond to paint a portrait of him as Christ somewhat in the style of Dürer, but with the dreamy landscape evoking Palmer's visions of Shoreham itself. In general, the subjects of their work were either biblical (for example, Palmer's *The Repose of the Holy Family*, 1824–5, or Richmond's *Christ and the Woman of Samaria*, 1828), or else they evoked the mystical and other-worldly vision in the near-at-hand. Palmer's *Coming from Evening Church* (1830) is an ethereal portrayal of villagers in indistinctly antique costume streaming out of the parish church, its spire and the trees embracing it bathed in a rich and mysterious moonlight which makes the scene appear charged, wordlessly significant and holy. Calvert's engraving *The Ploughman, or Christian Ploughing the Last Furrow of Life* (1827), made shortly after the death of Blake and probably in tribute to him, is an allegory based on the biblical verse 'No man, having put his hand to the plough and looking back, is fit for the Kingdom of God' (Luke 9.62). The ploughman,

* Beluah (in Hebrew meaning 'married') is a name given in Isaiah to the holy land of Israel to which the Jews would return after the Babylonian captivity. It is the name given by John Bunyan in *Pilgrim's Progress* to the peaceful and pleasant land next to the Celestial City. Palmer's use of it alludes to both of these texts.

cutting his furrows, is as the engraver or printmaker making incisions in copper or a woodblock; fully given to his activity, again set in a charged and numinous landscape, he is granted a beatific vision of Christ as the Good Shepherd, blessing his work and guaranteeing its value.

The Ancients only continued to create such works until the late 1830s, at which point financial and other pressures led them to turn to more mainstream styles of art. Their work became a powerful influence for a later wave of twentieth-century Neo-Romantic printmakers and artists such as Robin Tanner, Graham Sutherland and Eric Ravilious, but remained little cherished during their own time. It was not until the middle of the nineteenth century that a new generation of artists attempted again to challenge the dominance of 'the clear and tasteless poison of the art of Raphael', as John Ruskin put it.[36] Many of their inspirations again came from Christian material and thinking.[37]

In 1848, a circle of young painters and former Royal Academy students – including John Everett Millais, William Holman Hunt and Dante Gabriel Rossetti (who owned some of Blake's papers and studied them closely) – formed the Pre-Raphaelite Brotherhood. They desired to escape the ossified conventions of the Royal Academy and its institutional veneration of the 'great nobleness' and 'great style' of Raphael. Many productions of their age lacked 'ideas ... and character ...', were 'merely smooth and prettyish', 'self-parading and learned by rote', and were deficient because they discouraged artists from acting upon their 'own perception and study of nature', in the words of William Michael Rossetti, another member of the Brotherhood.[38]

The Brotherhood desired, ahead of anything else, a return to what was 'direct and serious and heartfelt'. Instead of the superficiality of the academic conventions, they wished to create art that had contemporary relevance, moral force, a sense of earnestness and seriousness. They found such an earnestness and moral force in the religious art of the medieval age and early Renaissance, hence the designation of their group as 'Pre-Raphaelite'. Their work tended to imitate this earlier archaic style and draw from the rich reservoir of neglected Christian artistic symbolism which was then being rediscovered and popularised by writers such as Anna Jameson and Lord Lindsay. This was combined with an intense observation of nature and a sympathy to detail, which was primarily inspired by John Ruskin. In his early work, *Modern Painters,* he called for contemporary artists to 'go to nature in all singleness of heart, and walk with her laboriously and trustingly, having no other thoughts but how best to penetrate her meaning, and remember her instruction, rejecting nothing, selecting nothing, and scorning nothing; believing all things to be right and good'. This call, at its heart, came from a Christian religious urge. In painting a landscape, for example, Ruskin insisted 'on the necessity, as well as the dignity, of an earnest, faithful, loving, study of nature as she is, rejecting with abhorrence all that man has done to alter and modify her', as only such faithfulness to nature would convey the 'faultless, ceaseless, inconceivable, inexhaustible loveliness, which God has stamped upon all things, if man will only receive them as He gives them'.[39]

The Bible and Christian subject matter formed one of the leading themes of the Pre-Raphaelites' art. Their early paintings created a shock. For example, Millais's *Christ in the House of His Parents,* exhibited in 1850, depicts Christ as a young boy in His father's carpentry workshop. It captures an uncomfortable moment where Christ has hurt the palm of His hand on a nail sticking out of a door, and other members of the family stop their work to comfort Him. The incident and its setting troubled many established commentators for its apparent banality, as well as the awkwardness and lack of conventional beauty of the careworn holy characters, far removed from the conventional grandeur and nobility of Raphael. Instead, the painting is heavy with foreboding, as Christ's injury, the concern of His mother Mary, and the other tools around the workshop – symbolic of the instruments of His Passion – all evoke and foreshadow His crucifixion and death.[40]

In the early years of the Pre-Raphaelite Brotherhood, its members were attracted to religious subjects, but more for the seriousness evoked by ideas of religion rather than an interest in religion itself. Amongst a number of its artists, this approach changed over time so that they evinced a real concern with Christianity itself and finding a new approach to religious painting. William Holman Hunt was particularly conspicuous in this concern. His early dedication to becoming the 'Painter of Christ', as he was described by one art historian at the end of the Victorian age, appears early in his visionary work *The Light of the World* (1851–4), depicting Christ as a patient and kindly but penetrating figure, bearing a lantern and knocking at a door overgrown with weeds in the hope of a response. Hunt, as he confessed to friends, painted the work in response to a spiritual inspiration. Such inspiration is visible in the work's intensity, but Hunt did not simply rest in this.

In 1854, he travelled to the Middle East to see for himself the landscapes and setting of the scriptural narrative, and he also immersed himself in contemporary biblical scholarship. His intent was to create a vision of Christ that offered an intensity of spiritual vision on the one hand, whilst still being true to the latest developments in the understanding of scripture and the history of the region. The works he created following this time showed the stamp of this research. *The Shadow of Death* (1869–73) represents Christ as a Middle Eastern carpenter pausing for prayer in His workshop, the shadow of His pose and the tools darkly suggesting the crucifixion to come. Hunt had based the painting on drawings of an actual workshop he had seen in Nazareth, as well as up-to-date knowledge of historical costume. Such attention to historical detail gave his work a striking sense of authenticity and freshness. His paintings became widely popular. Originals were in demand via galleries, and thousands of prints and engravings were sold for display in homes and schools. *The Shadow of Death*, with its carpentry shop and Christ resting from toil, was commonly to be seen in the homes of manual labourers. In 1904, he made a large copy of *The Light of the World*, which was seen by at least four million people on a world tour before being put on permanent display in St Paul's Cathedral.[41]

As the Pre-Raphaelite artists found a necessary seriousness and inspiration from looking back to medieval Christian art, the architects of the age did likewise. Augustus Pugin, a pioneer of the Victorian Gothic

Revival, argued in the 1830s that the 'pointed' period of medieval architecture from the thirteenth and fourteenth centuries should be considered the apogee of English design, and the model to be followed. 'On comparing the Architectural Works of the last three centuries with those of the Middle Ages, the wonderful superiority of the latter must strike every attentive observer', he stated confidently in his hugely influential book *Contrasts*, which included illustrations juxtaposing medieval churches, houses and other public buildings with more modern, and in his view inferior, equivalents. Architecture, he claimed, reflects the morality of the age, and the 'faith, the zeal, and above all, the unity of our ancestors ... enabled them to conceive and raise those wonderful fabrics [such as the great cathedrals] that still remain to excite our wonder and admiration'. Gothic was the archetypal style of Christianity and England, and pursued in a proper spirit it also had the capacity to elevate the society around it. He envisaged that the new sorts of building required by a modern society could be designed with such a Gothic spirit: 'There is no reason in the world why noble cities, combining all possible convenience of drainage, water-courses, and conveyance of gas, may not be erected in the most consistent and yet Christian character.'[42]

Pugin's early death in 1852 at the age of 40 cut short his career and precluded him from creating much in the way of such work – although the Gothic elaboration of the Palace of Westminster stands as his greatest achievement – but his ideas served to influence a later generation of architects. Sir George Gilbert Scott, in a chapter on the 'Architecture of the Future' in his 1857 *Remarks on Secular and Domestic Architecture*, argued that in the face 'of all the worldliness and self-seeking of our age, our secular arts' should be:

> legitimate offspring from a sacred stock ... The style which is best for the church, must be equally so for the palace, the court of justice, the market and the dwelling house. It must embrace also engineering works – as bridges, viaducts, and railway constructions. It must influence the character of our commercial structures, as warehouses and factories, and

> our agricultural buildings and labourers' cottages; yet it must be so elastic as to shape itself afresh for every one of these purposes . . .[43]

This later generation of architects, such as Scott, William Butterfield, George Edmund Street and Alfred Waterhouse, drew deeply from the Gothic style (both English and also the Italian thanks to the advocacy of Ruskin) and created large swathes of now familiar town and cityscapes – St Pancras Station, the Royal Courts of Justice and the Natural History Museum in London, Manchester Town Hall, not to mention scores of churches, university and school buildings, civic offices and court houses, branches of banks and insurance companies, railway stations, hospitals, prisons, as well as domestic dwellings. The Victorian streets and skylines, many of which survive today, were those secular 'offspring from a sacred stock'.[44]

Burning Bushes in Cookham

One may think at first glance that the art of the twentieth century, with its embrace of modernism, the abstract, and its general rejection of traditional ideas, would draw little from Christian cultural or spiritual inspirations. Yet, recent scholarship is increasingly recognising that English art of the period might be thought of as both a secular and sacred offspring from a sacred stock. Well into the first part of the century, the education of the most prominent English artists continued to lay an emphasis on Renaissance paintings with their religious subjects. From the 1890s to the 1930s, teachers at the Slade School of Fine Art – whose pupils included Graham Sutherland, Stanley Spencer and Winifred Knights – required their students to study Italian old-master drawings and to emulate them. Some, including Winifred Knights in particular, were able to spend time in Rome as part of their training to carry out such work. This was one particular factor that inspired leading artists to continue to use Christian imagery and biblical scenes in their art. A great deal of Winifred Knights's painting draws from Christian subjects, such as *The Deluge* (1920) on the theme of Noah's Flood, or *The Marriage Feast at Cana* (1923), where Christ turned water into wine. Although she repeatedly returned to scriptural material, it was not necessarily because she was exploring a personal faith – indeed, she ceased to be a churchgoer – but she still found in biblical stories the scope to explore her own immediate experiences of life, as well as weighty ideas of art and culture.

In *The Deluge*, where there is no sight of the ark (indeed, the perspective of the viewer might be the view from the ark itself), we are presented with the sight of a number of ordinary people, and a dog, rushing from ordinary houses and factories, desperately trying to reach high ground to escape the coming inundation. Although the limited colour palette, muted light and shade, and the sense of the characters as being suspended in motion, give the painting a dreamy, other-worldly feel reminiscent of early Italian Renaissance frescoes, particularly those of Piero della Francesca, there is no clear sign of the divine presence. Indeed, there is no sign of the conspicuous sin or wickedness of those about to be drowned. In fact, a number of the characters are based on Knights's own close relations. The whole composition suggests a meditation on the way in which the vast impersonal horrors of the First World War engulfed all people indifferently and without mercy. Knights herself had close experience of this on the home front, where she endured a number of Zeppelin raids and personally witnessed the catastrophic explosion at the East London Silvertown munitions factory in 1917 which left dozens of people dead and hundreds injured.[45]

Whilst some artists drew from scripture not necessarily as an investigation of Christianity per se, but saw in it the capacity to contemplate other fields or verities – as John Napper said of his frequent use of the Bible, 'it's part of one's folklore ... it's an enrichment ... I'm not talking about religion as religiosity but I am concerned with the eternal truths that exist in the imagination'[46] – many other twentieth-century artists still used their art as an expression of a spiritual engagement with the Christian religion itself. In some cases, the engagement was far from orthodox and deeply troubling. The prolific sculptor, designer and printmaker Eric Gill (perhaps best known for his 1933 statue of Prospero and Ariel outside the BBC Broadcasting House in London, as well as his creation of the Gill and Perpetua fonts) was fundamentally motivated by his Catholic Christianity. He saw creative activity and the engagement with workmanship – 'happy, intense absorption' brought as close as possible to perfection – as a state of being with God. He founded religious communities for creative artists, including at Ditchling in Sussex, which combined artistic work with the daily singing of the monastic office. Yet he also, perhaps as a means of rationalising his strong libido, developed a theory (perhaps under the influence of the Indian philosopher Ananda Coomaraswamy) that the enjoyment of human love was a participation in and glorification of divine love. His theory acted as a justification to himself for his unrestrained sexual activity, which extended to the abuse of his own daughters, and dog.[47]

Some of the works of Gill's contemporary Stanley Spencer were also dedicated to the 'beauty and sanctity of sex'. However, the deep sensuality of Spencer's works rests on his overwhelming perception of the holy in all things. For many years he lived in the village of Cookham near Maidenhead, and painted grand compositions where biblical scenes were enacted in the immediate locality of his own time. Christ preaches at the Cookham regatta, carries the Cross down Cookham High Street, and is crucified there on a pile of workmen's rubble with the local housetops in the background. In every case, the scenes are filled with Cookham villagers. Local carpenters with ladders follow Christ towards the site of His crucifixion. Curious housewives stare from their windows and local rooftops as He is nailed to the Cross by a brewer. In the churchyard, bathed in an uncanny light, the graves and tombs are burst open by the parish's departed, amongst them Spencer himself and his wife Hilda. Their immediate actions are mundane – they look at their headstones, brush off the earth, smell flowers and adjust their collars – but the whole is suffused with a feeling of serenity and the sense of all things at hand being numinous and sacred. 'When I lived in Cookham', he wrote in 1934, 'I was disturbed by a feeling of everything being meaningless. Quite suddenly I became aware that everything was full of special meaning, and this made everything holy. The instinct of Moses to take his shoes off when he saw the burning bush was very similar to my feelings. I saw many burning bushes in Cookham. I observed the sacred quality in the most unexpected quarters.'[48]

Such a capacity was shared by another contemporary, David Jones, whose work ranged from long-form poetry to prints and watercolours, which share the dreamy and mystical intensity of William Blake. Jones, who fought on the Western Front in the First World War, had a form of epiphany in the trenches one evening when, looking for firewood, he stumbled on a priest in vestments with candles celebrating a mass in a ruined farmhouse, whilst war-weary soldiers kneeled to receive the bread and wine. The sight of the timeless sacred ritual amongst all the destruction convinced him that one might experience the love of God in the midst of sin and total desolation. He became focused on the idea of God's incarnation in Christ, which was an important influence on his creative ideas and his belief in the 'unity of all made things'. 'The painter', he wrote, 'must deny nothing, he must integrate everything . . . it is this . . . gathering all things in that torments the artist.'[49]

Even where later generations of artists inclined towards idioms that were less figurative and more abstract, the biblical narratives were still a source of inspiration. The sculptor Henry Moore, although not a practising Christian, dwelled on the theme of the Madonna and Child, with several secular 'mother and child' statues preceding an explicitly religious work on the subject for St Matthew's Northampton unveiled in 1944. Graham Sutherland produced a Crucifixion for the same church in 1946. Seeing the crucifixion as the greatest of sacrifices, it gave him scope to meditate on the trauma of the Second World War. His studies for the body of Christ included sketches of wartime victims from Italy who had been emaciated with hunger, along with Matthias Grünewald's harrowing sixteenth-century depiction of Christ crucified on the Isenheim Altarpiece. These were combined with his striking use of thorns, an element which he stressed to signify the immense suffering of humanity. Later, in his great tapestry of *Christ in Glory* (1962) in the post-war Coventry Cathedral, he sought to unify in the face of Christ a combination of victory, serenity and compassion.[50] Also in the cathedral's baptistery, the versatile artist John Piper created an overwhelming abstract stained-glass window with a suffusion of colours; the quality of light that came through stained glass, remarked Piper, was something that he tried to capture in painting: 'you could say trying to approach the unapproachable'.[51]

That Christianity has been able to provide perennial, and sometimes surprising, inspiration to artists is something I can see by looking at the churches near to my home. In Axminster, the chancel arch attests to the centuries-old rediscovered frescoes of pre-Reformation devotion. Yet, in my own rural church of St Michael's Shute there also hangs in the chancel a modern work, commissioned in 2000 to commemorate the millennium: a Crucifixion etched on a metal sheet in a network of geometric, coloured patterning like stained glass. It echoes the same altarpiece of Grünewald that Sutherland drew from, as well as Piper's windows in Coventry. It was created by an Exeter-based artist, Mousa al-Kordi, a Muslim born in Palestine.

5

A Holy Landscape

Here is Made Manifest the Covenant to You

In every church, art offered an opening for the people to apprehend the divine. As a tenth-century inscription over an arch at Breamore Church in Hampshire reads, 'Here is made manifest the covenant to you'. Yet, Christianity did not confine its gaze just to the images within churches. It found for the holy in the English landscape itself 'a local habitation and a name'.[1]

Simply by virtue of being one of the country's oldest and most widespread institutions, the Church has naturally left a profound mark on the landscape. The more than 10,000 parish churches which form part of the panorama of nearly every rural village, every town and city; the cathedrals and cathedral closes, minsters, abbeys, chapels, ruined monasteries and priories either standing alone in the wild or built into the body of later dwellings; vicarages and parsonage houses, parish boundaries, pilgrimage routes, the vast wastelands and tracts of moor and marsh in northern England turned into still-productive farmland by the patient work of the Cistercian order* over the Middle Ages; the towns and conurbations which owe their existence to the trade and settlement around minster and monastic foundations; the idea of the parish itself based around a church and manor house which, since about the tenth century, has been the primary unit of rural social identity and cohesion – all of these are

* The Cistercians were a reformed monastic order founded at the end of the eleventh century; they had a strong belief in the value of manual labour and agricultural work.

part of the Church's contribution to the English landscape, without which its character would be profoundly different. But the influence of Christianity on the landscape goes beyond this. As with the art in the buildings, Christianity before the Reformation sought to discover and show the presence of the divine in the terrain and the landscape itself.

Before the arrival of St Augustine, the pre-Christian Anglo-Saxons had a keen sense of the sanctity, or else the uncanniness, of places. This sense is reflected in Anglo-Saxon literature, albeit written down after the advent of Christianity. In *Beowulf*, the lair of Grendel is an unnerving expanse of 'wolf-haunted slopes, windy headlands, dangerous swamps' where one sees 'fire on the flood' – the dark waters of the stagnant marsh apparently on fire with the rising gases of decomposition. So disturbing a place is this lair that 'the strong-horned stag, hard-pressed by hounds . . . would sooner give up his life on the riverbank than hide his head here'.[2] The malign mode of a demonic presence in a wilderness is brought out explicitly in the biography of an eighth-century hermit, St Guthlac, who retreated to a small isolated cell on top of a prehistoric burial mound in the fearful waterlogged fens at Crowland in Lincolnshire. One night, when at vigil, his cell was suddenly invaded by 'horrible troops of foul spirits' which entered through 'floor holes and crannies' and the 'openings of the wattle-work'. They were 'ferocious in appearance, terrible in shape with great heads, long necks, thin faces, yellow complexions, filthy beards, shaggy ears, wild foreheads, fierce eyes, foul mouths, horses' teeth, throats vomiting flames, twisted jaws, thick lips, strident voices, singed hair, fat cheeks, pigeon breasts, scabby thighs, knotty knees, crooked legs, swollen ankles, splay feet, spreading mouths, raucous cries'. From his hermitage they gathered him up and carried him to the gates of hell but, thanks to the strength of his faith and the assistance of St Bartholomew, he was able to overcome them.[3]

Soon after Augustine's arrival, Pope Gregory came to the view that his missionaries should not attempt to destroy and leave derelict the shrines and sacred places of England's pre-Christian cults. In a letter to Mellitus, first Bishop of London, sent in 601, Gregory advised:

> ... let the idols that are in them be destroyed; let water be consecrated and sprinkled in the said temples, let altars be erected, and relics placed there ... it is requisite that they be converted from the worship of devils to the service of the true God; that the nation, seeing that their temples are not destroyed, may remove error from their hearts, and knowing and adoring the true God, may the more freely resort to the places to which they have been accustomed ...

If, before, they had been accustomed to slaughter cattle, build huts for festivals and feast by these shrines in honour of the earlier deities, they should be allowed to continue these practices, but in honour of God, the 'Giver of all things ... to the end that, whilst some outward gratifications are retained, they may the more easily consent to the inward joys'.[4]

Thus, over the following centuries a new Christian geography settled on the landscape. Places once hallowed in pagan times could now become sites of sanctity for Christians under the new dispensation. Others, not before revered, now emerged as locations where people could seek, with Christian prompting, a particular presence of holiness. The ruins of Roman villas, considered to have a certain numinous awe, perhaps on account of their use after Roman times as burial sites, often attracted the building of Christian churches or chapels; over 200 examples of this are known. Many more were established near springs and sources of water, which had widely been regarded as portals to the sacred plane in pre-Christian Iron Age Europe. Others appear to have been set up near venerable trees, or on high places.[5]

Often, pious stories attach to the landscape to explain the origins of its sanctity and add to its richness. Sacred trees became associated with the actions of saints. Tales abound of holy men – Aldhelm, Cynehelm, Eadwold – striking the ground with their staffs which then held fast and miraculously grew into luxuriant ash trees. At the spot where the Christian King Oswald of Northumbria fell fighting his pagan rival Penda at Oswestry, an ageless ash tree likewise sprung up with a healing spring at its base. Holy wells often had associations with female saints.

Frideswide, the eighth-century patron saint of Oxford, in response to her prayers was granted a spring at her hermitage in Binsey which, according to a twelfth-century chronicler, 'gives healing to the many who drink from it'.[6] Indeed, springs often arose where the heads of decapitated female saints fell to the ground, such as Winefride, Juthwara and Sidwell. But such extremities were not always needed for their sanctification. Aelfric of Eynsham argued that Christ's blessing of the waters of the River Jordan left all sources of water blessed, thus confirming the veneration of all wells and springs.[7] Beyond this, even the passing touch of a saint could reveal the sanctity of a place. St Mildrith, a seventh-century descendant of King Aethelbert who became abbess of the nunnery of Minster-in-Thanet, on disembarking from a boat at Ebbsfleet, left the imprint of her feet on a hard white rock 'as if implanted in fresh snow or mud', causing the place to become a site of veneration, where people flocked seeking cures by rubbing the rock and singing litanies.[8]

The adoption of the old shrines and sacred places by the new religion was not simply a matter of opportunism. It was not the case that the doctrines of early Christianity were uninterested in the claims of place, but that the faith was nevertheless motivated to rebrand venerable locales through practical expediency. Christianity in England, from the time of Pope Gregory until the Reformation, drew from its own teaching ideas which led to the notion of holiness of place. Such ideas are manifest in the story of Aethelthryth, wife of King Ecgfrith of Northumbria, who became Abbess of Ely and died in 696. Sixteen years after her death, according to Bede's *History*, her wooden coffin was opened so that her remains could be transferred to a stone sarcophagus. When her body was taken out, it was found to be 'as free from corruption as if she had died and been buried on that very day'. The wound from facial surgery she had undergone in her final days to relieve pain from a tumour had healed, and even the linen clothes in which she had been buried appeared 'entire and fresh'.[9] Aethelthryth's preservation illustrated beliefs expressed by Pope Gregory about the connection between the body and the soul, and the fate of the bodies of the especially holy. Whilst the soul of the saint after death resided in heaven, there still remained some connection between the soul and the body for them, such that their bodies would indicate the soul's presence in heaven by way of incorruptibility or wonders at the site of their burial. Close contact with them could occasion miracles. In the case of Aethelthryth, this included cures from diseases by touching her linen burial clothes, or relief from eye complaints for those who lay their heads on her old wooden coffin to pray. The vigour of the soul of the saint, as with King Oswald, is signalled by the flourishing of nature and lush grass vegetation nearby. The locality of the burial itself became a portal to paradise, and by it one could hope that the saint was especially receptive to prayers for intercession.[10]

Places associated with the life and death of saints thus became points of attraction in the landscape. Even before the building of churches, they would have been sites of devotion and pilgrimage. The routes to them in themselves, or indeed the known journeys of saints, could also attract a sense of sanctity and change the landscape. In Cornwall, hundreds of stone wheel crosses survive from the eleventh to thirteenth centuries, mostly on the junctions of routes that point towards ancient churches. The rest of England had similar markers in wooden or stone crosses on such routes. Stone crosses once marked a trail of sites known from the journey of St Cuthmann, born in the south-west, who travelled as a beggar to Steyning in Sussex where God directed him to build a hermitage and a place of worship. Stone crosses likewise once marked the stages of St Aldhelm's 34-mile funeral procession along the south-west of the Fosse Way from Doulting to Malmesbury in the eighth century. These still stood, said the twelfth-century chronicler William of Malmesbury, in his own time, and many with serious illnesses even then eagerly sought them out as places to pray for miraculous cures.[11]

The attraction of the saints and their associated holy places was also at the root of an especially visible change to the landscape: the rise of the churchyard as a favoured place for burial. In the earliest centuries after the arrival of Augustine, burial in a minster close to the body or relics of a saint was relatively rare, a privilege generally enjoyed only by monks, clergy and the pious nobility. However, by the late ninth century, particularly as the network of parish churches started to spread, rites developed in England for the consecration of churchyards. The land around the church was deemed holy, not just the church itself. The old, detached Anglo-Saxon burial grounds were gradually abandoned, and burial of faithful lay people in the churchyard became the normal custom. Only those who died as outcasts or criminals continued to be buried on the margins in the old burial grounds or on the distant boundaries of the parish, on which spots descended an unsettled sense of the fearful and sinister which still lingers in the popular imagination.[12] An Anglo-Saxon poem, 'The Wife's Lament', may have been written in the persona of someone buried in such a place, in a fearful landscape bereft of Christian consolations: 'The dales are dismal; the hills loom up, / hostile outposts, overgrown with briars; the habitation is joyless . . .'.[13]

Whether the doctrines of medieval Christianity caused particular points in the landscape to be revered as beacons of sanctity or shunned as dark closes of foreboding, the iconoclasm of the Reformation had, as one of its objectives, the desire to extinguish any sense that the landscape, or any part of it, could possibly be sacred. 'The finite cannot contain the infinite' is a phrase often used to sum up the thoughts of Jean Calvin, who scoffed at the idea that local shrines might be responsible for miracles, or that any devotion expressed at them was given to God Himself behind the physical place, rather than the place in itself. As George Fox, the founder of the Quakers, said later in the seventeenth century, the ground on which the 'steeple houses', as he contemptuously described churches, stood was no more sacred than the hill around them. Yet, no matter how many wayside crosses were smashed, holy wells defiled, or chapels watching over the site of a saint's triumph or martyrdom pulled down, Protestant reformers were unable to expunge the idea of the sanctity of the landscape; rather, they continued to embrace it.[14]

For one thing, despite the official injunctions in the 1540s and 1550s that parishes should 'utterly extinct and destroy . . . all . . . monuments of feigned miracles, pilgrimages, idolatry and superstition', the reformers were surprisingly unwilling to destroy such monuments 'utterly'.[15] The stumps of broken crosses, the blank visage on a statue where the face of an angel or apostle once looked down, the shattered roofless walls of an abbey or wayside chapel – all of these were turned to serve as trophies of the victory of the Reformation, and as 'monuments' of the reformers' 'indignation and detestation against them'. Puritans kept pieces of broken stained glass 'to show the generation to come what God hath done for us', and the vision of monastic ruins could move them to declare that 'every stone hath a tongue to accuse the superstition, hypocrisy, idleness, luxury of the late owners'. Even as late as the nineteenth century, writers could say of the ruins, 'we may glory that the abodes of tyranny and superstition are in ruin'.[16]

As much as the ruins on the landscape were a mark of triumph for the reformers and a sign of puritanical barbarism for those with High-Church sympathies, they later came to be a distinctive mark of the beauty of the English landscape. In 1782, the young author J.H. Pott (later Archdeacon of St Albans) wrote on the benefits that the English landscape offered to artists. Aside from the country's 'beautiful verdure', the atmospheric 'fogs and damps' and, more positively, the 'great variety and beauty of our northern skies . . . nearly unknown to the placid southern hemisphere', he highlighted 'the many beautiful and venerable ruins' of Gothic architecture 'everywhere to be seen'. In them, he said, there was 'an awful romantic wilderness . . . that moves the mind very powerfully'.[17] Pott's older contemporary William Gilpin, who is often credited with conceiving of the idea of the 'picturesque', went so far as to allude to Oliver Cromwell's 'picturesque genius' and hail Henry VIII since no other person had 'contributed more to adorn this country with picturesque ruins'. As much as Gilpin's statement may seem tongue-in-cheek, the monastic ruins became a spiritual and artistic inspiration for many, from the great vogue for paintings and engravings of such ruins in the landscape at the end of the eighteenth century to William Wordsworth's meditations on Tintern Abbey. Gilpin himself gave voice to the mixture of aesthetic and spiritual solace that was to be found in them: 'A ruin is a sacred thing. Rooted for ages in the soil; assimilated to it; and become, as it were, a part of it; we consider it as a work of nature, rather than of art. Art cannot reach it.'[18]

But it was more than in the later reaction to the monastic ruins that reformed English Christianity found a spiritual re-engagement with the landscape. Despite the notion that 'The finite cannot contain the infinite', Calvin nevertheless argued that the physical world was 'a lively image ... in the which God shows and declares himself: For albeit he be invisible in his essence, yet he shows himself by his works, to the end we should worship him'. Thus, although no one place or shrine should be thought of as sacred, the whole world was a sign of God's nature. Many Protestant reformers rejoiced to worship in the open air, in imitation of Abraham and the ancient patriarchs. 'The ploughman', declared Bishop John Hooper in 1547, 'be he never so unlearned, shall better be instructed of Christ's death and passion by the corn that he soweth in the field, and likewise of Christ's resurrection, than by all the dead posts that hang in the church.' His contemporary, Bishop James Pilkington, disdaining Pope Gregory's idea of pictures being books for the unlettered, argued that the 'goodly books' for the poor were the sights of the natural world: sun, moon, stars, fishes, birds, beasts, herbs, corn, grass, trees, hills and rivers. The idea of God's design as being visible in the landscape and order of the universe became a given for natural philosophers in the seventeenth and eighteenth centuries, and was a spur to scientific investigation of all things. The eighteenth-century clergyman William Derham, one of the earliest people to make an accurate measurement of the speed of sound, expressed his approval of those 'curious and ingenious Enquirers' that sought to pry into God's works, for 'the more we pry into, and discover of them, the greater and more glorious we find them to be'.[19]

Such enquiry was not just the preserve of high-minded scientists or natural philosophers. Christian thought promoted the simple act of gardening as a meritorious business that could be freighted with contemplative profundity. Mankind sprang from the Garden of Eden where Adam was required 'to dress it and to keep it', and Christ spent His last free hours at prayer in the Garden of Gethsemane. Thus the garden became an especial place to meditate and seek the intimations of paradise, and another popular substitute for those who once would have sought the presence of the divine by pilgrimages or visits to shrines.[20] 'When I was in my earthly garden a-digging with my spade', wrote the seventeenth-century dissenter Roger Crab, 'I saw into the Paradise of God from whence my father Adam was cast forth.'[21] His contemporary, the poet Henry Vaughan, described a similar experience of the English garden as the place for a religious encounter in his poem 'Religion':

> My God, when I walk in those groves
> And leaves thy spirit doth still fan,
> I see in each share that there grows
> An Angel talking with a man.

6

A Holy Time-Scape

In the endless round of bad news we are enduring in the 2020s – wars or the threat of wars, climate change, pandemics – it is easy to get the impression that we are living in the last times. However, it is also easy to forget that the world should already have ended: on 1 January 2000, at the very stroke of midnight. The 'Millennium Bug', or the 'Y2K Bug', is little discussed today, but in the late 1990s it was the cause of almost universal panic. Governments and corporations across the globe feared that the computers on which humanity was by then dependent would not be able to cope with the year change from '1999' to '2000'. Many had been programmed to incorporate just the last two digits of the year in their software. Experts therefore believed that the movement from '31/12/99' to '01/01/00' would cause the computers to reset or break down. They forecast the systems that ran everything, from the banks and financial markets to power generation, telecommunications, transport, healthcare and defence systems, would seize up in the very first moment of the year 2000, with cataclysmic results. In 1996, one US consulting firm forecast that the problem would take $600 billion to fix.[1]

As it turned out, nothing happened. The fears were wildly overblown, and the world carried on as normal. Despite this, the whole affair offers a striking lesson about our relationship with the calendar: even in a secular context, many people still have a strange and overwhelming instinct to assign significance to particular years, often on the basis of the pattern of their numbers. In the 1990s, in addition to fears over the Y2K Bug, there was a widespread belief that the coming of the year 2000 would be somehow momentous or meaningful. This was based not on any overt association with the year being the conventional date for the 2000th anniversary of Christ's birth, but rather on the roundness of the number itself.

This reflex, to see a significance in particular years and dates, comes to the contemporary secular world by way of Christianity. The fears and hopes about the year 2000 were a modern variation of responses to the calendar that were explicitly based on Christian thought. In the tenth century, the approach of the year 1000 brought an expectation of the Second Coming of Christ and a new age.[2] Some historians attribute the rise of papal power and religious reforms of the period as being a response to this belief. Similarly, after the Restoration many believed that 1666 would usher in the Second Coming, as it contained '666', the biblical number of the Beast. The onset of the Great Plague in 1665–6 and the Great Fire of London in 1666 seemed for a time to confirm this.[3]

In the seventeenth century, the poet John Donne asked: 'What if this present were the world's last night?',[4] a question that has never ceased to obsess many Christians, particularly those with overlapping interests in prophecy and politics. From archbishops to scientists and eccentric visionaries, multitudes have pored over the texts of scripture in an attempt to predict when the end of days might come. The Jacobean chronographer James Ussher, Archbishop of Armagh, forecast 1997. Isaac Newton's calculations pointed to 2060. Newton's contemporary, William Lloyd, Bishop of Worcester, announced to a possibly bemused Queen Anne in 1712 that Christ would return in 1716, and that the city of Rome would then be consumed by a fire from heaven to mark the beginning of his 1000-year reign.[5] The eighteenth-century visionary Joanna Southcott, who started life as a shop-girl in Devon but later founded a religious movement with thousands of followers (which survives to this day), claimed that she was the 'Woman of the Apocalypse' as described in the Book of Revelation, and that she herself (at the age of 64) would give birth to the new Messiah in London on 19 October 1814.[6]

'The end of the world is nigh' is a cry still made by strident evangelists in our own age. The American pastors Jerry Falwell Sr and Pat Robertson famously fixed the date of the Last Judgement for 2000 and

2007 respectively. However, these high-profile claims about the date of the apocalypse lead to a more profound point: Christianity has had a deep and abiding impact on the way we perceive and relate to time. It is not just the expectation of the end of days (although this appears before Christianity) or indeed that our dating system numbers the years from the putative birth of Christ. The cycle of the day, the week, the year, feasts, fasts, festivals, the seasons of life and the perception of eras have all been moulded over centuries by a response to Christian doctrines and traditions. And even though many of the shared rituals associated with these calendrical turns of time have ebbed away, marked only as small print in our pocket diaries, their echoes and absences continue to trouble modern society.

The Acceptable Year of the Lord

An account of the impact of Christianity on time in England best starts with the Venerable Bede in the eighth century. Like other writers before him over centuries, he faced a difficult problem when describing historical events: how should one number the years?

Writers in the ancient world and late antiquity had a range of options, with a complexity and scale of choice that make the head spin. One could use the *Annus Mundi* (AM, year of the world), a chronology based on early Jewish and Christian scholarship that counted the years from the alleged beginning of the world – though there was no general agreement on when this took place. Bede claimed it to be equivalent to 3592 BC; others held it to be as early as 5509 BC, with other options in between. One might encounter in various records the use of the Greek Olympiad system, a four-year cycle that started in 776 BC, although this had petered out by around AD 400. Another possibility was *Ab Urbe Condita* (AUC), from the traditional date of the foundation of Rome (753 BC). There was the indiction system, a 15-year cycle based on regular Roman tax reassessments (though this itself, confusingly, had three variations).

Other reckonings were made from the dates of the Roman consuls (who changed annually) or the Roman emperors. Bede encountered dates calculated from the beginning of the reign of Augustus or Tiberius, and from the deaths of Antony and Cleopatra, when Egypt became a Roman province. Another popular system (*Annus Martyrum* or *Annus Diocletiani*) reckoned from the beginning of the reign of Diocletian (AD 284) in honour of the Christian martyrs who perished in his late persecutions. For more recent events, the dates at which the various Anglo-Saxon kings came to the throne were also used (and there were of course many overlapping kings in different kingdoms). Aside from these, one overtly Christian system that had some currency in late antiquity was based on the year not of Christ's birth, but of His crucifixion (the *Annus Passionis* system), which scholars generally agreed took place in the fifteenth year of the emperorship of Tiberius. Along with many others, there was also the *Annus Domini* (AD) system, a not particularly popular newcomer in Bede's time.[7]

The AD system, dating the years from the time of Christ's birth, was not invented by Bede. It seems to have been first conceived by a monk called Dionysius Exiguus, who lived on the Black Sea coast in the early sixth century. He developed the system simply to create tables for calculating the date of Easter in future years, rather than for any historical purpose. He objected to using the *Annus Martyrum* system, as it seemed to commemorate the oppressive Diocletian as much as the Christian martyrs. Although Dionysius's scheme for calculating Easter was adopted by the Roman Church, his AD system was initially little used for recording dates; it was Bede who first exploited its full potential.[8]

In his historical works, including the *Ecclesiastical History of the English People*, Bede started to quote the dates of events not just using the regnal years of kings and emperors, but also in the AD system. His pioneering work marked both new and current events, as well as the tangle of earlier chronologies and dating systems, which he used to work out the AD dates for historical incidents; thus, he calculated that the Emperor Claudius concluded his invasion of Britain in AD 46; that the Roman withdrawal from Britain was AD 409; and that St Augustine's arrival on the shores of England from Rome was AD 597.[9]

Bede's achievement had many practical benefits, and quickly spread in popularity. His work cut through a morass of confusing and overlapping regnal dates and indiction cycles to bring the events of history together on one clean, transparent timeline. It also confounded the Jerry Falwells and Pat Robertsons of Bede's age – 'lewd rustics' in the words of Bede – who argued that the Second Coming was imminent in their own era. Because of their interpretation of ideas in the Book of Daniel, such people believed that the final judgement would come 6000 years after the Creation and would thus be a time swiftly approaching. Bede's centring of the calendar on the birth of Christ drew the attention of these millennial thinkers away from using the Creation as the moment from which to calculate the end of times. Christ's birth as the new starting point of the calendar postponed any fears of an immediate end of the world, and AD 1000 – centuries after Bede's time – became the new focus of apocalyptic interest.[10]

But Bede's use of AD had a much wider spiritual and ideological significance. It offered an unprecedented widening of perspective. For Bede, Christ's incarnation was the most important moment in universal history. The plotting of every other historical event – the fall of Rome, the coming of the Saxons, the arrival of St Augustine – in terms of the date of Christ's incarnation instead of the accession of emperors or the Roman tax cycle served to connect all of these happenings to the appearance of Christ on earth. The events Bede narrated in his *Ecclesiastical History of the English People*, tied by the new calendar to the coming of Christ, were now presented as the working out over time of the salvation promised by Christ to the English. All that took place (and particularly that which took place in English history) had a cosmic importance. The new calendar signified that England was not a distant island: it was connected to Rome, Jerusalem, Bethlehem and to the purposes of heaven.[11]

For Bede, time itself had a sort of sanctity. Its movement and its cycles, properly understood, were – even from the moment of creation – a sign of the work of Christ. In another of his tracts, *The Reckoning of Time*,

Bede justified the idea that Easter should be celebrated on the first Sunday after the first full moon following the vernal equinox. Christ's resurrection, he reasoned, should be associated with the fullness of the moon, which shone with the borrowed light of the sun, signifying how at the Resurrection (which took place at night) Christ gave a light for the Church and its saints to reflect. The Resurrection taking place after the vernal equinox, when days begin to exceed the nights in length, signified the triumph of light over dark. Similarly, he argued, the same order of celestial events would have been seen in the creation story as described in Genesis – the vernal equinox falling on the fourth day, with the making of the sun and the full moon. Even in the first week of creation, the cycles of time were set up to reflect the forthcoming Passion of Christ.[12]

Before Bede there had been heated controversy over the date of Easter. Irish Christians generally followed a different system for calculating the date of Easter from those in the Saxon kingdoms, who for the most part followed the system of Dionysius Exiguus, which had been approved by Rome. The Synod of Whitby in 664 established that the Roman system would be followed in Northumbria (where the controversy was most acute), and hence in the British isles more generally. Although this was a settled matter by Bede's time, it was a point of utmost importance to him on which he lavished his attention: Easter had to be celebrated at the right moment. It was not just a matter of Christian unity across all lands. It was also a matter of Christians acting in accordance with the very order of the cosmos and time. The celebration of Easter in particular, hence other Christian festivals, at the correct time, linked English Christians not just to those elsewhere in the world, but also to the very patterns and rhythms of creation, ordained by God at the origins of time itself.[13]

Red-Letter Days

By the end of the seventh century, Christian ideas of time were already beginning to influence the calendar. The law codes of King Ine of

Wessex (*c.*693) and King Wihtred of Kent (*c.*695) provided that Sunday should be a day of rest, and that anyone caught working or travelling on business could face a fine or the lash. The first known regulations of the English Church about Sundays and festival days come from the Council of Clovesho (747). Here, some of the ideas about what activities and behaviour are appropriate on a Sunday start to be articulated:

> ... it is ordained that the Lord's day be celebrated by all, with due veneration, and wholly dedicated to divine service. And let all abbots and priests, on that most sacred day ... instruct the servants subject to them, from the oracles of Holy Scripture, in the rules of religious conversation and of good living. It is also decreed that on that day ... the priests of God do often invite the people to meet in the church, to hear the word of God.

Christmas and the birthdays of saints were to be kept in the same way, with the celebration of masses, following the pattern of the Church in Rome.[14]

Just over a century later, the law code of King Alfred (887) set out 37 holidays (apart from Sundays) to be enjoyed by all free men. These included 'twelve days at Christmas', Good Friday, 'the anniversary of St Gregory; seven days before Easter and seven days after; one day at the festival of St Peter and St Paul; and in autumn, the full week before St Mary's mass; and one day at the celebration of All Saints'. These holidays were not available to slaves, who were permitted holidays only on four Ember Days, or days of penitence, which were allotted once a quarter; however, they were allowed on those days 'to sell anything which has been given to them in God's name, or which they are able to acquire by their labour ...'.

This anomaly was ironed out in the following century. A stream of laws and rules issued by kings and Church councils repeated the idea that Sundays and festival days should be times of rest, where no labour, commerce or travelling for work should be allowed at all, by anyone. In particular, said Abbot Aelfric of Eynsham in the latter part of the tenth century, 'servile work' should cease on the days around Easter, 'because at that season all the world was freed from captivity to the devil'. Rest from work not only allowed time for attendance at church but was seen as a way of echoing the freedom and ease of heaven on earth.[15]

Further rules issued at the Council of Eanham in 1009, under the influence of Archbishop Wulfstan of York, filled out the picture of how Sundays and festivals should be kept: 'Let Sunday be strictly observed, as becomes that festival, and let men carefully desist from trafficking and county courts, and hunting bouts and worldly works on that holy-day.' A fast was to be kept every Friday, the day of Christ's crucifixion, 'except it be a feast [day]. And let ordeal and oaths and marriage be always forbidden on high festival days, and on the solemn Ember Days ... And it is also fit that there be common peace and concord to all Christian men on these holy tides, and that all law-suits be put far away.' Courts in England still do not sit on Sundays, on Good Friday or on Christmas Day.[16]

By the end of the tenth century, the English ritual year had broadly taken shape, with times allocated to penitence and fasting, such as Lent and Advent, high festivals at Easter and Christmas, as well as various saints' days and other festivals – for example the Annunciation and Michaelmas – which fell close to the equinoxes and solstices.

As a number of these festivals were placed at the turning points of the seasons and the agricultural year, many have argued that they are nothing more than pagan rituals linked to fields, farming, fertility or the conjuring of departed spirits lurking under a Christian veneer. Indeed, the appropriation of pagan festivals by Christian missionaries in England may seem to have been an official policy. Bede himself records a letter that Pope Gregory sent around 620 to Mellitus, the third Archbishop of Canterbury, offering advice about how to make conversions to Christianity easier:

> because the [pagan Anglo-Saxons] are in the habit of slaughtering much cattle as sacrifices to devils, some solemnity ought to be given them in exchange for this. So on the day of the dedication or the festivals of the

> holy martyrs . . . let them celebrate the solemnity with religious feasts . . . let them slaughter animals for their own food to the praise of God . . . It is doubtless impossible to cut out everything at once from their stubborn minds.[17]

In this line of argument, it is often claimed that the Christian celebration of Easter in England is merely the reincarnation of a pagan spring festival dedicated to a goddess named Eostre. The proof offered is that the Anglo-Saxon name of the month in which Easter was celebrated – *Eastermonath* – was, as Bede attests, drawn from this goddess and then applied to the Christian festival of Christ's resurrection. This differs from other European languages, which draw their word for Easter from the Latin *Pascha*, derived from the Hebrew *Pesach*, meaning 'Passover'.

But, in reality, this lingering belief that many Christian festivals such as Easter and Halloween are just pagan celebrations in different dress, and that their rituals and symbols – Easter eggs and rabbits, or candles in pumpkins – derive from pre-Christian custom, almost entirely evaporates on closer inspection. For a start, almost nothing is known of the Anglo-Saxon pagan festivals, or of their gods. As an example, the goddess Eostre mentioned by Bede occurs nowhere in any surviving literature from the period, nor is there any other mention of her festivals. By Bede's time, her memory was no more than a name and Bede himself seems vague about her. Indeed, she may never even have existed. Bede's idea that Eastermonath was named after a goddess may well have been a conjecture, deriving her name from the month rather than vice versa.[18]

Although a number of important Christian festivals have been placed on or close to significant dates in the astronomical calendar because of their symbolism – for example Easter and the Feast of the Annunciation close to the vernal equinox; and Christmas on the Roman date of the winter solstice, on which an earlier pre-Christian festival may also have sat – the way they were celebrated, their rituals, symbols and much of their significance visibly derive from Christian ideas rather than from any pagan origin. Such festivals and rituals were, for the most part, laid down in England during Anglo-Saxon times, and then widely elaborated during the medieval period, from which we have by far the best and most vivid evidence about them.

Anyone who picks up a legal or Church document from the medieval or Tudor age – or even personal records from that time or later – will see that they are frequently dated by reference to Church festivals. A payment may fall due on Lammas Day* or one of the traditional 'Quarter days' – Lady Day,† May Day, Michaelmas or Christmas. A court may be recorded as sitting on 'the Wednesday after the feast of All Saints'. Court terms, along with some school and university terms, still start on (or close to) Michaelmas, St Hilary's day or Trinity Sunday, from which a number of these institutions still name their terms. London's greatest fair from the Middle Ages to Victorian times was Bartholomew Fair, held on the saint's day of 24 August. Long remembered in Oxford were the St Scholastica's Day Riots on 10 February 1355 (sparked by the poor quality of wine served by the Swindlestock Tavern to the undergraduates) when nearly 100 people were killed.

A glance over medieval calendars or later almanacs gives a bewildering list of the saints and festivals to be celebrated over the course of the year. But the round of these festivals demarcated the year, and served as a visible demonstration of the sacred nature of time, telling the story of Christian salvation. Each of the saints' days and festivals had distinctive

* Lammas is derived from the Old English *hlāfmæsse* ('loaf-mass'). It is usually celebrated on 1 August, around half way between the summer solstice and autumn equinox. Its purpose is to offer blessings for the first fruits of the harvest.

† Lady Day, celebrated on 25 March, is another name of the Feast of the Annunciation, commemorating the visit of the Angel Gabriel to the Blessed Virgin Mary to announce that she would be the mother of Jesus. It was also, until the adoption of the Gregorian calendar in 1752, the start of the official new year in England, and hence the date often used for the start of contracts and fiscal assessments. After 1752, when 11 days were removed from the old Julian calendar to correct for the new Gregorian one, the dates for the assessment (Old Lady Day) then fell on 5 April, which still marks the end of the English tax year, and is the reason why income tax is still assessed up to this date annually.

ceremonies and rituals often rich with colour, light, sound and movement, not to mention texture, smells and meaning. The deep appeal to the senses, their profusion and the communal experience of these rituals make it no wonder that the English population generally perceived time with reference to them. There are far too many in the calendar to describe anything but a fraction of them. Yet we can choose a few to understand how, for hundreds of years, a pageant of Christian thought and imagery shaped the popular sense of time, and also how, even after the Reformation suppressed many of these rites, their echoes continued to linger in the course of the English year.

The Fate of Four Calendar Rituals

CANDLEMAS

Candlemas commemorates the visit made by the Virgin Mary to the Temple in Jerusalem 40 days after the birth of Christ. Under Jewish law, she was required to purify herself by offering a sacrifice, and to present Christ as her first-born son. According to Luke's Gospel, when Mary entered the Temple with her son, He was hailed as the Messiah by a devout old man named Simeon, who called Him 'a light to lighten the gentiles.'

As this is said to have happened 40 days after the birth of Christ, it is celebrated on 2 February – 40 days after Christmas Day. It is known to have been an important festival in Jerusalem by the end of the fourth century, and by the middle of the fifth century lighted candles were held during the services there on that day to evoke Simeon's words. In 541, the Emperor Justinian ordered solemn processions on the day in the Eastern Roman Empire to seek deliverance from plague. And by the time of Bede, Candlemas was being celebrated in England with both of these ingredients.

Candlemas occurs when the days begin to lengthen, and the first signs of life – tree buds and wildflowers – start to appear in the fields. It was thus taken to mark the beginning of spring, and was the moment at which cattle were moved from their winter pastures, then made ready for sowing. In this context of the ebbing away of winter cold and darkness, the emotional effect of the Candlemas rituals must have been profound, evoking as they did the idea of the coming of a divine light into the world. On the day before Candlemas, everyone was restricted to bread and water. On the day itself, all parishioners were obliged to take a candle to church and process with it to the altar. They paid a penny for the privilege. The candles were placed in the church sanctuary, where the priest blessed them with incense and holy water. They would then be retrieved by the parishioners, who might carry them in procession around the church, light them before a statue of the Virgin Mary, or take them home as a means of protection. The candles, after their blessing, were believed to ward off evil and the devil, and so they were lit also during storms or in times of sickness, and placed into the hands of the dying.

In the century before the Reformation, the processions of candle-bearing parishioners to their churches grew ever more elaborate. In some towns and cities, guilds put on pageants in which one of their members would dress as the Virgin Mary with a doll of the infant Christ in her arms. She would be accompanied by Joseph and Simeon, or the Three Kings, emperors, various saints, bishops and angels, escorted by musicians and elaborate racks of candles. The services would be followed by great municipal feasts and general merriment in the streets. The message of the Christian rituals went hand in hand with the joy at the return of spring and coming warmth.[19]

PALM SUNDAY

Palm Sunday marks the story of Christ's triumphal entry into Jerusalem on a colt shortly before He was arrested and crucified. According to John's Gospel, Christ was greeted by crowds waving palms they strewed before Him, and shouting 'Hosanna: Blessed is the King of Israel that cometh in the name of the Lord'.

The event is celebrated on the fifth Sunday of Lent, which is the week before Easter Sunday, and would have signalled the approaching end of the fasting and privations required by the Lenten season. The expectation of this joy would have been reflected in nature. By this moment, spring would be in full vigour, with blossom and new leafage rising on the trees.

The rituals of the day were some of the longest in the Christian calendar. How fully they were observed would have been according to the resources of each church and parish, but the most striking part was universal: the blessing and processional carrying of branches. These were used to imitate the palms carried by the crowds in Jerusalem, which were of course not generally available in medieval England. Instead of palms, people gathered fronds of willow, box, yew or other evergreens, which they presented to the clergy to be blessed. As a result, the day was locally known also as 'branch', 'willow' or 'yew' Sunday.

The ritual is first recorded in England in the mid-eighth century, and, as with Candlemas, it grew ever more elaborate throughout the medieval period. Processions of clergy and parishioners went about outside the churches bearing the branches, stopping to hear biblical readings and choirs singing anthems. Flowers and cakes might be thrown to the crowds from above the church door, before the processions entered to hear a mass and the whole of St Matthew's Gospel sung in chant. Whilst this was done, the congregation would arrange their branches into small wooden crosses, which the priests would bless with incense and holy water. As with the candles from Candlemas, people believed these crosses to be protective. Often, they were displayed above doors or kept in purses. Whilst the festival commemorated an important moment in the narrative of Christ's life, it served to tie this moment to a communal exaltation in the progress of spring.[20]

GOOD FRIDAY AND THE EASTER SEPULCHRE

In southern England, around the mid-tenth century, a number of churches developed a striking ritual to re-enact the burial and resurrection of Christ. The ritual spread throughout most of the country over the course of the Middle Ages. On Good Friday (the Friday before Easter Sunday), the priest, barefoot and wearing a simple surplice, would take a communion host which had been blessed and dipped in consecrated wine the previous day, place this in a casket, wrap it in cloth, and take it to the north side of the chancel. Here, a miniature tomb or sepulchre would have been prepared. This might originally have been a plain stone coffer or a wooden chest, though over time a number of these sepulchres became highly elaborate, gilded and decorated with stone arches and statues, set in the tombs of wealthy benefactors or, in one case, in a crystal container stowed in the breast of an image of Christ. Into this sepulchre the priest placed the casket containing the communion host, along with a crucifix that had been venerated by the congregation and washed with wine. He then covered the sepulchre with a fine cloth, often red velvet or richly painted. Candles were placed around it, and a number of parishioners, fortified by bread and ale and warmed with pans of hot coal, settled down to keep a watch alongside it.

Vigil was kept until early on the morning of Easter Sunday, when the priests would enter the church for the first service: matins. They would light candles, process to the sepulchre, bless it with incense and genuflect before it, then open it to remove the casket with the host, which they would then take to the altar. Suddenly, a great impression of life would enter the church, with the priests joyfully singing the *Christus Resurgens*: 'Christ rising up from the dead henceforth dies not . . . alleluia!' – the first time that singing would have been heard in the church since the start of Good Friday. Likewise, the bells which had been silent since that time were rung, and the ornaments, statues and crucifixes around the church which had been covered in heavy dark cloth since the beginning of Lent were swiftly uncovered. Shortly afterwards, the parishioners would be invited to partake in the mass – the only day in the year when, according to medieval custom, they were allowed to eat the host. At other times, only the priest was permitted to consume it.* It should be remembered that in the Middle Ages the communion host and wine were seen as the literal body and blood of Christ. The custom of the Easter sepulchre was a vivid drama where, for the medieval parishioners, Christ Himself was

* There were very rare exceptions to this rule, which was also gently relaxed in the fifteenth century.

present being buried and rising again, as He did in the gospel narrative, bringing an overwhelming blaze of light, sound and colour. Their consumption of the host marked the end of the Lenten fast, and the prospect of renewed pleasure in the full blossoming of nature.[21]

ALL SAINTS AND ALL SOULS

Although they are celebrated consecutively on 1 and 2 November, and connected in terms of their ideas, the festivals of All Saints and All Souls arose in different ages, and originally had different places in the calendar.

In the Mediterranean world, by the end of the fourth century, churches had begun celebrating a festival in honour of the martyrs who had died under the pagan emperors; however, for centuries the various churches were unable to settle on a shared date to mark the occasion, and might celebrate it at any time between Easter and Pentecost. But by the end of the eighth century in England and parts of Germany, the festival was being celebrated on 1 November, and was broadened to honour not just the martyrs, but all who had attained sainthood.

In 998, Odilo, the Abbot of Cluny, devised a commemoration that was far more ambitious in scope than that of All Saints. He set aside a day for his monks to pray for 'all the dead who have existed from the beginning of the world to the end of time'. Cluny's 'daughter houses' across Europe all followed this lead; thus, this new festival became popular throughout the Christian world. Odilo had originally placed the festival in February, but as it was complementary to the Feast of All Saints, it was decided they should be held alongside each other. The change of date made sense both spiritually and practically. The bereaved could pray to the saints to intercede for the salvation of the departed souls then believed to be in Purgatory. The sombre nature of the season, with the onset of autumn, the falling of leaves and the coming of dark, cold weather, called to mind not only human mortality, but the need to preserve life and light against the harshness of oncoming winter. It evoked then, as now, not only the sense of death, but also the need to rally against death with brightness, warmth and defiant celebration.

Accordingly, the rituals of the two days mixed both of these ideas. Churches bought in extra stores of candles so that on All Saints' Day they might be brightly illuminated. Torchlit processions were common, and some parishes and city councils laid on grand entertainments, with music, spiced cakes, wine and bonfires. Towards the end of the day, which was the eve of All Souls' Day, began the most important custom: church services with prayers for the dead, after which the bells tolled late into the night, to comfort the souls in Purgatory. Another practice was to bake bread or cakes to be handed out to the poor, which was also thought to help bring souls out of Purgatory, and to encourage the poor to pray for the souls of the departed.[22]

What Doth the People on these Holidays?

Though the medieval Church united the festal and the spiritual in the observance of the cycles of time, these comfortable bonds were broken apart by the Protestant reformers, who were contemptuous of the idea of sacred time. The biblical scholar William Tyndale, in a debate with Sir Thomas More, argued that Christ's view of the Sabbath as 'made for man, and not man for the Sabbath' negated the concept that any one day was holier than another. Festivals and holy days were celebrated by mere convention, not because there was anything intrinsically sacred about them. Any day, he said, could be the 'Lord's day', and one could even have a ten-day week with two Sabbaths if society so desired.[23]

This point of view gained currency in the 1530s. Hugh Latimer, the reforming Bishop of Worcester, fulminated in a sermon before the clergy at the opening of Parliament in 1536 about the evils of the festivals: 'what doth the people on these holidays?' he asked. 'Do they give themselves to godliness, or else ungodliness . . . God seeth all the whole holidays to be spent miserably in drunkenness, in glossing, in strife, in envy, in dancing, dicing, idleness, and gluttony. He seeth all this, and threateneth punishment for it.' For Latimer, it was not just that the holidays encouraged impiety, but also injustice and poverty: 'in so many holidays rich and wealthy persons ... flow in delicates, and men that live by their travail, poor men ... lack necessary meat and drink for their wives and their children, and ... they cannot labour upon the holidays, except they will be cited, and brought before our Officials.'[24]

The idea that spirituality, carousal and the cycle of time could fit together sat ill with the new thinking. The belief that the profusion of holidays was harming the gathering of the harvest and the economic prosperity of the nation added impetus to the will for reform. At first, moderate restraints were placed on the traditional festivals by King Henry VIII in 1538–9. The sterner Protestant government of his son, Edward VI, entirely forbade the Candlemas, Easter and Halloween rituals in 1548. They were briefly permitted again under the Catholic government of Queen Mary (1553–8), but the ban was again enforced in 1559 after the start of Elizabeth I's reign.[25] Yet these prohibitions could only go so far; though the rituals disappeared from the churches, they re-emerged in country lanes and private homes. Their deep and long-held mark on the calendar and in the minds of the people meant they could not so easily be effaced. For centuries afterwards they continued – in attenuated forms – to give their character to the cycle of the English year.

At Candlemas, instead of the presentation of candles in churches, candles were given as gifts within the home, a custom observed until at least the late eighteenth century. In Lyme Regis, it was known as a tradition at that time for each household to light a candle on that day and stand around it drinking. As late as 1853 it was recorded that candles would be lit in the villages along the Trent in Nottinghamshire. Palm Sunday rituals survived in the same way. Throughout England in the eighteenth century, people went out into the countryside to fetch foliage of willow and hazel then in bud. The branches, often fashioned into crosses, tied with blue and pink ribbons, were used as lucky charms to decorate houses – a custom known well into the nineteenth century.[26]

The rituals concerning the Easter sepulchre linger in the calendar even to the present. Thanks to the veneration of the host on Good Friday and its subsequent resurrection, a general belief arose that any sort of biscuits, bread or buns baked on that day – but only if marked with the sign of the cross – had especially beneficial powers. These included the capacity to cure diseases, particularly intestinal disorders. When hung up in a house, they could turn away bad luck. Customs recorded by nineteenth-century folklorists included a Good Friday loaf being kept in a tin for the whole year to bring good fortune to a household; the year-old bread was then moistened, re-baked and shared by all members of the family on the following Easter Sunday. The person who received the slice with the cross was regarded as being especially fortunate; in some places, a slice was also kept to be thrown in neighbouring rivers as a protection against floods. These special loaves baked on Good Friday were known as 'Hot Cross Buns' by at least the early eighteenth century. They became a traditional morning or lunchtime meal across the country on that day, even if their sacred origins in the Easter sepulchre ritual were forgotten. London bakers in the 1700s did not hesitate to commercialise the custom, and the street vendors' cry 'One a-penny, two a-penny, Hot Cross Buns' soon became a familiar nursery rhyme. Modern commercialism has dissociated the buns almost completely from the day, and they are now available year-round.[27]

All Saints and All Souls have similarly marked the calendar down to the present, but their influence is more complex, and perhaps even more telling of the ways Christianity has affected English attitudes towards time. The festival of All Saints was maintained in the Church calendar after Elizabeth I ascended the throne in 1558, but only to commemorate the saints as human beings of outstanding godliness and piety. They were no longer to be seen as semi-divine intercessors. And with the Reformation's official rejection of the doctrine of Purgatory, prayers for the departed were no longer conducted, and with the disappearance of Purgatory, the tolling of bells and all such associated rituals were also prohibited.

However, of all of the customs of the pre-Reformation Church, those performed in comfort of the dead were the hardest to stamp out. The fear of and reverence for the departed had as strong a hold over the popular mind than any diktat of government. Bells were still rung at night in defiance of Church authorities well into the 1580s, and on at least one occasion, on All Saints' Day in 1587 at Hickling in Nottinghamshire, a rowdy group of villagers assaulted a clergyman who tried to prevent them from ringing.

Yet, as it became impossible over the course of the sixteenth century to offer due reverence to the dead within the churches, people started to develop other rituals on the day to fulfil this need. In many places a custom arose that at midnight families would assemble in fields or on hills, where one representative of each would light a large bundle of hay on the end of a pitchfork and hold it in the air. The family would then kneel in a circle around it and pray for their departed friends and relatives until the fire guttered out. This custom was attested in the nineteenth century, not just in areas where Catholicism survived, but throughout the country. The places where this ritual took place were often dubbed 'Purgatory Field', a name still found in Lancashire and Hertfordshire.

In tandem with these midnight prayers, the custom of handing out bread and cakes in return for prayers continued uninterrupted. By the end of the seventeenth century these were known as 'Soul Mass Cakes'. Households baked them, according to the antiquary John Aubrey, in a 'high heap'. Visitors were obliged to take one and say the rhyme: 'A soule-cake, a soule-cake, Have mercy on all Christen soules for a soule-cake.' It continued to be observed throughout the nineteenth century, where groups of poor people would go 'Souling' from door to door on All Saints' Eve (Halloween) to beg for Soul Cakes and other food. Although the component of prayer for the dead had for the most part ebbed away by the end of that century, and it became a time where raucous licensed begging could legitimately occur, the origins of the custom in rituals tied to the Christian calendar remained obvious.[28]

This tradition, like many others, fell into decline by the start of the 1900s, perhaps because of the changes in English society wrought by industrialisation and modernity. It received a second wind in England in the first part of the twentieth century thanks to large-scale immigration from Ireland, where similar rituals over All Saints and All Souls had flourished. And in addition to the poor begging food and gifts to pray for the departed, other customs also emerged. The thought that the dead were particularly present during those festival days led to bands of the living dressing up in outlandish costumes to ward off any of their spirits that might have been ill-disposed. It was a short step from this to mummery and prank-playing. Hollowed-out turnips with grotesque carved faces and candles inside lighting the way for those outside, and with tricks including blowing smoke through key holes, stopping up chimneys, allowing horses out of stables, and breaking bottles to imitate the sound of smashing windows. This Halloween tradition was further strengthened thanks to its popularity in the USA – which again arose from Irish immigration – which in its turn influenced English culture from the 1980s onwards. It was also in the USA that the more readily available pumpkin became a substitute for the turnip.[29]

Happy Holidays?

Since the 1980s the popular observance of Halloween, with dressing up as ghouls and trick-or-treating, has come under attack from evangelical groups, who claim that these customs are pagan and pre-Christian in origin. They condemn the raucous festivities and behaviour which are often the mark of the evening, and argue that it is inappropriate to commemorate such a day in this way. They make constant efforts to propagate 'Light Parties' for children in opposition to more conventional Halloween parties. Whilst such arguments are without basis in fact or history,[30] they do point to a lasting anxiety in the national psyche that finds its origins in the Reformation. The sudden assault on the order of the calendar and its communal celebrations founded in Christian observance led to a number of lingering wounds: to an unravelling of the customs of church life and popular festivity; to the sense that cheerful pleasure in response to religious festivals might somehow be wrong; to the difficulty of setting aside time as sacred and still, instead of busy with secular matters; and to the struggle of finding agreeable times and occasions for communal celebration.

One manifestation of this anxiety is the English tendency to believe in a happier past. Although nostalgia is a constant of human nature, in the case of England it is especially tied to the watershed of the Reformation with its abolition of many festival days, particularly because these were often an occasion for charity and good cheer. Invocations of a lost golden age became common in the sixteenth century. 'Vor when we had the old Law', said a ballad of the 1590s describing the pre-Reformation age, 'a mery world was then: and every thing was plenty, among all sorts of men.' As early as the 1550s, the physician John Caius looked back to 'the old world, when this countrie was called merye Englande'.[31]

Such talk of the disappearance of 'Merry England' became a commonplace of English literature. Successive generations looked back to an era they usually placed just before their own, where England was a country of cheery yeomen and maypole dancing, social order and plenty. Ben Jonson evoked 'a happy age, when on the plains / The woodmen met the damsels, and the swains ...'. Dryden, in the late 1600s, looked back to the beginning of that century, 'when our age was in its prime, / Free from rage and free from crime, / A very merry, dancing, drinking, / Laughing, quaffing, and unthinking time'. In the early nineteenth century, William Wordsworth praised a 'Merry England, in old time'.[32]

Even if the idea of Merry England owes much to nostalgia, the Reformation undeniably made it more difficult for the English to unite around events in the calendar. From the late sixteenth century, festivals were prone to becoming times of contention rather than unity. Attempts were made by the Stuart kings in alliance with the more traditionalist clergy to revive some of the old festivities connected with the Church year. They called for the revival of maypoles and games, the 'cakes and ale' that earlier had gone hand in hand with religious feasts. They hoped to show that such common festivities and rejoicing did not just belong to Catholic traditions and adherents of the pope. They also hoped that such pastimes would bring social cohesion and keep the people in 'harmless action', as the Duke of Newcastle said to Charles II, 'which will free your Majesty from faction and rebellion'.[33]

Those with Puritan sympathies reacted strongly against this movement. The celebration of saints' days was, in the words of one Puritan text, 'devil-born heathenism'. Maypoles, according to another Puritan declaration from the Civil War, were a 'heathenish vanity'. Even after the Restoration in 1660, the cultural tension did not abate. In 1661 a clergyman from Cheshire, Adam Martindale, fulminated against local youths who had set up a new maypole, 'a relic of the shameful worship of the strumpet Flora in Rome'. It is perhaps no surprise that by the eighteenth century the Church played little role in popular festivities even on the highest traditional feast days.[34]

Puritan doctrine opposed the celebration of saints' days, but – despite Tyndale's earlier contempt – it did approve of the strict observance of the Sabbath. From the end of the 1500s, Puritan preachers condemned the way people generally spent their Sundays: 'full heathenishly, in taverning, tippling, gaming, playing and beholding bear-batings and stage-plays, to the utter dishonour of God', and 'their revelling day' passed with 'bowls, dicing, carding, dancing, drunkenness and whoredom'. The Sabbath, they insisted, was not for such leisure, nor for sports or other pastimes. Rather, the rest from work was to be given to religious labour. Sunday, said the Puritan leader William Perkins, 'should be a day set apart for the worship of God and the increase in duties of religion', with secular work a sin on that day, when it should instead be used to read sacred texts, to pray, meditate and listen to sermons. Indeed, according to Lincolnshire cleric John Cotton in 1614, it was unlawful to pass a Sunday without hearing at least two sermons.[35]

This Puritan approach to the Sabbath gained wide popularity in Victorian times, despite earlier opposition particularly in the seventeenth and eighteenth centuries, and remained deeply influential well into the twentieth century, helping to generate the archetypal quiet English Sunday devoid of amusements; a day on which, in the words of the children's writer Alison Uttley: 'Nobody ever read a newspaper or whistled a tune except hymns.'[36]

Although the celebration of saints' days had ebbed away by the end of the seventeenth century, and the Sabbath became the main outlet for rest and the time for religious devotion, this did not mean that there were no efforts to create other moments in the calendar for shared festivity, to fill the unsatisfying void. The authorities, in an attempt to remedy this, established new festivals in their place; however, instead of being dedicated to saints or biblical episodes, the new trend was to commemorate significant royal events or moments of national deliverance, a change that began to make England's calendar distinct from mainland Europe's, which still followed the old Catholic observances. This did not mean that the royal and national events were seen to be secular; instead, they were understood as marks of divine favour and providence for a reformed Protestant nation.

The first of these new festivities appeared around 1570. On 17 November, the anniversary of Elizabeth I's accession to the throne, a custom arose of ringing church bells and holding special services, as well as public feasting and drinking. The occasion became known as 'Crownation Day', and by the second half of the queen's reign it was widespread throughout England. The festival gave thanks for the Tudor dynasty and also for Elizabeth's protection of the Church.

Holidays commemorating royal events proliferated. Celebrations were held on 7 September (Elizabeth's birthday) and, in the following reigns of King James and Charles I, parishes were encouraged to ring their bells and hold festivities on the anniversaries of the kings' accessions and birthdays. After the Restoration, 30 January, the anniversary of the execution of Charles I, was dedicated to 'Charles, King and Martyr', and observed with prayer and fasting. By contrast, 29 May, the anniversary of the Restoration of Charles II – as well as his birthday – became 'Oak Apple Day', marked with special services and feasting. St George's Day (23 April) also regained some significance, as the day chosen by Charles II and James II for their coronations.[37]

As for national moments of deliverance, the first to be marked was the defeat of the Spanish Armada in 1588. Various cities, including Norwich and Salisbury, set aside an annual 'triumphing day' to commemorate the

English victory. Shortly afterwards, the unmasking of Guy Fawkes's conspiracy to blow up king and Parliament on 5 November in 1605 – again seen as an act of divine protection for a pious Protestant nation – led the following year to the establishment of 'Gunpowder Treason Day'. Special prayers authorised by Parliament were offered in churches, along with commemorative sermons. The rich performed annual acts of charity and made gifts to the poor 'so that Guy Fawkes's treason should never be forgot'. The day itself was not a holiday, but it came close to taking on the character of the earlier saints' days, almost as if an unintended substitute for the feasts of All Saints and All Souls held days earlier. Bells rang, feasts were held and, in the words of the London author and printer Michael Sparke, God was to be praised 'with bonfires, trumpets, shawms and psalms . . . on the fifth of November yearly and forever'.[38]

Despite how enthusiastically these celebrations were embraced, there were differences in spirit to their pre-Reformation antecedents. The new festivities, arising as many did from recent moments of dispute, often fostered division as much as unity. In the 1620s and 1630s, when the Stuart monarchs made overtures to Catholic Spain and France, Gunpowder Treason Day became a particular moment of contention. Puritans used the day to preach sternly against the danger of 'popery and superstition'. By contrast, preachers loyal to the court played down the fact that the day commemorated the foiling of a Catholic plot, and instead emphasised that it marked God's deliverance from treason and treachery to the king, as well as the need for loyalty.

Likewise, in the 1670s and 1680s, when fears were rife of Catholic plots, November pageants with the burning of the pope in effigy often degenerated into outright riots. In 1682, London filled with bands of young apprentices overnight, 'where marching through the streets they broke down several windows of those they knew to be popish and popishly affected, and those they got into their hands they most soundly beat' or, breaking into the houses of those they suspected of Catholic sympathies, 'they brought forth chairs, stools, beds, etc, of which they made a great bonfire, and calling for drink drunk rounds of the destruction of . . . the pope'.

Such violence persisted into the eighteenth century. In 1709, the High Church Anglican Henry Sacheverell preached a 5 November sermon comparing the Gunpowder Plot to the execution of Charles I, arguing that the bloodthirstiness of those 'enemies of Church and Government' who put the king to death was shared by the 'factious and schismatical impostors' of his own time – the non-conforming 'false brethren' such as the Presbyterians, Quakers and Baptists. Against these, he called for Anglicans to lead 'an army of banners'. The sermon set London in a frenzy, and started a train of events which led to riots not only in the city itself in 1710, but across the country. These only came to an end in 1715 (although there were sporadic outbreaks of unrest even afterwards), when Parliament passed the Riot Act.[39]

Whilst some of these festivals proved emotive, others proved ultimately to be evanescent. Queen Elizabeth's Crownation Day went through revived periods of popularity in the seventeenth century when its celebration was seen as a tacit rebuke to the Catholic tendencies of the Stuarts. Oak Apple Day and the solemnities of Charles, King and Martyr, remained popular for a time, particularly amongst Tory sympathisers. Yet interest in these festivals waned by the nineteenth century, when formal state observance of them was abolished. Only Guy Fawkes Night remains popular, perhaps because the lengthening nights and cold naturally incline people to collective acts of celebration and memory. The density of popular festivals round the beginning of November with memory at their heart – Halloween, Guy Fawkes Night and Armistice Day on 11 November – may bear witness to this.

Some do still celebrate Oak Apple Day and Charles, King and Martyr – commemorations that may yet last longer than those generated in our own time. As I write this (on 14 May), the Anglican calendar celebrates St Matthias the Apostle (a feast the Church moved recently from 24 February); however, one also has the choice of celebrating, amongst many others, International Chihuahua Appreciation Day, International Dylan Thomas Day, National Dance like a Chicken Day and World Topiary Day. I also note with sorrow that I missed out on celebrating World

Penguin Day. It remains to be seen whether any of these will still be celebrated four centuries hence. However, this modern approach to festivals and the calendar is the ultimate result of the struggles of the sixteenth and seventeenth centuries. Instead of festivals that celebrate a collective religious tradition and that derive their customs from the stories of that tradition, the new trend was that any number of new festivals could be conjured up, based on contemporary events. Their comparative inability to generate cohesion and a deep shared experience is one of the long legacies of the Reformation's assault on the Christian calendar of the Church.

7

My Song Is in Sighing

By the Middle Ages Christianity, with its calendar of festivals and dating system, had given England a new way of relating to time. During the same period, thanks to the flowering of an emerging movement of English spiritual writers, Christianity also offered England a new way of rising above time, and apprehending the world of the timeless and divine.

This great flowering of English spiritual literature began to manifest itself in the latter part of the fourteenth century. It arose in a period of social upheaval, economic turmoil and widespread distress. In that era, England was suffering the aftermath of the Black Death (1348–50), in which two million people, around a third of its population, had died. The years afterwards saw the Peasants' Revolt (1381), where the lower classes rebelled against the imposition of unfair taxes and wage restraints. They also saw another challenge to the established order with the development of the Lollard movement, which questioned the authority of the clergy, the validity of Church ritual, and the right of the Church to forbid the translation of the Bible into English.[1]

Against this disordered and chaotic background, spiritual writers professed to help anyone who sought a direct experience of the transcendent and heavenly in the midst of mortal existence. Their works plotted a path for Christians to proceed from the active to the contemplative life in which they could ultimately perceive, however fleetingly, God Himself. They described the spiritual journey to this destination, with its trials and dangers, warning of the need for humility, the belief that none could pursue such an undertaking without being called by divine will and that, even if the destination was reached, it was beyond the field of human description.

Yet to those who were able to follow this path, they would discover a joy and assurance which nothing in their earlier lives could parallel.

A twentieth-century criticism of English Christianity has been that it is a religion lacking in spirituality. This is a refrain which became common after the First World War and the rise of the psychoanalytic movement, with its heightened concern for the self. Christianity, says the complaint, was unable to offer any satisfactory means for people to process the horrors of the trenches, or to come to terms with the challenges of modernity and its purportedly deeper awareness of the interior life. The confusion of the times did not mean that there was no such thing as the spiritual or transcendent; however, there was nothing in Christianity that could assuage the spiritual needs arising from the turmoil of the age, and one had to look outside of Christianity for genuine spiritual or religious experience. Spirituality and Christianity appeared to part ways. In the words of the 1920s writer John Middleton Murry: 'I am not a Christian, I am not anything, but I have been forced to the conclusion that I am religious.' Many sought the goal of becoming an 'integrated self' at one with the universe, finding, in the words of the author Katherine Mansfield, 'moments, instants, gleams, when' one felt 'the possibility of something quite other', or, as her contemporary Virginia Woolf described, the sense 'that behind the cotton wool [of daily existence] is hidden a pattern; that we – I mean all human beings – are connected with . . . '.[2]

In pursuit of this 'pattern', Woolf worked as a writer, finding in this practice a 'rapture' that would put the 'real thing' of her vision 'into words'. Mansfield, by contrast, followed the Armenian theosophical guru George Gurdjieff, who was highly influential in the earlier twentieth century in Europe and America. Some years later, in a similar search for spiritual wisdom, George Harrison of The Beatles gave impetus to the trend of going to India to study Transcendental Meditation under the Maharishi Mahesh Yogi. Nonetheless, those who chose to follow other practices and traditions neglected the fact that within English Christianity there was indeed a home-grown body of spiritual and mystical writing and practice that in its depth and sophistication could match any of these rivals, even amongst the mayhem of modernity.[3]

The texts of the great spiritual flowering of the fourteenth century were born in an age of widespread death, suffering and upheaval, as shattering as anything endured by the early twentieth century. They also offered, within a Christian framework, the same survey of the nature of the self and its connection to 'the possibility of something quite other' in 'instants [and] gleams.' Their writers offered knowledge of such spirituality to all, not just to an educated clique. Some of the movement's most respected proponents were women. This body of writing, indeed, contains some of the first great works of literature by women in English, and throughout its texts there is a heightened awareness of the feminine in the Christian spiritual path.

Since in the present day many still proclaim a cleavage between the Christian and the spiritual, often in the formula 'I'm spiritual, but not religious,' it is more necessary than ever to revisit the works of these earlier Christian mystical authors where there was no such division. For them, the world of spirituality and contemplation was not just an obvious part of Christianity but something that lay at its deepest heart. Their work is one of the great literatures and treasures vouched to the English tradition. As one of their number, Julian of Norwich, said, God was 'homely';[4] thus, the spiritual journey many modernists have pursued to the East or elsewhere can just as easily be made at home, without leaving the English shore.

Roots of the Flowering

It is never easy to explain why certain moments in history are marked by great flowerings of cultural creativity. In the case of medieval English spiritual literature, the first reason may have been a renewal of interest in love.

The twelfth century in Europe was known as a time of artistic and intellectual renaissance, including the emergence of Gothic architecture and new approaches to law, philosophy and science, and a revival of the study of Classical Latin authors. Of these, Ovid was one of the most popular. His playful and sensuous portrayal of love in the pagan world – particularly in his spoof instruction manuals for lovers, the *Ars Amatoria* and the *Remedia Amoris* (the *Art of Love* and the *Cure of Love*) – enraptured medieval readers. Whilst the medieval audience had the capacity to enjoy such profane depictions of love, there was also an instinct to sublimate and sanctify them. From the same period in secular circles, the nobler vision of courtly love was given shape in knightly romances and troubadour poetry. And in churches and monasteries, analogous ideas of a sacred love between the Christian devotee and the heavenly creator came to the fore in sermons and devotional writing.

One pioneer of this thought was the Cistercian abbot and writer St Bernard of Clairvaux. Sprung from a noble Burgundian family and highly educated, he would have been influenced by the broad interest in the new theme of love. This became manifest in his own writing. In the 1130s, he composed a series of sermons on the biblical Song of Songs, an ancient love poem. Throughout these sermons, he argues that man's paramount goal is the restoration of his original likeness to God, which he once enjoyed before the Fall and the coming of sin into the world. Love was the force that would bring this to pass. The love for God would be the remedy to restore this pristine likeness, and this love would first be apprehended through love of one's neighbour and love of one's self, for which self-knowledge was needed.

For Bernard, the crucifixion was, more than anything, a sign of God's love for humanity; Bernard's meditations on the Cross, therefore, go beyond the physical sufferings of Christ to dwell on the spiritual love for humanity expressed in the Passion, and how it stirs up the love of humanity for God in response. Bernard's experience of Christ is 'like honey in the mouth, song in the ear, and jubilation in the heart'. It is a love that knows no bounds. It is 'headlong, vehement, unrestrained'. In the end, it is a love which is reciprocated, and tends towards a reunion of the lover and the beloved. As much as the human soul cries out for God, so God too longs for the human soul.[5]

Bernard's stress on the idea of love between the creator and the created, his sensuous manner of expression and his sublimation of the erotic had a lasting effect on other Christian writers throughout the Middle Ages, and have often been described as 'feminine'. His influence filtered through to England thanks in part to the presence there of the Cistercian order. English members of the order continued to write in the same vein, developing and popularising his approach. Aelred, Abbot of Rievaulx in North Yorkshire, whose reputation was such that he was venerated as a saint after his death in 1157, began one of his works, the *Speculum Caritatis* (*The Mirror of Charity*), with a passionate invocation of the love between God and the created man:

> ... May Your voice sound in my ears, dear Jesus, and teach me how my heart should love You, how my mind should love You, how the bowels of my soul should love You. May my inmost heart of hearts enclose You, my one and only true treasure, my sweet and lovely joy. But what is love, my God? If I am right, it is a strange delight of the spirit, ever sweeter as it is chaster, ever gentler as it is truer, ever gladder as it is wider: it is the savour of the heart which You inspire, for You are sweet, it is the eye by which You see, for You are good, it is a place that contains You who are everything. For he who loves You knows what You are: and as he knows You, so he loves You, for You are earthly love, You are divine love. These are the riches of Your house, with which Your lovers are made drunk, losing knowledge of themselves that they may come to You ...[6]

Other potent ideas mixed with these Cistercian notions of the passionate desire for God, the hope for union between the humbled self and God, and the belief that knowledge of God could only be obtained through love. Some were derived from an ancient set of texts, the *Corpus Dionysiacum*, which became highly influential during the medieval period. These were attributed by scholars in late antiquity to Dionysius the Areopagite, a character from the Acts of the Apostles, who is said to have been converted to Christianity by St Paul during his visit to Athens; however, in reality they were written under this pseudonym by an anonymous author probably in the late fifth century AD, melding together ideas from pagan Neoplatonic philosophers with Christian thinking.

Dionysius was, more than anyone, responsible for propagating the concept of negative or 'apophatic' theology, also known as the '*via negativa*'. The word 'apophatic', from the Greek for 'unable to be spoken', points to the belief that God is of an entirely different order to the perceptible and finite world, thus fundamentally unknowable using the normal means of human language or senses. In Dionysius's words:

> . . . [God] is neither darkness nor light nor truth nor error; He can neither be affirmed nor denied; nay, though we may affirm or deny the things that are beneath Him, we can neither affirm nor deny Him; for the perfect and sole cause of all is above all affirmation, and that which transcends all is above all subtraction, absolutely separate, and beyond all that is.

Granted, God may be manifest in the created world, for '. . . he goes forth in an unlessened stream into all things that are . . .', but these are merely fragmentary shadow-like glimpses 'in things divided'. To get beyond these echoes and refractions to apprehend His true essence and reality, one has to give up on knowledge or the intellect, and instead turn to pure experience through what Dionysius calls 'the eyeless mind'. Through a process of meditation and contemplation, in which the subject moves away from trying to define or understand God as being one thing or another, one moves to a pure experience of God simply as being, untrammelled by any finite ideas or definitions. One has to go 'unknowing' towards 'Him who transcends all being and all knowledge'. It is only by 'the unceasing and absolute renunciation' of one's self and all things that one could be 'borne on high, through pure and entire self-abnegation, into the superessential radiance of the divine darkness'. For those who could follow this path to its conclusion, there was a reward in an ecstatic, glorious and indescribable union with the divine: 'By the inactivity of all knowledge one is united . . . to the altogether unknown, and by knowing nothing, knows above mind.'[7]

These powerful ideas, where detachment from the world was required to pursue an engagement with God through contemplation, were suited ideally to the trend from the twelfth century in England for religious devotees to become hermits or recluses. For some, it was not sufficient to live the monastic life; a fuller withdrawal from the world and a solitary existence were not just the surest way to salvation, but the best way to commune with the divine. In the words of the eleventh-century Italian monastic reformer Peter Damian, who strongly influenced this movement: 'The hermit's cell is the meeting-place of God and man, a cross-roads for those who dwell in the flesh and heavenly things. For there the citizens of heaven hold intercourse with men, not in the language of flesh, but by being made manifest, without any clamour of tongues, to the rich and secret places of the soul.'[8]

The growing popularity of solitude was catered for partly by the rise of new monastic orders, such as the Carthusians and Premonstratensians, which allowed their members to live as hermits within monastic precincts, though a number of people chose to enter the solitary life outside the monastic sphere. Some were originally monks who then moved into separate hermitages. Others were lay people. Whilst some lived in harsh and isolated spots, for example the itinerant seafarer Godric of Finchale who spent 60 years in a hermitage in a bend of the River Wear in County Durham, others, like Julian of Norwich, would confine themselves within cells or small dwellings built on to churches in towns and cities. Many of these hermits, known as 'anchorites' or 'anchoresses', were women. By the fourteenth century, less of a provision had been made for nuns, with the result that women who wished to give themselves fully to religious devotion found it easier to engage in this life as hermits rather than nuns.[9]

Whether people entered the solitary life as monks or else from a lay background, they often required advice or spiritual counsel to support them in this endeavour. And when they became spiritually adept themselves, they could dispense such advice to others on the same path, or to clergy or lay people who wished to benefit from their insight. Much of this advice was given by word of mouth. Godric of Finchale, for example, was known to have counselled St Aelred of Rievaulx, but we know nothing of its substance. However, some was given in the form of poems and written treatises.[10] One earlier example is the *Ancrene Riwle* (*The Rule for Anchoresses*), which was written by an anonymous author, probably in the West Midlands in the early fourteenth century, for three sisters who had entered the solitary life. Already, in the midst of its strict instructions for self-mortification and the avoidance of sin, there are signs of the mix of ideas from the Cistercian tradition and the writings of Dionysius about the intense apprehension of the divine: 'After the kiss of peace in the Mass, when the priest takes communion, forget the world, be completely out of the body, and with burning love embrace your Beloved who has come down from heaven to your heart's bower, and hold Him fast until he has granted you all that you ask.'[11]

As the fourteenth century went on, it was in this context that a number of great texts would emerge, offering the advice and vision of these contemplatives especially for those who wished to follow similar paths. From this time, although there is a mass of poetry and other texts that could be discussed, here we can turn in particular to the writings of three great authors which can still speak to our own present time of turmoil.

Richard Rolle

Varying amounts are known about these three. Of one – the author of *The Cloud of Unknowing* – not even the name has been recorded. However, of the life of Richard Rolle, although he is the earliest, much detail remains. Not only does he leave allusions to the development of his own writing, but also, by the end of the century he had become a candidate for sainthood; thus, a good deal of biographical information was preserved.[12]

Rolle was born around 1300 in Thornton Dale near Pickering in

Yorkshire, from a relatively poor family. Nevertheless, he must have showed considerable talent at an early age for, when he was 13 or 14, he was sent to study at Oxford with financial support from an aristocratic cleric, Thomas de Neville, who later became Archdeacon of Durham. As a student, Rolle acquired a thorough grasp of Latin, a smattering of Greek (unusual for the period), and deep knowledge of scripture, philosophy, theology and music. By the age of 18 he seems to have become disillusioned with university life; the rigidly intellectual tendencies in scholastic theology repelled him, as did covetous members of the clergy. He left without a degree and returned to Yorkshire, where he decided to lead a reclusive life. On reaching home, he took two pieces of his sister's clothing and a hood belonging to his father, and fashioned them into some sort of hermit's outfit – behaviour that caused his sister to flee in horror. He then went to live in the wilderness.

After some time, he was recognised by some of his Oxford contemporaries when he was invited to preach one day, probably at the church in Pickering. His preaching had such a powerful effect on the congregation that he was offered patronage by a rich official called John de Dalton, who gave him board and lodging. For the rest of his life, Rolle seems to have been under the protection of a number of such patrons, for whom he would have preached and offered prayers. He seems to have moved away from John de Dalton after a few years because he felt tempted by a young woman in his household, and for a time he struggled to deal with his sexual desires. Later in his life he describes himself in Latin as a '*castratum*' – probably by way of a metaphor rather than literally – saying that by then he had nothing to offer anyone by way of physical attachment. Indeed, some of his patrons appear to have been women, and in the 1340s he was settled at the village of Hampole near Doncaster, where he became a spiritual counsellor for a community of Cistercian nuns. To one of them, Margaret Kirkby, who chose to follow the vocation of a hermit, Rolle addressed a number of works in English on the spiritual life. He died in 1349, almost certainly as a result of the Black Death.

Some time after he had been taken under John de Dalton's patronage, following a long period of devotional exercises and self-denial, Rolle underwent a mystical experience whilst at prayer:

> I was sitting in a certain Chapel, and while I was taking pleasure in the delight of some prayer or meditation, I suddenly felt within me an unwonted and pleasant fire. When I had for long doubted whence it came, I learned by experience that it came from the creator and not from creature, since I found it ever more pleasing and full of heat. Now from the beginning of that fiery warmth, inestimably sweet, until the infusion of the heavenly, spiritual harmony, the song of eternal praise, and the sweetness of unheard melody, which can be heard and experienced only by one who has received it, and who must be purified and separated from the earth, nine months and some weeks passed away.
>
> For when I was sitting in the same chapel, and was reciting psalms as well as I might before supper, I heard above me the noise of harpers, or rather of singers. And when with all my heart I attended to heavenly things in prayer, I perceived within me, I know not how, a melody and a most delightful harmony from heaven, which abode in my mind . . . meanwhile wonder seized me but I was taken up into such joy, and that God should have given me gifts which I knew not how to ask for, nor had thought that any, even the most holy, would receive such in this life.[13]

This direct encounter with the divine – its nature, the longing for it, how man might put himself in a position to receive it – forms much of the substance of the body of writing that Rolle produced. Some of it was in the form of Latin commentaries on scripture or autobiographical accounts of the spiritual journey. Some was in the form of English poetry or treatises, addressed either to a general audience or to specific people, perhaps Margaret Kirkby or others in her position, who were following the same devotional path. Throughout the fourteenth century, his writings became widely popular.

One mark of Rolle's work is its simplicity and directness. The passionate and sensual longing for Christ, characteristic of Bernard of Clairvaux, is manifest in his poetry, and its unvarnished intensity can be well appreciated in the original Middle English text:

My sange is in sighing,
My life is in langing,
Till I thee se my king,
So faire in thy shining,
So faire in thy fairehed.
Intil thy light me lead,
And in thy luve me feed.
In luve make me to speed,
That thou be ever my meed.
When will thou come,
Ihesu, my joy,
And cover me of care,
And give me thee,
That I may see,
[thee] living evermare?[14]*

Even though some of his work was in Latin or apparently scholarly in nature, such as his biblical commentaries, and drew from his wide education and reading, he was adamant that his writing, and indeed the experiences he underwent, was not 'for philosophers ... nor the wise of this world' but directed at 'the simple and unlettered, who endeavour to love God better rather than to know many things'. Such things could not be grasped by 'those disputants who are expert in all knowledge, but inexpert in the love of Christ'. The route towards this direct encounter lay through the practice of contemplation. Rolle explains the necessities for embarking on this way. 'A man must be truly turned to him and in his innermost mind turned away from all visible things before he can

* Langing – love-longing; fairehed – beauty; meed – reward; cover me of – recover me from.

experience the sweetness of divine love, even a little.' All devotion had to be turned towards the divine and away from the material, so that the seeker might avoid taking 'pleasure in the emptiness of visible life instead of truly happy love'. This beginning was one of pain and tribulation, with strict self-discipline essential. 'First ... a man [must] exercise himself unceasingly for many years in praying and meditating, scarcely taking the bare necessities for his body.' Nor could one expect to develop quickly, 'since it is well known that contemplation is attained after much time and much labour'. Moreover, these efforts could not guarantee even the attainment of the contemplative state: 'for it is not within man's power to receive it, nor does a man's toil, however long he spend, merit it, but it is given of God's goodness to his true lovers'.[15]

The contemplative life, said Rolle, had three parts: reading, prayer and meditation. 'In reading, God speaks to us; in prayer we speak to God. In meditation, angels come down to us and teach us so that we do not err; in prayer they go up and offer our prayers to God.' Each led to the other. 'To reading belongs reason or the inquisition of truth ... To prayer belongs praise, song, surpassing in beholding, and marvel ... To meditation belongs the inspiration of God, understanding, wisdom and sighing.'[16]

As for what a devotee actually experienced if they were able to enter into the full state of contemplation, Rolle, in the tradition of Dionysius and the *via negativa*, ultimately declined to give any full definition. 'If it be asked what is contemplation, it is hard to define', he confessed.

> Some say that contemplative life is nought else but knowledge of things to come and hidden: or to be void of all worldly occupation: or the study of God's letters. Others say that contemplation is the free sight into the visioned truths of wisdom, lift up with full high marvel. Others say that contemplation is a free and wise insight of the soul all spread about to behold His might. Others say, and say well, that contemplation is joy in heavenly things. Others say, and say best, that contemplation is the death of fleshly desires through the joy of the mind up-raised.[17]

Even though Rolle declined to offer a clear definition, he resorted to the sensual language of Bernard of Clairvaux to give an impression. Often, he combined ideas of music and of love to evoke the contemplative state:

> To me it seems that contemplation is the joyful song of God's love taken into the mind, with the sweetness of angels' praise. This is the jubilation that is the end of perfect prayer and high devotion in this life. This is the ghostly mirth had in mind for the Everlasting Lover, with great voice out-breaking... Marvel not if melody be sent to the soul thus ordinated in love [since] ... When she also loves unceasingly and burningly [then] meditation is turned in to songs of joy, and nature is renewed and enveloped in heavenly mirth.[18]

However, the 'angels' music' or heat enjoyed by the contemplative was not to be understood as that enjoyed by the senses. It could only be perceived in a mystery:

> This delight, certain, which [the contemplative] has tasted in loving Jesus, passes all wit and feeling. Truly I can not tell a little point of this joy, for who can tell an untold heat? Who lay bare an infinite sweetness? Certain if I would speak of this joy unable to be told, it seems to me as if I should empty the sea by drops, and fasten it all in a little hole of the earth.[19]

Rolle's work remained popular in England until the Reformation, his manuscripts not only kept in monastic libraries, but also circulated widely amongst clergy and lay people, particularly in the north. Editions were made by early printers at the end of the fifteenth century in London, Oxford, Paris and Cologne, and again on the continent in the sixteenth and seventeenth centuries. Even after the Reformation in England, copies of his writing were to be found as far afield as Prague and Bohemia, Spain, Italy and Sweden. In England, his simple style influenced John Wycliffe's clear and direct biblical translations. Given the use made of Wycliffe's translation in the development of the King James Bible, Rolle's work may be seen as one of the Authorised Version's early progenitors. His effect on subsequent generations of English spiritual writers was also profound. Even if they described the paths towards mystical experience in different ways and to an extent reacted against the way he described the contemplative state, his tendency for simple expression became the standard.

The Cloud of Unknowing

Despite the fact that it is one of the most powerful tracts on mysticism and spirituality of the earlier English Christian tradition, a wealth of research has been able to establish no more than a set of probabilities about the author of *The Cloud of Unknowing*: that he was likely male and a priest, and lived in the East Midlands in the second half of the 1300s.[20] Nothing he writes in any of his works – which also include a translation of Dionysius, as well as *The Epistle of Privy Counsel* and *The Epistle of Prayer* – hints at his identity. However, given not just the title but also the tenor of his principal tract, this anonymity was almost certainly part of his intent.

For all this, the author's learning, humour and strength of character remain distinctive. As with Rolle, the *Cloud of Unknowing* author mostly wrote tracts to give personal advice to particular devotees in pursuit of the solitary Christian life. If anything, the *Cloud* author's advice was even more concentrated and direct than Rolle's. He prescribed those who sought the direct experience of God a primary exercise, based on the Dionysian idea that nothing in the material or temporal world could be a full expression of the divine: 'Lift up thine heart unto God with a meek stirring of love, and mean Himself and none of his goods.' Devotees must detach themselves from any comfort or rest in the material world, or even intellectual understanding which was derived from mortal observation.

> Look that thou loathe to think on aught but [God] Himself, so that nought work in thy mind nor in thy will but only Himself. And do that in thee is to forget all the creatures that ever God made and the works of them, so that thy thought or thy desire be not directed or stretched to any of them.

The result of this concentration on God and the forgetting of the material and temporal would initially result in a sort of obscure agony: 'At the first time when thou dost it, thou findest but a darkness and as it were a cloud of unknowing, thou knowest not what, saving that thou feelest in thy will a naked intent unto God.' In this state, the devotee attempts to still the normal ways of apprehending the world, through the understanding and imagination: 'this darkness and this cloud . . . hindereth thee, so that thou mayest neither see him clearly by light of understanding in thy reason, nor feel him in sweetness of love in thy affection'. Without the reassurance of the normal faculties of reason or imagination, this 'cloud' could feel comfortless for the devotee:

> And therefore shape thee to bide in this darkness as long as thou mayest, ever more crying after him whom thou lovest. For if ever thou shalt see him or feel him as it may be here, it must always be in this cloud and in this darkness . . . smite on that thick cloud of unknowing with a sharp dart of longing love . . .[21]

All rational beings, says the *Cloud* author, have two main faculties for apprehension: knowing and loving. Knowing, dealing as it does with the finite and distinct, is unable to apprehend the divine. Loving, however, is capable of this. 'Of God himself can no man think. Therefore I will leave on one side everything I can think, and choose for my love that thing which I cannot think. Why? Because he may well be loved, but not thought. By love he can be caught and held, but by thinking never.' However many thoughts or meditations should occur to the devotee about the nature or attributes of God – His sweetness, mercy, grace, kindness – rather than just God Himself, they also have to be covered with the cloud of forgetting. If any such thought should emerge, one should 'go on to say [to it] "Get down", and proceed to trample on it out of love for God; yes, even when such thoughts seem to be holy, and calculated to help you to find God'. It is the 'naked intent, directed solely towards God', and Himself alone, that is wholly sufficient.[22]

The *Cloud* author eschews any long or complex prayer to express this intent. It should be summed up in a short word, he says, preferably of one syllable.

> The shorter the word the better, being more like the working of the Spirit. A word like 'God' or 'love' . . . Fix this word hard to your heart, so that it is always there come what may. It will be your shield and spear in peace and war alike. With this word you will hammer the cloud and the darkness above you. With this word you will suppress all thought under the cloud of forgetting. So much so that if you are ever tempted to think what it is that you are seeking, this one word will be sufficient answer. And if you would go on to think learnedly about the significance and analysis of that same word, tell yourself that you will have it whole, and not in bits and pieces. If you hold fast, that thought will surely go. And why? Because you refuse to let it feed on the helpful meditations we spoke of earlier.[23]

Even if the devotee could trample down all distracting 'holy meditations' on the attributes of God rather than God Himself, 'there still remains between you and God the stark awareness of your own existence', warns the *Cloud* author. 'And this awareness, too, must go, before you experience contemplation in its perfection.' Such awareness can only be extinguished through divine grace, which the contemplative must be willing to receive. At the base of such willingness must be 'true sorrow, perfect sorrow' filled with 'holy longing' from an awareness of one's separateness from God: 'All other sorrow in comparison with this is a travesty of the real thing. For he experiences true sorrow, who knows and feels not only what he is, but that he is.'[24]

The final destination of the devotee on this journey is a oneness with God 'in spirit, in love, and in harmony of will'. The *Cloud* author is wary of those who see physical feelings or exterior phenomena, particularly the sensation of heat or fire, as being marks of the successful end of this path. His own allusion to what one might ultimately experience by way of this oneness is expressed with considerable reserve:

> At such a time, [God] may, perhaps, send out a shaft of spiritual light, which pierces this cloud of unknowing between you, and shows you some of his secrets, of which it is not permissible or possible to speak. Then will you feel your affection flame with the fire of his love, far more than I can possibly say now. For I dare not take upon myself with my blundering, earthly tongue to speak of what belongs solely to God.[25]

The works by the *Cloud* author, like those of Rolle, circulated widely in England up to the Reformation, and were also important texts for English Catholic recusants on the continent afterwards. Following their republication in the modern age, they became an inspiration for many twentieth-century poets including Wallace Stevens and T.S. Eliot, whose protagonist in 'The Love Song of J. Alfred Prufrock', like the dedicatee of the *Cloud*, was a 24-year-old man on a difficult spiritual journey. Eliot quotes the *Cloud* in the *Four Quartets*, mindful of the idea of the naked intent: 'With the drawing of this Love and the voice of this Calling.'[26] But, as a text, the *Cloud* was able to reach even beyond Christian readers. Whilst the Benedictine historian David Knowles called it 'the most excellent work on contemplative prayer ever written in the English language', the Buddhist writer Anne Bancroft saw it as a parallel to many teachings of Zen.[27]

Julian of Norwich

Our third author, Julian, was probably born in Yorkshire around 1342. We know nothing of her earlier life except that she was devout, and appears also to have been close to her mother. Though she claims to have been 'unlettered', she had a formidable intellect, literary talent and knowledge of Christian doctrine. It is not for nothing that Rowan Williams, the former Archbishop of Canterbury, once said that her writings 'may well be the most important work of Christian reflection in the English language'.[28]

Sometime in her youth she had, by her own account, asked God for three favours: first, to be granted a 'bodily sight' of Christ's Passion, so she could share in His sufferings by love; second, to undergo 'bodily sickness', so that by enduring the pains of imminent death she could be purged from all attachment to earthly things; and, third, for three 'wounds' – of sorrow for sin, of compassion to suffer with Christ, and finally of longing for God Himself. She tells us that her prayer for the first two favours had passed from her mind but that, in May 1373, when she was 'thirty years old and a half', these prayers were answered. She was struck down with an illness that laid her prostrate for three nights. During this time, she was closely tended by her mother. On the fourth night she received the last rites. After that: 'I lingered two or three more days, and on the third night was quite convinced I was passing away, as were those around me.'[29]

The parson was called again to be with her. He brought a crucifix, which he held before her face as her breath and eyesight were failing. Soon, she saw a play of luminescence around the cross, whilst everything else in the room went dark, then suddenly her bodily pain ceased. She remembered her desire to be wounded with compassion to suffer with Christ, and at that moment the crucifix appeared to change: 'And in this suddenly I saw the red blood trickling down from under the garland of thorns hot and fresh and right plenteously . . . like to the drops of water that fall off the eaves of a house right after a great shower of rain . . . and for the roundness, they were like to the scale of herring.'

It was from this point that she experienced a series of 15 mystical revelations, or 'shewings'. They came in a rapid succession, the first at around 4 a.m., the last on the following night. Throughout them, as far as can be understood, the sight of Christ's head on the crucifix was always visible to her, whilst in her mind there were 'words' and 'ghostly shewings'.[30]

After this was over, her pain returned for a time, and she began to doubt their reality. A cleric visited her at this point to ask after her health, and she said: 'I had raved during the day.' She fell asleep, and suffered further dreams of being under assault by a devil, who filled the room with a fire and foul stench. But after further visions and revelations she stopped doubting the truth of what she had seen. Her work, written and revised over a number of years, was a relation of and meditation on these 'shewings', with one overarching theme:

> Wouldst thou witten thy Lord's meaning in this thing? Learn it well: love was his meaning. Who shewed it thee? Love. What shewed he thee? Love. Wherefore shewed he thee? For love . . . Thus it was I learned that love was our Lord's meaning. And I saw full surely that ere God made us he loved us; which love was never slacked nor ever shall be. And in this love he hath done all his works; and in this love he hath made all things profitable to us; and in this love our life is everlasting. In our making we had our beginning; but the love wherein he made us was in him from without beginning: in which love we have our beginning. And all this shall we see in God, without end.[31]

The idea of the need to abnegate the created world in pursuit of God, which appears in Dionysius and again with such austerity in *The Cloud of Unknowing*, is not absent from Julian; however, it is presented in her work with a strikingly different emphasis. In one vision, she was shown 'a little thing, the size of a hazelnut, on the palm of my hand, round like a ball'. She looked at it thoughtfully and asked what it was. The answer came that it was 'all that is made'. She was astonished that it continued to exist and that it did not suddenly disintegrate because of its insignificance. Nonetheless, it came to her in the shewing that despite its smallness and fragility, it was sustained by the love of God; to it, He was 'Maker, Keeper, and Lover'. Although she finds the necessity of realising the 'littleness of creation' and 'to see it for the nothing that it is before we can love and possess God who is uncreated', she does not neglect the sense of God being present in His created works through love. The created world, for her, is still a manifestation of God.[32]

The connection of God to man and creation through love finds a startling expression in the idea of God and Christ as 'mother' as well as 'father'.

The concept had been expressed by the eleventh-century Archbishop of Canterbury St Anselm in his theological work, but the importance Julian laid on the idea of motherhood may well have come through the closeness of her relationship with her own mother, who tended her through her illness. Julian extends maternal connections far beyond the domestic setting. The Virgin Mary is 'our mother in whom we are all enclosed' and 'she that is mother of our Saviour is mother of all that shall be saved in our Saviour', but, more than this, Christ 'our Saviour is our own very mother, in whom we are endlessly borne'. Even more strikingly, she fixes on Christ the idea of the mother breastfeeding her child:

> The mother may give her child suck of her milk, but our precious Mother, Jesus, he may feed us with Himself, and doeth it, full courteously and full tenderly, with the Blessed Sacrament that is the food of life ... This fair lovely word, 'Mother', it is so sweet and kind itself that it may not verily be said of none but Him; and to her that is very Mother of Him and all ...[33]

The closeness of God and man in Julian's vision, and its deep optimism – 'our very Mother, Jesus, he – all love – beareth us to joy and endless living' – imbues her work's every aspect. Man's first sin was not through some innate inclination to evil, but came about by man striving too hard to follow the divine. Sin was 'behoveful' as it allowed God and Christ to demonstrate their love for man – indeed, to fulfil a deep longing of God – by the incarnation and crucifixion. This opportunity for the display of love was a better outcome for creation than if there had never been Original Sin. 'It is an endless liking to me', says Christ to Julian in a shewing, 'that I ever suffered passion for thee: and if I might suffer more, I would suffer more.'[34]

However, in Julian's own mind there was an almost unresolvable tension between the fullness of God's love and Church doctrine – which she claimed to be punctilious in accepting – which taught that some sinners would be condemned to eternal damnation. One of the shewings presents a dialogue between Julian and God, where she presses Him about why sin and suffering were allowed into the world, and of those who would be damned because of it. To all of her questions, God offers a similar refrain: 'It is sooth that sin is cause of all this pain; but all shall be well, and all shall be well, and all manner of thing shall be well . . . That which is impossible to thee is not impossible to me: I shall save my word in all things, and I shall make all things well.' Hence, Julian follows the lead of the *Cloud* author and accepts the ultimate unknowability of God: 'For I saw soothly in our Lord's teaching, the more we busy us to know his secret counsel in this or any other thing, the farther shall we be from the knowing thereof.'[35]

Julian had a wide reputation in her own time, though enclosed as an anchoress at St Julian's Church in Norwich by 1404, from which she draws her name (her original name is unknown). Another spiritual writer and traveller of the time, Margery Kempe, records in 1410 being bidden by divine inspiration to visit 'Dame Jelyan' who 'was expert in such things and good counsel could give.'[36] Her writing never fell out of circulation in England, although, like other medieval texts of this sort, it grew greatly in popularity from the nineteenth century, and has continued to have a deep impact on English culture and its Church. The early-twentieth-century writer on mysticism Evelyn Underhill called Julian 'the first real woman of English letters.'[37] She was an inspiration to T.S. Eliot in the darkest days of the Second World War, and her statement that 'All shall be well' was repeated in 'Little Gidding' from the *Four Quartets* to express a stirring of optimism in the midst of despair. Likewise, her life and writings have given rise to a host of creative works, including music by Thomas Adès, novels by Iris Murdoch, and plays and films by other writers. Her experience was used to support the movement to allow women to be ordained as priests in the Church of England. Most recently, her words were broadcast around the world during the coronation of King Charles in 2023. Embroidered on the screen that shielded the king when he was anointed at the most sacred moment in the service was the assurance she had heard in her shewings: 'all shall be well, and all manner of thing shall be well.'

8

His Words Were with Power

As a former schoolmaster, I am a reasonable connoisseur of children's excuses. I have heard my fill of unaccountable bowel movements getting in the way of punctuality for lessons, and meticulously done homework being destroyed by dogs, woodworm, nitric acid, computer viruses or international crime syndicates. But for their erudite ingenuity in excuse-making, I tip my mortar board to a pair of seventeenth-century youths, Nicholas Lucas and William Mattock, from the village of Williton in Somerset. In 1633, this pair got in trouble with the local authorities for breaking a church window when playing ball. Determined not to take the blame, Mattock launched a clever defence. 'Where is the church? The church is where the *congregation* is assembled though it be at the beacon on the top of the hill of Quantock.'[1]

Mattock's smart quibble distinguishing the physical building from the concept of the Church didn't help them much: they were chased by the constable and ended up being summoned to court in Taunton. However, it casts a striking light on the intellectual atmosphere of the time. The idea that the Church was simply a congregation of its people who were all equal before God was deeply provocative. It challenged the traditional idea that it was a hierarchical organisation overseen by bishops and priests, who were God's mouthpieces, whose power was manifest in buildings and ceremonies.

One place in which this controversy originated was in the new translations of the Bible. In 1534, almost exactly a century before this incident, the brilliant scholar William Tyndale, influenced by Martin Luther and ideas of the Reformation as well as his deep linguistic knowledge, issued his English translation of the New Testament – an act that was then still illegal under English law. In it, he translated the Greek word *ekklesia* as 'congregation', rather than the more conventional alternative 'church'. Thus, in Tyndale's version of St Paul's Letter to the Ephesians, the 'congregacion', not the 'church', was said to be the 'body' of Christ.[2] His translation of Christ's commission of the Apostle Peter in chapter 16 of Matthew's Gospel is '... upon this rock I will build my congregation' rather than the more usually recognised 'my church'.[3]

The English Tudor establishment saw this as a damnable heresy, not to mention a threat to the Church's power and social stability more generally. The arrival of Tyndale's translation was the harbinger of a 'pestilent sect' in the words of Sir Thomas More, and the use of 'congregacion' a deliberate and provocative mistranslation.[4]

In the 1520s and the early 1530s, when Tyndale sparred with More and the English bishops, deep knowledge of the Bible and these complex controversies were open only to a select few who had the benefit of long scholarly and linguistic training in the universities. Well within a century, there had been a profound change. Scriptural ideas and their attendant controversies were now in the hands of every member of society down to the lowest country urchins, and even furnished them with the means and boldness to argue with and defy authority – even when they were simply trying to find an excuse to deal with a broken window.

When quarrelling with a priest in the 1520s, Tyndale vowed 'If God spare my life, ere many years I will cause a boy who drives a plough to know more of the scriptures than thou dost.'[5] Mattock's cocky excuse shows not only that Tyndale's vow was thoroughly fulfilled, but also how the placing of this deep knowledge of the Bible in the hands of all classes during the sixteenth and seventeenth centuries left a deep and lasting mark on the way that the English think, speak and behave.

Holy Writ in Englische Wole Make Cristen Men at Debate

Long before Tyndale embarked on his translation in the 1520s and 1530s, the Bible was seen by the Church hierarchy as a dangerous text.[6]

Throughout the Middle Ages, it was available in its fullness only to a very limited class of people, nearly all clergy, who had both access to rare physical copies, and the education to read them – nearly every copy was in Latin.

This is not to say that ordinary people had no knowledge of the Bible or were denied access to scripture. They would hear fragments translated in preaching at church services or in mystery plays, quotations in poetry or devotional literature. At every level of society, people were expected to know the Lord's Prayer in Latin and its English meaning, along with the meaning of other prayers and tenets of the Christian faith. The wealthier and more educated might even see translations of psalms and quotations from the gospels in a Book of Hours.[7]

However, especially by the end of the fourteenth century, this access to scripture was carefully curated. In the latter half of that century, a group around the Oxford theologian John Wycliffe argued that 'hooly scripture conteyneth al prophitable treuthe' and that it was 'leful [lawful] and nedful to the pepel for to knowe Goddis lawe and the feith of holy chirche in here langage'. The Bible, argued Wycliffe, was free from error. In it the truth was to be found, rather than in the Church or any of its traditional interpreters or intermediaries. Bishops and even the pope should be judged against the yardstick of the Bible, rather than claiming any sole right to determine its meaning. This was something that any faithful layman could do, if they set themselves to understand its style and logic in humility.[8]

Thus, the circle around Wycliffe set to translating the Latin Bible into English, and circulating it amongst their followers – known as the Lollards – who sought wider religious reforms. For decades afterwards, these translations were passed around and read at secret house meetings, where dissenting groups of laymen would discuss their meaning or even preach to each other about them.

This direct access to the biblical text gave these small groups the impetus to generate their own ideas on all manner of things. One man, William Wakeham of Devizes, who had attended many secret English

Bible-reading groups with weavers at a house in Marlborough in the early 1400s, admitted that the Bible had made him think that 'the earth was above heaven', that 'the soul of man is the church of God' and that 'it is no better for laymen to say the *Pater Noster* in Latin than to say "bibull babul"'.[9]

The weavers of Marlborough were not alone in drawing new ideas from the Bible. In 1395, leading members of the Lollard movement presented to Parliament their *Twelve Conclusions*, a call for thorough reform of the Church and wider society. The Church in England, they said, had become 'blynde and leprouse'. There was no basis in the Bible, they argued, for the orders of bishops or priests which they then had. Many of the ways in which priests ministered – exorcisms and hallowing of objects in church, hearing confessions, and claiming that the bread and wine in communion were actually changed into the body and blood of Christ – were closer to necromancy than 'holi theologie'. Priests should stop involving themselves in temporal offices. They should be allowed to marry, as their customary vow of celibacy 'inducith sodomie in al holy chirche'. The same went for women who took religious vows of chastity, as this led to illicit affairs, abortion and the 'sleyng of children' before 'thei ben cristenid'. The people should also avoid pilgrimages, and most importantly warfare. Manslaughter caused by battle or laws of justice in any temporal or spiritual cause without special revelation 'is expres contrarious to the newe testament' which was a 'lawe of grace and ful of mercy'. Indeed, Christ's teaching 'most taute for to loue and to haue mercy on his enemys, and nout for to slen hem'.[10]

Parliament roundly ignored these demands. Such ideas would have fundamentally changed the order of medieval English society. It is little wonder that voices were raised against the Lollards complaining that 'holy writ in Englische wole make cristen men at debate' and lead them 'to rebelle ageyns her sovereyns'.[11] These worries were not without foundation. The ideas of the Lollard movement played their part in the Peasants' Revolt of 1381. Other Lollard uprisings took place well into the first half of the next century.

The response of the English authorities to these threats was stern. In 1401, Parliament passed an act making seditious heresy a crime. Lollard texts were to be collected up and burned. Anyone who failed to surrender such texts and renounce their heretical views would also be condemned to the stake. The Church quickly followed suit. In 1409, the Archbishop of Canterbury, Thomas Arundel, established the Constitutions of Oxford, which forbade anyone from making new literal translations of the Bible without special permission from a bishop. The possession of these texts and their public readings were made illegal, on pain of excommunication.[12]

These fierce laws meant that for the rest of the 1400s, no one attempted to make any further English translations of the Bible. As many as 250 of Wycliffe's manuscripts continued to circulate underground, but sheer practicality was against them making any profound impact. Aside from the danger of making a copy, the sheer expense and difficulty of copying the texts by hand, combined with the low literacy of the population, meant that the audience of the Lollard translations of the Bible remained strictly limited.

Christ Wishes His Mysteries to Be Published

The times, however, did not remain unchanged. By the beginning of the 1500s, new ideas were turning the intellectual climate of Europe. The recovery of Classical texts and the knowledge of ancient Greek prompted a widespread reassessment of how the faithful should approach the Bible. 'Honourest thou the bones of Paul hid in a shrine, and honourest thou not the mind of Paul hid in his writings?' asked the great scholar Desiderius Erasmus in his hugely popular 1501 book the *Enchiridion*, a short manual discussing how Christians should face the temptations of the world and the devil.[13]

The unvarnished text of scripture in itself began to take centre stage. The old medieval approach that the Bible could only be interpreted under guidance of approved Church precedent, using the complex system of the

Four Senses,* came under challenge.[14] 'False expositions . . .', grumbled Tyndale, '. . . and vain opinions, pertaining as much unto the healing of a man's heel, as health of his soul . . .'.[15] Instead, argued Erasmus, 'Christ wishes his mysteries to be published as widely as possible. I would wish even all women to read the gospel and the epistles of St Paul, and wish they were translated into all languages of all Christian people . . .'. Anticipating Tyndale's desire for the ploughboy to be better versed in scripture than the priest, Erasmus also wished 'that the husbandman may sing parts of [the gospel] at his plough, that the weaver may warble them at his shuttle, that the traveller may with their narratives beguile the weariness of the way'.[16]

In 1516, Erasmus published a new and improved text of the Greek New Testament. Relying on this, in 1522 Martin Luther made a translation of the New Testament into German. Like Erasmus, he wanted the text to be accessible to all people without the mediation of the Church. Also like Erasmus, he believed that the Holy Spirit would aid them in the interpretation of the scripture. The traditional machinery of the Four Senses, laboriously expounded in the universities, could now be discarded. If the Holy Spirit could reach into the heart and mind of every believer, so could a copy of the physical text now easily make it into their hands. Unlike in Wycliffe's times a century and a half earlier, the new technology of the printing press eliminated the practical difficulties of copying and circulating the text. No longer were books the expensive and laboriously produced preserve of the highest elites.[17]

England was not immune to these changes. Tyndale encountered the ideas of Erasmus and the new learning during his time at Oxford, where he began his university education in 1505. In 1523, after many years of study, Tyndale petitioned the Bishop of London, Cuthbert Tunstall, for permission to embark on an English translation of the scriptures – the

* The Four Senses method held that there were four ways in which each event or idea in scripture was to be interpreted. These were the literal, the allegorical, the moral and the anagogical.

prohibition of the previous century was still fully in force. When this request was diplomatically declined, Tyndale headed for the continent, where he made translations of the New Testament in full and parts of the Old Testament, as well as writing a number of religious tracts. These he had printed primarily in Antwerp and smuggled over to England in their thousands. Full copies or flat printed sheets waiting to be bound were hidden in barrels or casks marked as wine or oil, concealed in sacks of grain, flour or hides, or wooden chests with false sides and secret compartments.

Tyndale's New Testaments began to arrive in England around March 1526, where they were met with fury by the senior clergy. 'Pestiferous and pernicious poison', fulminated Bishop Tunstall, who rounded up the London booksellers to watch impounded copies being thrown on a ceremonial bonfire outside St Paul's. 'He burnt the New Testament', remarked Tyndale dryly in a 1530 tract, 'calling it *Doctrinam peregrinam*, "strange learning"'.[18]

Tyndale himself met his end in the flames in Antwerp in 1536. Under diplomatic pressure from England, he was hunted down, interrogated and executed for heresy by the local authorities. His last words were reputedly 'Lord, open the King of England's eyes'.[19] In this prayer, he was not to be disappointed. Just two years later, in 1538, Henry VIII's minister Thomas Cromwell ordered every parish in the country to buy English translations of the Bible and set them up in 'some convenient place' to be available for all parishioners. Henry VIII himself, although he strongly disliked Lutheran ideas, had no option but to appoint reform-minded clergy and ministers over the course of the 1530s; these were the only people who would support him in his desire to break with Rome and thus secure his divorce from Catherine of Aragon and marriage to Anne Boleyn. The relaxation of these scruples was the price he had to pay in the hope of securing a male heir.

In Every Alehouse and Tavern

After Cromwell's order of 1538, there was to be no return. From the publication of Tyndale's New Testament to the beginning of the English Civil War in the following century, around two million English Bibles or parts of Bibles were printed. The population of England during this period was around six million. There was also a proliferation of translations: the Matthew Bible, the Coverdale Bible, the Great Bible, the Bishops' Bible, the Geneva Bible, the Douay-Rheims Bible, the King James Version. No other book came close to the prominence or ubiquity of the English Bible. It could be read anywhere and heard anywhere. Even if one could not read or acquire a copy, the Church set a cycle for the New Testament to be read aloud three times throughout the year at its services, the Old Testament once, and the Book of Psalms once every month.[20]

The new English liturgy also was replete with quotations from scripture. The Book of Common Prayer, created by Archbishop Thomas Cranmer and first published in 1549, was the sole prayer book authorised for use in church, aside from brief interruptions during the time of the Catholic Queen Mary (r.1553–8) and the republican Commonwealth period (1649–60). It remained so until the twentieth century. Like the Bible, it was also vastly popular, being found not just in churches, but also in private houses for family use, with around 200,000 copies being printed in the time of Elizabeth I alone.* The new simplified daily pattern of English services created by Cranmer – matins (or morning prayer) and evensong (or evening prayer) boiled down from the more complex seven daily Latin services of the pre-Reformation Sarum Rite – not to mention the communion service and the 'occasional offices' of baptism, holy matrimony and the burial of the dead, fixed certain lines of scripture or lines closely derived from scripture in the collective English memory through

* It must be acknowledged that the Book of Common Prayer was not immediately welcomed with open arms by everyone. The imposition of the new English prayer book provoked an armed uprising in Devon and Cornwall in 1549, with the people demanding that 'we will have the mass in latten, as was before.'[21]

constant repetition. 'I know that my redeemer liveth . . . The Lord gave, and the Lord hath taken away', read the sentences at the beginning of the burial of the dead, quoting from the Book of Job, or 'ashes to ashes, dust to dust' referring to verses of Genesis and Ecclesiastes.

Soon after official sanction was given for the publication of the Bible in English, Henry VIII began to suffer remorse. In 1541, he confirmed Cromwell's order, commanding the 'setting up' of 'the Bible of the largest and greatest volume, to be had in every church'. Yet, at the same time, he considered issuing a proclamation which bid those who had 'any doubt . . . touching the sense and meaning' of the scriptures to avoid trusting too much to their 'own mind, fantasies and opinions', nor 'open reasoning in your open Taverns or Alehouses'. Instead, they should rather turn to 'such learned men as be or shall be authorised to preach' and who had 'discreet quietness and sober moderation'.[22]

In his last speech to Parliament in 1545, it seemed that his creeping fears had been realised. 'I am very sorry to know and hear', he complained, 'how unreverently that most precious jewel, the word of God, is disputed, rhymed, sung, and jangled in every alehouse and tavern, contrary to the true meaning and doctrine of the same . . .'. His fears went beyond the simple profanation of scripture. 'Although you are permitted to read holy scripture and to have the word of God in your mother tongue', he told Parliament, 'you must understand that it is licensed you so to do, only to inform your own conscience and to instruct your children and family, and not to dispute and make scripture a railing and a taunting stock against priests and preachers, as many light persons do.'[23] In other words, his profounder worries were grounded in the knowledge that allowing the common people access to scripture gave them an unprecedented and uncontrollable way to challenge traditional bearers of authority.

This negative reaction was not confined to the king. 'What thinges haue we gotten by the scriptures beyng in englysh these yeares past?' asked one John Standish, a canon of St Paul's. The English Bible had turned the traditional order of things upside down: 'seruauntes stubbourne, frowarde and disobedieent to theyr masters and mastres, fleshly liberty, contempt of all godly order, losse of deuotion and godlynes, prayer and fastyng set at nought, and vnbrydled boldnesse to all mischefe'. This was all because the scripture, beyond the control of the Church authorities, gave people the capacity and confidence to question the received order of things, and to hold their own independent opinions: 'O howe manye scrupules and doubtes haue spronge in manye mens heades (whiche neither they nor their fathers euer imagined before) through the scripture in Englishe? How many alterations, scismes, and deuisions amonge the simple haue rysen, yea betwene man and wyfe, maister and seruant?'[24]

But from a different and more positive perspective, this unbridled boldness, these alterations, schisms and divisions, caused by the new Bible in English, were the beginning of a political and intellectual emancipation. In the words of a modern historian of the English Bible, David Daniell, the age – particularly after the accession of Elizabeth and into the Jacobean era – was one of 'free discussion' replete with a 'sense of liberty, the release of being able to say things without a charge of heresy'. There were censors, but their attention was for the most part confined to the danger of sedition rather than heresy. This being so, the time saw 'a new inventiveness, a release of imagination into . . . English words' where 'the liberated mind and spirit ventured largely'. It was a new environment in which new ideas about politics, authority and society could be debated on a wide scale as never before.[25]

The Bible itself became a source and ground for political ideas and debate over the coming centuries. An introduction to one edition of the Geneva translation declared that scripture was a guide 'to commonwealths and governments . . . magistrates (good and evil), peace and war'. Different translations were coloured by different viewpoints about the right sources of authority. The Geneva Bible, translated by Protestant scholars in exile during the reign of Henry's Catholic daughter, Queen Mary, inclined to words that undermined the old structures of power: not only 'congregation' instead of 'church' but also 'senior' or 'elder' instead of 'priest', 'washing' for 'baptism', and 'love' instead of 'charity'. It also used the word 'tyrant' around 400 times; this was absent from the

King James Version.[26] The Geneva Bible was designed to be a book for home use, smaller in size (even coming in an abridged pocket version for Parliamentarian soldiers during the Civil War) and with copious illustrations and maps to illuminate the topography and culture of the Holy Land. It was also covered in marginal notes, to aid interpretation of difficult matters – 'some . . . very partiall, vntrue, seditious, and sauouring too much of daungerous and trayterous conceit' later complained King James I.[27] A number could indeed be read as giving succour to dissent against kings. 'Thus', read one note on a wicked deed of Jezebel in the First Book of Kings, 'ye worldlings contrary to Gods commandment . . . obey the wicked commandments of princes, then the just lawes of God.'[28]

With the Bible in common circulation, it became the basis for a centuries-long debate about who could rightfully wield authority, and how the people should relate to it. Tyndale himself, despite his defiance of English law by translating the scriptures, was a strong supporter of obedience to the civil powers. He laid out his political views in a 1528 book, *The Obedience of a Christian Man*. Scripture, he argued, showed that hierarchy was a fundamental part of the universal order. The Fifth Commandment, to 'honour thy father and mother', ordained the submission of children to their parents. The consequences of the Fall in the Book of Genesis, along with other statements from St Paul's letters, likewise required the submission of wives to their husbands. From St Paul also came the call for servants to obey their masters, along with the broader idea in the Letter to the Romans that as all civil government is ordained by God, no one should resist their kings or princes, even if they should behave as tyrants.[29]

It is perhaps no surprise that Henry VIII is supposed to have enjoyed Tyndale's tract: a book 'for me and all kings to read' he is reputed to have said.[30] In 1534, *The King's Book* was published in Henry's name, which developed these ideas even further. In the Fifth Commandment alone, it argued, was all order and hierarchy crystallised: '. . . by these words father and mother, is understood not only the father and mother . . . but also princes and all other governors, rulers and pastors . . .'.[31] Already, the foundations were being laid for ideas of the divine right of kings.

But this was not the only message of scripture on the subject. Authority was not only about the enjoyment of obedience and rights. 'As Christ loved the congregation, and gave himself for it', wrote Tyndale, so Christian kings should also 'give themselves altogether' to the welfare 'of their realms after the ensample of Christ'. The king was but a 'servant, to execute the law of God, and not to rule after his own imagination'. Every office has a duty. Masters had to be kind to their servants, husbands love their wives, landlords not oppress their tenants. Kings had duties, according to scripture, but this left the question of what should be done if they failed to perform them. What if they ruled wickedly after their 'own imagination'? In this event, argued Tyndale, one might not comply. If a king commanded evil, the people could legitimately refuse to obey 'and say "We are otherwise commanded of God"'. Such refusals, however, could only be passive. The authority of kings 'may not be resisted: do they never so evil'.[32]

The next generation of thinkers, particularly English Protestants who were exiled under the Catholic Queen Mary, took this doctrine much further. John Ponet, Bishop of Winchester, who fled to Frankfurt when Mary came to the throne, asked what the people should do when an unjust ruler despoiled them of their goods and money, and used it not for the common good but on 'whores, whoremongers, dice games, cards, banklet-ting, unjust wars, and such evils and mischiefs . . .'. In such cases, he recalls that 'The history of kings in the Old Testament is full' of the 'deposing of kings, and killing of tyrants', which 'most certainly confirm it to be most true, just and constant to God's judgment'. If a king ruled unjustly and failed to act for the good of his people, he betrayed his office and should be held accountable like any private citizen: 'the magistrate's doings [should] be called into account and reckoning, and their vices corrected and pun-ished by the body of the whole congregation or commonwealth'.

Ponet's fellow exile, Christopher Goodman, who had been Lady Margaret Professor of Divinity at Oxford, was even clearer on the peo-ple's duty to make active resistance against wicked rulers. Drawing on Old Testament examples, he argued that 'when the Magistrates and other officers cease to do their duty' then they forfeit their positions. The people 'are as it were, without officers'. In these circumstances 'God giveth the sword into the peoples hand', and the people themselves 'become immediately their head'.[33]

Masterless Men

Now that scripture had placed 'the sword into the peoples hand', their scope for action was wider than simply deposing wicked kings. It gave them the capacity to set themselves up as independent authorities, and determine, based on their own reading of the Bible regardless of any Church teaching, how best they were to live. Their readings of particular texts – for example, the story in the First Book of Samuel which relates that God did not wish to appoint a king, and only consented to put Saul on the throne because of the foolish demands of the people, or the requirement in Acts 2 for the early Christian community to eschew private property and have all things in common – made the scriptures an engine for dissent.

In October 1580, the Bishop of Ely, Richard Cox, complained about a number of unusual tomes that had been discovered at the house of John Bourne, a glover from Wisbech. They had been concealed in different places around his house, 'some behynde a Chymney in his kitchen, some in his dye house under hassockes, other in a wooll chamber, between a bawke and a wall'. The books, written by a German mystic called Hendrik Nicholis, were expositions of scripture written in a flowery and often elusive style, suggesting their direct illumination from God Himself. Indeed, the texts spoke of a quest for unity with God where the believer would be 'Godded with God'. Later accounts of this strand of belief showed it to be radically different to conventional Christian doctrine. 'They doe hold that all things are Common . . . alltogether denyinge all prayers & the Resurrection of the body, or any heauen or hell . . .'. The current world was all: '. . . what is in this life & what the Scripture doth speake of is begun & ended in their bodies here as they doe liue:

As heauen is when they doe laugh & are merry & hell when they are in sorrowe & paine . . . .'[34]

The followers of these ideas, called the Family of Love, although described by Bishop Cox as a 'damnable sort of heretiques', were often prosperous and educated people. Some were even members of the Yeomen of the Guard, close to Queen Elizabeth I herself, and allowed to retain their positions with only a token rebuke for their unorthodox faith. This may have been because the members of this movement were content to work out their beliefs in private and to adhere to outward proprieties and social norms.

However, not everyone behaved like the adherents of the Family of Love. Over the course of the sixteenth century, and even more into the seventeenth century, new sects and divisions arose in English Christianity.

One indistinct group, the Ranters, which may have had its origins in the Family of Love, held that God was Reason and present in all things: 'man and beast, fish and fowl, and every green thing, from the highest cedar to the ivy on the wall . . . this dog, this tobacco pipe, he is me and I am him . . .'. As Christ was present in all, and all things were pure, they saw themselves as being liberated from conventional moral restraints. Ranters frequently met at taverns, where according to one account 'they took tobacco and drank ale' in their meetings, and 'were grown light and loose'. 'My spirit dwells with God', said the Ranter prophet Abiezer Coppe, 'sups with him, in him, feeds on him, with him, in him. My humanity shall dwell with, sup with, eat with humanity; and why not', he said, echoing Christ in the gospels, 'with publicans and harlots?'[35]

Equality was frequently the most striking feature of many of the new Christian sects and groups. The Quakers refused to observe social convention and received hierarchies. They refused to raise their hats to those above them in the social pyramid, and addressed them in familiar rather than respectful language. They had no qualms about interrupting clergy during services and challenging them to debate. Women, as well as men, were equally entitled to speak during their informal services.[36]

The Diggers were inspired by a clothing apprentice turned cow herder, Gerrard Winstanley, who had prophetic revelations and was also motivated by the biblical vision of the early followers of Christ holding all things in common, as described in chapter 4 of the Acts of the Apostles. 'All the earth should be made a common treasury of livelihood to whole mankind, without respect of persons', he preached, and in order to bring this about in 1649 he set up an agricultural commune on waste land on St George's Hill in Surrey, where 'every one shall put their hands to till the earth, and bring up cattle, and the blessing of the earth shall be common to all'. They were soon harried off the land by local property owners and scattered.

The Diggers appeared to be an offshoot of a larger amorphous group, the Levellers, who were also primarily concerned with ideas of equality that they found in scripture. One of them, William Walwyn, wrote that the essence of Christianity was in 'universal love to all mankind without respect of persons, opinions, societies' and even 'churches or forms of worship'. However, the Levellers were more interested in the constitutional and legal implications of these ideas. The equality of all people, they argued, meant that they could be subject to no authority except by consent. During the Civil War, they called for more fully representative government with wide suffrage, biennial elections and parliamentary constituencies that properly reflected the population.[37]

Shall I Disown Them Because They Will Not Put Off Their Hats?

After the beginning of the seventeenth century, some of these Christian dissenters began to call for an even more striking change in English society. In 1612, the English Baptist Thomas Helwys wrote that the king's power extended 'to all the goods and bodies of their servants', but not to their spirits. Therefore, he said, all religions, provided that they were peaceable, should be tolerated: 'Let them be heretikes, Turcks, Jewes, or whatsoever it appertynes not to the earthly power to punish them in the least measure.'[38] Shortly afterwards, a member of his congregation, Leonard Busher, repeated his call. In a 1614 tract entitled *Religious Peace; or, a Plea for Liberty of Conscience*, he called for the king and Parliament 'to permit all sorts of Christians; yea, Jews, Turks, and pagans, so long as they are peaceable, and no malefactors'. He, along with some other contemporary writers, argued that 'persecution for religion is to force the conscience; and to force and constrain men and women's consciences over a religion against their wills, is to tyrannize over the soul, as well as over the body'.[39]

These tracts were initially ill-received. When a slightly later writer, Roger Williams, published a more substantial tract reprising these ideas in 1644, Parliament ordered it to be burned. Yet, the simple fact of the translation of the Bible made these calls for toleration – at least for Christians – ever more difficult to ignore. By the middle of the seventeenth century, sects such as the Ranters, Levellers, Quakers, Diggers, Anabaptists, Antinomians and other indistinct and evanescent groups made up perhaps just a few per cent of the English population. They had a host of divergent views on the conduct of life, the place of laws, social order, morality, the role of the Church. Yet, these ideas were difficult to challenge because many of them were primarily derived from a reading of the Bible. In the words of John Milton, 'the whole Protestant church allows no supreme judge to rule in matters of religion, but the Scriptures themselves, which necessarily infers liberty of conscience'.[40]

With the Civil War, discussions of politics began to feature the notion that some form of tolerance of dissent and different political and religious opinions was going to become a necessity for orderly government. Such toleration certainly owed something to pragmatism. With an increasingly fractured set of approaches to Christianity, and the decline of other sources of religious authority aside from scripture – the English episcopacy, for example, had been abolished in 1646 – it was increasingly difficult to enforce any uniformity of belief.

Yet, arguments for liberty of conscience and religious toleration also came from the text of scripture itself. It was a generally received tenet of Protestant doctrine that all Christian believers formed a priesthood in their own right. Chapter 2 of the First Epistle of Peter, a text often quoted by Protestant thinkers in this context, described all believers as 'a spiritual house, an holy Priesthood', who were made 'to offer up spiritual sacrifices acceptable to God by Jesus Christ'. This being so, it followed that those in authority should be wary of repressing anyone who claimed to be speaking in God's name; anyone professing Christianity and offering a view of religious matters based on scripture might be speaking a holy truth, inspired by God. Some thinkers recalled Christ's refusal in Luke's Gospel to call fire down on a Samaritan village, thus implying a command of love for those of a different belief. The parable of the wheat and the tares in Matthew's Gospel gave a message that the godly and ungodly should be allowed to develop in peace as they pleased in this life; judgement would belong to God in the next world, not to the secular authorities of this world. Throughout the New Testament, the lesson came that Christians should be gentle, and share their doctrines with meekness rather than main force.[41]

Such were the thoughts of Milton and also, to an extent, of Oliver Cromwell, who himself became an advocate for liberty of conscience during and after the Civil War. He did not, to be sure, tolerate Catholicism or Anglican episcopalian approaches to Christianity on the grounds that these might repress other Christians from expressing the truths they found in scripture under the inspiration of the Holy Spirit. He also condemned the Ranters for their immorality and their subversive disdain for the law. Yet, seeing godliness as he did in all 'men that believe the remission of sins through the blood of Christ' rather than in any particular sect or form of worship, he was content to allow liberty of conscience and toleration for any Protestant group provided they accepted the doctrine of the Trinity. This left the way open for Presbyterians, Baptists, other independents and, despite some friction with the Commonwealth government, also Quakers. Cromwell himself employed Quakers in his household and when challenged on this replied 'Shall I disown them because they will not put off their hats?'[42]

John Locke, often hailed as the first 'secular philosopher', is usually credited as being the intellectual architect of the liberal order of modern politics. It was partly thanks to the influence of his *Letter Concerning Toleration*, written in 1685 and published four years later, that the 1689 Toleration Act was passed, allowing freedom of worship to Protestant dissenters who at least accepted the Trinity, provided that they pledged allegiance to the Crown. Locke's ideas became pervasive over the course of the eighteenth century in both Britain and America, and religious tolerance and liberty of conscience – provided that one accepted the authority of the civil magistrate in non-religious matters – were entrenched on either side of the Atlantic. Other restrictions on non-Anglicans (including Catholics and other Christians who did not accept the doctrine of the Trinity) – for example, their right to attend universities and hold public office – were done away with by the early part of the nineteenth century. Yet, many of the ideas expounded by Locke on political order – the general equality of mankind, the capacity of governments to be removed by society should they fail in their duties to those societies, the need for civil authorities to restrain themselves from involvement in matters of conscience or religious worship unless they should threaten domestic order – had all been articulated decades beforehand in the debates generated by the translation of the Bible into English. '[The] question of liberty of conscience . . . has for some years been so much bandied amongst us', Locke commented at the beginning of his earlier 1667 *Essay Concerning Toleration*. These concepts, so familiar a part of modern British, and indeed American, political principles, found their origins, and underpinning, in the English version of scripture.[43]

These Words Walk Very Goodly by the Hearer's Ear

The English translation of the Bible did not just give our two seventeenth-century window-breaking Somerset schoolboys a taste for independent-mindedness. It also gave them the language in which to express their freedom of thought.

Their retort to the complaint that their ball game had broken the church window certainly referred to the controversial difference between the idea of a church and a congregation. Yet, that was not the whole of its biblical grounding. The statement that 'The church is where the *congregation* is assembled though it be at the beacon on the top of the hill of Quantock' goes further. It seems to allude to the words of Christ Himself in the Sermon on the Mount that the congregation of Christians were 'the light of the world' and 'A city that is set on an hill' which 'cannot be hid'.

If a biblical turn of phrase was the first thing that came to mind for these two youths, it should be no surprise. Sir Thomas More, railing against Tyndale's choice of words in his translations, jibed that 'all England list now to go to school with Tyndale to learn English'.[44] Before too long, this was the case. Although a host of translations were made over the course of the sixteenth and seventeenth centuries, many of them closely followed Tyndale's original. Around 80 per cent of the King James Version, for example, follows Tyndale's initial translation. Tyndale set the lasting standard for not just English biblical translation, but the way that the English language itself was to be spoken and written at a vital moment in its development.

Just after 1500, the poet John Skelton, who was also tutor to King Henry VIII in his youth, wrote with some disdain about the quality of the English language. 'Our naturall tong is rude', he said, such that even if new words were introduced it would be hard to rescue or revive it. It was 'rusty', 'cankered', full of awkward words. If he wished to write 'ornatly' he would not be able to find the right 'Termes to serve [his] mynde'.[45]

Skelton's comments reveal a sense of English linguistic and cultural inferiority. At this time, Latin was still the country's pre-eminent language in terms of learning, culture and official communication. French, Spanish and especially Italian were the modern European languages which possessed the most cultural cachet. English, at that moment, lacked any substantial corpus or tradition of literature,* and thus any obvious indigenous models for new authors in English to model their style or diction on.

Thus, when Tyndale was working, he had, as he wrote in the preface to his translation of the New Testament, 'no man to counterfeit'. He had to generate a new style of English that was going to be answerable to the challenge of translating the scripture, the word of God.[46] Tyndale was deeply learned in the Renaissance traditions of formal Latin and Greek rhetoric, and there would have been a temptation for him in translating the Bible to follow the most esteemed Classical prose authors, such as Cicero or Demosthenes, with long and complex sentences full of subordinate clauses, and grandiloquent vocabulary also derived from Latin and Greek.[47] But this is not what he did. With his intention that the scriptures could be understood as much by the ploughboy as by the learned cleric, he took as his inspiration the everyday rustic speech of his native Gloucestershire. He avoided obscure Latinate vocabulary and long sentences and paragraphs which those imitating the Roman author Cicero liked to use. Instead, his preference was for shorter, direct phrases, using simpler, more common words of Old English origin. His idiom has a rugged directness, immediate and dignified, made all the more memorable and striking through his mastery of rhythm and cadence. The verses in chapter 4 of Luke's Gospel describing Christ's teaching are not just a sample of Tyndale's style, but might almost stand as a monument to it: 'And all bare him witness and wondered at the gracious words which proceeded out of his mouth and said: Is not this Joseph's son? . . . And they were astonished at his doctrine: for his preaching was with power.' As Sir Thomas More grudgingly conceded, Tyndale's 'words walk very goodly by the hearer's ear'.[48]

Tyndale had a genius for bringing out of the scripture an endless stream of memorable, pithy sayings. The influence of his Gloucestershire

* Even Chaucer could not easily fulfil a literary canonical role in Skelton's time. Although his *Canterbury Tales* were first printed by Caxton in 1478, his complete works were not printed before 1532 and only circulated in manuscript.

upbringing, with his exposure to the language of the region's significant clothmaking industry and other crafts, played its part in this. All trades passed on their practical wisdom by near-proverbial statements in heightened language, often rhythmical and sometimes with rhyme: 'Of a ragged colt comes a good horse', 'measure twice and cut once', 'early a master, long a knave'.[49] Tyndale's translations echo this proverbial speech: 'No man can serve two masters', 'Care not then for the morrow but let the morrow care for itself', 'Judge not that ye be not judged'.

But in addition to this, Tyndale also had a remarkable talent for rendering Hebrew idioms into English. He believed that 'The properties of the Hebrew tongue agree a thousand times more with the English than with the Latin', and by keeping close to them in his English translation, he created a new strain of biblical diction which became an intrinsic part of the English language. For example, the earlier Wycliffe version, translated from the Latin version of Genesis, wrote 'And God said, Be made light; and made is light.' Tyndale, translating directly from the Hebrew original and keeping closely to it, wrote 'let there be light, and there was light'. Similarly, he often preserved a Hebrew turn of phrase called the 'construct', where Hebrew would incline, for example, to say 'a woman of beauty' rather than 'a beautiful woman'. This gave rise to a whole host of English phrases: 'a mighty man of valour', 'the fowls of the air', 'the fishes of the sea'. Tyndale preserved the breathless but vivid Hebrew tendency to narrate stories by saying 'and . . . and' with new sentences rather than making a host of prolix sub-clauses: 'And the Lord God called Adam and said unto him where art thou. And he answered . . .'. He also preserved the tendency to repetition: 'And will love thee, bless thee and multiply thee . . .'; and inverted word order: 'Upon thy belly shalt thou go: and earth shalt thou eat', God tells the serpent, and Adam and Eve, 'earth thou art, and unto earth shalt thou return'.[50]

Under these influences, Tyndale, and the later sixteenth- and early-seventeenth-century translators who followed his manner towards the translation of the King James Version, created a diction which became a standard for good English: direct, unadorned, rugged, but still elegant and supple; understated, but dignified. This new English was a far cry from the rusty, cankered tongue of Skelton. After Tyndale, English certainly had the 'Termes' to serve any mind. From Tyndale's work and influence also came hundreds of biblical sayings and proverbs which have entered into the sinews of the English language: 'how are the mighty fallen', 'to pour out one's heart', 'to go the extra mile', 'the apple of one's eye', 'to lick the dust', 'no peace for the wicked', a 'wolf in sheep's clothing', 'the parting of the ways', 'fight the good fight', 'a law unto himself', 'of making books there is no end'.[51]

Likewise, the Book of Common Prayer, inspired by such principles, added its own stock of highly memorable lines inspired by scripture to the standard canon of English quotations. Matrimony was undertaken 'for better for worse, for richer for poorer, in sickness and in health ... till death us do part'. The service demanded of those who knew of 'any just cause why [the couple] may not lawfully be joined together, let him now speak, or else hereafter for ever hold his peace', and implored 'Those whom God hath joined together let no man put asunder'. When, in 1938, the Prime Minister Neville Chamberlain thought that his agreement made with Hitler in Munich would stave off another European war, he declared on the steps of Downing Street that it would bring 'peace for our time' – quoting the response used daily at morning prayer and evensong: 'Give peace in our time, O Lord ... Because there is none other that fighteth for us, but only thou O God.'

In the century after Skelton complained about the scantiness of the English tongue, there was a profound change of mood. Around the 1620s, the poet George Herbert wrote in 'The Sonne':

> Let forrain nations of their language boast,
> What fine varietie each tongue affords:
> I like our language, as our men and coast;
> Who cannot dresse it well, want wit, not words.

The work of Tyndale and successive translators of that time had turned English into a language fit for the Bible and fine writing. This, and the new availability of the scriptures, whose close detail was now common knowledge amongst all English-speaking people, was the foundation for a newly confident body and tradition of modern English literature. The invitation implicit in the translation of the Bible – to share the text, to ponder its messages and ideas – as well as the variety of material it made available – stirring tales of heroism and deceit, songs, poems, stories and parables with meditations on every turn of the human condition, histories and explorations of morality and politics, society, kingship and battle, visions of the divine, the Creation, the path to salvation, the world to come – prompted an outpouring of literary creativity, and opened pathways that English writers would explore for generations to come.

To the sermons, plays, poems, paraphrases of psalms, songs, meditations, tracts, satires, stories and ultimately novels from that time to the present day which owe their origins to the inspiration of the Bible, one can only make a gesture here, so vast are they in number and variety (though there will be a longer introduction to the great devotional and mystical poetry of the age in Chapter 10).[52] Here, there is room to speak briefly of just a few of the most well-known and influential authors who wrote in the sixteenth and seventeenth centuries in the immediate aftermath of the Bible's translation into English. For them, the Bible is a perpetual theme, and an endless source of new ideas. Shakespeare alludes to it incessantly, whether in the sublimest moments of tragedy: 'Most sacrilegious murder hath broke ope The Lord's anointed temple and stole hence The life o'th'building'; or through the mouths of clowns: 'You may tell every finger I have with my ribs', says the hungry clown Lancelet in *The Merchant of Venice*, in a scene which itself parodies the blessing given by Jacob to his sons at the end of Genesis.[53]

Not only does the Bible provide Shakespeare with allusions, but the deepest themes of his work.[54] The lament of Job underpins the 'to be or not to be' soliloquy of Hamlet and the wider progress of his character, balancing the desire for death after adversity with the need to stand his ground, and to tell and justify his story. Job likewise inspires the whole of *King Lear* in its meditation on the need for self-abnegation and self-emptying,* as does the Epistle of St Paul to the Philippians (2.6–9), where he speaks of how Christ,

> being in the form of God ... made himself of no reputation, and took upon him the form of a servant, and was made in the likeness of men: And being found in fashion as a man, he humbled himself, and became obedient unto death, even the death of the cross. Wherefore God also hath highly exalted him, and given him a name which is above every name.

As Lear, who has been cast out into the storm on the heath and brought face to face with his kingdom's paupers, exclaims:

> Poor naked wretches, wheresoe'er you are,
> That bide the pelting of this pitiless storm,
> How shall your houseless heads and unfed sides,
> Your looped and windowed raggedness, defend you
> From seasons such as these? Oh, I have ta'en
> Too little care of this! Take physic, pomp.
> Expose thyself to feel what wretches feel,
> That thou mayst shake the superflux to them
> And show the heavens more just.[55]

The stories of scripture offered authors the scope for a profound and radical exploration of the human condition. The tale of the Creation in Genesis provided John Milton the outline for *Paradise Lost,* where he expands the biblical narrative to offer a close examination of the psychology of the fallen state.[56] Satan complains of the dissociation and alienation within his spirit, which he can only ease by harming others:

> ... the more I see
> Pleasures about me, so much more I feel

* Called 'kenosis' by theologians, from the Greek word for 'emptying'.

> Torment within me, as from the hateful siege
> Of contraries; all good to me becomes
> Bane, and in Heav'n much worse would be my state . . .
> For only in destroying I find ease
> To my relentless thoughts . . .[57]

Rather than in the story of the Creation, Milton's contemporary John Bunyan found inspiration for understanding the human condition in another biblical notion: pilgrimage, and the story of a journey.[58] In his early writings, he likened the life of the Church to the movement of the Israelites from Egypt across the Red Sea to the Promised Land in Canaan, or their return from exile in Babylon to Jerusalem. Such an idea was echoed in the New Testament, where the Epistle to the Hebrews said the generation of patriarchs – Cain, Abel, Noah, Enoch, Abraham, Sarah – had seen God's promises 'afar off' and were thus 'strangers and pilgrims on the earth' who 'desire a better country, that is, an heavenly' (11.13, 16).

Bunyan's *Pilgrim's Progress*, which first appeared in 1678, saw the flowering of this idea in his work. 'This book will make a traveller of thee', he wrote in the preface, 'with sound and honest gospel strains.' Bunyan was from a poor family, and his only education was a brief spell at a village school. Unlike Milton, he had no access to Latin, Greek and Classical literature. Yet, he made up for this with his overwhelming knowledge of scripture, gained through private study. At the time he came to faith 'I was then never out of the Bible', he said, 'either by reading or meditation'. From the King James Bible, the version Bunyan knew most intimately, came not only the idea of the perilous journey for the *Pilgrim's Progress* but also its language. Bunyan wove scriptural quotations into the text at every turn: in the first paragraph, we see the hero, Christian, 'clothed in rags [and] a great burden upon his back', snippets plucked from Isaiah and the Psalms, and his first words are the anguished cry 'What shall I do?', a shortened version of the fearful question of St Paul's jailer in the Book of Acts: 'What shall I do to be saved?' Even when he is not directly quoting, the vocabulary, cadences and vigorous, homely style of the King James Version are permanently present. At the River of Death, for example, 'They then addressed themselves to the water: and entering, Christian began to sink, and crying out to his good friend Hopeful, he said "I sink in deep waters, the billows go over my head, all his waters go over me".' All of Christian's exclamations here are a mixture of quotation, imitation and allusion to the Book of Psalms. In the words of one historian, Bunyan 'had lived in the Bible til its words became his own'.[59]

The literary form of *Pilgrim's Progress* was also drawn from biblical example. Its use of allegory to chart the journey of a soul through the difficulties and snares of earthly life to a place of salvation – passing from the starting point of the City of Destruction via such spots as the Slough of Despond, the Valley of the Shadow of Death, Doubting Castle, By-Path Meadow, the Enchanted Ground and the famous Vanity Fair, encountering such characters as Hopeful, Faithful, Lord Hate-Good, Mr Worldly-Wiseman, Mr Honest, Mr Valiant-for-Truth, Mr Stand-Fast, Mr Feeble-Mind and Mr Despondency – Bunyan owes to the lead of scripture. 'I find', he writes in the preface, 'that holy Writ in many places, / Hath semblance with this method, where the cases / Doth call for one thing to set forth another.' Although Bunyan may have also read earlier examples of allegory in surviving medieval popular knightly romances, it was Christ's model of putting 'truth within a fable' by speaking in parables that led Bunyan to adopt this method in his work.

As much as this form may seem rigid and gauche to modern tastes, Bunyan stressed that his writing would help his readers 'find [themselves] again' in a way that was 'pleasant, yet far from folly', and cause them 'in a moment' to 'laugh and weep'. Far from being restrictive, the allegorical tale, together with the energy of Bunyan's biblical style, allows – as with *Paradise Lost* – for a profound survey of Christian's psychological travails. As an example, when Christian is struggling by the entrance to hell in the Valley of the Shadow of Death, Bunyan strikingly discerns the greatest threat to his resolve. As he faces a teeming company of fiends leaping out of the flames, it appears that 'Christian was so confounded, that he did not know his own voice ... Just when he was come over against the mouth of the burning pit, one of the wicked ones got behind him, and stept up softly to him, and whisperingly suggested many grievous blasphemies to him, which he verily thought had proceeded from his own mind.' Bunyan's allegory allows him to delve into the deepest fears and to confront the sharpest forms of mental anguish.[60]

Rather than its close grounding in scripture narrowing its interest, *Pilgrim's Progress* has been generally acknowledged as the second most popular work in English behind the Bible itself over the period since its publication in the seventeenth century. It has constantly been in print, and has been translated into 200 languages. A nineteenth-century Dean of Chester, J.S. Howson, said that it offered 'common ground for persons of the highest education, and for those whom we commonly term the working classes.' Its broad appeal lies not just in the vigour of the story or the moral quality of the text. Although Bunyan did not involve himself in ordinary politics, his treatment of the market town of Vanity Fair – where 'all such Merchandize [is] sold, as Houses, Lands, Trades, Places, Honours, Preferments, Titles, Countries, Kingdoms, Lusts, Pleasures, and Delights of all sorts, as Whores, Bauds, Wives, Husbands, Children, Masters, Servants, Lives, Blood, Bodies, Souls, Silver, Gold, Pearls, precious Stones, and what not' – not to mention his insistence on his personal right to preach and interpret scripture despite his lack of social position, clerical orders or elite education, made him and his work a hero for radicals. 'Christ's little ones,' he says, 'are not gentlemen' but 'sins are all lords and great ones.' The Chartist leader Thomas Cooper described *Pilgrim's Progress* as 'the book of books,' and the twentieth-century Marxist historian E.P. Thompson saw it along with Thomas Paine's *Rights of Man* (1791) as 'one of the two foundation texts of the English working-class movement.'[61]

At the same time, Bunyan's book followed trade and the flag. It was a common possession of those who made the British Empire, as well as its overseas subjects. British soldiers in the First World War trenches drew on their reading of *Pilgrim's Progress* to make sense of their experiences. Inscribed in the cupola of the dining room of Haileybury School – a leading place for the training of imperial officials – as a memorial to the war dead, are the lines from the moment where Valiant-for-Faith passes on his sword:

> 'My sword I give to him that shall succeed me in my pilgrimage, and my courage and skill to him that can get it. My marks and scars I carry with me, to be a witness for me that I have fought His battles who now will be my rewarder.' So he passed over, and all the trumpets sounded for him on the other side.

As much as it could be hailed as a radical text, it was also the totem of a muscular Christianity.

Above all, this work, which 'seems to be a complete reflection of scripture', in the words of Matthew Arnold, went on to inspire countless authors and cultural works in its turn. *Pilgrim's Progress* has been accounted a forerunner of the modern novel, particularly with its development of self-conscious and introspective characters. Its narrative of the holy call and the pilgrim's voyage has been adopted throughout the corpus of English literature, from Little Nell's journey out of London to the Midlands in Dickens's *Old Curiosity Shop*, to that of Dorothea Brooke in George Eliot's *Middlemarch*, Charlotte Brontë's *Jane Eyre*, to Mark Twain's *Huckleberry Finn*, and Billy Pilgrim in Kurt Vonnegut's *Slaughterhouse-5*. One other enthusiastic reader of Bunyan was the Victorian author L. Frank Baum, who published *The Wonderful Wizard of Oz* in 1900. Everywhere in Oz are the traces of Bunyan: the Scarecrow is drawn from Mr Feeble-Mind, the Tin Man is Mr Great-Heart, and the Lion, Mr Fearing. They are led by Dorothy, the equivalent of Bunyan's hero Christian, on a pilgrimage in the face of temptations and perils – imprisonment in the Doubting Castle for Christian, and the Castle of the West Witch for Dorothy. The yellow-brick road to the Emerald City of Oz is Bunyan's own path to the Celestial City, itself an image of the New Jerusalem delivered from heaven in the Book of Revelation.[62]

9

Let Everything That Hath Breath

In my daughter's primary school there is a piano. It is not, as with my own primary school in the mid-1980s, in pride of place in the middle of the school hall. Rather, it has been wheeled to the dead end of a corridor and left to gather dust and lost property.

In my own time, the piano was the mainstay of the school assembly. Try as one might, it is impossible to remember a word of the improving messages broadcast to us by the earnest and frustrated head teachers. But the music will always abide. Every day, proceedings began with a teacher striking up one of the old standards – 'When I Needed a Neighbour', 'Kumbaya', 'Lord of the Dance', 'He's got the Whole World in his Hands'. Three hundred voices plunged in after the piano without restraint, sometimes with actions. No one ever needed to be reminded of the words.

The songs were all hymns, of course, though hardly the most ancient. Every day there was an act of worship, and it was carried by the music. The tenor of the hymns became more traditional when I moved to an older prep school with a chapel, which we attended daily at half past eight every morning. Their tunes and lyrics became a part of schoolboy banter. 'To be a pilgrim . . .' became in our hands (for unknown reasons) 'To be an aardvark . . .'. The first line of 'The Day of Resurrection . . .' was irreverently finished off with '. . . we get our Easter eggs . . .'. 'We plough the fields and scatter the good seed on the land . . .' was often ironically sung to anyone unfortunate enough to turn up with a bad haircut.

At senior school in the 1990s, where the foetid dormitories hummed with a constant mix of Eric Clapton and Snoop Dogg, even the moodiest teenagers would be moved to song and lip-quivering displays of sentiment when the first chords of 'Jerusalem' or 'I Vow to Thee, My Country' rolled down from the great organ in chapel. Not even the most cynical could resist joining in lustily with the full-throated climax of 'Dear Lord and Father of Mankind' – '. . . Speak through the earthquake, wind, and fire . . .' – followed by the repeated final line in theatrical sotto voce – '. . . O still small voice of calm!'

Not that the music in chapel was simply hymns. After a couple of years, I found myself conscripted into the chapel choir after excessively hanging around the music school (a place untroubled by Snoop Dogg, with excellent radiators, and, if you knew where to look, free Nescafé). My desire for peace, warmth and coffee, added to the pleasure I already had in singing from primary school, set me on a lifelong journey of musical discovery. Soon, I had encountered everything from the great English choral composers of the sixteenth and seventeenth centuries – Thomas Tallis, William Byrd, Orlando Gibbons, Thomas Weelkes – and Gregorian chant to later stalwarts such as Charles Villiers Stanford, Hubert Parry and Herbert Howells. We toured around cathedrals to sing evensongs, not just agreeably missing afternoons of lessons, but also discovering a spiritual solace in the music and liturgy that stood against the tides of adolescent misery and difficulties beyond. Works on a grand scale were also part of our repertoire: J.S. Bach's *St John Passion*, George Frideric Handel's *Messiah*, and an eccentric contemporary gospel oratorio about David and Goliath, parts of which sounded like something that might be played in a strip club (one slightly unhinged tenor managed to remove his trousers in the back row during the dress rehearsals).

Now that the piano at my daughter's primary school sits closed at the end of its corridor, peeping sadly from under a welter of forgotten cardigans and odd wellington boots, I cannot but wonder at the changed soundscapes of that generation, or its scantier opportunities for music-making and the discovery of a huge tapestry of musical heritage – changed in a way that is arguably unlike anything experienced in England over previous centuries. From time to time a computer, rather than a pianist, is hauled in to accompany collective singing with a tinny MP3, but using repertoire not just secularised, but also, so it seems, carefully sterilised to avoid any snatch or echo of the old traditional tunes. The mention of 'Kumbaya' or 'When I Needed a Neighbour' will draw blank looks from my daughter. Anything older seems now to be treated as a threat. The profound gravitational pull that Christianity had on the manner that music was made in England, and the chances it gave for everyday people to hear or make an extraordinary range of music, seems on the verge of a tragic disappearance.

Ful Murily than Wolde He Synge and Crie . . .

The musical experience of a child six and a half centuries ago is captured, like much of everyday life, in Chaucer's *Canterbury Tales*. The Prioress tells of a seven-year-old boy, son of a widow, who sits 'in the scole at his prymer'. Certainly, there is no piano, but it is a fundamental part of his education to learn how 'to syngen and to rede'. As he works away at his 'litel book', almost certainly getting to know his letters, he overhears the older boys learning a hymn from their antiphoner, the 'Alma Redemptoris Mater', in honour of the Blessed Virgin Mary. Transfixed by the melody, he had soon learned the tune and words of the first verse by heart just by listening; but this was not enough for him. He accosted one of the seniors, and asked him to explain what the Latin meant, because he himself had not yet learned the language. When told that the song was 'maked in reverence / Of Cristes mooder . . .' his enthusiasm to memorise the whole thing became unbounded. He vowed to learn the entire hymn by Christmas under his own steam, even if he forgot about learning his primer and ended up being 'beten thries in an houre' for this neglect of the set curriculum.[1]

The young schoolboy soon learned the hymn, and sang it twice a day – not at church, but to pass the time when commuting 'To scoleward and homward whan he wente'. The music of Christian devotion is often heard out in the streets or in people's homes, amongst the dances and love songs enjoyed by those such as the Squire, who is 'Syngynge ... or floytynge [fluting], al the day'. It is not just at services that one hears 'freres in the chauncel gonne synge'. In the Summoner's Tale, a mother sings the 'Te Deum' over the body of her son on the way to burial. In the Miller's Tale, the 'poure scoler' of Oxford sits in his digs singing the 'Angelus ad Virginem' as he strums a 'gay sautrie' (a sort of proto-lute). Music is part of the standard expectation of the people from the church. The Friar 'hadde a murye note', the Prioress sang 'ful weel' the 'service dyvyne', and even the hideous Pardoner, who makes a living through the sale of false relics, charms his customers with his matchless singing of 'an offertorie'.[2] A bad cleric, in the words of Chaucer's younger contemporary William Langland, doesn't know how to chant or sing a scale, and doesn't even know properly the 'Paternoster as the preest it syngeth'.[3]

It is through the Church and Christian worship that much music entered English life, and also through the needs of the Church and worship that such music developed and changed. The first stratum of such music is in the 'Alma Redemptoris Mater' of the enthusiastic schoolboy and the 'Te Deum' of the grieving mother. Both of these, in Chaucer's tales, would have been sung as plainsong. It is a style of music that needs little introduction, although in the sound world of the present day it is often torn from its Christian context. One might hear it as the background music in the relaxation room of a health spa, or surreptitiously appropriated for the more contemplative types of 1990s pop. For all of its contemporary and new-age treatment, it is the most ancient surviving form of music: liturgical texts sung unaccompanied in a single, often sinuous line; the rhythm led not by a regular beat but meandering freely to the stress of the words; its scales drawn from the modes of the ancient Greeks, which often sound to modern ears somewhere between joy and melancholy.

This style, called 'Gregorian chant' after Pope Gregory, was brought to the British isles in the wake of St Augustine's mission in 597. It was championed in Canterbury by Augustine's successors, who held fast to it for its association with Rome, and who preferred it to other styles that were then current in Christian worship on the Celtic fringes. In 747, at the Council of Clovesho, Archbishop Cuthbert of Canterbury committed to follow the method of chanting and the liturgies drawn from the Roman examples.[4] This prescription set the direction for English church music for hundreds of years to come. The growing network of monasteries propagated the style of music, sung throughout the day in the seven offices and the mass. After the Norman Conquest, some cathedrals started slowly to develop the liturgy and the chants that had been passed down. Exeter, York and Salisbury were in the lead of such developments, but it was the music and style of worship from Salisbury – known as the 'Use of Sarum' or the 'Sarum Rite' – which became the most popular, and was followed by many local churches around England until the Reformation. The tunes of 'Alma Redemptoris Mater' and the 'Te Deum' sung in Chaucer's time were likely those which can still be found in the voluminous tomes of the Sarum Rite.

Yet, even if deeply traditional plainsong was at the base of English church music for hundreds of years, the music of the churches was by no means simple or static. Chaucer himself describes another style of singing, although in 'The Book of the Duchess' he imagines it being the product of the birds sitting on the roof outside his chamber rather than of clergy in a church. The musicians sing together, but each in their own individual way, to create a 'moste solempne servise . . . that ever man . . . had herd . . .'. Some of the singers 'song lowe, / Som high', but 'al of oon accord'. It created a sound that was 'a thyng of heven . . .'.[5]

Even before the Norman Conquest, some monasteries set boys to sing the lines of plainsong together with the deeper-voiced monks, but at a higher pitch. At first, the higher and the lower voices sang strictly in parallel, but in time, and with experimentation, the singers discovered ways that their lines could be made independent of each other, but still maintain an agreeable harmony. Simple polyphony was born. Further vocal lines, higher and lower, could be added, and new tricks introduced, such as different voices exchanging the original underlying plainsong melody whilst other voices rested. By Chaucer's time, polyphonic singing had already reached a high level of sophistication, such that he described it elsewhere as the 'voys of aungel'.[6] Although the emergence of western polyphony in this fashion was by no means unique to England – France and Italy could also boast of their own traditions – in certain periods English polyphony was seen as being at the cutting edge of the art, and particularly daring in its exploration of discords. The English choral composer John Dunstable, who lived in the first half of the fifteenth century, was regarded as a pioneer in the development of musical harmony, influential across Europe. The labour of choral composition, at that time, was not unworthy of the English kings themselves – two movements of a mass setting, written by either Henry IV or Henry V, survive in the opulent Old Hall manuscript, kept in the British Library.

Whom Do You Seek in the Sepulchre?

One might imagine plainsong as being restrained and understated. Yet, this is far from the case for the surviving chants of the Sarum Rite. Throughout them, the melodies paint and highlight the emotional freight of the scriptural and devotional texts of the liturgy: Christ's wonder and thankfulness to God the Father for the miracle of His resurrection, the Virgin Mary's fear and anxiety on the appearance of the Angel Gabriel, or the comfort she later draws from his reassurance. The liturgy and chant together have an inherently dramatic quality. Even when a single singer or a choir chant in unison, the melodies evoke the nature and feelings of different characters in arguments and dialogues: everything from the desperate pleading of Moses to God on behalf of the Israelites to the joy of the steward at the marriage at Cana when he tastes the miraculous wine created by Christ.

The dramatic quality of the chant and liturgy is one of the original sources of English theatre itself. By the end of the tenth century, the practice was established of re-enacting the discovery of Christ's empty tomb on Easter morning as part of a service. One text, the Winchester Troper, records that a cleric or monk was sent to sit in front of the church's Easter sepulchre, holding a palm, playing the part of the angel who waited in Christ's empty tomb. Three others would approach him in imitation of the three women who went to anoint Christ's body. '*Quem quaeritis* . . .' sang the first cleric. 'Whom do you seek in the sepulchre, O Christians?' A sung dialogue would then unfold: 'Jesus of Nazareth who was crucified, O heavenly one . . .'; 'He is not here! he is risen as he foretold! Go, announce that he is risen from the dead!' Together, they would then go to the choir singing an anthem in praise of the 'strong lion . . . the Son of God . . .' and return to the Easter sepulchre, flinging aside its curtains to show how it was empty. All others responded by singing the 'Te Deum', and causing all the bells to chime together.[7]

Throughout the Middle Ages, the music and liturgy of the church increasingly inspired independent drama outside the church in imitation of its rituals, particularly in connection with seasonal celebrations. Medieval devotional texts stressed the benefit of each Christian making Christ 'hym-self present in his thoghte as if he saw [Him] fully with his bodily eghe . . .', in the words of the popular fourteenth-century *Meditationes vitae Christi*. From the 1350s, town guilds are recorded staging grand pageant-like processions in imitation of the Candlemas liturgies commemorating the presentation of Christ in the Temple. Guild members dressed as characters in the story – the Virgin Mary carrying a doll of the infant Jesus, Joseph, the old prophet Simeon in the temple – went through the streets accompanied by candle-bearers, and the chanting of the song of Simeon, the 'Nunc dimittis'. Such events continued to develop into actual plays with texts based on scripture and the liturgy, even concluding with dancing and the playing of minstrels in the records of the Beverley Candlemas Guild, '*cum gaudio*' – 'with joy'.[8]

By the 1500s, mystery plays celebrating the great feasts of the Church year – Christmas, Easter, Corpus Christi – were widespread throughout England. Many were accompanied by the singing of carols – catchy songs written, in all likelihood, by those in the Church or with a clerical education, but for popular enjoyment, and perhaps even to be accompanied by dances.[9] A number of carols from this time and context remain as standards in the choral repertoire. Often, they are haunting. The 'Coventry Carol' recalls Herod's massacre of the innocents:

Oh sisters two, what may we do
To preserve on this day
This poor youngling for whom we sing
Sleep well, lully, lullay . . .

Their intensity often comes from the distillation of biblical and devotional imagery. Frequently, their texts even mix English with Latin snippets drawn from the wider liturgy – a style called 'macaronic' – again signifying their Church origins:

There is no rose of such virtue
As is the rose that bare Jesu;
   Alleluia.
For in this rose contained was
Heaven and earth in little space;
   Res miranda.
By that rose we may well see
That he is God in persons three,
   Pari forma.
The angels sungen the shepherds to:
Gloria in excelsis deo:
   Gaudeamus.
Leave we all this worldly mirth,
And follow we this joyful birth;
   Transeamus.

Despite official disapproval after the Reformation, English towns and cities were tenaciously proud of the staging of the mystery plays, and they were performed into the 1580s. Their mixture of drama and song, grounded in the texts of scripture and the liturgy, would have been fresh in the memory of the great generation of Elizabethan dramatists. William Shakespeare, growing up in Stratford-upon-Avon, was only a short journey from Coventry where the plays survived until 1579. In his plays, as well as those of Christopher Marlowe and Thomas Kyd, there are echoes and references to this earlier tradition – the behaviour of the powerful echoing the instability of Herod or of Pilate, or suggestions of the slaughter of the innocents in *Henry V* or *Macbeth* – aside from the formal mixture of drama and song.[10]

Do You Hear the People Sing?

The rich and intricate style of polyphony that was developing across Christian Europe in the Middle Ages had one particular foe: the pope himself. In a decretal issued in 1325, Pope John XXII grumbled at length about new fashions in church music. Its singers' voices 'run about all over the place and won't be quiet, their ear is drunk with melody rather than soothed, and they copy in their gestures what they sing from their mouths ... the required end of devotion is abandoned, and a wanton lasciviousness is encouraged ...'.

The big problem for this pope was that the new-fangled music, with its ornate textures and myriad voices – unlike the old-fashioned plainsong – hid the original melodies and the words that went with them. One ended up simply enjoying the music, instead of it being a means of worship or devotion.

In this, the pope was in complete agreement with the fourteenth-century English reformer John Wycliffe, who felt deep guilt at actually taking pleasure in the music he heard in church: '... As oft as the song delighteth me more than that which is sungen', he said, quoting the fourth-century Church Father St Augustine, 'so oft I acknowledge I trespass grievously.'[11]

As much as the English Reformation two centuries after Wycliffe was able to efface many of the sensory modes of worship – the incense and paintings, the processions, prostrations, statues and vestments – it was impossible for it to stop the use of music, even if it was pleasing. St Paul himself, in the Epistle to the Ephesians, gave his approval to praise in song: 'be filled with the Spirit', he wrote, '... in psalms and hymns and spiritual songs, singing and making melody in your heart to the Lord ...'. St Augustine also admitted, 'when I remember the tears I shed at the Psalmody of [the] Church, in the beginning of my recovered faith, and how at this time, I am moved, not with the singing, but with the things sung when they are sung with a clear voice and modulation most suitable, I acknowledge the great use of this institution ...'.[12]

Unable to gainsay these authorities, the reformers came up with a classic English compromise. When sacred texts were set to music, recommended Archbishop Cranmer to King Henry VIII in 1544, they should 'not be full of notes'. Instead, they should have 'as near as may be, for every syllable a note'. Queen Elizabeth I went along with this. In 1559, at the beginning of her reign, she commanded that 'there be a modest and distinct song, so used in all parts of the common prayers in the Church, that the same may be plainly understood, as if were read without singing ...'. Just as long as it could be 'understood and perceived', it would be 'permitted that in the beginning, or in the end of common prayers ... there may be sung an Hymn, or such like song, to the praise of Almighty God, in the best sort of melody and music that may be conveniently devised ...'.[13]

Even if musicians were soon to disregard his injunction, Cranmer's call 'for every syllable a note' fundamentally shaped the character of music in England for generations to come. Over the turbulent middle of the sixteenth century, out went the legacy of complex and winding polyphony where the voices 'run about all over the place'. Acres of gorgeously illuminated old antiphoners and other manuscript books with the legacy of hundreds of years of composition were torn out of the monasteries, cathedrals and parish churches. Highly trained singers, singing teachers and composers were pensioned off out of the service of the Church and left to find their own way. Church organs – which were becoming increasingly widespread by the beginning of the 1500s – were taken out or left to rot. And the choirs whose song oft delighted Wycliffe against his better desire were run down nearly to extinction.

Yet, there came in their place 'modest and distinct song'. With the near complete disappearance of parish church choirs, complex polyphony and Latin liturgy, there was a vacuum to be filled. This was done by the ordinary people, who until this time had for the most part been silent in church. The London diarist Henry Machyn, writing in September 1559, gives perhaps the first account of congregational singing: 'the nuw mornyng prayer at sant Antholyns . . . begyne to rynge at v in the mornyng; men and women all do syng, and boys'. In March the following year, 1560, he fills in a little more detail about what they sang: 'after the sermon done they songe all, old and yong, a salme in myter [psalm in metre], the tune of Genevay [Geneva] ways'. In the same year, the Bishop of Salisbury, John Jewel, wrote a letter describing the runaway popularity of song amongst the people: 'As soon as [the people] had once commenced singing publicly in only one little church in London, immediately not only the churches in the neighbourhood, but also distant towns, began to vie with one another in the same practice.' The people did not keep their singing just indoors in the church either: 'You may now see sometimes at Paul's Cross,* after the service, six thousand persons, old and young, of both sexes, all singing together and praising God.'[14]

These 'psalms in metre' were primarily what Queen Elizabeth's 1559 command had in mind for the 'Hymn, or such like song'. Almost immediately, a new book – *The Whole Book of Psalms Collected into English Metre* – was published to satisfy the voracious popular appetite for religious music. This book, usually known as 'Sternhold and Hopkins' after its first authors, went through over 700 editions between 1562 and the end

* Paul's Cross was an open-air pulpit outside St Paul's Cathedral renowned as a popular gathering place for public sermons.

of the seventeenth century (it isn't difficult to find copies in antiquarian bookshops). Its huge repute made it the cornerstone of English church music for nearly three centuries. Even into the 1800s, until an ecclesiastical court found otherwise in 1820, many believed it was the only hymn book that could lawfully be used in Anglican worship.[15] Some literary types were sniffy about its quality. John Donne complained: 'And shall our Church, unto our Spouse and King / More hoarse, more harsh than any other, sing?' Another seventeenth-century writer, George Wither, who was frustrated at the failure of his own version of the psalms to dent the popularity of Sternhold and Hopkins, grumbled that it was 'full of absurdities, solecisms, improprieties, nonsense and impertinent circumlocutions to more than twice the length of their originals.'[16]

Despite this, the wider public loved it. It recast the 150 psalms from the Old Testament in simple language with strong rhythms that could be sung without difficulty. The first verse of the well-known Psalm 23 (The Lord is my shepherd) becomes:

> My shepheard is the living Lord,
> Nothing therefore I neede,
> In pastures fayre with waters calme
> He set me for to feede.

Various editions united these with easy tunes which were either brought from Protestant communities on the continent (hence the reference to Geneva by Henry Machyn) or even old pre-Reformation plainsong melodies adapted. One of its Genevan tunes, 'the Old Hundreth', best known for its connection to the hymn 'All People that on Earth do Dwell', has been used by many composers including Felix Mendelssohn and Ralph Vaughan Williams, and remains popular to this day.

For centuries, these psalms were sung by high and low, learned and unlettered. From the sixteenth century onwards, diarists record them being sung by ordinary people not just in church, but after supper on Sunday, or on the road to and from church. Sir John Falstaff, in Shakespeare's

Henry IV Part I, alludes to their popularity amongst the artisanal classes: 'I would I were a weaver; I could sing psalms or anything . . .'. Jesting reference is made in *The Winter's Tale* to a sheep shearer who 'sings psalms to hornpipes'.[17] At the same time, the early-seventeenth-century Yorkshire diarist and aristocrat Lady Margaret Hoby records that she scarcely sang anything except the psalms. At many schools, as the Elizabethan statutes of Kirkby Stephen School require, 'Every morning and evening . . . the scholars . . . and the schoolmaster shall go from the schoolhouse into the parish church . . . and there sing together one of the psalms . . .'. Through the Civil War, they were still used by both Parliamentarians and Royalists. In the calmer eighteenth century, Alexander Pope evokes how the psalms remained particularly dear to country folk: 'Hopkins and Sternhold glad the heart with psalms', and thus, he suggested, the translation could not be without merit: 'How could Devotion touch the country pews, / Unless the Gods bestow'd a proper Muse?'[18]

No matter one's background, the metrical psalms were a prayerful way of expressing thoughts and emotions on all manner of situations and experiences. The parson or his parish clerk was responsible for choosing which psalms to sing for each service, and it was possible to find something to relate to any event or human problem. In a 1685 manual for parish clerks, the psalms were indexed by subject. One could pick a suitable psalm for any and more of the following eventualities: angels, atheists, blazing stars or comets, conspiracies, dark cloudy weather, earthquake, idolatry and its punishment, promises made good, prosperous estate of wicked men, watchfulness over the tongue, and whirlwinds.[19]

Their universal applicability, grounded in biblical authority, would have been part of their appeal, but it was also the simplicity of their language and settings which made them some of the most popular pieces of text and music in England for hundreds of years. Over this time, they were one of the fundamental shared English cultural experiences, one of its 'great commonplaces' in the words of one scholar. Although hardly known now, they have left their mark on the English language and its literature. Not only did their simple rhythms (usually ti-tum ti-tum ti-tum ti-tum) have 'an important influence in strengthening the iambic tendency of English verse' and their language establish 'a kind of norm for plain diction in verse' but, perhaps more importantly than either of these, they offered a musical emancipation to the English.[20] Any concern or emotion which could be found in the encyclopaedic interest of the psalm book was worthy of song by the people, in church or at home. Where once they remained silent, they now had liberty to sing.

The Image of my Heart is Painted in Them

Recently, a church organist in a village near me passed away. She was in her mid-nineties and had played for nearly all of her life. I was later contacted by her daughter, who wanted to give me her entire collection of music scores amassed over nearly a century. 'My brothers want to put it on the bonfire otherwise', she explained. As I write, my desk is surrounded by at least a dozen large boxes of sheet music, as yet unsorted. But another part of the collection was easier to deal with: her hymn books. I have ranged them on top of my piano. Their number and variety are astonishing. There is no trace of Sternhold and Hopkins, but one can find, amongst others, *The Army & Navy Hymnal, Songs of Praise (with Music), Hymns Ancient and Modern, The English Hymnal, The New English Hymnal, Congregational Praise, English Praise, The Methodist Hymn Book, The Salvation Army Tune Book, The Anglican Hymn Book*. Look inside any of them, and they each boast scores of editions and reprints. Their vast proliferation is an incontrovertible proof of John Betjeman's statement that 'Hymns are', or at least once were, 'the poems of the people'.[21]

The displacement of Sternhold and Hopkins by new collections of hymns, not based on strict translations from psalms, came from not a reaction against its principles, but a desire better to fulfil them. From its earliest days, the congregational singing of metrical psalms may have been received with popular enthusiasm, but it was hardly the highest art. One observer, Elias Hall, a musician in Oldham writing in 1706, put his view of the practice more directly: 'Then out the people yawl an hundred parts, / Some roar, some whine, some creak like wheels of carts . . .'.[22]

These problems were all a legacy of the Reformation. Organs, which might have supported congregational singing, had generally disappeared from parish churches by the 1580s. Choirs likewise were now for the most part confined to cathedrals and the Chapel Royal. Whilst in these places, from the Elizabethan period onwards, there was room for composers such as Tallis, Byrd, Gibbons and later Henry Purcell to develop a new repertoire of English sacred music, this was not generally at the time heard beyond the cathedrals. Few ordinary people had any musical education, and many could read neither text nor music. To get a congregation singing, the parish clerk would 'line out' the psalm, that is sing two lines to the congregation which they would then sing back, after which he would sing the next two lines in turn. In practice, the stronger singers would leap in on the first note, and then wait for the rest to join them before they then moved to the next note, again waiting for the weaker singers to reach it. Without any organ or choir to keep them in time, they sat on each note for two or three seconds. As a result, singing metrical psalms became an interminably slow process. On 6 January 1661, Samuel Pepys recorded that it took an hour for the psalm to be sung at St Olave's, Hart Street, in London. On top of this, as another observer, Thomas Symmes, complained: 'The rules of singing not being taught or learnt, every one sang as best pleased himself, and every leading-singer, would take the liberty of raising any note of the tune, or lowering it, as best pleased his ear; and add such turns and flourishes as were grateful to him . . .'.[23]

Worn down by this less than satisfactory situation, many clergy began to take their own action. In 1700, the vicar of Old Romney wrote to a friend:

> when I first came to my parish, about 10 years ago, I found, to my great grief, the people very ignorant and irreligious; the place of divine worship indecently kept . . . so that at first, I began to teach three or four youths the skill of singing psalms orderly, and according to rules, which greatly

tended, through the grace of God, to awaken affections towards religion, and to give 'em a relish of it.

Those 'three or four youths' formed the kernel of a new religious society intended to bring about 'a general reviving of piety, and a solemn observance of the public ordinances of God . . .', particularly with the proper singing of music in church services.[24]

These societies spread quickly. With them, choirs began to return to parish churches in the early part of the eighteenth century. Itinerant singing masters, armed with new teaching methods, worked to ensure that choristers were properly trained. Choirs also began to be accompanied by small bands, often composed of bass viols, oboes and bassoons. Until the mid-nineteenth century, these choirs were placed in large, elevated galleries at the west end of the churches, after which time they were moved back to the chancel, where the choirs had originally been before the Reformation.

These 'West Gallery' choirs could often be too independent-minded for the liking of the clergy. In 1822 at Camerton near Bath, the rector John Skinner complained that 'During the evening service . . .' of Sunday 14 July, '. . . the singers, who have been in a state of constant intoxication since yesterday, being offended because I would not suffer them to chant the service after the first lesson, put on their hats and left the church . . .'.[25]

Yet, George Eliot and Thomas Hardy depict them with deep sympathy as an integral part of rural English life. Certainly, they were the principal means whereby many of the working classes were able to make and enjoy music. In 1769, Parson Woodforde of Castle Cary in Somerset, who was also the subject of a choir walkout, listed his singers as including 'John Coleman, the baker', several farmers and 'Farmer Hix's son'. In 1770 at Welford, Northamptonshire, the choir was led by 'Mr Archer's steward, honest John Heath', whilst a gamekeeper played the oboe, and a gardener the bassoon. Their independence of spirit should hardly be a surprise. For many of them, as one historian of English music, Nicholas Temperley, remarked, '. . . this sort of singing or playing in church was the highest accomplishment of their everyday lives. Small wonder that any attempt to interfere with it met with the strongest resentment and resistance.'[26]

From these religious societies and choirs comes the origin of the many provincial English choral societies and festivals which still survive to this day. At Eccles, near Manchester, in 1792, four church choirs banded together to sing large oratorios by George Frideric Handel and Joseph Haydn. In the 1830s at Ellenbrook, also near Manchester, a society of instrumental players and church singers was formed, many of whose members 'were handloom weavers, who made music a special study . . .'. With 'constant practice' they 'became good performers, and had a large experience and knowledge of Handel's music, Dr Croft's, Dr Greene's, Dr Boyce's, Dr Nares', Kent's, Webbe's, and other anthems.'[27]

As the needs of Christian worship helped to propagate musical skills and knowledge more widely throughout English society during this time – thus laying the groundwork for the further development of hymn singing – it also gave an impetus to generate new material for congregations to sing, beside the old metrical psalms. However, as during the eighteenth century it was still believed that only the metrical psalms were permitted to be sung during Anglican services, this development's first stirrings had to find expression outside the formal context of the established Church.

A story is told of the eighteenth-century nonconformist cleric Isaac Watts that, when he was a young man of 22, he remarked to his father as they were walking home from a chapel service that he found the singing of the metrical psalms hard going. 'Then give us something better, young man!' replied his father, probably facetiously. However, Watts took him at his word. By the next service he had written a new hymn of his own inspiration, not based on the translation of a psalm:

> Behold the glory of the Lamb
> Amidst the Father's throne;
> Prepare new honours for his Name
> And songs before unknown.[28]

His presumption that human compositions – rather than the divinely inspired words of the metrical psalms and scripture – should be used to honour God during services unsettled many. However, he had choice words for those who thought this way. 'They will venture to sing a dull [metrical psalm] or two at Church, in Tunes of equal Dulness; but still they persuade themselves and their children that the beauties of [poetry] are vain and dangerous. All that arises a degree over Mr Sternhold is too airy for Worship, and hardly escapes the Sentence of *unclean* and *abominable*.'[29] To the contrary, the material of Christianity might form 'many poems' that could 'call back the dying Piety of the Nation to Life and Beauty ... make Religion appear like itself, and confound the Blasphemies of a profligate World ignorant of pious pleasures ...'.[30] The 'Doctrines of our Holy Faith', he argued, could wear a 'Delightful Dress'. But, more importantly, as he said of a group of his poems, 'the Image of my Heart is painted in them'.[31]

Led on by these principles, particularly that there should be room for the expression of the personal, the heartfelt and a sense of spontaneity, Watts began to pour forth lyrics for new hymns: 'O God Our Help in Ages Past', 'When I Survey the Wondrous Cross', 'Jesus Shall Reign Where'er the Sun', 'Joy to the World'. If Watts won for himself the reputation of being the father of English hymnody, he was soon followed over the course of the eighteenth century by other Methodist and nonconformist writers whose works, following the same principles, have endured to this day. From Charles Wesley, brother of the founder of Methodism John Wesley, we have 'Hark the Herald Angels Sing', 'Lo! He Comes with Clouds Descending', 'Love Divine, All Loves Excelling'. John Newton, a hard-bitten sailor who underwent a dramatic conversion on a foundering slave ship, immortalised his experience in 'Amazing Grace'. Augustus Toplady, the curate of Blagdon near Cheddar Gorge in Somerset, who was driven to take shelter in a small cave in the craggy landscape of his parish during a violent storm, was stirred by the incident to write 'Rock of Ages, Cleft for Me'.

These writers insisted that the new hymns, written with simple lyrics as they were, have simple tunes that could be sung easily by the people, not just the choirs or the musically trained. Such simplicity was intended to reflect the idea that such hymns were heartfelt and spontaneous. It was also, as the Wesley brothers maintained, an aid in teaching people about the Christian faith.

At first, during the eighteenth century, these new hymns were sung at informal outdoor Methodist meetings or in chapels. By the beginning of the nineteenth century, evangelical Anglican clergy had seen the enthusiasm which these hymns generated and started to bring them into formal church worship, despite the lingering impression that they were not a permissible part of established Church liturgy. However, after they were found to be lawful for use in Anglican churches in the 1820 court case, these strictures were lifted. Two further developments also added to the sharp growth in their popularity. The return of the pipe organ to churches throughout the 1800s, replacing the West Gallery bands, made it easier to provide support for whole congregations to sing together. A revival in pre-Reformation traditions also gave an unexpected fillip. The body of hymns from the Sarum Rite, which had been omitted from the Book of Common Prayer by Cranmer, was rediscovered and gave reassurance that there was a proper precedent for the use of such personal hymns in English churches, as well as material for new writing derived from them.[32]

With these factors all in place, the Victorian age saw the great flowering of the English hymn. The demand encouraged creativity. New hymns could be expressions of personal devotion or anguish – for example 'Abide with Me' (Henry Francis Lyte), 'Nearer My God to Thee' (Sarah Flower Adams) or 'Lead Kindly Light' (Henry Newman), all written as the author struggled with illness or the prospect of death. They might be scholarly translations, such as 'O Come Emmanuel' and 'Jerusalem the Golden' by the prolific John Mason Neale (also the author of 'Good King Wenceslas'). They might be particularly designed with children in mind, for instance 'All Things Bright and Beautiful' or 'Once in Royal David's City' (Mrs Cecil Frances Alexander), as was 'Onward, Christian Soldiers' ('knocked off . . . in about ten minutes' by Sabine Baring-Gould, so he later recalled, as a processional hymn for Sunday school pupils to walk to church). Some may have no special backstory, save a particular moment of random inspiration: 'The Day Thou Gavest Lord is

Ended' (John Ellerton) or 'Eternal Father Strong to Save' (William Whiting). The composers of the age, such as John Stainer, John Bacchus Dykes, Sir Hubert Parry (who wrote the tune for William Blake's poem 'Jerusalem') and Sir Arthur Sullivan, responded in kind, writing clear and simple hymn tunes that combined popular appeal with a sense that they were still a creation of high art.[33]

The music historian Andrew Gant remarked that the Victorian hymn writers did for the English 'what opera did for the Italians'. Their hymns succeeded 'because they filled a hole not just in British religion but in British life'.[34] Even now, this whole tradition of English hymnody is an integral presence, and it is difficult to envisage so many scenes of English life and public ritual in its absence. What else could replace it? From ceremonies of remembrance ('O God Our Help in Ages Past', 'Eternal Father Strong to Save') to sporting finals ('Abide with Me' and 'Jerusalem', not to mention the often raucous reworded versions of 'Guide Me O Thou Great Redeemer'), to Christmas ('O Come Emmanuel' and 'Once in Royal David's City' amongst many others) or funerals ('Lead Kindly Light' and 'All Things Bright and Beautiful'), these hymns offer a potent mixture of vigour and stately simplicity, combined with prayerfulness and deep emotion behind a veneer of restraint.

But although one can trace this lineage back nearly half a millennium to the Reformation – a distinct tradition which enfranchised the English people with a right to musical self-expression and gave them a musical language to deal with the deepest profundities of experience – it is not a tradition which has been cherished in this age. The thought of Watts's 'O God Our Help in Ages Past' takes my mind back to the last time I sang it. It was in a crowd of several thousand people outside Exeter Cathedral on the day of the proclamation of King Charles's accession to the throne. The text of the proclamation had been read by the civic dignitaries and, after calls of 'God Save the King', the crowd was invited to sing Watts's hymn accompanied by the cathedral choir. I belted the hymn out as if I were back in my school chapel. No one else in the crowd seemed to sing at all. My daughter looked at me quizzically.

10

My Unpremeditated Verse

When Old St Paul's Cathedral was destroyed in the Great Fire of London in 1666, only one memorial survived the flames: that of the poet John Donne, dean of the cathedral from 1621 to 1631. The memorial, which can still be seen in the south quire aisle, is haunting to behold. In white marble, delicately carved by the master mason Nicholas Stone, it depicts a life-size Donne shrouded in a sheet except for his face, which wears an expression of serene delight. The Latin epitaph above explains that he is gazing 'on Him whose name is Rising'.

The statue always had a measure of fame, and not just because of its fine quality – 'It seems to breathe faintly, and posterity shall look upon it as a kind of artificial miracle', as Donne's friend, Sir Henry Wotton, said of it. Commissioned during the last few weeks of Donne's life so that a sketch of his likeness could be made for the sculpture, Donne, although wracked with pain from stomach cancer, modelled for the artist. He would warm his large study with charcoal fires, undress, wrap himself in the winding sheet, arrange his hands 'as dead bodies are usually fitted' and, looking east as if expecting the Second Coming, composed his features in the guise of joyful tranquillity.[1]

The statue says much of Donne's courage in the face of death, with his epitaph reminding passers-by of his status as a clergyman, of his learning, the royal favour he enjoyed from King James I, and his confidence in the Christian message. Yet, the ensemble betrays nothing of what he is best remembered for: his poetry, which was instead memorialised by the 'Elegy upon the Death of the Dean of Paul's', written for him by his younger contemporary Thomas Carew, a penetrating judge of literature, who sharply articulated Donne's literary achievement:

> The Muses' garden, with pedantic weeds
> O'erspread, was purg'd by thee; the lazy seeds
> Of servile imitation thrown away,
> And fresh invention planted . . .

Donne's 'brave soul' could fathom, articulate and teach 'the deep knowledge of dark truths . . . / As sense might judge what fancy could not reach . . .' and bend 'Our stubborn language' to 'the awe of thy imperious wit . . .'.

Carew lamented that poetry would go into a decline with Donne's passing: 'The reverend silence that attends thy hearse . . . did proclaim in a dumb eloquence / The death of all the arts . . .'. Yet Carew's lament was overstated. What his lines discerned was a mark not just of Donne, but of the poetry of their age. In England, from the latter part of the sixteenth century into the second half of the seventeenth, poetry enjoyed a golden age. T.S. Eliot (here interpreted by the critic Louis Martz) discerned its main characteristics:

> . . . an acute self-consciousness that shows itself in minute analysis of moods and motives; a conversational tone and accent, expressed in language that is 'as a rule simple and pure'; highly unconventional imagery, including the whole range of human experience, from theology to the commonest details of bed and board; an 'intellectual, argumentative evolution' within each poem, a 'strain of passionate paradoxical reasoning which knits the first line to the last' and which often results in 'the elaboration of a figure of speech to the farthest stage to which ingenuity can carry it'; above all, including all, that 'unification of sensibility' which could achieve a 'direct sensuous apprehension of thought, or a recreation of thought into feeling'.[2]

Donne, best known for the love poetry written during his youth, wrote the great bulk of his output, both poetry and prose, on the themes of Christianity, a fundamental ingredient of the poetic efflorescence of the period. If this was a golden age of English poetry, it was also a golden age of Christian poetry that, as Carew wrote of Donne, sought to probe and put into words 'the deep knowledge of dark truths'. The literary legacy of this period is one of the great components of the English canon, and owes its origins and vitality to the poetic engagement with the intellectual and spiritual currents of the Christianity of the time. Such is its richness in language, in thought and in spirituality, that – no matter one's religious background – the poetry of that time can speak to readers in the present day.

O That I Were an Orenge-Tree

I struck the board, and cried, 'No more;
              I will abroad!
What? shall I ever sigh and pine?
My lines and life are free, free as the road,
Loose as the wind, as large as store.
      Shall I be still in suit?
Have I no harvest but a thorn
To let me blood, and not restore
What I have lost with cordial fruit?
      Sure there was wine
Before my sighs did dry it; there was corn
   Before my tears did drown it.
    Is the year only lost to me?
      Have I no bays to crown it,
No flowers, no garlands gay? All blasted?
           All wasted?

. . .

But as I raved and grew more fierce and wild
      At every word,
Methought I heard one calling, *Child*!
      And I replied *My Lord*.

These lines are an extract from a poem called 'The Collar' by George Herbert. It may have been written in the small parish of Bemerton, a low-lying and rather marshy area of countryside on the banks of the River Nadder, just south-west of Salisbury. Here, Herbert spent the last four years of his life as rector. It was an out-of-the-way sort of place. Aside from visits to Salisbury twice a week to hear evensong at the cathedral and play music with the choristers afterwards, and perhaps the occasional trip to his kinsman, William Herbert, the third Earl of Pembroke, at Wilton House nearby, Herbert's outward life would have been regular and unostentatious. 'The Countrey Parson,' wrote Herbert in a manual for clergy, 'is exceeding exact in his Life, being holy, just, prudent, temperate, bold, grave in all his ways,' given to '... Mortification in regard of lusts and affections, and the stupifying and deading of all the clamorous powers of the soul ....'[3]

This image of Herbert as a quiet and reserved country clergyman is belied by the passion and boldness he displays in his poem. He is unafraid to confront God, to complain of the frustrations of life in God's service, the times of sterility and the periodic sense of God's absence. His complaints pour out in verse that seems driven into wild and dramatic irregularity by the outpouring of his frustration, but which is nevertheless tightly controlled. The imagery seems simple, the sort of material that would be every day at hand in rustic life – wind, thorn, blood, harvest, fruit, wine, corn, tears, garlands, flowers – but in nearly every case it is carefully designed to refer to the Bible, the Book of Common Prayer and church liturgy. Herbert's anger and his questioning is enough to press God into giving a reply, but one freighted with ambiguity that poses as many questions as it might resolve: 'Methought I heard one calling ....'

* * *

At the beginning of this period, it might have been difficult to believe that there would be a great flowering of English religious poetry. In 1580, the Elizabethan courtier, poet and all-round hero Sir Philip Sidney complained in his highly influential *Defence of Poesy* that 'idle England' should 'be grown so hard a stepmother to poets' and that it could 'scarce endure the pain of a pen';[4] however, despite this gloom, the conditions for such a flowering were well in place. England, by this time, was a rising European power. English also was gaining wider acceptance as a language for learning and poetry in educated society. A little before Sidney wrote his *Defence*, the poems of the courtiers Sir Thomas Wyatt and Henry Howard, Earl of Surrey, were published. Both pioneered the use in English of the Petrarchan sonnet and, in Howard's case, unrhymed blank verse inspired by the Latin of Virgil. Their publisher, Richard Tottel, wrote in an introduction to their work, 'That our tongue is able . . . [in poetry] . . . to do as praiseworthily as [contemporary Italian and Latin poets, the verses of Wyatt and Surrey] . . . show abundantly'.[5] Soon afterwards, in 1589, author George Puttenham published *The Art of English Poesy*, challenging the primacy of Latin and Greek: 'Why may not the same be with us as well as with them, our language being no less copious, pithy and significative than theirs?' In this, he agreed with Tottel: 'our tongue is most fit to honour Poesy, and to be honoured by Poesy'.[6]

Whilst the poet, said Sidney, might freely range 'within the zodiac of his own wit' and bring forth 'quite anew, forms such as never were in nature, as the heroes, demi-gods, cyclops, chimeras, furies, and such like', he argued that '[t]he chief, both in antiquity and excellency, were they that did imitate [in their poetry] the inconceivable excellencies of God'. Sidney argues that the biblical King David was one such of these, a poet by virtue of his reputed authorship of the Book of Psalms, as were 'Solomon in his Song of Songs, in his Ecclesiastes and Proverbs; Moses and Deborah in their Hymns; and the writer of Job'. He adds that the parables of Christ are memorable thanks to their poetic nature, and that Christianity is the fittest subject for verse. The poetry of scripture, said Sidney, might bring joy and consolation when necessary, and new poetry should sing 'the praises of the immortal beauty, the immortal goodness of God who giveth us hands to write, and wits to conceive; of which we might well want words, but never matter; of which we could turn our eyes to nothing, but we should ever have new budding occasions'. Indeed, in the act of making (which is the original Greek meaning of the word 'poetry'), the poet comes closest to imitating God, 'when with the force of a divine breath [the poet] brings things forth far surpassing [nature's] doings.'[7]

The poets of this period, in spite of Sidney's understatement, lacked neither words nor matter. Thomas Plume, Archdeacon of Rochester, wrote in 1675 that the English clergy and gentry at the beginning of the seventeenth century were 'the most learned of the world', when greater numbers than ever had access to higher education thanks to the growth of the two universities, Oxford and Cambridge.[8] Classical texts and theological material from antiquity to the present time were available in profusion thanks to the developments in printing, and virtuosic mastery of languages, whether ancient or modern, became highly prized. Most of all, thanks to the presence of the English-language Bible and Book of Common Prayer in every parish, the knowledge of scripture became near universal, estimable not only for its own spiritual merit but also as a shared point of reference amongst the learned as well as wider society.

Yet, though the Bible was a fundamental spur to poetry in this age, it did not mean – as Herbert's poem above shows – that this poetry was a pale imitation of scripture, or an uncomplicated echo and acclamation of Christian dogma. Rather, its biblical origins provided an impetus, on occasion, for the opposite: complaints against God, the embrace of contraries and ambiguity, and expressions of confusion, bewilderment and despair. Differing views of Christ and scriptural events in the four gospels and New Testament epistles allowed for a similar variety of poetic responses. The Old Testament books of Ecclesiastes and Job legitimated critical scepticism and, in the case of the latter – 'I would order my cause before him, and fill my mouth with arguments', thunders Job (23.4) – determined questioning of God. Most of all, the Book of Psalms, which, as the Church Father St Athanasius said, 'portray in all their great variety the movements of the human soul',[9] gave a precedent for the angry expression of grievance or hopelessness as much as praise and thanksgiving.

Thus, as much as Christ calls out, quoting the beginning of Psalm 22, from the Cross – 'My God, My God, why hast Thou forsaken me?' – so the poets of the seventeenth century were emboldened to confront God or to express anger, hopelessness and deepest frustration. From this, John Donne openly expresses his exasperation with God in 'Holy Sonnets': 'Thou hast made me, and shall Thy work decay?' (I). And 'Except Thou rise and for Thine own work fight, / O! I shall soon despair, when I shall see / That Thou lovest mankind well, yet wilt not choose me . . .' (XIV). So Herbert cries out 'No more . . .' in 'The Collar', or, in 'The Search',

> Whither, O, whither art thou fled,
> My Lord, my Love?
> My searches are my daily bread;
> Yet never prove.
>
> My knees pierce th'earth, mine eies the skie;
> And yet the sphere
> And centre both to me denie
> That thou art there.

The poetry expressing such frustration can even come close to seeming unhinged – indeed, in 'Employment (II)' Herbert asks

> O that I were an Orenge-tree,
> That busy plant!
> Then should I ever laden be,
> And never want
> Some fruit for him that dressed me . . .

Nevertheless, the poets maintain throughout an extraordinary command of language and form, with a premium given to clarity of expression and the creative use of English as they attempt to grapple with questions of the divine. Much of this can be attributed to the increasing self-confidence expressed about the English language. 'Hail native language' wrote Milton in 'At a Vacation Exercise', addressing the English tongue as a student at the age of 19 in 1627. English, in his view, was now able to 'cloath [his] fancy in fit sound' and furnish him with the 'best aray' to deal with the most profound questions of theology and philosophy, not to mention having the capacity to rival Greek and Latin in the greatest literary genre of epic:

> Such where the deep transported mind may soare
> Above the wheeling poles, and at Heav'ns dore
> Look in . . . [and]
> . . . sing of secret things that came to pass . . .
> And last of Kings and Queens and Hero's old

As bold as these poets might have been to express moments of despair, their deep engagement with the English language often leads them to moods of high playfulness. In another poem, 'The Pulley', Herbert plays with the word 'rest' as he contemplates why mankind cannot find contentment within his mortal lifespan:

> When God at first made man,
> Having a glasse of blessings standing by;
> Let us (said he) poure on him all we can:
> Let the worlds riches, which dispersed lie,
> Contract into a span.
>
> So strength first made a way;
> Then beautie flowed, then wisdome, honour, pleasure:
> When almost all was out, God made a stay,
> Perceiving that alone, of all his treasure,
> Rest in the bottome lay.
>
> For if I should (said he)
> Bestow this jewell also on my creature,
> He would adore my gifts in stead of me,
> And rest in Nature, not the God of Nature:
> So both should losers be.

Yet let him keep the rest,
But keep them with repining restlesnesse:
Let him be rich and wearie, that at least,
If goodnesse leade him not, yet wearinesse
May tosse him to my breast.

In another of his poems, 'Heaven', in which he attempts to contemplate the nature of life beyond the mortal horizon, Herbert's wordplay becomes even more brilliant. He asks questions of heaven and is met in answer with an echo:

O who will show me those delights on high?
Echo. I.
Thou Echo, thou art mortal, all men know.
Echo. No.
. . .
Then tell me, what is that supreme delight?
Echo. Light.
Light to the mind: what shall the will enjoy?
Echo. Joy.
But are there cares and business with the pleasure?
Echo. Leisure.
Light, joy, and leisure; but shall they persever?
Echo. Ever.

Herbert's wordplay is a serious matter. It allows him to investigate the unfathomable, and bring an unexpected clarity to a field at the edge of human comprehension, allowing him to embrace ambiguity and paradox. It is the same in the case of Donne, here in a sonnet on the Annunciation of Christ's impending birth, addressed to the Virgin Mary:

Salvation to all that will is nigh;
That All, which always is all everywhere,

Which cannot sin, and yet all sins must bear,
Which cannot die, yet cannot choose but die,
Lo, faithful virgin, yields Himself to lie
In prison, in thy womb; and though He there
Can take no sin, nor thou give, yet He will wear,
Taken from thence, flesh, which death's force may try.
Ere by the spheres time was created, thou
Wast in His mind, who is thy Son and Brother;
Whom thou conceivst, conceived; yea thou art now
Thy Maker's maker, and thy Father's mother;
Thou hast light in dark, and shutst in little room,
Immensity cloistered in thy dear womb.

This playfulness ranges more widely than just wordplay. In a similar way, John Milton subverts the earlier dispensation of pagan gods in his 'Ode on the Morning of Christ's Nativity', describing how the coming of Christ put all earlier divinities to flight:

The Oracles are dumb;
No voice or hideous hum
    Runs through the arched roof in words deceiving.
Apollo from his shrine
Can no more divine,
    With hollow shriek the steep of Delphos leaving.
No nightly trance or breathed spell
Inspires the pale-ey'd priest from the prophetic cell.
. . .
Nor is Osiris seen
In Memphian grove or green,
    Trampling the unshower'd grass with lowings loud;
Nor can he be at rest
Within his sacred chest,
    Naught but profoundest Hell can be his shroud:

In vain with timbrel'd anthems dark
The sable-stoled sorcerers bear his worshipp'd ark.

He feels from Juda's land
The dreaded Infant's hand,
The rays of Bethlehem blind his dusky eyn;
Nor all the gods beside
Longer dare abide,
Not Typhon huge ending in snaky twine:
Our Babe, to show his Godhead true,
Can in his swaddling bands control the damned crew.

Such poetry alludes to both scripture as well as wider intellectual currents, with, for example, Milton's use of Classical myth, and Herbert's use of ideas from St Augustine that relate to the notion of rest. However, this poetry is far more wide-ranging, and does not turn away from the tensions of an age where, in Donne's words in 'An Anatomy of the World', 'new philosophy calls all in doubt', with the rise of modern scientific method giving rise to angst and uncertainty:

The element of fire is quite put out,
The sun is lost, and th'earth, and no man's wit
Can well direct him where to look for it.
And freely men confess that this world's spent,
When in the planets and the firmament
They seek so many new; they see that this
Is crumbled out again to his atomies.
'Tis all in pieces, all coherence gone . . .

Indeed, Herbert was a close friend of the politician and philosopher Sir Francis Bacon, whose seminal work, the *Novum Organum*, published in 1620, outlined a new method for scientific enquiry. The Baconian Method, as it came to be known, demanded the collection of data by observation and the development of hypotheses based on that data to unearth the underlying cause of any phenomenon. Bacon's work was crucial for the development of modern science, yet it also had its effect on Herbert's poetry. One may take as an example his sonnet 'Prayer (I)', which investigates the nature of prayer in a Baconian, scientific spirit. It is, in sum, a series of hypotheses:

> Prayer the church's banquet, angel's age,
> God's breath in man returning to his birth,
> The soul in paraphrase, heart in pilgrimage,
> The Christian plummet sounding heav'n and earth.
> Engine against th'Almighty, sinner's tow'r,
> Reversed thunder, Christ-side-piercing spear,
> The six-days world transposing in an hour,
> A kind of tune, which all things hear and fear;
> Softness, and peace, and joy, and love, and bliss,
> Exalted manna, gladness of the best,
> Heaven in ordinary, man well drest,
> The milky way, the bird of Paradise,
> Church-bells beyond the stars heard, the soul's blood,
> The land of spices; something understood.

The poem runs through a sequence of striking physical images that attempt to pin down and elucidate the abstract essence of prayer, testing each one before moving on to one that might better fit its substance. Samuel Johnson lambasted the poetry of Herbert's era for this proclivity, complaining that in it 'most heterogeneous ideas are yoked by violence together; nature and art are ransacked for illustrations',[10] but it is this tendency to make hypotheses by using concrete ideas to illustrate and test the abstract that give it a particular appeal. Indeed, in many ways, the poem shows a thoroughly modern sensibility. For Herbert, prayer is scarcely submission or simple thanks, but rather a scientific quest in itself and a demand for answers: 'The Christian plummet sounding heav'n and earth.' Although scientific in spirit, it is hardly cool and detached, but wracked with passionate desire. His imagery turns to warfare and baroque violence: 'Engine against th'Almighty, sinner's tow'r, / Reversed thunder, Christ-side-piercing spear', as if, like the centurion Longinus who wounded Christ on the Cross, Herbert had to commit such brutality to get through to God. In the short round of the sonnet, Herbert cycles through the contemplative, the furious, and finally an ecstatic and blissful revelation, but even then still tainted with uncertainty; it is only 'something' understood.

This idea of 'Church-bells beyond the stars heard ... something understood' points to another engagement between these poets and new ideas of philosophy. In the mid-fifteenth century, a host of Classical texts including many of Plato's dialogues in Greek became available again in western Europe; many such texts were rediscovered in monastic libraries or sent from the Greek-speaking city of Byzantium as they sought help from western Europe against Ottoman Turkish attacks. Amongst these texts were interpretations of Plato by other commentators from late antiquity, including Plotinus and Porphyry of Tyre, and Iamblichus, which had a strong bearing on approaches to the fifteenth and sixteenth centuries' interpretations of the concepts of God and the relationship between God and the created world. These ideas, often described as 'Neoplatonic', had originally influenced a number of the Church Fathers in antiquity including St Augustine. They portrayed God as an uncreated unity, the 'One'. Because of His superabundance, God creates angelic creatures as emanations of Himself, and below these the visible world of creation. God is present, though not fully, in this visible world which echoes the heavenly world above. The visible created world is only an imperfect copy of the beauty of the heavenly world, but yet, in the words of a Latin saying '*sicut superius, sicut inferius*' ('just as above, so as below'), it imitates and points to the heavenly world above. Within man, there is a spark of the divine, and thus he has a fundamental urge to reunite himself with God, from whom he draws his origins. If man follows and cultivates this urge to transcend the created world, look to the heavenly and reunite with God, he will achieve fulfilment and contentment. If not, he descends further to the created world, submitting to the restless power of the material from where God is farthest.[11]

Sir Philip Sidney's allusion to the poet imitating God in the act of creativity is drawn from this intellectual stream.[12] Sidney's contemporary, the poet Edmund Spenser, who wrote the unfinished allegorical epic on Christian virtues, *The Faerie Queene*, was one of the earlier English writers to be influenced by this approach to Christianity. In his 'Hymn of Heavenly Beauty', for example, he dwells upon the nature of divine perfection in the world above:

> For far above these heavens, which here we see,
> Be others far exceeding these in light,
> Not bounded, not corrupt, as these same be,
> But infinite in largeness and in height,
> Unmoving, uncorrupt, and spotless bright,
> That need no sun t'illuminate their spheres,
> But their own native light far passing theirs.

How, asks Spenser,

> . . . can we see with feeble eyne
> The glory of that Majesty Divine,
> In sight of whom both sun and moon are dark,
> Compared to his least resplendent spark?

The answer, he says, is to start with the visible works of God in nature:

> The means, therefore, which unto us is lent
> Him to behold, is on his works to look,
> Which he hath made in beauty excellent,
> And in the same, as in a brazen book,
> To read enregister'd in every nook

> His goodness, which his beauty doth declare;
> For all that's good is beautiful and fair.

From a contemplation of the works of God, one can transcend to a contemplation and vision of God beyond them:

> Thence gathering plumes of perfect speculation,
> To imp the wings of thy high-flying mind,
> Mount up aloft through heavenly contemplation,
> From this dark world, whose damps the soul so blind,
> And, like the native brood of eagles' kind,
> On that bright Sun of Glory fix thine eyes,
> Clear'd from gross mists of frail infirmities.

These ideas of finding signs of God in His creation and using these in an attempt to reach God and the divine have an analogy in the ideas of the Christian sacraments, such as baptism and Holy Communion. The Catechism of the Book of Common Prayer, quoting from St Augustine, describes these as 'an outward and visible sign of an inward and invisible grace'. Poets, inspired by these ideas, began to find creation more generally such a sign, and it was a powerful motivation behind their work. It was another impetus for poets such as Herbert to latch on to striking but simple physical images to describe God and divine things – 'How fresh, O Lord, how sweet and clean / are Thy returns! even as the flowers in spring . . .' he observes in 'The Flower' – but also in their efforts to envisage the divine more broadly. The Hereford-born priest Thomas Traherne, who wrote poetry and poetic meditations in prose, expressed these ideas in writing that is both sublime but extraordinarily simple:

> You never enjoy the world aright, till the Sea itself floweth in your veins, till you are clothed with the heavens, and crowned with the stars: and perceive yourself to be the sole heir of the whole world, and more than so, because men are in it who are every one sole heirs as well as you. Till you

can sing and rejoice and delight in God, as misers do in gold, and Kings in sceptres, you never enjoy the world.

Till your spirit filleth the whole world, and the stars are your jewels; till you are as familiar with the ways of God in all Ages as with your walk and table: till you are intimately acquainted with that shady nothing out of which the world was made: till you love men so as to desire their happiness, with a thirst equal to the zeal of your own: till you delight in God for being good to all: you never enjoy the world. Till you more feel it than your private estate, and are more present in the hemisphere, considering the glories and the beauties there, than in your own house: Till you remember how lately you were made, and how wonderful it was when you came into it: and more rejoice in the palace of your glory, than if it had been made but to-day morning.

Yet further, you never enjoy the world aright; till you so love the beauty of enjoying it, that you are covetous and earnest to persuade others to enjoy it. And so perfectly hate the abominable corruption of men in despising it, that you had rather suffer the flames of Hell than willingly be guilty of their error. There is so much blindness and ingratitude and damned folly in it. The world is a mirror of infinite beauty, yet no man sees it. It is a Temple of Majesty, yet no man regards it. It is a region of Light and Peace, did not men disquiet it. It is the Paradise of God. It is more to man since he is fallen than it was before. It is the place of Angels and the Gate of Heaven. When Jacob waked out of his dream, he said '*God is here, and I wist it not. How dreadful is this place! This is none other than the House of God, and the Gate of Heaven.*'[13]

Similarly, the Welsh-born, Oxford-educated poet and physician Henry Vaughan expressed a heavenly vision of transcendence in 'The World':

> I saw Eternity the other night,
> Like a great ring of pure and endless light,
> All calm, as it was bright;
> And round beneath it, Time in hours, days, years,

Driv'n by the spheres
Like a vast shadow mov'd; in which the world
And all her train were hurl'd.

As well as the signs of the divine in nature around him, in 'The Waterfall' he wonders 'What sublime truths and wholesome themes / Lodge in thy mystical, deep streams', and in another poem, 'Rules and Lessons', he describes how, on an early-morning walk, he perceives a sense of all creatures knowing the essence of God:

Walk with thy fellow-creatures: note the hush
And whispers amongst them. There's not a spring
Or leaf but hath his morning-hymn. Each bush
And oak doth know I AM.

These poets found the divine not just in the realm of nature. Even the simple workaday business of life is infused with God's presence and divine significance. Herbert conveys this pivotal notion in 'The Elixir' with the image of the philosopher's stone, which can turn anything to gold. For Herbert, the capacity of man to see God in every humble thing and action is that 'famous stone' which makes every lowly thing noble and priceless:

A servant with this clause
makes drudgery divine;
who sweeps a room, as for thy laws,
makes that and the action fine.

As much as the poetry of Herbert and Vaughan draws from the Neoplatonic, it is still closely wedded to scripture. The definition of God as 'I AM' is the name God gives Himself in Exodus 3.14, and the idea of all creatures, and even springs and trees, voicing praise is expressed in Psalm 148: 'Praise him, all ye heavens: and ye waters that are above the heavens ... Praise the Lord upon earth: ye dragons, and all deeps; Fire and hail, snow and vapours: wind and storm ... Mountains and all hills: fruitful trees and all cedars; Beasts and all cattle: worms and feathered fowls ...'. In this sight of the divine in nature, and also a particular sense of the capacity of youth to attain an unadulterated vision of God, Vaughan's 'The Retreat' proclaims:

> Happy those early dayes! when I
> Shin'd in my Angel-infancy ...
> When on some gilded Cloud, or flower
> My gazing soul would dwell an hour,
> And in those weaker glories spy
> Some shadows of eternity ...

Vaughan is a precursor of the nature poetry of William Wordsworth and the Romantic movement of the nineteenth century, if not a direct influence on them. Wordsworth is known to have possessed a copy of his work. Coleridge did much to repopularise Herbert, calling him 'exquisite master ... scholar ... poet ... [and] the perfect well-bred gentleman'.[14] Keats's great odes, 'To a Nightingale' and 'On a Grecian Urn', ring with echoes of Herbert's poem 'Jordan (I)', 'I envy no man's nightingale or spring ...'.

If the poets of Vaughan's age looked outwards and found God in nature, new developments in Christian thought prompted them to look inwards as well. Intellectual currents across the different Christian traditions, to which all were subject regardless of affiliation, prompted a heightened concern with the individual and introspection. The Protestant doctrine of justification by faith alone made the study of the mind and conscience of each Christian a matter of paramount concern. At the beginning of his *Institutes of the Christian Religion*, the sixteenth-century Swiss religious reformer Jean Calvin wrote that 'true and solid Wisdom consists almost entirely of two parts': not just 'the knowledge of God' but also that 'of ourselves'.[15] This found a parallel in the growing practice of meditation and spiritual exercises which developed across both Protestant and Catholic traditions. In both cases, albeit with different emphases, all sides called for each individual Christian to consider their own self in relation to each biblical scene and each biblical teaching. William Tyndale advised those reading the Bible, 'As thou readest therefore thinke that every sillabe pertayneth to thine own selfe, & sucke out the pithe of the scripture.'[16] The Neoplatonic ideas influencing Christian theology also contributed to this approach. In accordance with the idea that each person possessed a fragment of the divine dwelling within, and that the creation below was a reflection of heavenly reality, introspection and self-examination were a vital necessity to come to an essential knowledge of the godly.[17]

Poets such as Herbert and Donne were fully alive to these currents of thought, and they were a profound influence on the poetry and wider literature of their age. Donne, speaking in a sermon on King David – the writer of the Psalms, and therefore the archetypal poet – said that he '… was not onely a cleare Prophet of Christ himselfe, but a Prophet of every particular Christian; He foretels what I, what any shall doe, and suffer, and say … David speaks prophetically, as well as personally, and to us.'[18] With this precedent, Donne did not hesitate to delve into himself; to speak with shocking honesty, almost like a psychological analysis, of what he did and suffered personally, his inner life and the difficulties and intricacies of his belief, such as in 'Holy Sonnet XIX':

> Oh, to vex me, contraryes meet in one:
> Inconstancy unnaturally hath begott
> A constant habit; that when I would not
> I change in vowes, and in devotione.
> As humorous is my contritione
> As my prophane Love, and as soon forgott:
> As riddlingly distemper'd, cold and hott
> As praying, as mute; as infinite, as none.
> I durst not view heaven yesterday; and to day
> In prayers, and flatt'ring speeches I court God:

To morrow I quake with true feare of his rod.
So my devout fitts come and go away
Like a fantastique Ague: save that here
Those are my best dayes, when I shake with feare.

The poetry of the era is large enough to encompass even an understanding of hostility to the divine. In *Paradise Lost,* Milton sets out with the mission of justifying 'the ways of God to men.'[19] Whilst Milton was not, as William Blake says, 'of the Devil's party without knowing it',[20] he still allows Satan to express his agonised reactions to God and His creation, and explains why Satan finds relief in working his corruption. His expressions of anxiety (taken here from Book 9 of *Paradise Lost,* when he surveys the newly created earth) at moments strangely echo those of Donne:

With what delight could I have walkt thee round
If I could joy in aught, sweet interchange
Of Hill and Vallie, Rivers, Woods and Plaines,
Now Land, now Sea, & Shores with Forrest crownd,
Rocks, Dens, and Caves; but I in none of these
Find place or refuge; and the more I see
Pleasures about me, so much more I feel
Torment within me, as from the hateful siege
Of contraries; all good to me becomes
Bane, and in Heav'n much worse would be my state.
But neither here seek I, no nor in Heav'n
To dwell, unless by maistring Heav'ns Supreame;
Nor hope to be my self less miserable
By what I seek, but others to make such
As I though thereby worse to me redound:
For onely in destroying I finde ease
To my relentless thoughts . . .[21]

But if such poetry, prompted by the changes in its approaches to the Christian message, allows for these deep explorations of the self and even for expressions of dark and paralysing angst, it also provides resolutions which offer a stilling of the self and its anxiety: a sight of simple connection between the fearful, alienated individual, and the transcendent bounty of the divine. There is perhaps no better expression of this than in Herbert's 'Love (III)':

Love bade me welcome: yet my soul drew back,
    Guilty of dust and sin.
But quick-ey'd Love, observing me grow slack
    From my first entrance in,
Drew nearer to me, sweetly questioning,
    If I lack'd any thing.

A guest, I answer'd, worthy to be here:
    Love said, You shall be he.
I the unkind, ungrateful? Ah my dear,
    I cannot look on thee.
Love took my hand, and smiling did reply,
    Who made the eyes but I?

Truth Lord, but I have marred them: let my shame
    Go where it doth deserve.
And know you not, says Love, who bore the blame?
    My dear, then I will serve.
You must sit down, says Love, and taste my meat:
    So I did sit and eat.

11

But Oh! Who Shall Convert Me?

There is a teenager in my house. It is a joy experienced by many. There are also liberal deposits of unwashed crockery in unexpected corners, mounds of decomposing laundry, fridges and food cupboards that empty with remarkable alacrity, days of leisurely existential despair cast in the half-light of winking electronic devices, communication not in tongues but in the sort of lowing one might hear from an indignant yak in the high mountains of Tibet, and things that go bump in the night.

It has not always been the case that the English teenager has been at liberty to rot himself for long days at home with indulgent ease. Take, for example, this testimony given by one James Doyle to the Children's Employment Commission of 1863:

> I am thirteen ... I do not know how long I have worked. I wedge clay for a thrower. I come at 6. At Baker's I used sometimes to come at 5.30 am. About two or three days a week I used to come home at 5.30. I sometimes give over at 6.30; sometimes at 7 or 8. It was 8 last night ... I go to dinner at 1. I always go home to dinner. I come back at 2. I get 4/6 a week. I can't read. I go to school sometimes on Sundays.

Despite his frequent 12-hour working days, Doyle was rather more fortunate than many of his agemates because he lived at home with his parents. In the early nineteenth century, as soon as teenagers of Doyle's social class were able to work, their childhood was over. They were liable to be sent away to seek an occupation. They had to find their own meals and lodgings, and also activities and amusements for their scanty free time. All of this was often without any family or adult assistance, even though these teenagers might have to venture to unknown towns or cities for their employment.[1]

The fact that we now cherish and coddle the teenage years, rather than thinking them a ripe moment for the young to be sent away to work back-breaking shifts in ceramics factories, is a striking change in public opinion which occurred over the course of the nineteenth century. Yet, this is just one of many such alternations in popular sentiment at that time whose legacy to us is the general moral code of English society today.

During that time, the slave trade and then slavery itself were abolished across the British Empire and suppressed by the British Navy throughout the world more widely. The English gave up on bear-baiting, cock-fighting and setting dogs on fire for amusement. They eschewed duelling. They reacted against sexual exploitation, particularly of girls and vulnerable women. They sought to lessen the burdens of endemic poverty amongst the working classes, which had been aggravated by the Industrial Revolution, rural enclosures and rapid urbanisation. They tried to lessen the prevalence of public drunkenness, especially amongst children. For the sick, the aged, the infirm, pregnant women, the blind, the deaf, disabled, orphans and prisoners they strove to improve the treatment and life chances. No longer was there widespread indifference to the indigent aged and terminally ill being left to perish in workhouses, or those with learning difficulties being left shackled and abandoned amongst the mentally ill, both to be treated as beyond hope of recovery. In every case, there was a fresh ethic of care and concern, a new and restless impetus to make things better.

Those who dedicated themselves to improving English society were not reticent about the pre-eminent source of this impetus. For example, Sarah Martin of Great Yarmouth, who became known for her philanthropic work in prisons and amongst the poor of her town, recalled at the end of her life what led her to commit herself to the service of the disadvantaged. On a 'fine Summer Sunday' in 1810, as a 19-year-old orphan, she heard a sermon preached on a verse of St Paul's Second Letter to the Corinthians: 'Knowing therefore the fear of the Lord, we persuade men.' The sermon had an overwhelming effect on her. 'It was then,' she said, 'that the Spirit of God sent a ray of light upon my guilty soul, slave of Satan . . .'. She spent months studying the Bible and other theological works, and after a year of spiritual struggle she experienced a profound revelation: '. . . whilst experience had shewn my utter destitution before God, I rejoiced to see my eternal salvation secure on the ground of God's free and sovereign mercy . . .'. The 'high assurance' that she was saved, and that 'Christ was mine,' which was 'an ocean of comfort from the rock of my strength,' did not, however, leave her complacent. 'I wished to give proof of my love, and desired of the Lord to open privileges to me of serving my fellow creatures, that happily I might, with the Bible in my hand, point others to those fountains of joy, whence my own so largely flowed.'[2]

Martin's conversion is an epitome of English experience at the time. In the late eighteenth and early nineteenth centuries, the country saw a radical change in the way that it understood Christian practice. At the end of the 1700s, the anti-slavery campaigner William Wilberforce complained,

> It seems to be the commonly received opinion, that provided a man admits in general terms the truth of Christianity, though he neither know of nor consider much concerning the particulars of the system; and if he be not habitually guilty of any of the grosser vices against his fellow creatures, we have no great reason to be dissatisfied with him, or to question the validity of his claim to the name and privileges of a Christian.[3]

The titles of two particularly popular works on Christianity from the century before Wilberforce give a good idea of the tenor of the faith at this time: *The Reasonableness of Christianity*, by John Locke, and *Christianity not Mysterious*, by John Toland. The years after the English Civil War saw a widespread, although not universal, disdain of enthusiasm in religion as a reaction against the sectarian divisions of the conflict.

Instead, reason became the paramount guide in questions of interpreting questions of the divine. 'Reason is the only foundation of all certitude', argued Toland, and 'All the doctrines and precepts of the New Testament . . . must consequently agree with Natural reason, and our own ordinary ideas'. No one should unthinkingly trust in any personal, passionate and ineffable experience of the divine. Rather, 'Reason vouches the truth' of any revelation, said Locke, 'by the testimony and proofs that they come from God'.[4]

By the time of Wilberforce and Martin, these attitudes were changing. Many preachers, no longer fearful of enthusiasm, extolled the idea of 'vital religion'. Hannah More, another writer and philanthropist of this period, said that religion was not 'merely an opinion or a sentiment', nor 'an act or a performance', but 'a turning the whole mind to God'. Christianity, she said, should be 'the leading principle of all human actions, the great animating spirit of human conduct'.[5] The new mood, as Martin had expressed, was fixed on the deep guilt of the fallen soul, the 'slave of Satan'. The question which pressed most deeply on the mind in these circumstances, as John Wesley – an early forerunner of this approach – expressed in his diary in 1738, was 'but Oh! Who shall convert me?' Wesley felt this full weight of damnation, as he expressed in a letter to a friend: 'God is holy; I am unholy. God is a consuming fire; I am altogether a sinner, meet to be consumed.'[6]

There was, however, a way forward for those who sincerely asked 'what shall I do to be saved?' After the recognition of one's own deep sinfulness, one might experience, in the words of the famous hymn, God's 'Amazing Grace'. After Wesley's acknowledgement of his depravity, there came to him 'a voice saying, "Believe, and thou shalt be saved"'. It was not a matter of an intellectual assent to reasoned propositions. Instead, Wesley's complete belief and surrender in faith to God's mercy brought it about, as he described it, that sin no longer had dominion over him. 'I felt my heart strangely warmed; I felt I did trust in Christ, Christ alone, for salvation; and an assurance was given me that he had taken away *my* sins, even *mine*, and saved me from the law of sin and death.'[7]

Such a 'great change', as Wilberforce described it, was a common feature of this approach to Christianity, which came to be called 'evangelical'. This experience of a fundamental conversion was often one that came suddenly, in a moment, though after times of spiritual struggle, adversity or even illness. One follower of Wesley, Sampson Staniforth, underwent such a conversion whilst a soldier on active service:

> As soon as I was alone, I kneeled down, and determined not to rise, but to continue crying and wrestling with God, till He had mercy on me. How long I was in that agony I cannot tell; but as I looked up to heaven I saw the clouds open exceeding bright, and I saw Jesus hanging on the cross. At the same moment these words were applied to my heart, 'Thy sins are forgiven thee'. My chains fell off; my heart was free. All guilt was gone, and my soul was filled with unutterable peace.[8]

The soul of the convert might be filled with 'unutterable peace', but this did not mean that it was free from restlessness. In the words of Wilberforce, the converts 'dare not believe their title sure, except so far as they can discern in themselves the growing trace of this blessed resemblance' to God. Many were given to relentless self-examination, keeping diaries to judge their spiritual progress and the worthiness of their conduct. 'First, I lie idly in bed often and even generally longer than I need . . . I am not steady and punctual enough in reading the Scriptures . . . In my prayers I am idle . . . In my secret thoughts and imaginations I am far from having learned self-denial . . .' confessed Henry Thornton, an early-nineteenth-century evangelical banker in his private diary. The parable of the talents was a constant refrain. 'We shall give an account of our talents', wrote the philanthropist Sarah Trimmer, 'and receive a reward for them; not of merit . . . but of grace.'[9]

For the evangelicals, one of the very best ways of using one's talents was in unceasing charitable service to one's fellow man. The call to act charitably has always been a fundamental part of Christian ethics: 'Sell your possessions, and give to the needy' commands Christ in Luke's

Gospel (12.33). For the evangelical movement, however, it was of paramount importance. The work of charity was one of the best means at their disposal to carry on the work of evangelism. Martin spoke of how her work in the schools and prisons might 'point others to those fountains of joy'. Catherine Marsh, who worked amongst the navvies and labourers who were building the railways in the 1840s and 1850s, begged the privileged in society to 'alleviate their discomforts as far as lies in your power. Provide some little innocent pleasure ...' and then '... secure to them their Sabbaths; and hold forth to them the Word of Life'.[10]

But the evangelicals, driven by a close adherence to biblical scripture, were also moved to action by a belief in the dignity of all people. Genesis affirmed that man was made in the image of God, and Christ similarly in Matthew's Gospel declared 'Inasmuch as ye have done it unto one of the least of these my brethren, ye have done it unto me'. Thus, 'Blessed Jesus', wrote Sarah Trimmer, had 'directed thy disciples to regard the poor as thy substitutes'. Anthony Ashley-Cooper, seventh Earl of Shaftesbury and a leading evangelical social reformer in the nineteenth century, once addressed a crowd of 400 poor people in East London and told them that Christ Himself stood 'at the door of every house in Whitechapel ... if they would throw open the door "he would come and sup with them"'.[11] Each individual, through that association with the divine, was of infinite worth, and the way that the evangelicals offered charity to them was predicated on this idea. As beings made in the image of God, they were worthy of all respect. Alleviation of poverty made it easier for them to hear the word of God whilst they were unconverted. Being converted, they should also enjoy brotherly love from other Christians. And, regardless of whether they had been converted, the fact that they were each made in the image of God entitled them to be treated with dignity as *individuals*, with respect being given to their individual circumstances, difficulties and needs. This particular idea had a profound impact on the way that charity developed in England from the late eighteenth century, and its legacy is very much alive today.

Am I Not a Man and a Brother?

The idea of human dignity, before anything, drove the evangelical campaign against the slave trade. Wesley was one of the first to speak out against it in the eighteenth century, having personally seen the effects of the trade on a visit to Georgia in 1736. 'Did the Creator intend, that the noblest creatures in the visible world, should live such a life as this', he asked as he described the horrific living conditions of the slaves on American plantations in *Thoughts upon Slavery*, a pamphlet he eventually published in 1774. God was loving to every man, said Wesley, the father of 'the spirits of all flesh . . . who hast mingled of one blood, all the nations upon earth'. The practice of slavery and the slave trade, he argued, was an affront not only to the human dignity of those enslaved, but also to the dignity of those who were responsible for it. He quoted with approval the testimony of Hans Sloane, who had first-hand experience as a doctor on the slave plantations: 'Now must not the reasonable and humane nature of those who order these dreadful tortures, as well as those who execute them, be changed into devilish, who can thus put their fellow creatures to such extravagant, such exquisite torment?' The slave traders, he begged, should have regard to 'justice . . . mercy [and] the revealed law of God' and 'see that you invariably do unto every one, as you would he should do unto you'.[12]

Wilberforce, who was eventually to lead the campaign against the slave trade to success in 1808, followed the lead of Wesley. For Wilberforce, the quest to abolish the trade was also a vocation that arose from his evangelical faith. In his 1807 *Letter on the Abolition of the Slave Trade*, he declared that 'Christ has done away all distinctions of nations, and made all mankind one great family, [and] all our fellow creatures are now our brethren . . .'. Over the letter's 300 pages, Wilberforce advanced all the necessary economic and political arguments to show that the abolition of the trade was a practical and indeed sensible proposition, but the arguments from ethics and religion were its driving force. A verse of St Paul's Letter to the Colossians stood at the head of the letter: 'There is neither

Greek nor Jew, circumcision nor uncircumcision, Barbarian, Scythian, bond nor free: but Christ is all, and in all. Put on therefore bowels of mercies, kindness . . .'. Wilberforce claimed biblical authority for the view that the act of enslavement was one that destroyed the dignity of its perpetrators as much as of its victims. In Wilberforce's view, however, the guilt fell on not just the traders, but the whole country:

> the sufferings of nations are to be regarded as the punishment of national crimes; and their decline and fall, as the execution of His sentence . . . is not this then a time in which all who are not perfectly sure that the Providence of God is but a fable, should be strenuous in their endeavours to lighten the vessel of the state, of such a load of guilt and infamy?[13]

May You Not Still See Him a Saint?

The nineteenth century, which saw the abolition of the slave trade and slavery itself throughout the British Empire, also saw the establishment of many of the great national charities which still support the needy and disadvantaged today. From a very long list, one may pick out just a few of the most prominent: the National Society for the Prevention of Cruelty to Children (NSPCC) was founded in 1884, Barnardo's Charity for vulnerable children in 1866, the Royal Association for Deaf People (RAD) in 1841, the Royal National Institute of Blind People (RNIB) in 1868, the Young Men's Christian Association (YMCA) in 1844, the Salvation Army in 1865.

Except where there is an explicit reference to Christianity in the charity's title, one may be forgiven for not realising that there was any Christian motivation for their establishment. Indeed, whilst the history pages on their websites proudly proclaim the dates of their foundation and the names of their founders, rarely is any hint given of the evangelical origins of the charities of this period. The NSPCC mentions that its founder was the Reverend Benjamin Waugh, but nothing more of his religious background. Whilst Barnardo's glancingly alludes to a Christian ethic at its inception, their retelling of Dr Thomas Barnardo's story suggests that he had no more than a primal humanitarian urge to help the disadvantaged: 'When a cholera epidemic swept through the East End, leaving 3000 people dead and many orphaned children, the young Barnardo felt an urgent need to help . . .'.[14]

A closer look at the work and writings of these charities' founders offers a truer perspective of their motivations in helping the downtrodden. Eleven years before he founded the London Society for the Prevention of Cruelty to Children (which later became the NSPCC), Benjamin Waugh wrote *The Gaol Cradle: Who Rocks It?*, a work calling for children to have a separate justice system from adults. In its conclusion, he is explicit about what stirred him to work for the redemption of vulnerable children:

> Who can tell what, by transient knitting of soul and soul, has been done for a lad and for his God! One step beyond confidence in man lies the new and higher faith in God. Mutual hope in effort, and dejection in failure may at least bring within one step of the threshold of immortality. Fruitlessly you seek to see one a smith, may you not still see him a saint? Success is not the doing what one would; it is doing what one can. God is king. God is on the side of the heart, therefore somehow, love is victory.[15]

Waugh's motivation is little different from that of the earlier generation of evangelicals who saw to the abolition of the slave trade. Work with the outcast children served to recover their God-given dignity, as well as that of those who helped them. It elevated and brought society together in a Christian mould. It also cherished the individual capacity and potential of each downtrodden child, who cried out for help to bring them out of poverty to full fruition: 'It was an agony to [Christ] to see a sheep without a shepherd, an unhappy life without another life wiser and stronger to care for it . . .'.[16]

To discount the religious impetus in the foundation of these charities prevents one from realising how lastingly Christianity changed the treatment of the needy, and also how it left an enduring and profound mark on English life and culture. The work of Dr Barnardo is a striking illustration of this impact. Barnardo had never intended to have a career working with orphaned children in London. His intention had been to spend his life in China as a medical missionary. However, his encounter with a young homeless boy, Jim Jarvis, who showed him how many destitute children were living on the streets of the East End, led him to discard this ambition. Nonetheless, he saw his newly found desire to work amongst the poor youth of London as a holy calling, a 'Home Mission enterprise' in his own words.[17]

From 1870 until his death in 1905, Barnardo worked tirelessly to establish orphanages for poor and destitute children. However, the type of care and accommodation he created ended up being radically different to that which had been customary in the eighteenth and earlier nineteenth centuries. The older orphanages, in regulation and style, were more like barracks than places for the nurture of children. The orphans were subject to strict discipline, wore austere uniforms, and were trained to live in a spartan and frugal fashion that would reflect the humble position in life that they were expected later to occupy. Despite the uninviting nature of these institutions, it was a trial to get a place. Admission was based not on need, but on whether they were able to obtain a personal recommendation from a sponsor of the institution, or approval by vote of the subscribers. The most destitute were thus often turned away.

Barnardo's approach was different. He followed the lead of a small number of evangelical pioneers who were setting up new institutions for homeless children in the late 1860s, which themselves drew from the example of German evangelical charities. Almost from the beginning, Barnardo followed the principle that no child in need should be turned away. Need was to be the basis of helping a child, not whether they could garner the support of a subscriber or the votes of the sponsors. Rather than following the old model of large barrack-like orphanages and near military discipline, he took the view that orphans should be placed in an environment which was as homely and domestic as possible. As a result, over the course of the 1870s he adopted the approach of using 'cottage homes' to house the orphans. These were more compact institutions where smaller numbers of children were overseen by a foster father and mother, who could look after the emotional needs of the children and maintain their discipline without resorting to the stern order of the old orphanages. The children could choose their own clothes, visit others and have friends outside. The homes were integrated into towns and villages so that the children could attend the local school and church, so that they were not isolated from the community or widely branded as 'orphan children'. The 'cottage home' approach, aside from being better placed to see to the individual needs of each child, was also more practical than the old approach. New cottage homes could be established more cheaply and quickly than the earlier large orphanages. In such a way, this new child-centred approach, from which modern foster-parenting later emerged, displaced the old and foreboding institution of the orphanage.[18]

The Cup that Cheers but Does Not Inebriate

Although Dr Barnardo is best remembered for his work in developing children's homes, it was far from being the full focus of his attention. Late in 1871, Lord Shaftesbury asked Barnardo to investigate the causes for the homelessness and destitution of the children who came to his homes. His investigations revealed that at least 85 per cent of the children who turned up at his door 'owed their social ruin and the long train of their distresses to the influence, direct or indirect, of the drinking habits of their parents, grandparents or other relatives'.[19]

Barnardo was shocked at the finding but, given the social conditions of the working classes in the nineteenth century, he should not have been surprised. Alcoholism was ubiquitous, and endemic. A parliamentary report of 1854 found that there were 123,396 licensed pubs and beer houses in England for a population of around 18 million (in 2023, there were 39,404 for a population of around 56 million).[20] Coffee houses, cafes and cheap restaurants – now a staple of the high street – were almost unknown. The older coffee houses of the seventeenth and earlier eighteenth centuries had either turned into private clubs or higher-class eating houses, or otherwise dwindled away. The pub or beer house was often the only available resort. A witness who gave evidence for the parliamentary report described one of the many drinking houses near Waterloo Station:

> . . . it was a house very gaudily fitted up . . . I think I counted 50 persons in all drinking, and amongst the number were women with children in their arms. Upon one butt there was an infant fast asleep, and the father and mother were drunk by the side; against the counter was a little child, about four years old, fast asleep; they were serving as fast as they could . . .[21]

Alcohol, at this time, was a universal palliative for poverty, stress and illness. Tea and coffee were expensive, and drinking water often unsafe or unavailable. Pubs and beer houses were usually more warm, comfortable and attractive than many dwellings. Wages were often paid in them on Saturday afternoons, and drinking parties were the invariable accompaniment of changes in employment, baptisms, weddings and funerals, with family members of all ages present. When adults were unable or disinclined to go to the pub themselves for their drink, children were sent to collect it, and would drink it on the way home. When one publican warned a boy not to drink any of the beer he was carrying home, the child replied, 'I will fill it up at the water tap before I get there.'[22]

The proof of the clear link between alcoholism and the destitution of children immediately prompted Barnardo to become teetotal. Alcohol was a prime threat to the dignity and well-being of the children whom his Christian faith caused him to see as 'responsible beings, possessing immortal souls, with a future as lasting as eternity'. No work to support them, he came to insist, 'can ever be successful which does not place in its forefront a watchword of unquenchable opposition to the great drink traffic which sweeps so many unhappy young victims into its vortex'. This being so, he took prompt and direct action. At the heart of the East End was one of London's largest and most notorious pubs, the Edinburgh Castle: '... a flaming gin-palace', wrote Barnardo, 'with well-lighted and attractive frontage' behind which there was a bar and music hall 'of the most unenviable reputation ...'. It was filled with young men and women,

> ... a roaring drink-trade was going on, and on the stage songs were being sung which won applause in strict proportion to the filthy *doubles entendres* and questionable gestures with which they were plentifully besprinkled. Round the room were statues of the nude, which I suppose would be considered all the more artistic in that they were disgusting to decent people ...[23]

Against this 'citadel of the enemy', Barnardo set a siege. In August 1872, he pitched a large tent in front of the Castle. Here he preached, inviting others to forsake alcohol, as well as offering help to the needy; 4000 signed the pledge to give up drink. His campaign was so successful that the pub was forced to shut, and he was able to buy the freehold after a public appeal. The nudes were removed, and in their place it was decorated with the latest gas chandeliers and bright pictures of biblical quotations. The music hall became a church, and the rest of the premises offered education, tuition in reading, access to newspapers, support for the underprivileged and, above all, coffee. The gin palace became a 'Coffee Palace' which supplied 'the best class of eatables at the lowest possible remunerative prices', boasted Dr Barnardo. 'Their cleanliness and neatness present a high standard of domestic comfort to the working men who frequent them, while they also hold forth the advantages of a cosy club, with reading and recreation rooms, and without any of the pernicious drawbacks of the public-house.'[24]

Barnardo's embrace of teetotalism, his concern with the pernicious effects of alcohol, and his desire to reform the wider social culture around drinking, placed him in the vanguard of evangelical thought and action at this period.

Abstinence from alcohol had been advised by Wesley in the eighteenth century, the drinking of tea in the afternoon ('the cup that cheers but does not inebriate' in the words of evangelical poet William Cowper)[25] became the mark of religious dissenters by the 1840s, and temperance movements started to become more prominent particularly amongst evangelicals by the middle of the nineteenth century. One notable movement, the Band of Hope,* was founded in 1847 by the Reverend Jabez Tunnicliff and Anne Jane Carlile, to promote teetotalism amongst children; Mrs Carlile was led to this work by the sight of the child of a female prisoner licking up some whisky which had been spilt on the floor.[26]

In the second half of the century, these movements began to address the almost complete lack of outlets and resorts for those who wished to avoid alcohol. A new wave of coffee houses were opened in the mid-1850s, many by evangelical clergy or like-minded volunteers. In the latter part of the decade, temporary coffee huts started to appear wherever labourers, workers or commuters congregated, along with mobile coffee stalls, barrows or vans. Whilst Dr Barnardo was laying siege to the Edinburgh Castle, the evangelical writer and activist Elizabeth Reid Cotton was busy starting her own coffee rooms in Dorking. Open from 5 a.m. to 10 p.m., these offered, like Barnardo's Coffee Palace, inexpensive meals including bread, soup and cheese, tea, coffee and cocoa. In addition, they provided classes in reading, writing and maths, Bible studies, singing classes and even a savings bank where money not spent on alcohol could be kept. Descriptions she wrote of her coffee rooms in several best-selling books helped greatly to popularise the idea, and over the course of the 1870s thousands of new coffee rooms, grander coffee palaces, and cafes began to open throughout the country. In 1879, a new parliamentary report noted that the new 'coffee-taverns, cocoa houses and other places of entertainment' now rivalled the public houses, and were usually 'more roomy, more cheerful and better provided with general refreshments and with the means of agreeable relaxation than the generality of the public

* This still exists as Hope UK, a charity which deals with addiction in children.

houses'. It even noted that the public houses, under pressure from this new competition, had themselves started to sell coffee.[27]

Other Signs of the Great Change

The evangelical movement can claim the lion's share of credit for this wholesale change in the country's drinking and recreational culture, which also widely benefited its health, prosperity and general welfare. But the evangelical concern with individual dignity changed far more than the nation's drinking habits. Their work ranged across so many fields that one can do no more than give the barest outline of its impact. They endeavoured to offer schools for tens of thousands of destitute children, to prevent the sexual abuse and human trafficking of English girls to the continent, successfully campaigning to raise the age of consent for women to 16 and putting a legal burden on parents to protect their daughters from the danger of exploitation. They helped women escape from prostitution. They assisted young women and men working away from home with safe accommodation, food, recreation and company.

Their concern with the circumstances of each individual often led to their support becoming more specific and sustained; they realised that people in difficulty frequently needed continuing rather than one-off assistance. As well as helping the disadvantaged in prisons and campaigning for more humane treatment in custody, they were present in courtrooms as missionaries to help prisoners in the dock or who were being released. They were, by this token, the forerunners of the Probation Service, assisting convicts over a period of time to return to employment and society. Their help with the sick not only led to the establishment and funding of many hospitals and medical missions for the poor, but also strongly contributed to the principles of modern nursing – drawing from the earlier work of German evangelical institutions – with its scientific and devotional character. Outside the hospitals and medical missions, they likewise established the model for many types of long-term social care. They were at the forefront of developing district and domiciliary nursing, from the mid-nineteenth century ministering in workhouses and amongst the poor. They also laid down the pattern for modern antenatal care.

They took the lead in looking to the welfare and training of the blind (including the propagation of Braille), the deaf and those with physical or mental disabilities, finding ways to help them work and lead autonomous lives. They created separate homes to look after the poor who were dying and those with incurable illnesses, rather than leaving them to pass away in the harsh conditions of the workhouse. For the aged poor, they endeavoured to help them live independently in their own homes as long as possible; they were also at the forefront of the campaign for old-age state pensions, which started to be paid to the poor over 70 from 1909.[28]

Nobler, Deeper and Sterner Stuff

The evangelicals were not just concerned about the living conditions and morals of the poor. The change they wrought extended to the whole of society, both high and low.

Early in the morning of Whitsunday, 27 May 1798, two men, each accompanied by a friend, arrived on Putney Heath in separate horse-drawn carriages. Their presence was meant to have been a secret, but rumours had spread about their meeting and a small crowd had gathered in anticipation. Soon after the men had disembarked, each was offered a loaded pistol and took up his position at a measured distance. At a given signal, both men fired two shots; one of them fired in the air, not even trying to hit the other man. Neither man was injured, and all departed as quickly as they had arrived.

One of the men was William Pitt, the Prime Minister. The other was a Whig Member of Parliament, George Tierney. Their dispute had started in the Commons, where Pitt had accused Tierney of a deliberate attempt to endanger the defence of the nation during the debate on an emergency bill on naval manpower. Pitt's refusal to apologise led Tierney to accuse Pitt of impugning his honour, and the quarrel was moved from Parliament to the duelling ground.

Although Pitt was a close friend and ally of many evangelicals, including Wilberforce, this incident – although it was not an uncommon occurrence in the higher echelons of English society – appalled them. Hannah More, another member of Wilberforce's evangelical circle, complained 'What a dreadful thing, that a life of such importance should be risked (or indeed any life at all) on the miserable notion of false honour!' This was not the only objectionable thing about their meeting: 'To complete the horror, too, they chose a Sunday!'[29]

Duelling epitomised everything that the evangelicals thought was wrong about the culture of the English aristocracy. They disdained not just what they saw as the frivolity of much of English aristocratic life of the period – the hunt and the gaming table, the 'dice box and the turf' in the words of one tract[30] – but also the insistence on the maintenance of one's honour, slights to which had to be defended by duel. Duelling, they argued, was a fundamental offence against Christian principles of humility and forgiveness, and that forgiveness was the most gentlemanly way to respond to a personal slight.

Over the first half of the nineteenth century, the evangelicals not only successfully campaigned to make duelling socially unacceptable (the last duel in England was fought in 1852), but they also launched a more profound attack on aristocratic behaviour. After a visit to Eton College (where Tierney had been educated), Lord Shaftesbury complained about the inadequacy of the English aristocratic ethic:

> . . . it fits a man, beyond all competition, for the drawing room, the Club, St James' Street, and all the mysteries of social elegance; but it does not make the man required for the coming generation. We must have nobler, deeper, and sterner stuff; less of refinement and more of truth; more of the inward, not so much of the outward, gentleman; a rigid sense of duty, not a 'delicate sense of honour'.[31]

One way the evangelicals drove on their campaign to improve the ethics of the rising middle classes was to produce tracts on proper behaviour and conduct. The vogue for these grew hugely towards the end of the eighteenth century and throughout the whole of the nineteenth century. The way of life they advocated offered a very different set of virtues to the frivolous model of aristocracy.

Instead of chasing the vanities and fashions of the upper classes, argued the Reverend James Bean in 1808, the 'middle orders' should look towards the 'more substantial enjoyments which attend on probity, frugality, unassuming pretensions, moderate desires, plain manners, and Christian hopes'. They should pursue their work and callings 'without showing any signs that its avocations were irksome to them; as they are to the proud and idle. After the fatigues of business, instead of hurrying away, each one to his favourite haunt of dissipation, we should see them reposing in the bosom of domestic concord ... concluding their day with a frugal meal, and an act of family worship ...'. William Roberts, an evangelical author and barrister, wrote of 'The Christian Gentleman' in 1829 that '... however fervent in spirit, his professions range within the limits of a strict moderation ... he carries his religion, or rather the spirit of his religion, into all his ... converse with society ... his creed is written in his practice, and blazoned in his victories over pride, passion, and temper'.[32]

This constant message had its effect. In the words of one historian, 'between 1780 and 1850 the English ceased to be one of the most aggressive, brutal, rowdy, outspoken, riotous, cruel and bloodthirsty nations in the world and became one of the most inhibited, polite, orderly, tender-minded, prudish and hypocritical'.[33] Critics of the change lamented the heaviness of the Victorian Sunday, or the evangelical household where, as mocked by William Makepeace Thackeray, 'gravity fell on you; and decorum wrapped you in a garment of starch'.[34] But as much as one might satirise the evangelical ethos, the value of its contribution to the development of English society is undeniable. At this period, when the middle-class professions started to reform and organise themselves, it was from the evangelical lead that they took their ethics and codes of conduct. Surgeons, solicitors, engineers, bankers and others all banded together in professional bodies which based their codes of behaviour on the evangelical ethos. Changes in the army and civil service, which moved from older customs of aristocratic amateurism to dedicated professionalism, also followed this evangelical trend of seriousness. Anyone in public service, wrote the evangelical priest Robert Gisborne at the beginning of the nineteenth century, had to possess industry, the requisite talents for the job, and should 'scrupulously try himself in the balance of integrity, that he may discern whether he possess that upright simplicity and steadfast firmness of mind which may enable him to resist the allurements of personal emolument'. In this way, both at work and at home, the evangelicals took the lead in forming English middle-class morality, with all the lasting influence it had on civil society and social cohesion.[35]

12

A Priest to the Temple

Throughout the 1370s, repeated complaints were made to the Archbishop of Canterbury about the peculiar behaviour of a certain priest in Colchester named John Ball. On Sundays, he made a habit of lurking in churchyards around the town and surrounding countryside, waiting for the congregation to come out of mass. When they emerged, he would pounce on them and corral them into nearby cloisters, markets or suchlike spaces. His intention was to subject them to his passionate, and unauthorised, sermons.

'My good friends', he would say, according to the contemporary chronicler Jean Froissart,

> things cannot go well in England, nor ever will, until everything shall be in common; when there shall be neither vassal nor lord, and all distinctions levelled, when the lords shall be no more masters than ourselves . . . Why should we be kept in servitude? We all come from one father and one mother, Adam and Eve . . . Those lords are clothed in velvets and rich stuffs, decked with ermine and other furs, while we are forced to wear poor cloth. They have wines, spices, and fine bread, when we have only rye and the refuse of the straw; and, if we drink, it must be water. They have handsome seats and manors, when we must brave the wind and rain in our labours in the field; but it is from our labour they have the means to support their estates. We are called slaves, and if we do not perform our duty we are beaten . . .'[1]

John Ball's protestations of his own poverty were far from empty. There is no sign he had a permanent position as a vicar or rector of any parish.

Like many others, he probably had to make his way as a jobbing chantry priest or curate, deputising on scanty wages for a wealthy absentee. His pay might have been just a couple of pennies a day. Even if he had his own parish, it is likely that he had to make ends meet by ploughing the glebe land (land set aside for a priest's upkeep) himself, like the rustic folk around him. Whilst there were many rich magnates at the top of the Church, Ball was probably much closer to the 'povre persoun' (poor Parson) of Chaucer's *Canterbury Tales*, who was 'Ful looth . . . to cursen for his tithes' (loath to curse for his tithes) but 'koude in litel thyng have suffisaunce' (could make do with few possessions). In Christian charity, Chaucer's Parson would rather give out of his own income and goods 'Unto his povre parisshens' (unto his poor parishioners), than keep his wealth, although meagre, to himself.[2]

Ball's own revolutionary cry that the poor should no longer pay tithes to those who were richer than themselves did not find favour with the Archbishop of Canterbury, Simon Sudbury. Archbishop Sudbury cast Ball into Maidstone prison, and complained to his clergy that Ball was 'beguiling the laity with his invectives'. However, the laity had different ideas. One of those who had listened attentively to Ball's sermons was Wat Tyler. When the Peasants' Revolt broke out in 1381 with Tyler at its head, he and his fellow leaders determined that Ball should become the new archbishop in Sudbury's place. Given the unsettled conditions of the time, this was no idle desire. The rebels stormed Maidstone prison and freed Ball so that he could join the uprising. Now one of their number, Ball preached to Tyler's peasant army assembled on Blackheath, south-east of London, on 13 June 1381, and demanded of the crowd: 'When Adam delved and Eve span, / Who was then the gentleman?' All men were alike by nature, he told them. Bondage and servitude were brought in by wicked men against the will of God. The time had come to return to the original Eden-like state where there were no lords or slaves. The 'great men of the kingdom' – bishops, judges, lawyers – were to be cut away like 'noisome weeds' so that the common people would again have 'equal liberty, all one nobility, and like authority and power'.[3]

The next day, an angry mob broke into the Tower of London where Archbishop Sudbury was sheltering, dragged him outside, and hacked off his head. The Tower's guards put up little resistance. They were aggrieved with Sudbury (who was also Lord Chancellor) as much for his role in jailing Ball as his part in establishing the poll tax, which was one of the causes of the Revolt.

Ball's manifesto – that England should be ruled only by the king and faithful Commons, that serfdom be abolished, trade be free, land cheap, equal justice be available for all – was highly influential in his own day. It won him the widespread popularity which Sudbury so conspicuously lacked. It even came close to bringing about fundamental change in the nature of England. Two days after Sudbury's death, King Richard II started to issue charters ordering the end of serfdom, along with a promise that he would personally mete out justice to royal officials. Whilst the brutal suppression of the Peasants' Revolt, with Tyler's assassination and Ball's own capture and execution by hanging, meant that these reforms were rescinded whilst the ink was barely dry on the charters, Ball at least won lasting posthumous fame as a visionary, whose ideas anticipated the cry of the French Revolution: 'Liberty, Egality, Fraternity', or even the Marxist 'Workers of the world unite!'[4]

But beyond Ball's own legacy as a proto-revolutionary, his story has a wider message: one should not forget the indelible mark that Christian clergy have made on the development of English culture and history.

The First Estate

Throughout most of the history of England, in distant villages, towns or cities, wherever one saw a church tower or humble chapel, there too one would find members of the clergy. In John Ball's time, there may have been around 35,000 men in religious orders, and around 1500 nuns. This was about 3 per cent of the population.[5] Although numbers of clergy fluctuated throughout the Reformation, by the 1630s nearly every parish in England was overseen by someone with a university education. This formed a distinct class – the 'First Estate' – many of whom were little different from the people around them in terms of wealth, but with a higher level of education, greater leisure, independence, and bound by their vows to advocate and maintain Christian ideals and a charitable way of life that could often be at tension with the wider world.

Many did not always attain to these ideals. In 1250, for example, Robert Grosseteste, Bishop of Lincoln, wrote to the pope to describe his clergy as 'utterly sensual, given over to fornication, adultery and incest, sunk in every kind of gluttony, and . . . polluted with every sort of depravity and crime and abomination and . . . having "gone a-whoring with their own inventions"'.[6]

Modernity did not necessarily bring a universal reform of standards. At the end of the nineteenth century, for example, the author Sabine Baring-Gould records the story of a deathbed scene of a country parson, whom he calls by a pseudonym, Mr Winterton. 'What account can you render for the talents committed to your charge?' asks a visiting vicar who is preparing him for his passing.

> 'Use of my talents?' repeated the dying man. And then, thrusting his hands out from under the bedclothes, he said: 'I came into this diocese with nothing – yes, with nothing – and now', and he began to check off the names on the fingers of his left hand, 'I am rector of Eigncombe, worth £80; rector of Marwood, worth £450; rector of Westcote, worth £560; vicar of Barton, worth £300; and rector of Eastcote, worth a £1000. If that is not making use of one's talents, I do not know what is. I think I can die in peace.'[7]

Yet, not every member of the clergy was conspicuously 'polluted with every sort of depravity'. Not all were possessed by Mr Winterton's avarice. For all those sunk in the seven deadly sins, there were others more like Chaucer's Parson: 'a shepherde and noght a mercenarie'. Whilst their 'good ensample' was designed to draw 'folk to hevene', their effect on the world around them could be just as profound and lasting.[8]

Heavy Hearts in the Gathered Fields

In the Augustan age of English literature, during the earlier part of the eighteenth century, there was a vogue for creating comfortable and idealised visions of life in the English countryside. One can almost feel the indecent overexcitement of the poet James Thomson as he evokes a young couple working in the fields in summer:

> Now swarms the village o'er the jovial mead:
> The rustic youth, brown with meridian toil,
> Healthful, and strong; full as the summer-rose
> Blown by prevailing suns, the ruddy maid,
> Half-naked, swelling on the sight . . .

Thomson, and many others in polite society, were content to see the English countryside 'from dale to dale' as a place of 'happy labour, love, and social glee'.

George Crabbe, writing later in the eighteenth century, had little time for this cheerful view of rural England peopled with many a wealthy 'swain, / Pleas'd, and unwearied, in his guarded toil'.[9] He responded to these earlier portrayals with something rather more real. Instead of Thomson's prosperous villas, he describes the village poor-house: 'Theirs is yon House that holds the parish poor, / Whose walls of mud scarce bear the broken door . . .'. In such wretched places, where 'children dwell who know no parents' care', one also finds those too old, sick and infirm to work in the fields, left to die:

> Such is that room which one rude beam divides,
> And naked rafters form the sloping sides;
> Where the vile bands that bind the thatch are seen,
> And lath and mud are all that lie between;
> Save one dull pane, that, coarsely patch'd, gives way
> To the rude tempest, yet excludes the day . . .

Crabbe unsparingly describes the sight of one man dying alone in such a place, far different from Thomson's 'rustic youth':

> Here, on a matted flock, with dust o'erspread,
> The drooping wretch reclines his languid head;
> For him no hand the cordial cup applies,
> Or wipes the tear that stagnates in his eyes . . .[10]

Crabbe was born to a poor family in the Suffolk fishing village of Aldeburgh. He managed to get a good education locally and trained as a doctor's apprentice, but he remained almost destitute. Despite this, he started to write poetry. His literary talents were soon recognised by Edmund Burke and Samuel Johnson. He was ordained as a priest, and his new admirers were able to secure him a plum job as chaplain to the Duke of Rutland, and later other clerical posts.

Although he enjoyed this sudden change in his fortunes, he maintained an overriding concern for the poor. Rural life was undergoing a prolonged upheaval with the continuing enclosure of common land and the emergence of new industries and technologies. These changes brought about increased poverty and social dislocation, as he starkly described in his verse. His upbringing in hardship made him alive to the want all around him, but it was a Christian calling which motivated him to denounce the miseries wrought on the needy by the creeping arrival of modernity. Christian doctrine, he insisted, obliged those with wealth to help the less well-off. As a country rector, he himself was assiduous in looking after the welfare of his poor parishioners 'in the double capacity of physician and priest'. In the words of Crabbe's son, 'The contents of his medicine chest . . . were ever at their service; he grudged no personal fatigue to attend the sick bed of the peasant.'[11]

As freely as he gave this practical help, his literary depictions of the evils of poverty had the widest impact. He insisted that his poetry should be a clear vehicle for the observable truth around him, rather than any 'tinsel trappings of poetic pride'; it 'Tells how it came . . . That we are Men

& of the suffering Kind!'[12] This approach won his writing a stream of adherents, from Samuel Johnson to Lord Byron, who called him 'nature's sternest painter, yet the best',[13] and Jane Austen. His unrelenting realism made him a precursor of the work of George Eliot and Charles Dickens.

Many other clergy were outspoken in their calls for social reform. Sydney Smith, a younger contemporary of Crabbe, came, like him, from a modest background. During some parts of his earlier career, when he was rector of Foston in Yorkshire, it was recorded that he could no more buy white flour than any of his parishioners. Despite this, he was still tireless in ministering to their needs. He started vegetable gardens for them, experimented with diets to find those which were both the cheapest and most nutritious, acted as a doctor, and even took on the role of a magistrate to ensure that they were treated mercifully. Yet again, like Crabbe, his writings echoed like a clarion call far beyond his parish.

Smith was not afraid of speaking frankly to those under his care, when he thought they needed it:

> I don't like that red nose, and those blear eyes, and that stupid, downcast look. You are a drunkard. Another pint, and one pint more; a glass of gin and water, rum and milk, cider and pepper, a glass of peppermint, and all the beastly fluids which drunkards pour down their throats ... It is all nonsense about not being able to work without ale, and gin, and cider, and fermented liquors. Do lions and carthorses drink ale?[14]

Yet, his waspish and satirical tongue was most sharply turned in defence of the most wretched of the poor. Where a fine dinner, he wrote, 'includes everything of sensual and intellectual gratification which a great nation glories in producing', in the midst of this 'who knows that the kitchen chimney caught fire half-an-hour before dinner and that a poor little wretch of six or seven years old, was sent up in the midst of the flames to put it out? ... What is a toasted child compared with the agonies of the mistress of the house with a deranged dinner?'[15]

As for the man-traps and spring-guns that blanketed grand estates to ward off hungry poachers, he was forthright, and not swayed by any thought of upsetting the local gentry:

> There is a sort of horror in thinking of a whole land filled with lurking engines of death – machinations against human life under every green tree and guns in every dusky dell and bosky bourn . . . the lords of the manors eyeing their peasantry as so many butts and marks, and panting to hear the click of the trap and see the flash of the guns.[16]

Well into the twentieth century, there were many country clergy who were content simply to 'guzzle port with squire / And back and praise his damned opinions . . .' as the poacher Saul Kane said in John Masefield's poem 'The Everlasting Mercy'.[17] Yet, a vociferous minority were unrelenting in their calls for the better treatment of the poorer classes as they were buffeted by the economic changes of the industrial age. Their pleas on behalf of the downtrodden and defenceless in society have not lost their potency with the passing of time. In 1862, Charles Kingsley, rector of Eversley in Hampshire, took up the cause of the chimney boys in his novel *The Water Babies*. The world of the fairies, in the novel, was a metaphor for the Christian heaven, and populated with children who 'come to grief by ill-usage or ignorance or neglect . . . all the little children who are overlaid, or given gin when they are young, or let to drink out of hot kettles, or to fall into the fire; all the little children in alleys and courts, and tumbledown cottages, who die by fever, and cholera, and measles . . . which no-one will have someday, when folks have common sense; and all the little children who have been killed by cruel masters, and wicked soldiers'.[18]

Others took to the newspapers or other public platforms to excoriate injustices done to the poor. In 1864, shortly after Kingsley wrote *The Water Babies*, R.S. Hawker, the vicar of the remote parish of Morwenstow in Cornwall, condemned attempts to hold down the pay of farm labourers:

> I often think what heavy hearts there must be in the gathered fields – the toiling labouring husbandmen. They know well that the profit of all the

> increase is not for them, that they must still drag on life and labour to win their daily share of daily bread. There is not a clod in the furrow so hard as a farmer's heart.[19]

Lord Sidney Godolphin Osborne, Charles Kingsley's brother-in-law and rector of the Dorset parish of Durweston, wrote letters to *The Times* over a 40-year period, lamenting the living conditions of the working classes: 'Their wages have been brought below the minimum of healthy existence ... The villages in which they dwell have been turned into dirty undrained lanes, bordered with hovel homes ...'. Canon Edward Girdlestone, vicar of Halberton in Devon, who was known as 'the labourer's friend', confessed at a Church Congress in Bath in 1873: '... that last great day, when we all meet together, rich and poor, learned and unlearned, master and servant, pastor and flock, for my own part I feel, and I feel it terribly, that the man whom I shall fear most to meet on that great day is the labourer'.[20]

These clerical cries against social injustice were not without their practical effects. In 1784, the Reverend James Ramsay,* vicar of Teston in Kent, published a 300-page work entitled *An Essay on the Treatment and Conversion of African Slaves in the British Sugar Colonies*. Before he was ordained in 1761, he had worked as a surgeon aboard the Royal Navy warship HMS *Arundel*. Its interception of a British slave ship, the *Swift*, in 1759, changed his life. Such was his horror at seeing the conditions in which the enslaved Africans were transported that, after he left the Navy and was ordained, he volunteered to work amongst slaves in Caribbean parishes, acting as both a doctor and a priest. His Christian doctrine gave him a conviction that all people should be treated with equal dignity, and he made a point of inviting black and white people to attend his churches together. On returning to England in 1780 he was persuaded by his friend and patron Sir Charles Middleton, who had commanded the *Arundel*, and his wife, Lady Middleton, to write a first-hand account of the life of slaves in the British colonies.[21]

* Sometimes spelled 'Ramsey'.

Although some Quakers and nonconformists had written about slavery beforehand, this was the first occasion that a member of the Anglican mainstream had done so. Ramsay was frank in his description of the suffering of slaves. Any transgressions, for example, whilst the slaves were doing the hardest part of the work, collecting fodder for cattle, 'was followed with the smart of a cart whip' which 'cuts out flakes of skin and flesh with every stroke; and the wretch, in this mangled condition, is turned out to work in dry or wet weather, which last, now and then, brings on the cramp, and ends his sufferings and slavery together'.[22]

Ramsay's respectable position as an Anglican clergyman gave his writing a credibility and level of influence that was not easily available to works by nonconformists. Soon after its publication, dozens of petitions calling for the abolition of the slave trade were submitted to Parliament from all over the country. The work had an effect even before it was published. An early preview was seen in 1783 by Beilby Porteus, the Bishop of Chester, who later became Bishop of London. Strongly influenced by Ramsay's writings, Porteus delivered a sermon at St Mary-le-Bow in London where he described the slave trade as 'that opprobrious traffic, in which this country has for too long taken the lead . . .'. From his seat in the House of Lords for nearly the next three decades, he campaigned in the teeth of deep opposition for the abolition of the trade.[23]

These calls were not only heard in the Lords. In 1783, Ramsay's work in preparation also came to the notice of a young member of the House of Commons, William Wilberforce. Wilberforce visited Ramsay in Kent and over a long discussion asked him to relate everything he knew about the trade and the condition of slaves on the Caribbean plantations. After parting, Wilberforce inundated Ramsay with letters about the trade, and they continued to stay in touch. An informal group developed around Ramsay, nicknamed the 'Testonites' after his parish, which pressed Wilberforce to raise formal motions in Parliament towards the abolition of the trade. Wilberforce allied with his friend, William Pitt the Younger, who became Prime Minister in 1783, to work for abolition, and both men continued to draw on Ramsay's expertise.

Ramsay did not long survive the publication of his 1784 essay. However, he continued to write pamphlets against slavery until his death in 1789. Although his publications provoked a torrent of abuse from supporters of the trade – Ramsay described himself to Wilberforce as 'a marked man ... to whom it was good manners to say anything disagreeable however insulting ...' – his work left an indelible legacy. He not only laid the foundations for the long-running parliamentary movement against the slave trade and the institution itself, but also led others to research, campaign and establish associations such as the Society for Effecting the Abolition of the Slave Trade. The success of the movements which brought about the abolition of the trade in 1807 and the full abolition of slavery in the British Empire in 1833 owed much to the early courage of Ramsay in using his clerical position to bring the full horror of slavery to the attention of the public.[24]

The appearance of Kingsley's *Water Babies* was similarly not without practical social benefits. Its publication in 1863 stirred up considerable public concern about the plight of chimney boys, and in the following year the evangelical Christian reformer Lord Shaftesbury was able to pilot legislation through Parliament to restrict their use. The practice of sending children up chimneys was in the end completely outlawed thanks to a further law introduced by Lord Shaftesbury in 1875.

It was not the only endeavour in which Shaftesbury benefited from the support of clergy to push through social reforms. In the same period, Shaftesbury allied with successive bishops of London, Charles Blomfield and Archibald Tait, to work for better quality and more plentiful housing for the poor. They were able to secure laws to provide for the building of new lodging houses, their regular inspection, and measures to ensure the proper upkeep of rented property. They also fought against another serious related problem: the dispossession of tens of thousands of poor people who were moved out of slum houses, without compensation, for the building of new railway lines. Bishop Blomfield condemned the railway companies for the suffering of these disenfranchised masses:

> If they destroyed a rich man's residence, he was entitled to compensation, and, perhaps, it was of no consequence to him whether he removed to a distance of one mile or five miles; but if they turned a poor man out of his tenement he had no choice, he must of necessity live near to his employment, and thus was obliged to pay any price, however exorbitant, to secure shelter for himself and his family . . .[25]

As the nineteenth century went on, the Church became increasingly concerned with the social conditions of the disadvantaged. The practical actions of energetic individual clergy could leave a lasting effect. In the 1870s, Canon Samuel Barnett, who ministered in the impoverished slums of Whitechapel in London's East End, managed to secure a visit from the Home Secretary Richard Cross so that he could see for himself the 'ruinous and insanitary' houses where the annual death rate was 40 in 1000. The 'long and dirty tramp' on which Barnett took Cross through the crumbling tenements, where rooms were furnished with sacks of hay and where many inhabitants only had four square yards of space each, moved the Home Secretary to press for laws – known as 'The Cross Acts' – which made it easier for new dwellings to be built for the poor by local authorities. Barnett himself did not wait to rely on the actions of civic authorities, but went so far as to establish an early version of a housing association, the East End Dwellings Company, which built a number of high-quality houses and flats which were rented out even to casual and day labourers. Many of these still stand today.[26]

Barnett's work set an example for many others to follow. In the 1920s, Reverend Basil Jellicoe denounced the housing conditions around the London rail terminals of Euston and St Pancras as a 'blasphemy' which demeaned the sacred dignity of those who had to endure them. The devil, he said, made the slums. One of his fellow campaigners, Edith Neville, recorded

> our boiling indignation and sense of frustration as we realised how little most people knew or cared that a family of 15 lived in two smoky little

> attics with the rain pouring in on them, that babies born healthy died after a few months of life in damp cellar rooms, that young men and women were starting new families in conditions which should have shamed our great-grandparents . . .[27]

Jellicoe died in 1935, at the early age of 36. Yet, in the few years of his ministry he had been able to build hundreds of new flats for the working poor around the two railway stations, and also had founded several housing associations in London, as well as others further afield in Sussex and Penzance. As with Canon Barnett, he was able to draw visits from government ministers and members of the royal family, and his tireless fundraising – which he lightly described as a 'sanctified lark' – improved the living conditions and prospects for thousands of families over generations.[28]

The laments over the conditions for workers in factories and fields likewise gave rise to action in these spheres. In the early days of the trade union movement, one of the most vocal supporters of the Tolpuddle Martyrs – six Dorset farm labourers who had been sentenced to transportation in 1834 for joining a union – was the vicar of Warwick, Dr Arthur Wade. Wade, described as 'a mountain of a man', wearing full clerical dress and his insignia as a doctor of divinity, led an orderly protest of 50,000 people through the streets of London to Whitehall to present a petition to the Home Office seeking a pardon for the six men. The government, said Wade, should 'take the burden from the backs of the industrious and lay it on the broad shoulders of the rich . . . To withhold God's bounty from those who want is the highest treason against Heaven.' The public pressure led to their release in 1836.[29]

The same period saw the rise and fall of the Chartist movement in England, which called for greater political representation and economic rights for the working classes. In response to the movement's failure to make any progress in the face of strong parliamentary opposition, in 1848 the Reverend Charles Kingsley anonymously issued an inflammatory pamphlet addressed to the 'Workmen of England'. Signed 'A Working

Parson', it gave no quarter to those who wanted to stand in the way of reform:

> Workmen of England – You say that you are wronged. Many of you are wronged: and many besides yourselves know it. Almost all men who have heads and hearts know it – above all, the working clergy know it. They go into your houses, they see the shameful filth and darkness in which you are forced to live crowded together; they see your children growing up in ignorance and temptation, for want of fit education; they see intelligent and well-read men among you, shut out from a Freeman's just right of voting; and they see, too, the noble patience and self-control with which you have as yet borne these evils. They see it, and God sees it.[30]

Yet reform, he argued, would not come simply from the manifesto of the Chartists, but required the adherence to, and practical application of, Christian ideas and ethics. To bring this about, he founded the Christian Socialist Movement together with another cleric, Frederick Denison Maurice, and a campaigning lawyer named John Ludlow. From its origins in 1848, it endeavoured to improve the lives of working people by supporting the establishment of Working Men's Associations, workers' cooperatives (firmly embedding in the south of England a movement which was already widespread in the north) and friendly societies. These societies were supported by many members of the clergy far beyond the Christian Socialist Movement, and helped to insure members against loss of pay through sickness or damage to tools. They might also pay medical fees, or act as savings banks. A number still exist today, as does the cooperative movement. It was thanks to a parliamentary campaign staged by the Christian Socialists in the early 1850s that put cooperatives on a sound legal basis in English law.[31]

As the nineteenth century went on, in moments of tension between organised labour and the employers it was often the Church that was able to bring about a resolution. The most famous example of the time was the intervention of Brooke Foss Westcott, Bishop of Durham, in the miners' strike of 1892. A steep drop in the price of coal caused the mine owners of Durham to cut miners' wages sharply. The miners downed tools, and distress spread quickly throughout the area as ancillary industries ground to a halt. Suffering was acute in the absence of social security. Bishop Westcott, deeply troubled by the widespread misery, cajoled both sides into a series of meetings, where through an appeal to the humanity of the owners he persuaded them to moderate the pay cuts, thus bringing an end to the action. His settlement caused him to be cheered through the streets.[32] The Archbishop of Canterbury, Randall Davidson, was similarly acclaimed when he worked for conciliation during the General Strike of 1926, calling – in the teeth of opposition from the government, and even obstruction from the nascent BBC – for subsidies for the coal industry and better wages for miners.[33] His colleague and supporter, William Temple, who went on to serve as Archbishop of York and then Canterbury, made it a crucial part of his work to highlight the effects of unemployment particularly in the industrial towns, and to call for the decent treatment of workers and families using notions derived from Christian precepts.

The work of the clergy in great affairs – influencing Parliament, setting up housing and working men's associations, friendly societies, industrial conciliation – has left its visible mark on English history. Yet, for all that was effected in these high places, much more was done by others that was less conspicuously recorded, but which was no less important. The action of the clergy as a social support for their flock over time has consisted in countless acts of charity, often of life-saving significance for those who benefited. One should balance the accounts of the high work of archbishops with the deeds of a country parson such as R.S. Hawker as one that might speak for many. On cold nights, according to his biographer Sabine Baring-Gould, Hawker would worry about his parishioners who 'had not above one blanket on their beds' and would thus stamp around his parsonage 'collecting warm clothing and blankets, bottles of wine, and any food he could find in the larder', so that he could 'cheer' his people 'with port wine and cold pie'. Often he would repeat: 'If I eat and drink, and see my poor hunger and thirst, I am not a minister of Christ, but a lion that lurketh in his den to ravish the poor.'[34]

The Three Categories of Clergy

By the light of the full moon one July evening in 1825 (or 1826), a mermaid was sighted off the coast of Bude.

People who were walking by the coast were first arrested by the strains of an uncanny song, 'remarkable sounds, unlike the singing of mortal throats'. Several of the passers-by ran on to the beach, and with telescopes they scanned the rocks by the shore. Soon, they sighted the mermaid, sitting on a rock out at sea, combing her hair 'that hung in lank streamers' down her back. Moonbeams flashed from a mirror she was carrying, and for hours she carried on with her strange singing and disconsolate wailing.

Unbeknown to the onlookers, the mermaid was none other than a young R.S. Hawker, a little while before his priestly ordination. Earlier that evening he had swum or rowed to the rocky outcrop, covered his legs in an oilskin wrap, plaited a wig out of seaweed and, sitting otherwise naked on the rock, sang his strange songs, using his mirror to reflect the moonlight to the shore.

Over the next few evenings, the apparition reappeared, and the crowd of astonished onlookers grew with visitors from the villages nearby. Then, after several days, when Hawker had grown hoarse with singing, and slightly cold, he suddenly wound up the performance by singing 'God Save the King' and then plunging into the waves. The mermaid never returned again.[35]

Tales of Hawker's eccentricities are legion. He tried to cure his ailments by eating only clotted cream. He had ten cats which followed him to church, one of which he excommunicated when it killed a mouse during a service. Quite opposed to the fashion of the time he wore a yellow poncho around his parish, which as a hoax he told visitors was modelled on the vestments of early Celtic saints.

But he was far from being the only eccentric English cleric. Indeed, eccentricity was an acknowledged part of the territory. When Edward King was installed as Bishop of Lincoln in 1885, he was informed that there were three categories of clergy in his diocese: those who had gone out of their minds; those who were about to go out of their minds; and those who had no minds to go out of.[36]

This tendency towards eccentricity should hardly be a surprise, given the circumstances of the clergy. Most, by the 1700s, were well educated. After an intense period of study, generally at Oxford or Cambridge, and perhaps some experience of the wider world and other work, their acquisition of a permanent clerical position in a way spelled the end of their liberty. Most livings were rural and isolated. They may have had little chance of interacting with others of a similar level of education, save perhaps the local squire. From day to day they could act with relatively little oversight, and were masters of their time with more leisure available than most.

Such circumstances could prompt clergy towards megalomania and unusual behaviour. The Reverend John Froude, vicar of the Devon parish of Knowstone for the first half of the nineteenth century, had no compunction in burning down the hayricks of parishioners who were late with their tithes, digging holes in the road to prevent visits from his bishop, or making his curate drunk and hanging him up from a beam in an empty corn sack to stop him from leading evensong.[37]

However, they might equally encourage more harmless forms of eccentricity. Francis Pickford, rector of Hagworthingham, spent his later years in the 1880s taming squirrels. Thomas Massey, rector of Farringdon from 1857 to 1919, conducted services behind a screen in fear of being photographed, and spent nearly 30 years working hands-on with a bricklayer to construct the largest folly in England.[38]

Yet, more often than not, such eccentricity gave rise to an extraordinary creative legacy. When George Crabbe was not ministering to his flock or writing verse, his attention was occupied by beetles. In an essay on the natural history of the Vale of Belvoir in Lincolnshire, published in 1790, he carefully recorded more than 70 species of beetle that were to be found in the region. He is credited with discovering the first specimen of the forest caterpillar hunter beetle in his native Suffolk. He was also an avid collector of botanical specimens, even going so far as to write a treatise on the subject, which he unfortunately chose to burn because he did not have the capacity to translate it into Latin.[39]

There can be few collective bodies that have historically contributed more to scientific knowledge than the English clergy. Stephen Hales, the perpetual curate of Teddington from 1709 to 1761, can be credited with the invention of artificial ventilators, advances in the measurement of blood pressure, new types of forceps and catheters, the ideas that plants drew energy from light and that nerves transmitted instructions using electricity, as well as a whole host of discoveries about plant and animal physiology. He did this whilst acting as a dutiful pastor to his flock in Teddington, such that his friend, the poet Alexander Pope, said that if one wanted 'to draw the man who loves his God' he would make a copy of 'plain Parson Hale'.[40]

Edmund Cartwright, the rector of Goadby Marwood in Leicestershire from 1779 to 1802, transformed the weaving industry with his invention of the power-loom, thus managing to automate a process which many believed was too complex for a machine to undertake. John Beale of Yeovil was a renowned seventeenth-century authority on not only baptism and the Eucharist, but also cider production; his experiments with brewing and arboriculture led to the vast increase in the number of orchards in the West Country, as well as an improvement in the quality of English cider. John Henslow, rector of Hitcham in the mid-nineteenth century, whose interests ranged from archaeology to botany and mineralogy, was particularly interested in coprolites (fossilised dinosaur droppings) and his work established that many of these deposits in his East Anglian locality could be profitably converted into fertiliser on a commercial scale. He also left his mark as the mentor of Charles Darwin. Another close clerical friend of Darwin was Octavius Pickard-Cambridge of Bloxworth, England's leading expert on spiders, who described 932 new species in a host of published papers, not to mention his two-volume classic, *Spiders of Dorset*. Charles Butler, the seventeenth-century vicar of Wootton St Lawrence, is known as the father of English beekeeping. He was the first to discover, thus overturning an idea belonging to Aristotle, that bees were ruled over by a queen, and that drones are male. He not only used his observations of bees to admonish his parishioners in sermons ('Thou must not come among them smelling of sweat or having a stinking breath ... through the eating of leeks, onions or garlic ...'), but he also aimed for a complete reform of English spelling. '... Men should write altogeder according to de sound now generally received', he said, and one of the editions of his book on beekeeping, *The Feminine Monarchie* (which became a standard manual on the subject), was written using his new system of spelling.[41]

Amongst the welter of clerical antiquarians, archaeologists, ornithologists, historians, mathematicians, musicians, general scholars, artists, clock-makers, dog-breeders (the Jack Russell terrier was the eponymous creation of the nineteenth-century hunting vicar of Swimbridge in Devon), woodcarvers, plant-hunters, explorers and smugglers, one should also remember that the English parsonage house was a great cradle of literature. It is not just that the clergy themselves contributed great works to the English canon – many of them, such as John Donne and George Herbert, have already been mentioned in other chapters – but that the learned, leisured and high-minded atmosphere of the vicarage encouraged many who grew up in it as children towards literary creativity. Jane Austen was the daughter of John Austen, rector of Steventon in Hampshire, and her observations of clerical life thoroughly inform her novels. The novelist Samuel Butler grew up in the rectory of Langar in Nottinghamshire, Lord Tennyson in Somersby, the Brontë sisters at the Haworth parsonage, and Dorothy L. Sayers at Bluntisham-cum-Earith. Clerical life fascinated not only Anthony Trollope, but also George Eliot and Virginia Woolf, who became obsessed with the diaries of the unfortunate John Skinner, rector of Camerton; his tendencies to solitude, descent into madness and his suicide in 1831, she thought, echoed much in her own experience.[42]

To break through the tyranny of opinion, wrote John Stuart Mill, 'it is desirable ... that people should be eccentric'. Eccentricity, he went on, 'has always abounded when and where strength of character has abounded; and the amount of eccentricity in a society has generally been proportional to the amount of genius, mental vigour, and moral courage which it contained'.[43] Mill himself was a nonconformist, but by his own measure, the English clerical classes should not be remembered just as spiritual and moral leaders, campaigners for justice, dispensers of comfort and charity, or scientific and literary pioneers. Their habits of imitating mermaids, taking their cats to church or taming squirrels signify the English character of independent-mindedness and love of liberty in the same tradition, but perhaps more elegantly and gently, as John Ball's medieval cries for revolution.

PART TWO

What Christianity Still Can Give

13

The Problem: A Sickness unto Death

Why is English Christianity in Decline?

The historical eccentricities of the English clergy went far beyond obsessions with spiders and fossilised dinosaur droppings. On occasion, they would devote their energy to attacks on Christianity itself. One example is the early-eighteenth-century cleric Thomas Woolston. Woolston was originally a fellow of Sidney Sussex College in Cambridge, but he was deprived of his position there on account of reports that his 'mind was disordered'. He moved to London on a small allowance and became obsessed with the idea that the Christian scriptures could only be interpreted in an allegorical way. In the 1720s, he poured out several volumes of work, self-published, which argued against the literal truth of biblical miracles, and even against the gospel narratives of the Resurrection itself. These were, he said, 'Absurdities, Improbabilities and Incredibilities', and he claimed that the disciples 'unquestionably stole Jesus's Body away, in order to pretend a Resurrection'.[1]

The reception of Woolston's work was mixed. On the one hand, around 30,000 copies of his tracts were said to have been bought by a curious public. On the other, in 1729 he was convicted of blasphemy, fined, and committed to prison. His portrait was painted by the fashionable artist Bartholomew Dandridge, but he was also the subject of relentless satire. An anonymous ballad, perhaps written by Jonathan Swift or Alexander Pope, depicted him as a Mr 'Woolstain' throwing up over a number of fellow clergy in a tavern: 'Now Woolstain came to whisper him, / But puk'd full in his Face, / Till his Breast was fill'd with Phlegm, / As was his Soul with Grace . . .'.[2]

The abiding interest in Woolston's work is the fact that he appears to have been one of the first people, certainly in England, to predict that the emergence of rationalism and modernity would lead to the disappearance of Christianity. As Woolston's older French contemporary the philosopher Pierre Bayle argued, the ideas of religion would be seen as subordinate to the dictates of reason: '. . . Reason, speaking to us by the Axioms of natural Light, or metaphysical Truths, is the supreme Tribunal, and final Judge without Appeal of whatever is proposed to the human Mind. Let it never then be pretended more, that Theology is the Queen . . .'.[3]

Woolston's claims found favour with various members of the European intelligentsia. Frederick the Great of Prussia, writing to Voltaire in 1767, mentioned his understanding of Woolston's writings, and saw them as having predicted the end of Christianity by the twentieth century: 'The Englishman Woolston prolongs the duration of the *infâme** according to his calculation, two hundred years . . . he endeavoured to destroy the prejudice which serves as a foundation for this building. It crumbles down of itself, and its fall only becomes more rapid.'[4]

Woolston was one of the first to articulate what historians of religion have come to call the 'Secularisation Thesis' – the idea that with the rise of a modern society characterised by a scientific world view, industrialisation and urbanisation, the role of faith in that society would inevitably recede and eventually disappear. The appeal to scientific reasoning and knowledge would ultimately displace the flimsy and strained authority of revealed religious truths.[5]

This thesis has been popular from the eighteenth century well into the present era, not only in England, but across the West as a whole. In the early nineteenth century, Auguste Comte claimed that humanity was outgrowing its 'theological stage', and Friedrich Engels similarly predicted that the disappearance of religion, thanks to the onward march of socialism, would only be a matter of time. In the United States, Thomas Jefferson forecast in 1822 not the extinction of Christianity as such, but

* The 'infamous thing', which was how Frederick had begun to describe Christianity.

that by the end of the following generation no one would any longer believe in the divinity of Christ, and they would find many of the theological claims of Christianity to be implausible. In the twentieth century, such claims increased in frequency and volume. They were often made by anthropologists and historians of religion such as Anthony Wallace, who confidently argued that 'belief in supernatural powers is doomed to die out, all over the world', or Professor Bryan Wilson of Oxford who insisted that the 'rational structure of society itself precludes much indulgence in supernaturalist thinking'.[6]

These arguments came to a strident crescendo in the early part of the current century with the New Atheist movement, most forcefully expressed by scientists and polemicists such as Professor Richard Dawkins, Sam Harris or the late Christopher Hitchens. For this generation of thinkers, all religious faith took on a miasma of wickedness thanks to the Islamic inspiration of the 9/11 attacks on America. Religious belief, they insisted, was not only foolish, but actively dangerous: a 'persistently false belief held in the face of strong contradictory evidence', warned Dawkins in *The God Delusion*, suggesting that it was 'evil precisely because it requires no justification, and brooks no argument'.[7]

The Secularisation Thesis offers a comforting simplicity to those who ask why Christianity appears to be in decline. It paints the decay of the religion as an inevitable, organic process. Indeed, it implies that the disappearance of Christianity is even a mark of progress. The ebbing away of faith, it suggests, is a visible sign of civilisations discarding outdated and unreliable sources of authority and accounts of the wider universe, as humanity empowers itself with better and more credible explanations of the origins of things and its own place in the natural order. The assertion made by the thesis of religion's inevitable disappearance is, in a way, another facet of its attraction. If Christianity, and religion in general, is bound to disappear with the march of human progress, why even spend time worrying about it? Christianity may once have contributed to the development of the nation, or mankind more generally, but its time has now passed, and it is a childish thing that can be put to one side.

However, there are two significant problems with the Secularisation Thesis. First, if it were correct in its view that the spread of a 'rational' modern and scientific world view would lead to the inevitable decline of religious belief, then we would have seen over the last two centuries, with their unprecedented increases in the availability of higher education and scientific knowledge, the steady and irreversible disappearance of faith both in England and further afield. Such were the constant predictions of the proponents of the Secularisation Thesis, from Frederick the Great's understanding of Woolston that Christianity would last until the twentieth century, to Voltaire's view that it would disappear by the early nineteenth century, to Freud's assured, but slightly less specific, claim that Christianity would fade away 'soon'.[8]

However, this has not at all been the case. One way of looking at the matter is through statistics on church attendance and membership. Church attendance in England remained sustained and high throughout the nineteenth century. In a census held on Sunday, 30 March 1851, it was found that a figure equivalent to 59 per cent of the population attended church on that day – which might be adjusted to around 40 per cent on account of attendance at more than one service.[9] Attendance remained generally stable until the 1880s, at which point there was a gradual but not uninterrupted decline until the Second World War, a part of which may be accounted for by attendance simply being less frequent (for example, a decline in the custom of attending church twice a day) rather than a rise in complete non-churchgoing. Church membership appears to have been at a peak around 1904. The increase of urbanisation and greater availability of education did not harm the practice of Christianity or the widespread membership of churches.[10]

Data from a variety of sources – church membership rolls, attendance at Easter communion services, baptisms and church marriages – show that after the Second World War until the end of the 1950s there was a considerable rally in church attendance and activity. Other Western countries experienced a similar boom. In England, the evangelical revivalist crusades of the 1950s were the most conspicuous sign of this growth.

In 1954, nearly two million people came to hear the southern American Baptist preacher Billy Graham speak in London; 100,000 people attended one open-air service alone in Hampden Park Stadium. It was only from the early 1960s that all indications of church membership and attendance began to decline steeply. Between this period and 1984, Church of England membership fell by over 35 per cent. By 1995, it was 60 per cent lower than at the beginning of the century. A similar picture appears in other measures, for example attendance at Easter Sunday communion services. Despite the proliferation of education and the advance of scientific knowledge over the whole period, it was only from the 1960s that Christian religious observance suffered a drop, which was not steady – as predicted by the thesis – but vertiginous.[11]

The second problem with the Secularisation Thesis is that whilst traditional patterns of Christian observance – regular churchgoing, church membership, baptism and church marriage – may have declined, the belief in religious ideas has not. In 2022, a survey by the Theos think tank found that whilst around half of the UK population said that they had no religion, only half of that non-religious section of the population (dubbed the 'Nones' by the survey report) said that they did not believe in God. Of the Nones, 14 per cent said that they believed in a higher power, and 9 per cent said that they still believed in God. The view that humans were 'at heart spiritual beings' was taken by 36 per cent, and 42 per cent believed in 'some form of the supernatural'. These beliefs included 'the power of prayer' (17 per cent), life after death (20 per cent), heaven (11 per cent), reincarnation (16 per cent), ghosts (27 per cent), the 'healing power of crystals' (14 per cent) and the 'supernatural power of ancestors' (also 14 per cent).[12]

Whilst the Secularisation Thesis may well have been responsible for a part of the decline in English Christianity, it fails to explain the trends which have been observed over the last two centuries. Despite the spread of scientific knowledge and education, the adherence to Christianity remained prevalent for most of the period and even became more popular in the middle of the twentieth century, until it began to tail off sharply in the middle of the 1960s. On top of this, the broad retreat of Christianity in England since the 1960s has not led to a similar collapse in the popular propensity to accept religious ideas generally, even if they are not specifically Christian.[13]

The persistence of belief in religious ideas amongst the Nones, with a not infrequent acceptance of human spirituality, the possibility of God, higher powers, a heaven and the role of prayer, suggests that even if Christianity is currently in retreat, the capacity for religious belief remains. The rise of scientific thinking has not put paid to the need for religious belief. This being so, it would be reasonable to think that there is at least the potential for Christianity, or Christian ideas, to be accepted by a proportion of the Nones.

In a discussion of whether Christianity still has a role to play in English life, it is necessary to have a better understanding of what led it into retreat over the course of the twentieth century. What happened to English life during this period that the religion which for centuries had furnished the most fundamental tenets of English nationhood and law, culture and social life, came over the course of just a few decades to be neglected, abandoned and even treated by many with hostility? If we can understand the bifurcation between English life and Christianity which has taken place since the 1960s, and how an increasing number of people have found that Christianity no longer seemed to fulfil their spiritual or practical needs, we may be able also to understand what potential Christianity has to contribute more fully again to English life, both as a nation, and at the level of each particular individual.

The Crisis of Association

When I was a child visiting my grandparents' house in Yorkshire, one favoured way I had of passing the time on rainy afternoons was to seek out the surviving heirlooms they kept from previous generations of the family. As I hunted around in dusty cupboards and drawers, I would delight in unearthing mysterious, miscellaneous fragments of past lives

– a pair of spindly glasses like Schubert's, a beautifully made magnifying glass with a brass frame and polished walnut handle, old framed prints, a silver medallion on a chain, a silver-topped walking cane.

The most obvious, and most venerable, heirloom was the family Bible. This huge tome sat in a display cabinet under a small pile of other old books, surrounded by oddments of glassware and antique china. I had to ask permission to take it out of the cabinet, and my hands had to be washed and inspected before I could touch it.

The caution was understandable. Its opening pages recorded, in spidery copperplate, family births, baptisms, marriages and deaths back to the 1700s. It had to be protected from my grubby, infantile paws.

As I reflect now on these artefacts, some of which have been passed on to me, I realise that many of them have connections to Christianity and the Church. They demonstrate how many aspects of the lives of my forebears up into the early twentieth century were shaped and defined by their association with the Church and connected institutions. The marking of the milestones of each life by sacraments and church rituals – baptisms, marriages, funerals, all carefully noted in the family Bible – of course shows this most evidently. However, many of the other relics betray this also. The smaller volumes piled up in the cabinet were prayer books, hymn books, well thumbed, and other books given as prizes or gifts from Sunday schools, which were assiduously attended. The silver medallion was a St Christopher's medal, carried for protection; the biggest print was a Victorian copy of the *Madonna della Seggiola* by Raphael, the Virgin and Child with the Young St John. Even the silver-topped walking cane had its story connecting the life of my great-grandfather with the rhythms of Christian observance. 'He used to carry that when he was wearing his Sunday best to go a-courting my mother after church ...' recalled my grandmother.

There is nothing unique in this story. Many families across England will have similar heirlooms, artefacts and tales bearing witness to how the lives and leisure of their forebears were intimately bound up with and influenced by the country's Christian customs and institutions.

Before anything, these customs and institutions provided a moral definition and pattern to individual and national life. From the end of the eighteenth century to the middle of the twentieth, thanks to the all-pervasive strength of the evangelical revival heightened by the prolific circulation of cheap religious magazines and tracts, the English public generally defined their lives not only by the conventional sacramental milestones of baptism, marriage and church funerals, but also by the ideals of evangelical Christianity: a point of true conversion, repentance, and then a reformed life dedicated to the principles of self-sacrifice, sobriety, restraint, respectability and energetic service to others in the pursuit of moral improvement and the relief of distress.[14]

I remember the moral atmosphere of my grandparents' house from my visits in the 1980s and 1990s: an insistence on decorum, constant exhortations to self-improvement (everything from incessant demands from my grandmother that I wash behind my ears and eschew scruffy clothing, to making sure that I worked hard at school and got good exam results), a suspicion of alcohol, a quiet pleasure in simplicity, and a thrifty horror of unnecessary luxury. As I turn to some of the colossal volumes of evangelical tracts, stories and poems which had saturated national culture for decades before their birth in the 1920s, I can see how those long-standing evangelical ideals still dictated their outlook on life to the end of the twentieth century. 'The hands that do God's work are patient hands, / And quick for toil, though folded oft in prayer', begins one poem from the *British Weekly*, a Christian periodical published at the turn of the 1900s. Another tract exhorts us to

> See the temperate man entering his house to spend his evening with his family. How delighted they are by his presence! Some of the pence he has saved from the liquor vault have purchased a copy of some cheap and useful publications . . . He will have excitement and pleasure enough in his evenings at home, and, in his frequent walks abroad with his wife and children, pointing at the beauties of the heavens and the earth, and discoursing on the nature and design, so far as yet discovered, of the works of the Almighty.[15]

Such literature often depicted men as especially fallible, and women as holding a position of natural moral strength and responsibility. 'You can't depend much on father', a mother says to her eldest daughter in a poetic deathbed scene from the *British Weekly*, 'But just be patient, my child, / And keep the children out of his way, / Whenever he comes home wild . . .'. Female piety was more reliable, not to mention vital for society. 'The character of the young men of a community depends much on that of the young women', asserts one text. Mothers had a particularly heavy responsibility. For every mother 'it is to say, whether those who go forth from her fire side shall be imbued with sentiments of virtue, truth, honour, honesty, temperance, industry, benevolence and morality, or those of a contrary character – vice, fraud, drunkenness, idleness, covetousness'.[16]

The Christian culture of England in this period provided not only moral definition to the great mass of people, but also practical definition to the order of their lives. From the late eighteenth century onwards, the evangelical movement began to create a new 'associational ideal'. The congregations in churches and emerging groups of evangelical dissenters became not just centres for worship, but also groups for carrying out practical works of evangelism, charity and mutual support. Such work could be done more effectively by congregations working together rather than individuals acting alone. Around every church or chapel, a host of societies and alliances developed to give an effective and practical expression to the evangelical desire for doing good works and improving the local community.

From around the 1780s, the number of religious voluntary associations began to mushroom. Although evangelical conversion was experienced as a personal revelation, its results were expressed communally: the practice of religion became an intensely club-like affair. Such clubs and associations acted not only for the immediate ends of worship – building churches or chapels, financing preachers – but also for the benefit of what they saw as the lapsed and unconverted masses. From these early times, their members became Sunday school teachers, distributed improving tracts, set up savings schemes and penny banks. By the Victorian period, they had assumed a myriad of duties: teaching, medical work, combatting drunkenness, encouraging thrift and working for the relief of poverty.

Thus, the evangelical movement gave rise not only to the great charities described above in Chapter 11, but also led to every parish and nonconformist congregation spawning a teeming mass of groups committed to carrying out charitable endeavours. One might find 'Entrance Committees' to welcome people into churches, guilds pledged for general service to the congregation and locality, Sunday school groups, choir committees, a chapter of the Band of Hope for the promotion of temperance, sewing societies, young women's guilds, even elocution societies, rambling societies and orchestral societies.[17]

The evangelical movement made English Christianity – no matter which denomination one belonged to – an active, communal endeavour. Membership of the ubiquitous church clubs and societies helped to propagate an ethic of working for the collective good. They also, as suggested by the rambling and orchestral societies, were one of the main outlets for recreation. Church sports clubs were widely popular. A number of modern football clubs, including Everton, Fulham, Manchester City and Southampton, were originally established by churches (hence Southampton's nickname, 'The Saints', thanks to their foundation by St Mary's Church in the city). Many churches even ran dances for the young and other social events. It was at such an event, a garden fete and subsequent dance at St Peter's Church in Liverpool in 1957, that Paul McCartney first met John Lennon, who was playing in a skiffle band, thus laying the foundation for the establishment of The Beatles.[18]

The young enjoyed not only the church clubs and societies. Until the mid-twentieth century, churchgoing itself was one of the major arenas for leisure and socialising. Again, the tale of my great-grandfather going courting after church clutching his silver-topped walking cane was far from unique. 'All our romantic attachments were formed with those boys whom we met through the church', recalls one woman, Molly Weir, describing her childhood in the 1920s for a social history archive. 'All our religious observance, which played so large a part in our lives, became more thrilling and exciting when we would peep across at the lads under cover of our hymn-singing . . .'.[19]

The very act of going to church was, aside from any spiritual nourishment, an enjoyable pastime in its own right. Another woman, Nelly Messenger, speaking to a social history archive about growing up in the 1940s and early 1950s, explained how her friends would tour round different churches for pleasure, and '[j]ust to see what they were like. We would go to the Salvation Army one week, we would go to the Gospel Hall another week and the Methodist church another week, and one week we went to the Catholic church and it was absolutely full . . .'.[20]

As these congregations and church societies provided not only sources of authority, guidance, an opportunity to serve others and develop skills, socialise and enjoy moments of recreation, they were for many the most important institutions outside immediate family life. It is little surprise that these church associations also became the context for the development and expression of personal identity and self-esteem. My great-grandfather must have taken pleasure in promenading on Sundays with his silver-topped walking cane. Such pleasure appears to have been widespread. '[T]he one [day] I look forward to is a Sunday just for that – to keep my Sunday clothes on', recalled a working-class girl, Kate Langholm, born in 1914, who would go to every possible church engagement so that she did not have to change out of her Sunday best. First, she would attend an early mass with two Catholic friends, and then,

> When I came home I'd go to the [Protestant] church with my mother and then when I came home from that I kept on my clothes because I was going to the Sunday school, and then we went to Bible class at night. And the reason I went to all that was because I got wearing my Sunday clothes. As soon as I was finished from the Bible class you'd take them off, hang them up and put on your ordinary clothes. You weren't allowed your Sunday best for playing with . . .[21]

If we wish to find the most credible reason for the sharp collapse of Christian observance and identity from the 1960s, there is perhaps no better starting point than to consider the care with which Kate Langholm had to treat her Sunday clothes when she was a young girl. Along with the other women whose accounts are included above, like great swathes of the English working and lower-middle classes, their lives until the mid-twentieth century were marked by austerity. Money and material resources were in short supply, and there was little in the way of surplus. Sunday dresses had to be looked after carefully, as they were relatively expensive, and difficult to replace. Yet, from the late 1950s, a profound change began to occur in the experience of the lower and middle classes. As the Second World War receded into the distance, rationing was abolished and there were improvements in technology and manufacturing across the Western world. Access to higher education widened. Economies boomed, the population enjoyed near to full employment (in which many more jobs were in the more genteel service industries), and the old austerities began to give way to an unprecedented age of affluence. Luxuries which had only been available to the rich – cars, foreign holidays, easy long-distance travel, house ownership, other labour-saving devices – now became a part of everyday life for the many.[22]

One of the rapid innovations wrought by these developments in technology and affluence was in culture. The late 1950s and early 1960s saw the spread of not only the television, but also the vinyl LP, pirate radio stations and the pop concert. All at once, rather than needing to engage with the churches and their clubs, societies and dances for music and recreation, the affluent young had a choice. They could now enjoy music and socialisation at home with a record player or tuned in to the pirate stations, or else in another town or city at a concert. The style and choice of music, not to mention the codes of behaviour when socialising, were no longer overseen by the vicar or church volunteers. New mores and youth customs, unbound from the old restraints and morality, began to emerge. The lyrics of The Beatles' hit songs over the 1960s cycled through the themes of romantic and sensual love, rebellion against convention, anti-war protests, drug-taking, anomie, nostalgia, nihilism and eventually Eastern mysticism. Such motifs were reflected in the developing youth culture, with the rise of nightclubs, widespread experimentation with drugs, open sexual licence enhanced by the introduction of the female contraceptive pill (available after 1961), and the emergence of radical new fashions. The young, and women especially, now had a different context and narrative in which they could express their character and identity. Before, the customary path through life had solely been the parish church tea dance and Sunday best. With the 1960s, suddenly it could be a car ride to the pub and rock concert in a different town, enjoying the bright primary colours of a Mary Quant miniskirt.[23]

The new technologies and affluence which allowed the young to withdraw from the old structures of society, with its emphasis on rules and self-restraint for the benefit of the collective, were given further strength by profound changes in received ideas about human psychology.

In the earlier part of the twentieth century, it was generally accepted that self-control was an overriding necessity. Many psychiatrists, in response to the work of Sigmund Freud, believed that the human unconscious harboured dangerous and destructive forces which were best kept in check. Anna Freud, Sigmund's niece who became one of the leading lights of the psychoanalytic movement, propagated the view at this time that children who were strictly encouraged to follow the rules of accepted social conduct would do best at controlling the dangerous forces of the unconscious. This view was well in accord with the established and widespread Christian social ethic.

However, by the early 1960s, these views came under sustained attack by critics of the Freuds. Psychoanalysts including Wilhelm Reich and later the California-based Fritz Perls argued that the expression and satisfaction of the feelings and desires which earlier generations had sought to suppress should be pursued as the way to better mental health, fulfilment and freedom. External rules had to be shaken off. The new imperative was for self-expression and self-actualisation, with the prospect of personal and societal transformation.

This fundamental idea – the cherishing of the self and its desires before all things – spread rapidly during the 1960s and 1970s. Its adoption by the advertising industry furthered its reach and impact. Under the influence of this notion, advertisers began to segment their audiences into groups based on lifestyles, and to market to these groups not by convincing them that they had a practical need for new products, but because the products would appeal to their underlying values and promote their desires for self-actualisation, the satisfaction of which should be put before all else. The 1973 slogan for the new Access credit card summed up the spirit of the new age: 'It takes the waiting out of wanting.'[24]

A similar change affected the philosophy of education over the period. It can be seen in a comparison of teacher-training manuals. One of the most popular in the late nineteenth and early twentieth centuries was John Gill's *Introductory Text Book to School Education, Method, and School Management*. For Gill, education and moral instruction were intertwined. The Christian scriptures themselves laid the parameters for such instruction. Within the mind of every child was the 'image of Deity', but 'defaced'. It was the task of education to restore it. Education, therefore, embraced 'both time and eternity', and must also take a view of 'the good life'.[25] The notions of the good life, for which education must fit every child, were derived from the Bible and the example of Christ, which taught how to lead humankind back to God. From the same sources came the ideas of beautiful, good and true, which must also form a part of a rounded education. With a view to pupils being able to participate in the good life and appreciate the beautiful, good and true, the teacher had to inculcate in the pupil the ability to enjoy pleasures only when rightly ordered, and by the same token to fulfil their obligations to others and wider society. The late-Victorian inscription of a line of Tennyson over one of the gates of my school – 'The path of duty is the way to glory' – captured the spirit of the age perfectly.[26]

This can be contrasted with Percy Nunn's *Education: Its Data and First Principles*, first written in 1920, but which became particularly influential after the Second World War. For Nunn, education should not include the 'assertion of any particular ideal of life'. There must be no striving for anything shared or universal, no imposition of a standard set of ethics or character, and certainly not the inculcation of religious doctrine. The teacher must not claim any superior wisdom to the pupil, or expound the greater merits of an inherited canon. The real work of education was rather to offer the conditions and opportunities in which 'Individuality is most completely developed', regardless of any possibility of laying down any shared identity, moral or ideals. Pupils should cultivate their 'loves', but the objects of these loves were irrelevant, so long as they were nurtured to the full. The only measure of morality was the extent to which one cherished personal self-expression and a development of the self.[27]

Under the growing influence of this approach, although the 1944 and subsequent Education Acts obliged every school to provide a daily act of collective worship, most schools came to ignore this requirement. By the beginning of the current century, fewer than 20 per cent of schools observed the law on this point. The decline in such acts of worship, with the loss of associated Bible-reading and hymn singing, has contributed to the decline in general knowledge of scripture. The classroom has not made up for this. The Education Acts in force also oblige schools to provide religious instruction that acknowledges the 'religious traditions in Great Britain are in the main Christian'. However, the manner in which such teaching is done is delegated locally, and Christianity is often taught in an anthropological, abstract and detached fashion amongst many other religions and patterns of belief, rather than with a view to encouraging devotion and belief in it, as had been the norm before the middle of the twentieth century.[28]

The 1960s also saw an analogous change in the attitude of the Church of England towards its traditional theology and relationship with society. One particularly profound influence was the German theologian and pastor Dietrich Bonhoeffer, who had been imprisoned in 1943 and subsequently executed by the Nazi regime in 1945 for his alleged role in a plot to assassinate Hitler. Bonhoeffer's letters from prison were preserved by a friend and subsequently published in 1953. Bonhoeffer, writing in the bleak context of war and Nazism, considered how a religious life might be led in whatever uncertain world might come to pass after the end of the Second World War. He conceived the notion of 'religionless Christianity', in which devotees shared in the suffering of Christ by submitting themselves to endure a godless world in which there was no notion of religion. In the 1960s, Bonhoeffer's ideas were taken up and developed by other theologians, including John Robinson, who published the seminal book *Honest to God* in 1963, which popularised the ideas widely amongst the English audience.[29]

In tandem with Robinson and other contemporary theologians, a vogue of scepticism about inherited concepts of the Church and the divine developed amongst many clergy. They challenged traditional ideas of a transcendent God 'out there'. Instead, they adhered to the belief that Christ was immanent in the secular world, and that there were Christian tendencies present in all people, not just those who professed Christianity. This being so, they took as the overriding objective of Christian faith and practice to make the present world better. They tended to hold back from the rigid imposition of inherited ethical codes, instead arguing that morality had to be re-evaluated in the context of the times. They also grew increasingly critical of the traditional forms of the Church. The conventional liturgy, language, music, rituals, structures of authority, and the old ideas of the parish and congregation were increasingly treated with suspicion and disdain. The subsequent attempts to make the customs of the Church contemporary and relevant may have been done with the theological intention of signalling that all of society was holy and to appeal to the widest possible spectrum of people, but the long-term result was to erode the distinctive identity and culture of the Church, and make it appear to be more secular. With the loss of such distinction, and the relentless questioning of the value of the Church's traditions, it became difficult for many to think that there was any merit in membership of such an uncertain and seemingly evanescent institution.

During this period, Christianity went through a paradoxical change in its relationship with English society. The establishment of the post-war welfare state was, if anything, a triumph of a vision for society based on Christian principles, and worked out in the earlier part of the twentieth century primarily by members of the churches. The very phrase 'welfare state' was coined in the 1920s by William Temple, later to be Archbishop of Canterbury. Many of the ideas encompassed by this notion – the duty of service, the dignity of the person, the need for an economic system based on cooperation for the public good, the necessity of paying a living wage and ensuring that workers had time for leisure and recreation – were articulated in a highly influential report, *Christianity and Industrial Problems* (also known as 'the Fifth Report'), commissioned by the Church during the Second World War. Indeed, the Labour Party, which advocated for these changes, found its origins in Christian Socialism which was incubated in both the established Church and dissenting movements. Keir Hardie, Labour's first Member of Parliament, drew his principles of human equality and socialist ideas from a reading of scripture. Philip Snowden, Labour's first Chancellor of the Exchequer from 1924–9, said that his socialist views derived their inspiration 'more from the Sermon on the Mount than from the teachings of the economists.'[30]

However, as the state took over the responsibility for healing the sick, the care of the helpless and the relief of poverty, the Church, which since the rise of the evangelical movement had taken the forefront in fulfilling these roles, found itself shorn of another of its primary purposes.[31]

As the Church went into social retreat, having suddenly ceded its roles in welfare, culture, leisure and even apparently the maintenance of traditional forms of worship, it also found itself ever less able to enforce inherited norms of morality. The 1960s saw a whole raft of legislation that eradicated many of the long-standing legal strictures, based on Christian doctrine, which regulated personal moral conduct. The period saw the liberalisation of gambling, the decriminalisation of suicide, the abolition of capital punishment, the removal of legal barriers to homosexual practice, divorce, abortion, blasphemy, censorship of the theatre, lending on credit, alcohol licensing and Sunday trading. Over this time the established Church had to grapple with a number of new restraints:

the decline in church membership and religious practice; the increase in religious pluralism as a result of Commonwealth migration; and also the new tendency to determine personal morality on the basis of the discovery and satisfaction of individual desires rather than by looking to inherited codes which emphasised restraint and the needs of the wider community. Thanks to these, the Church took the view that it was no longer appropriate or indeed possible for it to seek to enforce the traditional moral standards through the law. It was not now the Church's function to pass judgement on particular incidents, said the Archbishop of Canterbury, Michael Ramsay, in 1971, but rather simply 'to state the Christian moral principles which bear upon present problems and to expose the trends which make for evil'.[32] The Church might raise its voice, but it was no longer a voice with power.

Society or Solitude?

It is not the volumes of Woolston, Frederick the Great, Voltaire, Comte, Jefferson nor Engels which explain the precipitous decline of Christianity, particularly in England, but rather the tale told by the relics in our grandparents' houses. The English population departed the churches not because of a carefully considered rejection of the notions of metaphysics or the possibility of a supreme being – indeed, many people of no religion still accept these possibilities – but because the sudden advent of new technologies and concomitant new ideas about human psychology in the 1950s and 1960s overturned the old order of society.

At this time, English society started to undergo what might be called a 'crisis of association'. Affluence and mobility increased markedly. New means of communication and entertainment became available. The accessibility of more reliable contraception made sexual choice and freedom a greater possibility. The disappearance of the threat of Nazism and foreign invasion made the old forms of cohesion seem less necessary, and the rise in immigration including those of different faiths made those old forms of cohesion seem more complicated and problematic. Above all, the change in psychological and moral emphasis from the belief that personal desires should be repressed for the benefit of social intercourse and cohesion, to the notion that such desires should be given free rein as the primary objective of each person, naturally made cohesion ever more difficult. The self began to matter more than society.

From this period onwards, a whole host of clubs and civic associations started to go into decline: political parties, Freemasonry, the Rotarians, the Royal Antediluvian Order of Buffaloes, learned societies, gentlemen's clubs in Pall Mall, working men's clubs, the Women's Institute, local sports clubs. No one seemed to want to join clubs anymore, and anything which smacked of the old establishment, with its notions of duty and self-sacrifice, was treated by many in the younger generation at the very least with suspicion and, not infrequently, mockery. It is not for nothing that the 1960s saw a boom in satire with *Beyond the Fringe*, *That Was the Week That Was* and later *Monty Python's Flying Circus*, with their acute ridicule of members of government, the British Empire, the monarchy, membership societies (one recalls the *Monty Python* sketch about the 'Royal Society for Putting Things on Top of Other Things') and of course the Church of England and its clergy.[33]

As the churches were, by their very nature, collective organisations with the character of clubs and societies, these new conditions made it almost impossibly difficult for them to continue to function. Congregation members, especially the young, began to seek satisfaction and fulfilment away from the churches, and as individuals rather than part of a group. Such a sudden decline could not but undermine the confidence of the churches. The effects of this included the rejection of old traditions of liturgy, music and culture, and the search for new outlets of activity which appeared to be more in keeping with the individualistic and secular ethos of the developing age. Beyond the churches, in the education system itself, the propagation of not only the faith, but even the tenets of the faith in terms of biblical knowledge and acquaintance with Christian doctrine also went into sharp decline, such that it began to pass out of common understanding.*

If these are indeed the primary reasons for the decline in English Christianity, then the prognosis may certainly appear bleak. It may appear insuperably difficult for the religion to play any role in society when so few wish to participate in the structures where it has been traditionally practised, where there is no general acceptance of the idea that morality should be imposed from external authorities over the desires of the self, and the very knowledge of the faith amongst the public is scanty. However, it may be that in the depths of these apparently hopeless problems, there are the signs of why Christianity may still be needed, and how it may still contribute to English culture and society which it did so much originally to form.

* This idea has been questioned,[33] but the practical challenges for anyone at present (which are even worse than in 2002) attempting to develop and maintain clubs, groups and societies make the thesis unexceptionable.

14

Identity: Whom Do Men Say I Am?

I recently asked an Anglican parish priest if they thought Christianity had anything to contribute to an understanding of English national identity. The reply was no more than pursed lips, a furrowed brow and embarrassed silence.

One can understand this disapproving response. In the moment I asked the question, I could almost sense by telepathy the host of scriptural and historical proofs crowding into my interviewee's mind, proclaiming the misguided nature of my question.

'There is neither Jew nor Greek, there is neither bond nor free, there is neither male nor female: for ye are all one in Christ Jesus', says St Paul in Galatians 3.28. 'And how hear we every man in our own tongue, wherein we were born?' ask the astonished multitude in Jerusalem when the Holy Spirit visits the apostles at the first Pentecost so that 'every man heard them speak in his own language . . . Parthians, and Medes, and Elamites, and the dwellers in Mesopotamia, and in Judaea, and Cappadocia, in Pontus, and Asia . . . Cretes and Arabians . . .' (Acts 2.6–11). These differences of language and tribe are reduced to nothing in the face of God's presence. Earthly kingdoms, indeed, are empty and deceptive. 'My kingdom is not of this world', says Christ in John 18.36. The Church Father St Augustine of Hippo spurned the earthly dominion of Rome and looked to the eternal City of God. Even in the best-known invocations of English or British patriotism written at the height of national self-confidence, one's attention is called to a higher loyalty than the temporal nation. 'I Vow to Thee, My Country' begins the famous hymn by Cecil Spring-Rice written in the same decade as the First World War, but, as the second verse goes on, 'And there's another country I've heard of long ago . . .'. No thought of any earthly allegiance goes without a suggestion of the heavenly realms beyond.

Even aside from any scruples the gospels might bring against interesting ourselves in English national identity, the very discussion of the subject now seems fraught with peril. One ever more popular reading of English identity is to see it as being a colonialist mindset to its most ancient roots. The will to colonise was expressed first in the unification of the various Anglo-Saxon kingdoms under the hegemony of Wessex, then the English 'internal colonisation' of the British isles – Wales, Ireland and later Scotland – not to mention the maintenance of territorial possessions on the French mainland until the Tudor period, and then finally the acquisition of an overseas empire from the middle of the sixteenth century.[1] From an identity so deeply and perpetually grounded in oppression – so contemporary discourse will tell us – no good or wholesome thing can emerge. Its maintenance is a historic injustice and a cause of shame. Better that the very idea is extirpated in the name of ending its tendencies towards perpetrating oppression.

For some, English national identity is evil and oppressive to its core. For others, it is nothing but a chimera. One school of historians, including the eminent Dame Linda Colley, argue that English national identity scarcely exists. The notion of national identities per se cannot be spoken of before the rise of the modern and centralised administrative state in the seventeenth or eighteenth centuries, by which time the idea of an England distinct from Britain had already passed. It was only in the 1990s with the rise of Scottish and Welsh devolution that the notion of an English national identity separate to a British one began to emerge in any widespread fashion, but such an idea, isolated from the concept of Britishness, struggles for articulation. In Colley's view, it would be best to avoid emotive discussions of national identity altogether in the future, and instead focus our thoughts on citizenship: '. . . on convincing all of the inhabitants of these islands that they are equal and valued citizens irrespective of whatever identity they may individually select to prioritise . . .'.[2]

Others go even further than Colley, arguing that not just English national identity, but all national identities are chimeras. The most prominent of this school was the political historian Benedict Anderson. Drawing from the Marxist idea that nationalism itself was conceived by exploitative capitalists to keep the global proletariat divided and thus stave off revolution, Anderson propounded the idea of 'imagined communities'. This view holds that the concept of nationalism only arose with the printing press and the capacity for mass communication, hand in hand with the development of European capitalism. Nationhood was a recent construction, grounded in the collective feelings that such mass communication could engender. The very act of reading a newspaper was akin to a daily religious sacrament, making one feel a deep sense of unity and communion with millions of other people one could not hope personally to meet or know, even to the extent of being willing to lay down one's life for them. Yet, such a collective sense was recent, manufactured and unreal.[3]

Even if one goes so far as to claim that any sense of national identity is an illusion, British identity (if not English identity) has been given some concrete reality and definition by diktat of law. The 2002 Education Act requires school curricula to promote 'the spiritual, moral, cultural, mental . . . development of pupils . . . and of society'. From this, according to subsequent government guidance, schools have a duty actively to promote 'fundamental British values', which are listed as being 'democracy, the rule of law, individual liberty, and mutual respect and tolerance of those with different faiths and beliefs'.[4]

When this guidance was promulgated, the Minister for Schools Lord Nash said that its purpose was 'to ensure children become valuable and fully rounded members of society who treat others with respect and tolerance, regardless of background'. An understanding of British values was designed to lead 'young people [to] understand the importance of respect and leave school fully prepared for life in modern Britain'. These values were articulated in the context of heightened concern about extremism and terrorism, particularly from Islamic fundamentalists and especially al-Qa'ida.[5] In 2011, Lord Carlile, the Independent Reviewer of Terrorism Legislation, commented that at the root of the government's counter-terrorism strategy was the assertion that 'extremism is the vocal or active opposition' to the fundamental British values articulated in the government guidance, and that such extremism bred terrorism. '[C]itizenship', he went on to say, 'excludes undermining the foundations of British society.'[6]

The articulation in law and government guidance of a set of British values, minimal as they are, illustrates a fundamental point. It may be very well to theorise away the idea of national identity, but in the practical context of maintaining a tranquil and cohesive state, there must be a set of shared ideas and notions which allow the citizens of the state to live together peacefully, and the machinery of state – its laws and its institutions – to function effectively. In the British context, if even a small minority of citizens refuse to accept the rule of law, democracy and tolerance, as the government guidance acknowledges, the security and orderly administration of the British state would become impossible. As the religious historian and father of social studies, Émile Durkheim, wrote in 1922, 'society can survive only if there exists amongst its members a sufficient degree of homogeneity; education perpetuates and reinforces this homogeneity by fixing in the child ... the essential similarities that collective life demands.'[7]

This list of British values is the only discernible and formal attempt by government to articulate, for the purposes of the education system and more widely, what characteristics are shared by the British, and thus what a British national identity might be. What is striking about it is the fact that it is extraordinarily pared down and abstract. Aside from the values being immediately expedient – they are articulated as a response to the threat of terrorism and British society unravelling in the face of extremism in the present moment – there is no wider attempt to account for how the values arose over time, their origins in the course of English and British history, how they relate more widely to British traditions, its land, life and culture, or indeed each other. It is not explained why these particular abstract notions, rather than any others, are British values, and why the British should adhere to them over any other approaches to life. In sample teaching material used to convey British values in schools, published by various official training bodies, there is little attempt to move beyond this somewhat pallid approach. Discussions of democracy might involve, for example, 'discussing how and why laws that relate to learner experiences were introduced'. On the rule of law, students could be encouraged 'to research health and safety laws which regulate industry or review the health and safety processes within their education or training institution' and, for individual liberty, discussions of 'the extent that this exists or is limited by regulation'.

In short, the official version of British identity has been boiled down to a few disjoined theoretical notions, to which any student or observer might well, like Shakespeare, respond: 'how I caught it, found it, or came by it, / What stuff 'tis made of, whereof it is born, I am to learn'.[8] We are given no more than a handful of tentative ideas, but there is no courage to offer any story behind them.

It is an unusual thing for a nation, a tribe, a collective, a city state not to possess and adhere to some sort of generally received foundation story – a narrative which accounts for the origin of the entity, and which gives some sense of its identity, character and purpose. Such stories belonged to societies and cities in the ancient as much as the modern world, and were never dependent on the contemporary technologies of the mass media for their generation or propagation. Ancient Rome told of its foundation by descendants of refugees from the destruction of the city of Troy. Athenians spoke of the founder of their city, King Erechtheus, as being born from its very earth, and claimed that they themselves were his descendants, so that they too were autochthonous, intrinsically of the land itself. The Old Testament (or Hebrew Bible) offers for the Jews the story of their origins from the rise of the patriarchs – Abraham, Isaac, Jacob – down to their freedom from Babylonian captivity. Tribal peoples, whether Native Americans or Afghans of the Frontier, have stories and myths to account for the origins and character of their groupings – in the case of many Afghans, surprisingly, descent from the lost tribes of Israel.

Such stories not only provide for each society's identity and coherence, but also its collective sense of direction and wider culture. The Roman myth, for example, in its rendering by the poet Virgil in the *Aeneid*, articulates the belief that Rome was not destined to excel in the field of arts or science (which would be left to the dominance of the Greeks) but rather that their duty was to bring law and peace to the world: 'to bring down the mighty and spare the conquered',[9] and to bear any suffering and privation in pursuit of that duty. In the modern age, the enlightenment ideals which express something of the national characters of France or the United States – 'liberty, egality, fraternity' or that 'all men are created equal' with the right to 'Life, Liberty and the pursuit of Happiness' – are abstract ideals not just conjured up from nowhere, but which are given vigour by the narrative of their birth in times of revolutionary change. Ideas of nationhood, as Professor David Cannadine said, have a 'real, palpable existence',[10] which Richard Weight, the historian of British identity, argues are grounded in earlier 'motifs, visions and ideals'.[11]

Until the profound changes in English society of the 1960s, as described in the previous chapter, there would have been no hesitation – whether in official or academic circles – in acknowledging the role of Christianity in any current account of national identity. For example, in 1948 the director general of the British Broadcasting Corporation, Sir William Haley, declared that the British were 'citizens of a Christian country' and therefore that 'the BBC – an institution set up by the State – bases its policy upon a positive attitude towards Christian values'.[12]

Contrast this with the speech given by Queen Elizabeth II to the two Houses of Parliament on the occasion of her Golden Jubilee in 2002, in which Her Majesty spoke of British values and identity in a time of change. The nation's enduring characteristics, 'that mark our identity as a nation and the timeless values that guide us', she identified in not only the institutions of the monarchy and Parliament, but also 'the traditional values etched across our history'. She saw the British as 'a moderate, pragmatic people, more comfortable with practice than theory . . . With an offshore, seafaring tradition we are outward-looking and open-minded, well suited by temperament . . . to our shrinking world.' She also spoke of the British characteristics of inventiveness, creativity, service, fairness, tolerance, and how the latter two contributed to 'the consolidation of our richly multicultural and multifaith society', and allowed this to happen 'remarkably peacefully'. Despite her own well-attested strong Christian belief, this reference to Britain as a 'multifaith' society was the only allusion she was at liberty to make to the role of any religion in this most formal statement of national identity, and how it might have shaped the values she identified as British.[13]

It is instructive that Her Late Majesty, in the absence of referring to the role of Christianity in creating the national values she described, felt compelled to give some account of their origins – their existence, she suggested, came from Britain's place as an 'offshore, seafaring' location. This nod to giving some sort of explanation for the origin of such values returns to highlight the problem that unless they have a deep foundation grounded in historical circumstances, they are unlikely to be generally or durably accepted. They exist rather as airy untethered abstracts, liable to be swept away and replaced by changing fashions and the pressures of the moment. If nothing makes tolerance, service, democracy or the rule of law into British values besides the proclamations of government or the cultural elite of the time, what is there to hold them in place?

Indeed, there are many indications that these values, vaunted as British, are altogether in decline. For example, regarding tolerance, a 2022 survey by the Higher Education Policy Institute found that, in comparison to a similar 2016 survey, undergraduates were ever more intolerant of those with opposing viewpoints.[14] This included 39 per cent of students believing that student unions 'should ban all speakers that cause offence to some students' (up from 16 per cent in 2016); 36 per cent believed that academics should be fired if they 'teach material that heavily offends some students' (again more than doubling from 2016), and nearly a quarter believed that some mainstream political parties should be banned from speaking at universities. Only a third of undergraduates agreed that in university libraries 'all resources should be included for the purpose of academic study, regardless of content'. As for the idea of service, surveys by the British government and the National Council for Voluntary Organisations in 2022 and 2023 have found that over the previous decade, formal volunteering declined by about 50 per cent.[15] The picture is little better for democracy as a British ideal. A survey conducted by Royal Holloway, University of London, in the run-up to the July 2024 UK general election found that around half of all young people aged 16–21 were disaffected with how democracy works in the UK, and a 2022 YouGov survey found that 55 per cent of young adults said that democracy 'served them badly'.[16] Even the very idea of taking pride in national identity is in decline. In 2018, a survey by YouGov found that only 45 per cent of 18–24-year-olds felt pride in their English identity. This compares to 72 per cent in the over-65s.[17]

An objective survey of English history cannot deny the fundamental role played by Christianity in the development of national institutions, culture and identity. Christianity conjured forth the very idea of English nationhood, and shaped its notions of kingship, law and the rule of law, education, literature, language, art, music and time. It is from the trauma of the Reformation and the Civil War that came the English tendencies towards moderation, as well as tolerance in religion – not just towards different forms of Christian practice, but even a developing openness to the practice of non-Christian faiths. English Christianity is deep in the foundations of contemporary party politics: the seventeenth-century division between High Church Anglicans and dissenters generated the split between the Tories and the Whigs, and Christian nonconformism was a strong influence in development of the Labour Party. It is from the promptings of the evangelical revival that many of the ethical codes came which have (despite the contemporary shifting of mores) underpinned the nation's politics, civil service, the financial world and the City of London, and its established professions. It was also responsible for the emergence of the national ethic of charity and service, especially thanks to the fundamental and inalienable dignity which it assigned to every person as being made in the image of God.

Christianity, therefore, must form a grand part of any overarching narrative of English national identity. It is an intrinsic part of the national story. It is only with an understanding of the scriptures, doctrines and history of Christianity that one can grasp a coherent, integrated and holistic sense of not only national values and their origins, but also English institutions and the inherited body of English culture. It is from the impetus of Christian faith that these values developed, and that much of the culture, ethics and mechanisms of social cohesion on which English society has been reliant have come. If these ethics, national values or mechanisms of cohesion appear to be in retreat at present, it would be not unreasonable to say that the decay of a shared understanding of Christianity, their general foundation, has played a significant part in such a decline.

This decay of a shared understanding of Christianity, as was discussed in the previous chapter, came not through a grand and principled rejection of the faith based on rational or scientific objections to its doctrine. Rather, it came about partly from the 1960s collapse of the social networks around churches which offered an arena for education about the faith and a place to enact its works, followed by a consequent collapse of confidence in national institutions to teach or proclaim the Christian faith as a normative part of English life and social practice. In an England where church attendance was in sharp decline, and ever more citizens from migrant backgrounds adhered to non-Christian faiths, the view took hold that the state had to be secularised. English identity and Christian practice began to drift apart, and the subsequent withdrawal of state support for the faith hastened its retreat, and – by the logic of a vicious cycle – further justified the notion that Christianity, as an ever more marginal belief, was irrelevant and unworthy of being counted a part of English identity.[18]

It is in this development that there is a fundamental flaw. Even if the numbers of practising Christians in English society are in decline, and even if there is an increasing number of migrants from other countries who do not adhere to the Christian faith, this does not take away from the fact that Christianity remains a part of English national identity, because of the role it has played in creating the institutions, culture, ethics and values of which all people in the country, to varying extents, are beneficiaries. Belief in Christianity may not be universal, but in all things English, it remains a universal presence.

This being so, it should not be wrong, especially in the world of education or the institutions of state, to incorporate Christianity into received accounts of English identity, where there is now little more than a void. An understanding of the tenets of Christianity should be seen not as a burden, a useless and outdated folly, but as a right and a benefit, regardless of whether one is a practising Christian or otherwise. A knowledge of Christianity gives an insight into the origins of English values, institutions and culture which might otherwise remain inexplicable and opaque. It illuminates how they are part of a more coherent whole. It demonstrates how, in the achievements wrought by England through Christian inspiration – the best of its culture and laws, the abolition of the slave trade, the countless acts of self-sacrifice and charity provoked by the Christian conviction of the dignity of every person – there may be cause for pride rather than unremitting shame in the idea of Englishness. It shows the possibility of an English identity which is not bound by ethnic descent; indeed, in the universalising tendencies of the religion, this knowledge even offers a way to negotiate between a national identity and supranational ideas of human belonging. Within England, regardless of one's class or descent, to offer knowledge of Christianity in England is to offer a means of navigating English culture and institutions which many might not otherwise possess: it is an act of inclusion, and makes possible stability in a situation of aimless and unrestrained change. Regardless of whether one accepts the faith, a knowledge of England's Christian background provides a more stable and continuous sense of connection with the culture of the past, and how this culture and identity can develop in the face of modernity whilst still retaining their fundamental essence.

15

Spiritual Space

A Voice in the Modern Wilderness

There are always moments from one's schooldays which stick indelibly in the memory – fragments which, either sublime or ridiculous, resist the tide of time and forgetfulness and refuse to go into dark oblivion. One recalls with a sense of divine justice the instant our Greek teacher's chair collapsed under him after he had quite unfairly berated us for doing no work before A-levels, or the time he excused himself for being late to another lesson with the explanation: 'I'm having trouble with chronic diarrhoea . . .' (his aged Labrador, not himself, he later explained).

One comment of greater metaphysical significance has always hung in my memory. It came in a GCSE biology lesson. Our teacher was a walrus-moustachioed fitness fanatic whose main topic of conversation was the Tour de France champion Miguel Induráin. When he departed from this perennial subject to focus momentarily on the GCSE syllabus, specifically the double-helix structure of DNA, there was a lesson where, having drawn his sketch of the complex molecule on the whiteboard, he stared at it sagely before turning back to the class and pronouncing his judgement with a grave nod and a slowly wagging finger: 'Ah yuh, water . . . and some chemicals. That's all you are. That's . . . *all* . . . *you* . . . *are*.'

I remember, as I sat in the front row of the biology lab, my sudden rising sense of indignant discomfort as he made this pronouncement. It was not just that this teacher presumed, in a very conscious and forthright way, to mock at and exclude the very possibility of any spiritual component to human life, to rail from a position of authority at the idea, as expressed by John Donne four centuries ago, that each of us might be 'a little world made cunningly / Of elements and an angelic sprite . . .'.[1] My indignance came also from the fact that this statement was made as if *ex cathedra*, without any desire for or expectation of contradiction. Indeed, in the pause that followed I summoned up a voice to challenge what he said, but was shushed and the lesson moved on. There was no room in the class for another point of view.

This one-sided exchange has taken on a somewhat nightmarish quality in my memory. It is not so much that the recollection of it brings in its train the sinister surroundings of the school biology labs, with their large collections of stuffed Victorian animals, fume cupboards, incubators and posters of how to lower one's resting heart rate to 28 beats per minute like Miguel Induráin, but rather that the whole incident prefigured in microcosm a deep and emerging tendency in modern society.

There is an overwhelming trend in this age to what the American historian Professor Jerry Muller has called the 'metric fixation'. The eminent British psychiatrist Professor Iain McGilchrist would call it 'left-brain thinking'.[2] Governance, industry, commerce, education, medicine, artistic creativity, human relationships and even personal satisfaction: all are now predominantly rated not by broad human critical judgement, not by the considerations of what in them might be ineffable or at least fuzzy – excellence, beauty, wisdom, justice, joy, morality, sublimity, sanctity – but only by what of them can be numerically measured. In schools and universities, primacy is given to exam results, league tables and the income of graduates rather than any notion of whether a student has experienced inspiration, or gained a deeper understanding of culture. Academic papers are rated (and funding accordingly allocated to university departments) not on the basis of their insight, but on their 'impact' – the prominence of the journal in which they are published, and the number of citations they receive. Online news articles are rewarded not for seeking out the truth but the number of clicks they amass, and every snippet of online conversation through social media is rated with likes.

Statistics and visible quantities are king. Little consideration is given to 'things unseen'. The objectives of all activities are consequently distorted as all effort is concentrated on manipulating their numerically measurable parts, rather than judging their outcomes as a whole. Exam cramming drives out deep engagement with school texts. Clickbait and listicles oust proper news. Public discourse fills with rage in the hunt for followers and engagement. Governments claim success when they have increased the figures for gross domestic product, regardless of whether the lives of the population have been made any better as a whole.

As with my biology classroom, it is ever harder to find a space to challenge the metric fixation or left-brained thinking behind this consensus in the political and public realm. Students must be directed towards STEM subjects, as these bring the most immediate tangible financial reward; the arts, humanities, music can be allowed to decline, no matter what immeasurable solace they bring to the students or wider benefits to society. In new buildings, the search for profit edges out the need for beauty, individuality or a reflection of a sense of place. In the sphere of human interaction – the building of communities, the development of friendship and even love – the efficiencies of technology and online communication have been allowed to seize control of the basic substance of relationships, leaving many of our personal dealings now feeling abstracted and denuded of broader and more nourishing complex substance. In all of these spheres and more, it is harder to argue for the value of the immeasurable when such deference is given to material and visible quantity.

The presence of Christianity in England offers a constitutional antidote to the ever-increasing consensus of the left-brained, metrically fixated consensus. It provides a protected, sacred space from which one can contradict and work against the constant refrain of the measurable, material world saying 'that's all you are'. The many statements of scripture – 'The Word was made flesh' (John 1.14); 'My kingdom is not of this world' (John 18.36); 'Man shall not live by bread alone' (Matthew 4.4) – present the cultural and spiritual grounds for a sustained critique of the dehumanising excesses of modernity. Christianity embeds in our national life a vital diversity of fundamental views.

On account of its position as the established faith, with – as continues to be one of the avowed aims of the Church of England – a 'presence in every community', Christianity has the capacity, first and foremost, to use this differing, spiritual viewpoint to offer practical support and solace to those for whom their material situation or wider life is a struggle. The spiritual space of Christianity continues to be a very real refuge in times of agony or trouble, and signals to all their fundamental value, regardless of the temporal judgement of society. The mere presence of thousands of church buildings, open daily for all comers to enter, sit and contemplate with no obligation on them to believe or think, or indeed buy anything, manifests this idea at its most basic. One chaplain said to me of his chapel, set within a historic and busy London institution:

> The presence of the [chapel] as a space within the precincts ... is an important thing. It is a visible 'statement', if you will, making clear the availability of the spiritual in the midst of daily life and quotidian concerns. People come into the church for all sorts of reasons besides services, whether to enjoy music or concerts, or just to visit and seek peace and quiet from a sacred space, where prayer has been valid as T.S. Eliot put it. The church is open to everyone, offering spiritual solace to anyone who needs it regardless of whether they subscribe to the Christian faith.

Spirituality, as one senior Anglican cleric commented to me, serves to confer a worth on people and communities, and the very church buildings perform this act by their simply being amongst the people and open to them, perhaps simply by the eloquence of their architecture and the collective memory of their meaning even if they no longer host the liturgy and services. 'Some years ago', he commented,

> I was involved in reviewing Canon Law as it pertained to redundant church buildings – and it was clear how passionately local (at any rate, rural)

communities wanted to see their building preserved, almost regardless of its actual use. Conversely, a church going to rack and ruin was seen as a profound offence and a symbol that the whole community was worthless.

Such spiritual space is also created by the practical daily work of thousands of clergy and volunteers ministering in parishes and chaplaincies throughout the country. The value of their work is not just the offer of a universal ministry to all in England, regardless of their faith or background, and that such ministry (following the example of Christ) is especially offered to those in distress – the bereaved, the dying, the sick, prisoners, the lonely, the outcast or those under heavy burdens of responsibility. It is that the character of this ministry contributes to both its recipients and national life something that is difficult to find elsewhere. As with the buildings, the contribution lies in a recognition of the worth of each person ministered to, which acknowledges their individual spiritual value and spiritual needs – things not tangible in a world where everything is increasingly measured by numbers and systems.[3]

It also, as another person who had worked in the armed services commented to me, is distinctive in that those in such ministry answer spiritually to an authority entirely outside the ordinary command structure or immediate temporal situation. 'The chaplain's life is to serve God, not the system or themselves – that is why they can speak truth to power and be the best person to be "a friend and advisor to all". The only guarantee that they are going to serve everyone is because they are serving God.' As for plans to introduce secular chaplains, he remarked 'Why bother going to a civvy in our uniform just because he's a friendly bloke? How is that distinctive to the ordinary secular structure of the forces, compared to a chaplain who believes in God?'

As one former hospital chaplain who had several years of experience in mental health wards put it to me, the patients she worked with were getting treatment, but 'there was something they weren't getting from the medical model'. Regardless of whether they were mentally unwell or had committed serious crimes, the ministry dealt in an acknowledgement that they were still human beings who needed the value of their lives and their stories to be understood, and to be received with love and grace. Such ministry might be manifest in the most simple ways: being available to stop and talk regardless of the timetables and pressures of hospital life; to listen without taking notes or making judgements; and to offer 'spiritual conversation' – a response from a spiritual perspective to enable people to consider 'how might they see themselves differently in the light of where God' might be with regard to their situation. The spiritual perspective brought something even to those without faith: 'the non-religious recognised something about the person who has faith ... they often seemed to want to borrow some of that faith'.

Yet such ministry, with its spiritual perspective, is equally available for those in positions of power, who, by the nature of their work, are weighed down with difficult or even agonising choices in the course of their duty. One priest who ministers in London's legal district told me that lawyers will certainly come to them in the church

> for guidance and support in the midst of stress or anxiety arising from their work whether at the Bar or on the bench of their very demanding work. This may raise difficult questions of ethics, sometimes touching on life and death, and there is the undoubted stress of being involved with people who are suffering in some terrible situations ... We are certainly not the only resort for those in the Inns who seek support, but we are distinct from secular counsellors. We can relate the problems and questions brought to us with the broader ideas of Christian ethics and behaviour, drawing on the example of Christ and the apostles. This being so, we can assist those in the legal profession who want to think more profoundly about their professional as well as personal lives and the contexts in which those lives are lived as well as understanding ideas about justice and fairness.

Where Christianity, thanks to its established status, still retains an active presence in the structures of state and government, its effects – as Walter Bagehot said of the English Constitution more widely – are both dignified and efficient.[4] For the former, Christianity continues to find a place in the daily and regular rituals of various national institutions. Regular services aboard Royal Navy ships and submarines are mandated by law – times which, one naval officer told me, have extraordinary value for service personnel regardless of their faith as being protected from distraction, and a comfort on which people 'often fall back when the chips are down'. In Parliament and local councils, every session and meeting begin with prayers. In the House of Commons, prayers are known to have been in regular use at the start of each day since at least 1558, if not earlier. Following recent calls for the practice to be ended, several members supported a motion in their favour, saying that they provided 'a time for reflection, perspective and calm ahead of the important work of the House . . .'.[5]

The Speaker's Chaplain, the Venerable Tricia Hillas, remarked to the press that many members would see their abolition as a real loss:

> The thing that people talk about most is, when there is so much demand on people and there is very little time for pause, that in itself, no matter actually what faith someone is – people of a range of faiths have argued for this – that actually having that moment is really significant, before the hustle and bustle . . . And actually, as I come out (of the chamber), often people will say 'Thank you for that' or 'Thank you for that piece of scripture', which is quite remarkable.[6]

Indeed, the prayers, which call for the government and Parliament never to 'lead the nation wrongly through love of power, desire to please, or unworthy ideals' but rather 'laying aside all private interests and prejudices [to] keep in mind their responsibility to seek to improve the condition of all mankind', serve to bring to mind a sanctified ideal of conduct and commonality that transcends party differences at the beginning of the parliamentary sitting, which might otherwise struggle to be recalled amongst the stress, distractions and temptations of day-to-day business.

Yet it is the fact that the Church of England still retains a formal place in Parliament, with 26 of its bishops given the right to speak and vote in the House of Lords, which may be seen as the most efficient part of Christianity's constitutional presence. It is perhaps this, more than anything else, which embeds a diversity of viewpoints in English public discourse. As one bishop, speaking anonymously, observed in a 2024 study on the role that they play in the House of Lords, whilst they could comment on social issues regardless of their constitutional position, 'if the bishops were taken away from the Lords they would be ignored . . . The presence of the bishops affects perceptions of the state. Government is answerable to a higher authority.'[7]

The bishops in the House of Lords are some of the few contributors to parliamentary debate – aside from the cross-benchers in the Lords, who act independently from party politics. The 2024 study, which examined their contributions in Parliament from 2021 to 2022, found that they had joined debates in a wide range of areas: nationality and borders, education, health and social care, crime and sentencing, the environment, gambling, assisted dying, child benefit and universal credit. Whilst they are active in the legislature, they exercise restraint, recognising the primacy of the Commons. They are not whipped and do not follow a Church of England line, but speak and vote according to their own consciences inspired by faith and the experience of ministering within their dioceses, sometimes taking opposite sides on the same issue. They also, via a parliamentary unit, consult with the leaders of other faith groups, as they take the view that they exercise the function of representing all faiths. As another bishop commented in the study,

> It is not our role to represent the Church of England in the House of Lords or our view of Christianity, but of faith and what it is to be part of humanity. The bishops can speak of the whole life of this country in a way that no other member of the House or group of peers can. They can bring into the arena of legislation a perspective of the most vulnerable in society.

Perhaps with this in mind, and their close connection with all manner of people and faiths throughout their dioceses, not only do bishops 'bring faith into the public square; [being] careful to speak about faith as a whole, not just the position of the Established Church', but, as another bishop said more succinctly and provocatively: 'We are the most democratic part of the House of Lords.'[8]

16

Moral Space

I Was an Hungered, and Ye Gave Me Meat

Most church services, near their beginning, have a confession. 'Almighty and Most Merciful Father, We have erred and strayed from Thy ways like lost sheep', begins the General Confession in the Book of Common Prayer, intended to be said every day at matins and evensong.

Whilst both priest and people alike are enjoined to confess their 'manifold sins and wickedness', it has not been uncommon to hear demands for the greatest expressions of repentance to come from the churches and clergy themselves. Such calls are not without foundation. Too often, the churches have 'erred and strayed' from the very paths of goodness and probity they are charged to proclaim.

In the churches, scandals of sexual abuse have cast a long shadow. Since the 1960s, there have been hundreds of complaints about individual clergy and church officers in the Church of England. Whilst in recent years there have been improvements in their procedures for safeguarding, 'the Church's neglect of the physical, emotional and spiritual well-being of children and young people in favour of protecting its reputation was in conflict with its mission of love and care for the innocent and the vulnerable', found the Independent Inquiry into Child Sexual Abuse in October 2020.[1] Similar flaws were identified by the 2024 Makin Report into the prolific abuser John Smyth QC. Its conclusion that the Archbishop of Canterbury, Justin Welby, failed to do everything within his power to alert the relevant authorities about Smyth's abuse, of which he had been made aware in 2013, led to the archbishop's resignation in November

2024, and called into question the credibility of other senior clergy of the Church of England.[2]

The Roman Catholic Church has trodden a similar path. In May 2019, the most senior Roman Catholic priest in England, Cardinal Vincent Nichols, said on the subject: 'We humbly ask forgiveness ... for our slowness and defensiveness and for our neglect of both preventative and restorative actions.' However, the same Independent Inquiry complained that the cardinal made 'no acknowledgement of any personal responsibility to lead or influence change[, n]or did he demonstrate compassion towards victims in the recent cases which we examined'. Overall, 'Real and lasting changes to attitudes have some way to go if the Roman Catholic Church is to shake off the failures of the past'.[3]

This is not the only recent example of ignominious behaviour by those in the Church hierarchy. The most conspicuous is that of the businesswoman and cleric Paula Vennells. Despite being an ordained priest in the Church of England, as CEO of the Post Office from 2012 to 2019 she presided over the wrongful prosecutions of hundreds of sub-postmasters for fraud and false accounting based on incorrect information from the faulty Horizon computer software, even though the problems with the system had been repeatedly brought to her attention. The prosecutions led to the loss of jobs, homes and livelihoods, bankruptcies, and even several suicides. Her behaviour was described by the former Member of Parliament Lord Arbuthnot as 'both cruel and incompetent'.[4] Although her competence was already being called into question towards the end of her tenure, and despite her relative lack of pastoral experience, she was shortlisted for the position of Bishop of London, and senior members of the Church paid considerable deference to her astringent and centralising ideas for the reform of Church governance.

As much as the Church of England as an institution has failed a number of its own most vulnerable members, it is even failing to look after many of its own clergy. The pressures placed on parish priests on account of the amalgamation of parishes, so that some might even be expected to look after seven or eight churches and different congregations spread over a wide geographical area, not to mention an increasing burden of bureaucracy and low wages such that some clergy even need charitable support to pay everyday bills, have caused a sharp decline in the number of people willing to train for ordination, and also a wave of mental health problems amongst incumbents. A 2023 Church of England survey found that 36 per cent of parish clergy were suffering symptoms of depression. One anonymous clerical writer has described on the Anglican Futures weblog how the new managerial fashion in the Church causes so much stress:

> The problem is that our bishops see themselves as managers – organising structures and attempting to fend off insolvency by sweating their assets. And so the most significant asset, the clergy, are just asked to do more; to take on more responsibility and stretch themselves more to keep the parish system going. Add to this the fact that decisions regarding deployment, re-appointment, and licensing of workers seem to occur behind a veil of secrecy, and you have the perfect cocktail for a collapse in mental and physical health and well-being.[5]

When the Church of England's recent record includes failures on sexual abuse, a lack of discernment regarding those admitted to positions of responsibility, and also a lack of a coherent direction about a number of contemporary moral issues, it may seem difficult to advance the proposition that Christianity still has a role to play as a moral guide or inspiration in English life. How can an institution which is still unable to agree amongst itself on the validity of women's ministry, and which is suffering even greater tensions over the question of same-sex marriage in church, pretend it has the capacity to offer any leadership to the wider nation in any matters of ethics or right conduct? Surely the only thing one can say to the Church at this point is 'Physician, heal thyself'.

That the Church has been unable to live up to its ideals in many cases is not to be disguised. As an institution, the Anglican Church cannot and does not claim infallibility in its actions or conduct. The abuse of power, the culture of excessive deference and the fear of speaking out in the face of hostile authority are an inescapable part of any sort of corporate life, no matter how elevated the institution's principles. Such, as the Church itself would be the first to admit, is the result of the fallen nature of humanity, and the Church, being an institution of humans, inspired as its members may be by the highest principles of Christianity, is in no wise immune from stumbling.

The Church, being human, will err, and being under the unaccustomed pressures of modernity will err all the more. The precipitous decline of Church membership since the 1960s is a situation the like of which the Church has never before confronted. This has led it, in somewhat of a panic, to attempt solutions inspired by the world of business and management quite alien to its fundamental values and purposes, harming both the clergy and congregations, despite its good intentions of restoring growth. The conflicts over women's ministry and same-sex marriage are also questions with which the Church has not had to grapple before the present age, but they are hard to resolve because they are grounded in a perennially difficult crux about the interpretation of scripture – do the various specific pronouncements of the Bible, especially in the New Testament, lay down moral strictures for all time, or do they need to be reinterpreted according to the changing circumstances of the moment?

However difficult and fundamental this question, it is perhaps on account of another effect of modernity – the relentless elevation of sex in all areas of public discourse – which makes it appear, to those both in the Church and outside it, that the Church is interested in little else at present, and unable to focus on anything aside from the question of same-sex relationships.

Yet, putting aside the inescapable failings, the all-too-fascinating discussions of matters of sex which expand to fill the spaces available in our already too narrow attention spans, and even the deeper question of the contexts of the interpretation of scripture, there are still more fundamental ideals of Christian morality unaffected by these areas of turmoil, which the Church still upholds and faithfully proclaims. It may not be so conspicuous, but the presence and witness of Christianity remain a moral inspiration, without which English society would be infinitely the poorer.

Beyond any subtle discussions of scriptural interpretation, and even beyond the Bible's most memorable and direct ethical statements – 'Blessed are the meek ... Blessed are the merciful ... Blessed are the peacemakers' – it is in the most basic elements of the Christian world view that the profoundest and most durable moral ideas have their roots. Man is made in the image of God, but estranged from Him because of Original Sin. To redeem mankind, God is made incarnate in the person of Christ, who is present on earth not in the pomp of riches or great estate, but ultimately as an outcast and crucified criminal, a suffering servant. Yet, for those who place their faith in Christ, 'to them', in the words of John's Gospel, 'gave He power to become the sons of God' (1.12).

There are two primary ethical consequences from these beliefs. The first relates to the nature of mankind, and the second to the nature of power. As regarding the first, man has an inalienable dignity, because he is made in the image of God. Moreover, even if he is estranged from God, he has the potential, thanks to the redemptive act of Christ's crucifixion, to enter into a closer relationship with God. This being so, no matter how low one has fallen or wickedly one has behaved, that potential for each individual to be redeemed by God's grace and to develop that deeper relationship with God is a confirmation of the dignity inherent in each person.

These ideas about the inherent dignity of each person and their potential for redemption – despite whatever their previous poverty, misfortune or wickedness may have been – were, ahead of anything else, responsible for motivating the evangelical movement from the eighteenth century onwards towards its great acts of charity and self-sacrifice. The duty of service and of cherishing our fellows came not simply from the commands of Christ expressed in the gospels, but because every person is made worthy by their connection with God. If they were in distress or had lost their worldly dignity such that they were unable to respect themselves or recognise their own relationship with God, there was an imperative to help them regain that worldly comfort and dignity so that they too could gain the space and capacity to turn their hearts and minds towards the divine.

More than this, as all people shared in the same relationship with God through being made in His image and by the offer of redemption, there was in the Christian view a brotherhood not just of all Christians, but indeed of all people, regardless of their faith or station. This too was a further compulsion towards charity and service.

The message of human dignity arising from the connection of every human with God is one that has had extraordinary power. It moved the evangelicals under the guidance of William Wilberforce to bring an end to the slave trade and suppress slavery altogether – 'Am I not a man and a brother?' as their famous portrait of a slave in chains proclaimed – and later to work for the great charitable endeavours and societal reforms of the Victorian age and beyond. It is also a message that can and does have great power today. It offers a grounding for the worthiness of each person that cannot be abridged or lessened. It rejects the idea of categorisations by wealth, ability, identity, celebrity, connections. It urges a vision of human fellowship against the compulsions to divide, and to act selflessly in the name of that fellowship so that the dignity of each of its members may be upheld.

It would not be difficult to find testimonies of how this principle has inspired many people to dedicate their lives to good works in the service of others. It is often cited as the motivating idea in the literature of many church and Christian charities. Yet, to see the still-pervasive influence of this notion, it is perhaps more indicative to look at the evidence of studies about the habits of charitable giving. A number of surveys carried out in the past decade have shown that practising Christians are more likely to give to charity than those who practise no religion. A 2024 survey found that greater engagement with Bible-reading and churchgoing was likely to lead to greater charitable giving, with those attending church at least once a month being likely to give over 6 per cent of their income to charity.[6] This is in contrast to the trends visible in wider society. Charity Commission research found that between 2011 and 2019, whilst average incomes grew by around 10 per cent, average donations fell by 20 per cent. Further work by the Office for National Statistics in 2022 showed that a majority of households now make no regular donations to charity, and of those that do, the donations are generally between 1 and 2 per cent of income.[7] Investigations about volunteering reveal a similar trend. The Community Life Survey 2016–17 found that Christians were more likely to volunteer than those with no faith, and that those who were more dedicated to their faith were also more likely to volunteer.[8]

Indeed, despite the corrosion of communitarian bonds since the 1960s and the consequent rise of individualism, the churches and Christianity have maintained against this decay not just a vision of community and fellowship, but an active endeavour to keep them a practical reality. Almost 12,000 churches are involved in assisting the national network of food banks, according to the Trussell Trust.[9] In 2022, nearly three million people sought help from churches on account of the cost-of-living crisis.[10] Many churches continue to provide not only food, but access to warm spaces, advice to those in need, and also regular support and companionship to combat the increasing scourge of loneliness. Recent research has found that around 2000 Church of England parishes have hosted or supported night shelters for the homeless.[11] With the Christian imperative for hospitality in mind, such help has also been offered to vulnerable refugees from conflict, including those from Ukraine and Afghanistan. Churches have helped them not just with the basic practicalities of food, clothing and shelter, but also with learning English to help them integrate into society. Such charitable work is not the purpose of the Church – it is ultimately the consequence of faith – but without such work society would be much the poorer. Christianity and the churches have held fast to the ideas of community and fellowship which, given the current trends towards loneliness and social atomisation, English society is coming to realise it needs more than ever.

The Christian message about human dignity brings with it not only the idea of duties to one's fellow man, but also a more secure concept of human rights. The emergence of such rights in English culture has owed much to earlier Christian origins, as has been argued in this book. However, in the contemporary age they are defined and enforced not on the basis of religion, but on secular legal conventions, principally the Universal Declaration of Human Rights (1948) and the European Convention on Human Rights (1950), the latter of which became a part of English domestic law with the Human Rights Act 1998. Yet, despite the grandeur of the titles of these instruments, beyond the force of legislation there is very little to underwrite them in a secular society. As the philosopher Alasdair MacIntyre strikingly argued in his leading work *After Virtue*, the belief in human rights in themselves 'is one with belief in witches and in unicorns'. The problem with them in a modern secular society, as MacIntyre and later Rowan Williams maintained, is that in such a society there are two measures of moral value – rights and utility. Both are guaranteed and administered by the state through law and bureaucratic mechanisms. Yet, as the rights of the individual and the utility of the state or the wider population are often in conflict, there is little to stand in the way of the state eroding the rights of the individual. Without an ultimate place to ground them that is beyond governmental diktat, they lie at the mercy of the state.[12]

A leading example of this problem is given by the current debate on assisted dying (or, more accurately, assisted suicide). The Universal Declaration may guarantee a right to life. Yet, as can be seen by the recent experience of Canada and the Netherlands, this does not stand in the way of an assisted dying law which creeps beyond an initial remit of helping the terminally ill to die, to those who are simply old, infirm, disabled, depressed, or those who have complex chronic medical conditions but who are poor and a burden to their families and medical authorities. People who may wish to live but feel pressured into ending their lives because of the cost they place on society find their own right to life overridden for the utility of the state and their dependants. Such rights, in the face of these pressures, are hardly meaningful.

Rights, ultimately, cannot exist without roots. As the philosopher Nicholas Wolterstorff has argued, they have to be grounded in something beyond the human. The Christian account of the inviolable dignity of every human based on their relationship with God – something which belongs to every individual, and which is not at all dependent on their wealth, station or abilities – places the fount of those rights in a stronger realm beyond the capacity to be changed or challenged by the fashions of the time or the immediate needs of a government. The presence of Christianity in the public realm reminds us that there is more to rights than simply the ascription of law, and provides a standard for such rights when the law or government might lose its way.[13]

The first ethical consequence of the Christian world view, as said earlier, relates to the question of mankind: his dignity, his duties and rights. The second relates to the idea of power in society. In the Christian faith, the power and leadership of Christ are displayed not by Him appearing in temporal glory or splendour, but rather in service and self-abasement: 'whosoever will be great among you, let him be your minister', He told His disciples in Matthew's Gospel, 'And whosoever will be chief among you, let him be your servant: Even as the Son of man came not to be ministered unto, but to minister . . .' (20.26–8). Or, as He told His disciples after He washed their feet at the Last Supper, 'If I then, your Lord and Master, have washed your feet; ye also ought to wash one another's feet' (John 13.14). That power, in the Christian account, appeared at its apogee when Christ died as a man disgraced and broken on the Cross.

This biblical pattern still sits at the very heart of the ritual of the English state. At the recent coronation of King Charles the first words spoken by the king were not to a lord or bishop but to a chorister, echoing Matthew's Gospel: '. . . I come not to be served, but to serve.' Then, to be anointed as king, he was stripped of his robes down to his shirt and even made to bare his chest in what amounted to a ritual humiliation, before being invested with the symbols of kingship and crowned.[14]

The fact that the central symbol of the Christian faith is its God as a man, humiliated and dead on a cross – something so familiar that it may easily be forgotten – is one that should constantly shock and surprise us. It stands as a sharp critique to any conventional idea of power, and a perpetual challenge to those who would wield it. The virtuous ruler acts in service not of himself, but of others. His pleasure is not in glorifying himself, but in embracing humility. His eminence comes not from what he takes, but from what of himself he is able to give. Such a vision offers an extraordinary and visceral check on the unrestrained exercise of a ruler's authority, demanding his care and concern for not just the mighty around him, but the very lowest. It tends one and all towards gentleness, reasonableness and moderation. Christianity maintains this vision as an established part of English life and culture, and its presence is, beyond argument, a constant and salutary contribution to the common national good.

17

Space between Faiths

We Do Hear Them Speak in Our Tongues

It's a story that comes round every year, with liturgical regularity. Someone, somewhere, is abolishing Christmas. A town council, we read in the papers, has renamed it 'Winterval', 'Winterfest' or 'Winter Night Light Festival'. A university publishes guidance that students and staff should speak of the 'Winter Closure Period' rather than Christmas holidays. A 'multicultural tree' pops up in a city square, decorated with tinsel and baubles. School nativity plays are curiously rewritten to include Elvis, footballers or spacemen. In a seasonal advertising campaign in 2017, the bakery Greggs was lambasted for substituting Christ in a manger with a sausage roll. The examples are legion.

As ever with such stories, the reality is usually not quite as extreme as the newspaper report. The original 'Winterval', for example, was a 1997 marketing initiative by Birmingham City Council to encourage people to the city centre, where a number of individual festivals would be celebrated, including Christmas. 'Christmas – called Christmas! – and its celebration lay at the heart of Winterval', insisted a council spokesman. '[T]here was a banner saying Merry Christmas across the front of the council house, Christmas lights, Christmas trees in the main civil squares, regular carol-singing sessions by school choirs, and the Lord Mayor sent a Christmas card with a traditional Christmas scene wishing everyone a Merry Christmas', said an official statement.[1]

Yet, for all that some of these stories are exaggerated, there is an undeniable underlying trend. This is a growing belief that the use of Christian and religious terminology, and, indeed, the very presence of religious rituals, traditions or ideas in the public sphere, is discriminatory and potentially offensive, particularly to those of other faiths. The National Secular Society, speaking of the long-standing custom of saying prayers in Parliament at the beginning of each day's sitting, said in 2020, 'This practice undermines efforts to ensure the UK's parliament reflects the interests of all its people, regardless of their religious beliefs or identities . . . .'[2] The same principle, they argue, obtains for the established Church the presence of bishops in the House of Lords, the formal Christian observances around Remembrance Sunday, the appointment of hospital chaplains. In 2018, Humanists UK described the legal requirement for collective worship in schools of a broadly Christian character as 'outdated' and called for them to be replaced with assemblies which would be more inclusive.[3] The 2022 'Inclusive Language Guidance' issued by the University of Brighton implied that the use of religious terminology could be seen as 'outmoded' and that 'alternative phrases' might 'help to foster an inclusive and diverse academic environment'.[4] In October 2024, the University of Nottingham placed trigger warnings on canonical pieces of medieval literature in their English course on the grounds that they contained 'expressions of Christian faith'.[5]

It might be predictable for a Member of Parliament to complain that such incidents are 'political correctness gone mad' and the work of 'policy wonks' wanting to strip the public sphere of all Christian religious symbols. However, this critique, from 2006, was made not by any fulminating bishop nor High Church Anglican, but by a Muslim Labour MP, Shahid Malik.[6] Such attempts to remove the established traditions from collective English life, he insisted, were neither desired by Muslims, nor of any benefit to them: 'Many fellow Muslims', he said, 'will be horrified the liberal PC brigade want Christmas cancelled to avoid offending us. We actually relish this time of year.' This strident sentiment was later echoed by the Muslim Council of Britain: 'Keep calm, it's Christmas . . . Who wants to ban Christmas? Not Muslims. None of us will be offended if you go ahead and enjoy the Christmas cheer.'[7]

Another politician of a different background who has consistently expressed his support for established Christianity is Rishi Sunak, the first Hindu Prime Minister of the United Kingdom. Whilst making no secret of his devout adherence to the Hindu faith, conspicuously displaying Diwali candles in the windows of Downing Street, he has repeatedly acknowledged the value and importance of Christianity to English life and identity. In an Easter Sunday message given in 2023, he said that the celebration 'gives us a chance to reflect on the considerable contribution Christian communities make to our national life, offering support and a sense of belonging to so many across the country ... Christianity and its values of tolerance, compassion and charity are embedded in our history and national fabric. Its values are British values.'[8] Christianity, he has argued, plays a fundamental role in creating an open society for the practice of all faiths. In an address to the nation given on the steps of 10 Downing Street in March 2024, in response to the increasing disorder in the regular anti-Israel marches which followed Israel's invasion of Gaza in late 2023, he said 'You can be a practising Hindu and a proud Briton as I am ... Or a devout Muslim and a patriotic citizen as so many are ... Or a committed Jewish person and the heart of your local community ... and all underpinned by the tolerance of our established, Christian church.'[9]

These statements by Malik and Sunak belie the claim of the secular and humanist movement that the institutional presence of Christianity makes English society exclusive and hostile for those, particularly migrants, of other faiths. If anything, it is the opposite. The removal of religious ideas and the awareness of religious history from the English public sphere actually make integration harder. For many migrants from outside Europe, coming from countries in Asia and Africa, where religious ideas are closely tied to notions of identity, morality and motivation, the complete absence of religion from public space and discourse seems unnatural, suspicious and even hostile. If religious ideas and practice are assumed by migrants to be a normal part of the public sphere, then their absence can lead migrants to believe there is something wrong with English society – that it is rootless, lacks merit or self-respect, and is not an example to emulate. By the same token, the lack of religious awareness – the idea that religion can be the prime motivation for behaviour and cultural assumptions – on the part of England as a host community can also lead to incomprehension of and hostility towards the religious newcomers. Though it may seem a paradox, the open presence of Christianity in public life, coupled with an awareness of the tolerance which it has evolved over the course of English history, offers a better hope for the integration of migrants and peaceful understanding between communities.

Dr Rakib Ehsan,* a British Muslim academic on social cohesion and race relations, agrees that an established Church and a strong presence of Christianity in the public sphere benefits rather than alienates members of other faiths:

> As a Muslim, I see much value in England's Christian heritage. To start, there is the overlap based on shared Abrahamic traditions. There are also similarities between Protestantism and Islam, especially Sunni Islam – such as a common reliance on textual criticism, opposition to the use of images in worship, and the rejection of monastic orders. More broadly, I believe there is a craving for a deep sense of meaning and belonging in the country at large. A modern Britain that is more at ease with its own Christian heritage and traditions would not alienate its religious minorities. Christianity, we should remember, promotes a wide number of virtues: the family, the wider community, civic action, contributions to the social good – these values are held strongly in many of our Muslim communities.

Indeed, he observes, there is the paradox that amongst British Muslim communities, many of the virtues preached by Christianity are better cherished than amongst the wider, more secularised and relatively individualistic English population:

* Dr Ehsan is the author of *Beyond Grievance: What the Left Gets Wrong about Ethnic Minorities*.

> When it comes to providing care for elderly relatives, giving charitable donations and sharing homemade food with those outside of their family, the rates are higher amongst British Muslims than the wider populace. We see the erosion of social bonds and intergenerational connections in the rapidly secularised mainstream, but Muslims are generally 'insulated' from this atomisation. If there were a greater collective ease about the conventional teachings of Christianity in English society, there would also be a better appreciation of Islam's place in modern Britain.

A shared appreciation of moral values is not the only thing that brings together minority faiths with Christianity:

> With rising ethnic and religious diversity, we need to be asking 'How do we cultivate a truly wholesome sense of national belonging? What does being British mean?' One component of this which can unite various groups is a shared interest in faith ... An inclusive appreciation of faith can transcend the tribal boundaries between different communities. First, there is the legacy of Christianity to England, with its shaping of how we work as a country: England's law, politics, culture, traditions, civil society. This ought to be an integral part of the English education system. It gives us a chance to work towards an idea of civic nationhood, where common beliefs and shared ideas can unite us, rather than the concept of ethnonationalism, which ties nationality to the exclusive idea of race and ancestry. Second, with growing levels of irreligiosity, we have witnessed the ascent of radical progressivism (the 'unholy trinity' of DEI)* – which is quasi-religious and puritanical – seeking to challenge traditional faith-based authority. Religious faith, for the Christian or the Muslim, brings with it a sense of hope and optimism; it can be an incredible source of resilience and determination. This is different from radical progressive thinking, which is ultimately defined by its doom-and-gloom pessimism, which in turn fuels the politics of victimhood and division. The aegis of Christianity as

* i.e. Diversity, Equity and Inclusion.

> an established religion allows those of different faiths, as well as even the moderate secular-minded – who see aspects of this progressivism and are alarmed by it – to come together.[10]

Dr Ehsan's observations are supported by opinion-poll data. For example, a survey conducted by Gallup found that Muslims in London were considerably more likely to express positive opinions of those who held strong Christian beliefs. It also found that Muslims were at least as likely to support the rights of those of other faiths to display their religious symbols as much as their own. In the words of the analysis of the survey, the expectation of Muslims 'of respect for Islam and its symbols extends to an expectation of respect for religion in general'.[11]

A Jewish scholar echoes many of the ideas put forward by Dr Ehsan:

> From a Jewish perspective, we would wish to support what you might call the 'particularity' of the place to which we want to belong. This would include its established authority and moral norms, and in the case of England, the moral norms that have been established by the Church of England are those to which we would also wish to subscribe. However, it is not just the moral norms from the Church of England which are in alignment with those of Judaism. It is also the way that the Christian heritage of England, and also the established nature of the Church of England and its stewardship, have created a benign climate for the practice of Judaism and other minority faiths. This presence of an established faith, which still preaches a morality concordant with Judaism, but which doesn't aggressively proselytise, is far preferable to the alternatives which might assertively insist on the primacy of the state's religion on the one hand, or which allow for complete moral laxity on the other.

The presence of an established religion which tolerates and supports others is, indeed, a more agreeable situation for minority faiths than an overridingly secular public sphere, as the presence of the established faith effectively legitimises the very presence and idea of *faith* per se, and therefore different faiths. The contrast is with the strictly secular public sphere in France, which outlaws all expressions of faith, and which thus has the practical effect of making the possession of any faith in itself appear potentially at odds with citizenship and national identity. 'A self-confident culture which accepts minorities can actually tolerate the minorities being different, whereas a plastic liberal universalism is only superficially tolerant and actually seeks to replace the minorities' norms with those of liberal universalism.'[12]

A senior Church of England cleric concurred with this sentiment – whilst modestly not wishing to 'overstate' the point:

> ... the leaderships of other major faiths ... feel more comfortable – even safe – in a society with an Established religion than in one with a specifically secular constitution ... It is, of course, a historic accident that the relationship between Church and State turned out as it did – but it remains a significant historical fact ... it is the 'coalition' nature of the Elizabethan Settlement which created the conditions for the Church of England to see its vocation in terms of the Common Good of the people of England rather than as securing the primacy of a single set of beliefs.[13]

The late Queen put the point succinctly in a speech to an interfaith gathering at Lambeth Palace in 2012:

> The concept of our established Church is occasionally misunderstood and, I believe, commonly under-appreciated. Its role is not to defend Anglicanism to the exclusion of other religions. Instead, the Church has a duty to protect the free practice of all faiths in this country ... It certainly provides an identity and spiritual dimension for its own many adherents. But also, gently and assuredly, the Church of England has created an environment for other faith communities and indeed people of no faith to live freely. Woven into the fabric of this country, the Church has helped to build a better society – more and more in active co-operation for the common good with those of other faiths.[14]

18

Spiritual Worth

In My Flesh Shall I See God

I am not a preacher. It is not part of my talents, nor indeed the remit of this book, to persuade anyone of the truth of the Christian faith. I am not here to argue the historicity of the gospels, the death and resurrection of Christ, the validity of miracles. I cannot lead anyone to a belief in the creeds of Christianity, nor can I cause anyone, like John Wesley or the evangelicals, to be born again. As Wesley himself would say, such is, if anything, a result of grace, a gift of the Holy Spirit: 'The wind bloweth where it listeth' (John 3.8).

But if one can make the case that for 1,00 years and more, Christianity has made the most fundamental contributions to the emergence, development and flourishing of England as a nation, and that in spite of the profound changes of the twentieth century, it still has an essential role to play in national life, one can also make that case that in addition to these instrumental contributions – identity, culture, morality – it still has a spiritual offering and benefit to all here, regardless of their background or faith. This, at least, I can still hope to argue.

For all the decline in church attendance and membership since the 1960s, the interest in the idea of the sacred has never declined. Indeed, the retreat of the churches is strangely paralleled with an increase in the concern with the holy. Research conducted at the turn of the millennium found that although church attendance had dropped 20 per cent between 1987 and 1999, reports of people undergoing 'spiritual experiences' increased by 60 per cent over the same period. The same research found that 55 per cent of those surveyed had found a transcendent meaning in the course of their own life that was not of their own making, 38 per cent had felt the presence of God, and a similar figure felt that they had received help through prayer. The number of people stating that they had undergone such experiences had close to doubled over the period.[1]

Nonetheless, such experiences are more and more being experienced outside the ambit of formal Christian or religious belief. As mentioned in Chapter 13, a 2022 Theos survey found that of those who belonged to no religion, 36 per cent believed that humans were 'at heart spiritual beings', and 42 per cent believed in 'some form of the supernatural'.[2]

Researchers who have interviewed those who describe themselves as spiritual but not religious frequently find that there is a belief in the transcendent which often struggles for clear articulation. As one person said to a researcher, 'I still do believe there's something . . . I mean I can't prove there is, but you know, I do, yes, I do definitely believe there is something, more to heaven and earth as they say, definitely.' There is often a striving for an engagement with that 'something' – a transcendent world which, in the absence of conventional Christian language, they might label as 'universal consciousness', 'driving force', 'divine energy'. Such a 'something' may be sought by any means from new-age rites to little domestic rituals, often in a space which becomes as if sacred – sitting on the doorstep after dark and staring at the sky, a recess of a garden, a place by the sea. When such rituals lead people to meditate and to feel a sense of connection to this 'something', the result is often described as one that brings both meaning and serenity: '. . . it is quite a spiritual feeling, that sort of peace that you get, that sort of peace with the world'. It may also bring about a sense of connection with the deep self: 'It's how you feel within yourself as well . . .'.[3]

The spiritual but not religious might find such a sense of peace and serenity even in conventional Christian rituals and sacred spaces – lighting candles in the parish church on Christmas Eve, a visit to a cathedral, the sight of a stained-glass window behind an altar: 'And I don't know what it was, but when I walked out of there I felt a hundred percent better. Just being there. I don't know if . . . I don't know, I can't explain it. I haven't got the words to explain it . . .' as one person said of contemplating the stained-glass windows in a church after the death of a relative.[4]

Yet, despite this, the general tenor of thought amongst the spiritual but not religious is that the conventionally religious are not at all spiritual. 'I think some people who are just religious, are just fanatical, aren't they? But I think if you're more spiritual, that's not, you're not fanatical, you're just, does that make sense?' said one person in a study. Others put the purported distinction more moderately: 'I think people that are spiritual that think a lot about lots of things. Whereas religious people just base their thoughts and stuff on God and traditional religious type things.' Somehow, for such people, Christianity is estranged from any idea of that transcendent 'something': 'Religious means that you go to church very regularly, you know, and you do all the things. And spiritual . . . I think that it's an awareness of knowing that there's something and you don't really know what you know, without going to church all the time.'[5]

A sense of spirituality might also bring with it a sense of morality: 'I think spiritual means do you feel there is something out there? Do you believe? Do you have an open mind about things? Do you believe in goodness, and in friendship, and in helping others?' This sense of spirituality might change the way that one connects with others: 'On the surface we might have those human connections, but without that kind of deeper connection with somebody it would be very shallow, and life would be sort of quite meaningless if we didn't have that with people.'[6]

Even if the spiritual but not religious consider themselves more open-minded and more moral, it seems that they are generally reticent to lend definition to their sense of the 'something'. Indeed, they are often hesitant even to discuss it. There is almost a taboo on sharing and explaining any such personal experiences of spirituality. One person who felt comfortable enough to describe their own personal sense of spirituality to a researcher went on to say why they could say nothing of it to their friends: 'I play, these guys I play football with on Sunday, you know, they'd think I was a lunatic if they could hear me sort of talking, you know . . .'.[7]

It is one of the more striking turns of the twentieth and early twenty-first centuries that not only the churches, but even Christianity itself are becoming dissociated from the fundamental idea of spirituality in the public mind. The reasons for this disconnection are perhaps to be found as a subset of the causes for the general decline in church attendance and membership from the 1960s as described in Chapter 13. The sudden development of alternative means of association, culture and recreation led to a withering of the means that churches might use – whether broad public knowledge of scripture, devotional literature, music – to transmit and propagate the idea of spirituality. All of this marked the loss of a shared cultural language which affirmed the idea of spirituality and made it a normal part of life to share it. On top of this, the general trends of attacking received ideas of knowledge and old institutions, along with the privileging of the experience and desires of the individual over collective and inherited experience, undermined the authority of the churches in the field. The post-1960s tendency was not to accept doctrines from traditional establishments or inherited canons, but either to defer to one's own feelings and intuitions, or else to look further afield. The failures of the churches after that time, whether financial or abuse scandals, or else a general running down of local networks and infrastructure (such as the Anglican parishes), or also of the theological, liturgical and cultural training of the clergy, have exacerbated the problem. The result is as the research has shown. There is a loss of the superstructure which made it possible for people to understand the offer of Christianity and spirituality. As a consequence, the public ever more look to themselves alone, or else to imported traditions, as with The Beatles following the maharishi, to assuage their spiritual longings.

As the search for spirituality becomes more individualised and estranged from an inherited and shared language anchored in wider cultural traditions, it becomes harder and more uncomfortable for people to articulate the nature of their spiritual longings or their spiritual progress, and, in a climate which privileges the immediate satisfaction of every matter of sensual desire and the veneer of the rational, every expression of a wider or less temporal longing brings with it a sensation close to shame.

For all of this breakdown of the last half-century and more – the overwhelming of the structures of the Church and its surrounding culture with the unaccustomed acid of new technology, the contempt of the old, the new insistence on the primacy of the individual over the inheritance of shared knowledge and experience – the spiritual insight of the Church and the Christian faith remains. It is a passionate and articulate expression of that longing for the 'something' which the spiritual but not religious deeply desire, but can barely put into words, and are fearful even to speak of. 'Like as the hart desireth the water-brooks: so longeth my soul after thee, O God', says Psalm 42. 'My soul is athirst for God, yea, even for the living God: when shall I come to appear before the presence of God?'

In the pursuit of that 'something', the presence of God, it falls to those on the Christian spiritual path to 'think a lot about lots of things'. 'Try me, O God, and seek the ground of my heart', demands the psalmist, 'prove me, and examine my thoughts.' In that pursuit of whom, through whom, and to whom 'are all things', as St Paul writes (Romans 11.36), there is an imperative towards the deep contemplation of all things, in which are hinted the presence of that God which defies all categories we can grasp or impose:

> Such knowledge is too wonderful and excellent for me: I cannot attain unto it . . . Whither shall I go then from thy Spirit: or whither shall I go then from thy presence? If I climb up into heaven, thou art there: if I go down to hell, thou art there also. If I take the wings of the morning: and remain in the uttermost parts of the sea; Even there also shall thy hand lead me: and thy right hand shall hold me. If I say, Peradventure the darkness shall cover me: then shall my night be turned to day. Yea, the darkness is no darkness with thee, but the night is as clear as the day: the darkness and light to thee are both alike. (Psalm 139)

That confusing, confounding intimacy with that 'something' – the distant God the knowledge of whom 'is too wonderful and excellent for me' but who is so close that He '. . . hast searched me out and known me', who 'knowest my down-sitting and mine up-rising, [and] understandest my thoughts long before' – finds its epitome in the figure of Christ crucified, who transcends the barriers between the human and the divine, the transitory and the eternal. 'Who', as St Paul wrote in the Letter to the Philippians:

> . . . being in the form of God, thought it not robbery to be equal with God: But made himself of no reputation, and took upon him the form of a servant, and was made in the likeness of men: And being found in fashion as a man, he humbled himself, and became obedient unto death, even the death of the cross. Wherefore God also hath highly exalted him, and given him a name which is above every name . . .' (Philippians 2.6–9)

In the mystery of the incarnation of Christ, 'the Word' who for love of man 'became flesh and dwelt among us' (John 1.14), there is offered a path to a spiritual unity, a reintegration with that 'something' from which the human spirit, confined by its temporal and evanescent frame, feels its profoundest longings. The incarnate Christ crosses every spiritual frontier. As He says in St John's Gospel, '. . . because I live, ye shall live also. At that day ye shall know that I am in my Father, and ye in me, and I in you' (14.19–20). In the act of communion, all are knitted together in Christ: 'He that eateth my flesh, and drinketh my blood, dwelleth in me, and I in him' (John 6.56). The exaltation of man in mutual fellowship, unity and love is the culmination of this path: 'Beloved, let us love one another: for love is of God; and every one that loveth is born of God, and knoweth God . . . If we love one another, God dwelleth in us, and his love is perfected in us' (1 John 4.7, 12).

These desires, for that 'something', for unity and spiritual integration, are still as much a part of human longing today as they were when the psalmist, the gospel authors and St Paul were writing. Such fundamental longings have not been assuaged by an abundance of technology, wealth or affluence, or the connectivity of social media, as passingly pleasing as they are. The message of integration, of the wholeness offered in the way of the Christian spiritual path, is presented to us not just in the raw and unmediated texts of scripture, but it is to be found given 'A local habitation and a name' in the generations and centuries of English culture and artistic creativity inspired by this message which, even though we are ever more estranged from it, lies close to hand and ready to inspire in its turn. For that longing for the 'something', for God, for which many still furtively and inarticulately strive, is declared and affirmed in the cries of the great poets, of George Herbert and John Donne calling 'Whither, O whither art thou fled, My Lord, My Love', or 'Batter my heart, three-personed God';[8] in the outpourings of the medieval mystics, of Dame Julian of Norwich and Margery Kempe; in the fragments of doom paintings and soaring spaces of the parish churches and cathedrals, or the canvases of the Pre-Raphaelite Brotherhood; in the longing of the music of Thomas Tallis, of William Byrd, of Orlando Gibbons, of Henry Purcell heard at evensong. And even the intimation of the height of that journey, the sense of wholeness and integration in the vision of the divine, that too is offered in a homely guise, whether in the puzzling and fiery simplicity of *The Cloud of Unknowing*, the poems of William Blake seeing heaven in a wildflower, Gerard Manley Hopkins finding the Passion of Christ charged in the 'achieve' of 'The Windhover':

> . . . air, pride, plume here
> Buckle! And the fire that breaks from thee then, a billion
> Times told lovelier, more dangerous, O my chevalier!

Or Thomas Traherne, apprehending with the vision of a child the presence of heaven all around: 'The corn was Orient and Immortal wheat . . . I thought it had stood from Everlasting to Everlasting. The Dust and Stones of the Street were as Precious as GOLD . . . The Green Trees which I saw them first . . . Transported and Ravished me; their

Sweetness and unusual Beauty made my Heart to leap, and almost mad with Exstasie . . .'.[9]

'Are not all His treasures yours, and yours His?' asks Traherne. The treasure of England is a spiritual tradition, proclaimed in a matrix of culture, which, if offered with confidence and approached with an open-minded patience, has the power to assuage and nourish those longings of the spirit so clearly present but which the demands of this age desire us to disregard. We need not think that England is brutish, or deficient in that which might feed and satisfy the spirit. Like Traherne, we may look beyond the garden gate, and see the dust and stones in our local streets as precious as gold, and the very trees here to make our hearts leap, almost mad with ecstasy.

Notes

INTRODUCTION: DEBT TO A DYING GOD

1 British Social Attitudes Survey, 2017; Sherwood, 2017.
2 Office for National Statistics (ONS), 29 November 2022.
3 Church of England, Press Release, 20 May 2024; Butcher and Swerling, 17 February 2024.
4 Bruce, 2003.
5 Edwards, K., 29 November 2022.
6 Good introductions to the history of Christianity in the other parts of the British mainland may be had for Wales in Lewis et al., 2022, and for Scotland in Kelly, 2018.
7 A striking overview of this work is given in Chula, 2023.
8 For further reading see Bassard, 2010.
9 Shakespeare, *Julius Caesar*, 3.2.84–5.

1 THE LAND OF ANGELS

1 Shakespeare, *Richard II*, 2.1.45–56.
2 Bede, *EH*, II.i; a version of the story is also given in the Whitby life of Gregory the Great; see Colegrave, 1968, ch.9.
3 An overview of the mission is given in Mayr-Harting, 1972, ch.3, 51–68.
4 Bede, *EH*, I.xxiii.
5 ibid., I.xxiv.
6 Adams, 2021.
7 For the background to Aethelbert and the early kingdom of Kent, see Yorke, 2003, 25–44.
8 Bede, *EH*, I.xxv.
9 ibid.
10 ibid.
11 Morris, 2021, 15.
12 Omrani, 2017, 333–7.
13 Morris, 2021, 17–18.
14 ibid., 20.
15 Zosimus, *New History*, VI.v.3.
16 ibid.
17 Morris, 2021, 22–3; Brown, P., 2013, 126–7; Ward-Perkins, 2000, 528.
18 Morris, 2021, 24; Innes, 2007, 320.
19 Gildas, *Works*, chs 23–6; Morris, 2021, 26–9.
20 Innes, 2007, 321.
21 See Bassett, 1989, 24–5.
22 Ward-Perkins, 2000.
23 Brown, P., 2013, 126; Innes, 2007, 333; Ward-Perkins, 2000.
24 Morris, 2021, 50.
25 ibid.
26 Procopius, *Vandalic War*, II.14.
27 Morris, 2021, 54–5.
28 ibid., 51.

29 Bassett, 1989; Morris, 2021, 51–3.
30 Rollason, 2012, 124–5.
31 Bassett, 1989, 4.
32 See the discussion in Wormald, 1999, 179–200.
33 Brown, P., 2013, 344.
34 Rollason, 2012, 119; Behr, 2000, 50.
35 Brown, P., 2013, 344.
36 Bede, *EH*, I.xxxii; Morris, 2021, 60.
37 Thacker, 2000, 259.
38 Bede, *EH*, II.x–xi.
39 Brooks, 2000, 225.
40 Bede, *EH*, I.xxxii.
41 *Gregorii I Papae registrum epistolarum*, Ep.11.35.
42 Wallace-Hadrill, 1971, 32; Higham, 1997, 98–102.
43 Eadmer, 'De reliquiis sancti Audoeni', quoted in Brooks, 2000, 230.
44 Brooks, 2000.
45 Thacker, 2000.
46 Brooks, 2000, 227–8; Bede, *EH*, IV.ii, for the spread of Roman chant in England.
47 Brooks, 2000, 245–6.
48 Brown, P., 2013, 349.
49 Bede, *EH*, I.xxxiv; Wallace-Hadrill, 1971, 78; McClure, 1983, 87.
50 Foot, 2017, 40–46.
51 Wallace-Hadrill, 1971, 73–4.
52 Bede, *EH*, III.ii.
53 ibid., III.vi.
54 ibid., II.xvi.
55 McClure, 1983, 91–2.
56 Bede, *EH*, III.vi.
57 Wallace-Hadrill, 1971, 78.
58 Aeddi, 1985, chs 19–20; Wallace-Hadrill, 1971, 63–4.
59 See Bede, *Epistle to Egbert*, in *EH*, II; and Innes, 2007, 364.
60 Wallace-Hadrill, 1971, 64–5.
61 Wormald, 1999a, 94; for Aethelbert's Law Code, see Attenborough, 1922, 4–17. A fuller discussion of the law is below in Chapter 2.
62 Wormald, 1983, 122; Boniface, Letters, no.73: Boniface to King Aethelbald of Mercia (746–7).
63 Bede, *EH*, I.i.
64 Yorke, 2001, 71–2.
65 Bede, *EH*, I.xiv.
66 Wormald, 2009, 24.
67 See discussion in Richter, 1984; Yorke, 2001; Wormald, 1983, and 1999, ch.14, 359–82, esp. 375–8; Brown, P., 2013, 351–2.
68 Bede, *EH*, I.vii.
69 McKinney, 2013, 47–8.
70 Foot, 1996, 27.
71 Alfred, Preface to *Pastoral Care*.
72 Foot, 1996; Wormald, 2009; Brooks, 2005.
73 Smyth, 1998, 39–43; Tombs, 2014, 78–9; for Aethelstan, see Foot, 2011; Holland, 2016.

2 TEACH ME THY LAWS

1 Taylor, M., 1991; Chapman, 2010.
2 For Mrs Donoghue's application, see 1930–31, *House of Lords Journal*, 163, at 128, 251, quoted in Taylor, M., 1991, 19.
3 *Donoghue v Stevenson* [1932] AC 562, at 580.
4 Castle, 2003, 211.
5 Atkin, 1932, 30.
6 Quoted in Castle, 2003, 212–13.
7 *R (Johns) v Derby City Council*

[2011] EWHC 375 (Admin.), at para.39.

8 Blackstone, *Commentaries on the Laws of England*, 1765–9, ch.2, quoted in Zimmermann, 2014, 162.

9 2 Swann. 487 (1754), at 490, quoted in Spiegel, 1984, 499.

10 *R v Woolston* 94 Eng. Rep. 655 (KB 1729), quoted in Zimmermann, 2014, 162.

11 *R v Taylor* 1 Vent. 293. 3 Keb. 607 (KB 1676).

12 *R v Love* (1651) 5 St. Tr. 43, 172.

13 Devlin, 1965.

14 Denning, 1989, 33.

15 *R (Johns) v Derby City Council* [2011] EWHC 375 (Admin.), at para.39; see also the discussion in Knights, 2021, chs 1–2.

16 Wallace-Hadrill, 1971, 32.

17 Bede, *EH*, II.v.

18 Wormald, 1999, 194–8; Wormald, 1999a, 101.

19 Berman, 1983, 53–4; Wormald, 1999a, 96.

20 Wallace-Hadrill, 1971, 33–44; Wormald, 1999a, 29–30; Brown, P., 2013, 345–6; Perks, 2013, 18–19.

21 Wormald, 1999, 374–5; Redgate, 2014, 68.

22 Wormald, 1999a, 101–2; Perks, 2013, 19–20.

23 1623, 21 James 1 c.28, An act for continuing and reviving divers statutes, and repeal of divers others, sections 6–7. For a history of sanctuary in England, see Everett, 2021.

24 Wallace-Hadrill, 1971, 149; Berman, 1983, 65; Foot, 1996, 31–2; Wormald, 1999a, 416–17, 422–3; Zimmermann, 2014, 149–51.

25 Prologue to the Laws of Alfred, 43, quoted in Jurasinski and Oliver, 2021, 259.

26 Perks, 2013, 28–9.

27 Quoted in ibid., 32.

28 Wormald, 1999a, 423.

29 Wormald, 2009, 25; Spencer, 2011, 20.

30 Wormald, 1999, 62; Wormald, 2014 chs 8–9; Lambert, 2017, 203–5.

31 Quoted in Wormald, 2014, 98.

32 Wormald, 2014, 138–40. For the medieval development of felony, including ideas of intentionality, see Papp, 2019.

33 Bede, *In regum librum xxx quaestiones*, xix, quoted in Foot, 2017, 43.

34 McClure, 1983, 92.

35 Quoted in Spencer, 2011, 28.

36 Baldwin, 2015.

37 See Zimmermann, 2014, 162–3; Vincent, 2017.

38 Quoted in Zimmermann, 2014, 163.

39 Berman, 2009, 238–44; Smith, D., 2017.

40 See Plucknett, 1926, or more recently Helmholz, 2009, for a discussion of the role of Coke in the development of judicial review.

41 *R (on the application of Miller) v The Prime Minister, Cherry and others v Advocate General for Scotland* [2019] UKSC 41.

42 Berman, 1983, 87.

43 ibid., 90–91.

44 ibid., 95–8, 113–15.

45 ibid., 437.

46 Criminal Justice and Public Order Act 1994, sections 34–9.

47 Shakespeare, *Hamlet*, 2.2.555–7.
48 Helmholz et al., 1997, ch.2, esp. 17–20.
49 ibid., esp. 21–4.
50 Pennington, 1998 and 2003.
51 Pennington, 2003, 118.
52 Volokh, 1997, 182.
53 Quoted in Sytsma, 2017, 178.
54 Sytsma, 2017, 178; Berman, 2009, 265.
55 Berman, 1983, 30.
56 ibid., 166.
57 Byrne, 2019, 44–5.
58 Quoted in Sytsma, 2017, 176.
59 *Earl of Oxford's Case* (1615) 21 ER 485.
60 Hedlund, 2015.
61 Berman, 2009, 337–43.
62 For Selden, see Witte and Berman, 2017; for Hooker, see Doe, 2017.
63 *Calvin's Case* (1608), 77 ER 377; Berman, 2009, 243.
64 Taylor, J., 1667, 176.
65 Berman, 2009, 320–1.
66 Witte, 1987; Berman, 2009, 245–8.
67 Berman, 2009, 320–4.
68 ibid., 328.
69 *Bird v Holbrook* 4 Bing. 628, 130 Eng. Rep. 911 (CP 1825); see Partlett, 2021, 266.
70 *Cowan v Milbourn* (1867) LR 2 Exch. 230.
71 See *Bowman v Secular Society Ltd* [1917] AC 406.
72 *Re G (Education: Religious Upbringing)* [2012] EWCA Civ. 1233 [2013] 1 FLR 677, paras 35–6.
73 *R (on the application of E) (Respondent) v Governing Body of JFS and the Admissions Appeal Panel of JFS (Appellants) and others* [2009] UKSC 15, para.157.
74 See, for example, Witte and Hauk, 2017.
75 Dent, 2017.
76 Helmholz, 1990, 58–60.
77 For example, see Helmholz, 2021.

3 ANGEL'S WIT AND SINGULAR LEARNING

1 Quoted in Brown, P., 2013, 356; see also Mayr-Harting, 1972, 153–4; Thacker, 2000, 260.
2 Bede, *Lives of the Abbots*, ch.2, Benedict.
3 Love, 2011; Brown, P., 2013, 356.
4 Brown, P., 2013, 357–8.
5 Procopius, *Gothic Wars*, I.16, quoted in Wormald, 1977, 98.
6 ibid.
7 Bede, *EH*, IV.ii.
8 Quoted in Dales, 2012, 61.
9 Alfred, Preface to *Pastoral Care*.
10 Morris, 2021, 235–8.
11 Bede, *Life of Cuthbert*, 165; Brown, P., 2013, 355.
12 Bede, *EH*, V.xxv.
13 Weber, 2019, 3.
14 Mayr-Harting, 1972, 195–9.
15 Aldhelm, *Riddles*.
16 Mayr-Harting, 1972, 201–04.
17 ibid., 204–9; see also Bischoff and Lapidge, 1995, esp. chs 2 and 4.
18 Mayr-Harting, 1972, 211–12.
19 Bede, *EH*, I.xxix.
20 Bolton, 1967, 53–4; Orme, 2006, 21.
21 Bede, *EH*, III.xvii; Orme, 2006, 21–2.
22 Orme, 2006, 30; Bischoff and Lapidge, 1995, chs 2–4.
23 Orme, 2006, 24.

24 ibid., 42–4.
25 Gwara and Porter, 1997; Dumitrescu, 2018.
26 Orme, 2006, 19–20.
27 Power, E., 1922, 237–84; Clark, 2008.
28 Orme, 2006, 279; Bailey, 2012, 159.
29 Clark, 2008, 156.
30 Orme, 2006, 237–44; for a local study, see Harvey, 2006, 120–31.
31 Orme, 2006, 225–35.
32 ibid., 39–40.
33 ibid.
34 See Pedersen, 1998, ch.5, esp. 152–4; Orme, 2006, 79–85.
35 Hunt, R., 1936, 36–7.
36 Pedersen, 1998, 160.
37 Orme, 2006, 259.
38 Knowles, 1955, 155–6; Pedersen, 1998, 174–7; Orme, 2006, 259–66; Clark, 2008, 165–7.
39 Orme, 2006, 273.
40 Brown, P., 2013, 479–89.
41 Hare, 2004.
42 Cynewulf, *Christ*, I.404–10, II.457–60.
43 'Hymn of Caedmon', quoted in Bradley, S., 1982.
44 North, 2013, 42–5.
45 Lindberg, 1987; Power, A., 2006.
46 See Oliver, 2004.
47 Catto and Evans, 1992, chs 3–4; North, 2013, 39–49; Pedersen, 1998, 291–2.

4 MIRRORS OF THE BLESSED

1 Bede, *EH*, I.xxv.
2 Brown, P., 2013, 344; Thacker, 2000, 259.
3 Mayr-Harting, 1972, 247–8; Innes, 2007, 357–60; Webster, 2017.
4 Bruce-Mitford, 1967; Brown, P., 2013, 358, 362–3; Morris, 2021, 85–7.
5 See Brown, M., 2017; Doan, 1982 (who disputes Coptic influence).
6 Brown, P., 2013, 371–2; Morris, 2021, 59.
7 Quoted in Denton, 1987, 22.
8 Quoted in Aston, 2015, 888.
9 Darby, 2013, 391–5.
10 See Camille, 1987, 33.
11 Quoted in Aston, 2015, 707.
12 Douie and Farmer, 1985, 140.
13 Henderson, 1999, 228.
14 Quoted in Stanbury, 2008, 21.
15 Quoted in Stanbury, 2008, 25; see also Reiss, 2008, 7–8.
16 Heslop, 1987, 27.
17 ibid., 31–2; see also Oliver, 2004.
18 Quoted in Aston, 2015, 25.
19 Thomas and Hessayon, 2009, 210; Walsham, 2011, 275.
20 Aston, 2015, 953–6; Hamling and Willis, 2023.
21 Fincham and Tyacke, 2007, 260.
22 Haynes, 2006, 121.
23 See discussion in ibid., esp. 1–14.
24 Sherlock, 2020, 170.
25 Hamling and Willis, 2023, 939–42.
26 Hamling, 2007.
27 Hamling, 2011; Davis, 2013; Walsham, 2020.
28 *Spectator*, 226, 19 November 1711; Haynes, 2006, chs 2–3.
29 Quoted in Haynes, 2006, 87.
30 Quoted in Giebelhausen, 2016, 23.
31 Quoted in Will, 1957, 341.
32 Will, 1957, 345.
33 Ryan, 2003, 161–6.
34 Ackroyd, 2024, 233–40.
35 Paley, 1989, 101; Owens, 2020, 192–8.

36 Ruskin, *Modern Painters*, 4.4.18, 61.
37 For Palmer, see Lister, 1984; Vaughan, 2015.
38 Giebelhausen, 2016, 67.
39 Quoted in ibid., 67–78; Beaumont and Thiele, 2023.
40 Giebelhausen, 2016, 108–25.
41 ibid., 179–85.
42 Pugin, 1843, 39; see Lang, 1966; Hill, R., 1999.
43 Scott, 1858, 274.
44 Cheshire, 2020.
45 Powers, 2019.
46 ibid., 28.
47 See MacCarthy, 1989; Harries, 2013, 58–63.
48 Quoted in Harries, 2013, 46.
49 Harries, 2013, 61–73.
50 Thuillier, 2015, 81–9.
51 Harries, 2013, 83–9.

5 A HOLY LANDSCAPE

1 Blair, J., 2005, 457.
2 Owens, 2020, 17–20.
3 Gittos, 2015, 33.
4 Bede, *EH*, I.xxx.
5 Blair, J., 2005, 376–8.
6 ibid., 378.
7 ibid., 487.
8 Gittos, 2015, 19–28.
9 Bede, *EH*, IV.xix.
10 Forbes, 2013, 270; Browett, 2017, 501, 508.
11 Blair, J., 2005, 478–80.
12 ibid., 228–45; Forbes, 2013, 275–86.
13 Quoted in Owens, 2020, 21.
14 Walsham, 2011, 84.
15 ibid., 98.
16 ibid., 147–51.
17 Owens, 2020, 125.
18 ibid., 152–9; Mayhew, 2004, 102–12.
19 Aston, 2015, 1001–2; Walsham, 2011, 388.
20 Walsham, 2011, 249.
21 Quoted in Poole, 2005, 12.

6 A HOLY TIME-SCAPE

1 Committee on Government Reform and Oversight, 1998.
2 See Frassetto, 2016, *passim*.
3 Keeble, 2002, 163–5.
4 John Donne, 'Holy Sonnet XIII'.
5 Snobelen, 2003, 545–51.
6 See Brown, F., 2002.
7 See Wallis, 2004, xxxiv–lxiii.
8 MacCarron, 2019, 136–9.
9 See esp. Bede, *EH*, V.xxiv.
10 Wallis, 2004, lxx.
11 See discussion in Liuzza, 2013.
12 See discussion in Bequette, 2002; MacCarron, 117–35.
13 Bequette, 2022, 36–7; Parker, 2023, 118–20.
14 Quoted in Kirkland, 2013, 39.
15 Kirkland, 2013, 44.
16 ibid., 46.
17 Bede, *EH*, I.xxx.
18 For Easter, see Hutton, 1996, 179–81; for the question of pagan origins more generally, see Hutton, 1996, 408–27, 1996a, 50–51, and 2013, 340–400.
19 Hutton, 1996, 139–45; Orme, 2022, 259–60; Parker, 2023, 86–9.
20 Hutton, 1996, 182–5; Orme, 2022, 274–5; Duffy, 2005, 23–7.
21 Hutton, 1996, 187–93; Orme, 2022, 277–8.
22 Hutton, 1996, 371–85; Duffy, 2005, 579–80.

23 Sommerville, 1992, 34.
24 Quoted in Sheils, 2013, 87–8; see also Duffy, 2005, 389–91.
25 Cressy, 2004, 13–33.
26 Hutton, 1996, 142.
27 ibid., 192–3.
28 ibid., 372–8.
29 ibid., 379–85.
30 See ibid., 408–27, 1996a, 50–51, and 2013, 340–400.
31 Thomas and Hessayon, 2009, 210–11; Hutton, 1996a, 89.
32 Thomas and Hessayon, 2009, 212–13.
33 Hill, C., 2014, 84.
34 Hutton, 1996a, 225; Hill, C., 2018, 154.
35 Hill, C., 2018, 143–4.
36 Quoted in Wigley, 1980, 185.
37 Cressy, 2004, 50–66.
38 ibid., 110–55.
39 ibid., 171–89.

7 MY SONG IS IN SIGHING

1 Knowles, 1961, 39–47.
2 Quoted in Owen, 2006, 173–4.
3 Owen, 2006, 166–76.
4 Julian of Norwich, *Revelations*, ch.5.
5 Riehle, 2014, 18.
6 Quoted in ibid., 2014, 23.
7 Knowles, 1961, 29–30; Cox, 1983, 74–6.
8 Quoted in Riehle, 2014, 6.
9 Riehle, 2014, 6.
10 ibid., 7–9.
11 Cox, 1983, 128–9; Riehle, 2014, ch.3.
12 For Rolle's biography, see Comper, 1933, part 1; Knowles, 1961, 48–66; Riehle, 2014, ch.5.
13 Quoted in Cox, 1983, 131.
14 'Ego dormio', Lyric ii, quoted in Comper, 1933, 231.
15 Rolle, *Incendium amoris* (*Fire of Love*), chs 31–2, quoted in Knowles, 1961, 60.
16 *De emendatione vitae* (*The Mending of Life*), ch.12, in Rolle, *Fire of Love*, 236.
17 ibid.
18 ibid., 237.
19 *Incendium amoris*, II.iv, in Rolle, *Fire of Love*, 145.
20 For *The Cloud of Unknowing*, see Cox, 1983, 134–40; Knowles, 1961, 67–99; Riehle, 2014, ch.7.
21 *The Cloud of Unknowing*, in McCann, 1924, ch.3, 11–12, ch.6, 24.
22 ibid., ch.7, 26.
23 ibid.
24 *The Cloud of Unknowing*, in Wolters, 2018, ch.44, 128–9.
25 ibid., ch.26, 100.
26 Eliot, *Four Quartets*, no.4, 'Little Gidding', V.25.
27 Knowles, 1934, 92; DiMaggio, 2013.
28 For Julian of Norwich, see Knowles, 1961, 119–37; Riehle, 2014, ch.9; Williams is quoted in Riehle, 2014, 200.
29 Julian of Norwich, *Revelations*, ch.3, quoted in Knowles, 1961, 122.
30 Quoted in Knowles, 1961, 123.
31 Julian of Norwich, *Revelations*, ch.86, quoted in Knowles, 1961, Introduction, 23.
32 Julian of Norwich, *Revelations*, ch.5.
33 ibid., ch.60, quoted in Knowles, 1961, 129.
34 Julian of Norwich, *Revelations*, ch.22, quoted in Knowles, 1961, 130.

35 Julian of Norwich, *Revelations*, chs 31–3, quoted in Knowles, 1961, 132.
36 Quoted in Julian of Norwich, *Revelations*, Introduction, 16.
37 Quoted in Riehle, 2014, 201.

8 HIS WORDS WERE WITH POWER

1 Quoted in Hill, C., 1993, 51.
2 Daniell, 1994, 122.
3 ibid., 240, 276.
4 Quoted in ibid., 267, 122.
5 Daniell, 1994, 79.
6 Aston, 1983, 13–15.
7 ibid., 108–9, 199–202; Duffy, 2005, 53–87.
8 Quoted in Aston, 1983, 14–15.
9 Aston, 1983.
10 ibid., 21.
11 ibid., 14.
12 ibid., 18.
13 Daniell, 1994, 64–74.
14 See ibid., 238–41.
15 Quoted in ibid., 37.
16 Daniell, 1994, 67.
17 King and Pratt, 2010.
18 Daniell, 1994, 191.
19 Quoted in ibid., 383.
20 Daniell, 2003, 121.
21 Cummings, 2016, 137.
22 Daniell, 2003, 228.
23 Norton, 2000, 165.
24 Bragg, 2012, 337.
25 Daniell, 2003, 121–2.
26 Craig, 1938.
27 Nicholson, 2003, 58–9.
28 Craig, 1938, 43–4.
29 Daniell, 1994, 223–49; Spencer, 2011, 68–70.
30 Quoted in Daniell, 1994, 242.
31 Spencer, 2011, 74.
32 Quoted in ibid., 70.
33 Spencer, 2011, 86–8; Skinner, 1978, 211–38.
34 Marsh, 1994, 18.
35 Hill, C., 1991, 197–213; Spencer, 2011, 121–2.
36 Spencer, 2011, 122; Hill, C., 1991, 231–48.
37 Spencer, 2011, 122–5; Hill, C., 1991, 107–28.
38 Coffey, 1998, 964.
39 ibid.
40 ibid., 965.
41 ibid., 967; Witte, 2008, ch.4; Spencer, 2011, 126–9.
42 Spencer, 2011, 125; for a nuanced discussion of the nature of Cromwell's toleration, see Worden, 2012, ch.3.
43 Spencer, 2011, 144–61.
44 Norton, 2000, 10.
45 Quoted in Daniell, 2003, 273.
46 Daniell, 2003, 274.
47 For Tyndale's education, see Daniell, 1994, 22–48.
48 Norton, 2013, 5.
49 Pantin, 1930.
50 Daniell, 1994, 284–308.
51 For a survey of such sayings, see Crystal, 2010.
52 For fuller surveys of this, see Lemon et al., 2009; Hamlin and Jones, 2010; Bragg, 2012.
53 Shakespeare, *Macbeth*, 2.3.77–9; *The Merchant of Venice*, 2.2.106–7.
54 See Hamlin, 2013, for a full treatment of Shakespeare and the Bible.
55 Shakespeare, *King Lear*, 3.4.32–41.
56 See Fisch, 1999.
57 Milton, *Paradise Lost*, 9.119–30.

58 See Hamlin, 2010.
59 Quoted in Bunyan, *Pilgrim's Progress*, 167.
60 Bunyan, *Pilgrim's Progress*, 68.
61 Mason, 2010, 153.
62 ibid., 159.

9 LET EVERYTHING THAT HATH BREATH

1 Chaucer, *Canterbury Tales*, 'The Prioress' Tale', 553, 517, 500, 516, 537–8, 542.
2 ibid., 549; 'General Prologue', 91; 'The Miller's Tale', 3656; 'The Summoner's Tale', 1866; 'The Miller's Tale', 3190, 3216, 3213; 'General Prologue', 235, 122, 710.
3 Gant, 2017, 31.
4 Wagner, P., 1907, 214; Gant, 2017, 8.
5 Gant, 2017, 32.
6 Chaucer, 'Parliament of Fowles', 191.
7 Flanigan, 1996; Petersen, 2000; Gant, 2017, 18–19.
8 Duffy, 2005, 20–22.
9 For a history of the carol, see Routley, 1959.
10 Davidson, 2016.
11 Gant, 2017, 25.
12 Augustine, *Confessions*, 10.33.
13 Smith, A., 1967; 1559 visitation injunctions, no.29, quoted in Gant, 2017, 105.
14 Gant, 2017, 108–9.
15 *Holy & Ward v Cotterill* [1820].
16 Hamlin, 2000, 38.
17 Shakespeare, *Henry IV Part I*, 2.4.6–7; *The Winter's Tale*, 4.3.46–7.
18 Pope, 1966, 'The First Epistle of the Second Book of Horace Imitated', ln 233–4.
19 Temperley, 1979, 88.
20 ibid., 57.
21 Betjeman, 2007, 21.
22 Quoted in Temperley, 1979, 91.
23 Temperley, 1979, 91–4.
24 ibid., 142.
25 ibid., 156.
26 ibid., 158.
27 ibid., 200.
28 Betjeman, 2007, 22.
29 Watts, 1799, vi.
30 ibid., xv.
31 ibid., xviii.
32 Temperley, 1979, 296–7.
33 For an overview, see Bradley, I., 1997; Watson, 1999 (who discusses the literary merits of the hymns, 1–21); Betjeman, 2007.
34 Gant, 2017, 304.

10 MY UNPREMEDITATED VERSE

1 Edwards, D., 2002, 132.
2 Martz, 1954, 2.
3 Herbert, 1652, ch.3.
4 Sidney, *Defense of Poesy*, in *Selected Writings*, 137.
5 Tottel, 1557, 'The Printer to the Reader', 2.3–25.
6 Puttenham, *Art of English Poesy*, 95.
7 Lewalski, 1979, 36–7.
8 In his biography of John Hacket, Bishop of Lichfield, quoted in Drury, 2013, vi.
9 Lawson, 1953, 103.
10 Johnson, 'Cowley', in *Lives of the English Poets*, 153.
11 Thompson, 1921.
12 Kaske, 2000.
13 Traherne, *Meditations*, I.29–31.
14 Coleridge, *Biographia Literaria*,

ch.19, quoted in Hooton, 1997, 37.
15 Calvin, *Institutes*, ch.1.1.
16 Quoted in Lewalski, 1979, 150.
17 Lewalski, 1979, ch.5.
18 Lewalski, 2013, 389.
19 Milton, *Paradise Lost*, 1.26.
20 Blake, *The Marriage of Heaven and Hell*, 'The Voice of the Devil'.
21 Milton, *Paradise Lost*, 9.114–30.

11 BUT OH! WHO SHALL CONVERT ME?

1 Heasman, 1962, 107.
2 Prochaska, 2008, 1–2.
3 Quoted in Bradley, I., 1976, 19.
4 Spencer, 2011, 156–61.
5 More, 1791, 59–60.
6 Smith, G., 1864, 133.
7 Wesley, *Journal*, 24 May 1738.
8 Bebbington, 2003, 5.
9 Quoted in Bradley, I., 1976, 23.
10 Bradley, I., 1976, 49–50.
11 ibid., 47.
12 Wesley, 1778, 57, 25, 56.
13 Quoted in Howse, 1952, 62.
14 https://www.barnardos.org.uk/who-we-are/our-history (accessed 18 November 2024).
15 Waugh, 1873, 223.
16 ibid., 225.
17 Wymer, 1954, 52–3.
18 Heasman, 1962, 97–101.
19 Winskill, 1892, 176.
20 Villers Committee, 1854, x; see also Winskill, 1892, 102, 224; 2023 figures given in Slow, 18 September 2023.
21 Villers Committee, 1854, 278, para.4737.
22 Quoted in Heasman, 1962, 135.
23 Barnardo, 1907, 96.
24 Winskill, 1892, 175; Heasman, 1962, 92.
25 Cowper, *The Task*, 4.37–8.
26 Heasman, 1962, 135–6.
27 ibid., 137–47.
28 For a broad overview of the subject, see Howse, 1952; Heasman, 1962; Bradley, I., 1976; Prochaska, 2008.
29 Howse, 1952, 121; Bradley, I., 1976, 152.
30 Bowdler, *Reform or Ruin*, quoted in Bradley, I., 1976, 152.
31 Quoted in Bradley, I., 1976, 153.
32 Bradley, I., 1976.
33 Perkin, 1969, 280, quoted in Bradley, I., 1976, 106.
34 Thackeray, *The Newcomes*, ch.2, quoted in Bradley, I., 1976, 26.
35 Bradley, I., 1976, 26–7, 156–78.

12 A PRIEST TO THE TEMPLE

1 Froissart, *Chronicles*, book 2, ch.73, 652–3.
2 Chaucer, *Canterbury Tales*, 'General Prologue', 478–90.
3 Quoted in Tindal Hart, 1980, 32.
4 Spencer, 2011, 54–6; Tindal Hart, 1959, 56–9.
5 Russell, 1944.
6 Tindal Hart, 1980, 26.
7 Baring-Gould, 1949, 143.
8 Chaucer, *Canterbury Tales*, 'General Prologue', 514–20.
9 Thomson, 'Summer', 352–6, 368–70, 1459–60.
10 Crabbe, *The Village*, 1.228–9, 232, 262–7, 268–71.
11 Quoted in Ripperger, 1934, 29.
12 Crabbe, *The Village*, 1.48; Crabbe, 'Tragic Tales, Why', 34–5.
13 Byron, *English Bards and Scotch*

Reviewers, 365.
14 Quoted in Smith, S., 1957, xii.
15 Smith, S., 1957, 298.
16 ibid., 236.
17 Masefield, 'The Everlasting Mercy', 887–8.
18 Kingsley, *The Water Babies*, 104.
19 Quoted in Tindal Hart, 1959, 60.
20 Tindal Hart, 1959, 59–61.
21 Howse, 1952, 12.
22 Ramsay, 1784, 74.
23 Howse, 1952, 31.
24 Shyllon, 1977; Atkins, 2019, 183.
25 Quoted in Wagner and Hunt, 1930, 106.
26 Wagner and Hunt, 1930, 102–4.
27 Quoted in Lloyd, 1966, 318.
28 Lloyd, 1966, 318.
29 Tindal Hart, 1959, 63.
30 Wagner and Hunt, 1930, 52.
31 ibid., 52–9.
32 Beeson, 2003, 160.
33 ibid., 54.
34 Baring-Gould, 1949, 75.
35 ibid., 15; Butler-Gallie, 2021, 4.
36 Brendon, 1975, 137.
37 Tindal Hart, 1970, 134.
38 Tindal Hart, 1959, 110.
39 Groves, 1907.
40 Tindal Hart, 1959, 74.
41 ibid., 72–84.
42 Jones, 2000, ch.10.
43 Mill, 1865, 39.

13 THE PROBLEM

1 Woolston, 1729, 29.
2 Quoted in Rogers, 2014, 85.
3 Bayle, *Philosophical Commentary*, 67–8.
4 Stark, 1999, 249–50.
5 Brown, C., 2001, 8–10.
6 Stark, 1999, 249–51.
7 Dawkins, 2006, 308.
8 See Heyck, 1996, for a useful discussion of the thesis.
9 Brown, C., 2001, 161–2.
10 Wolffe, 1994, 63–74; Brierley, 1998; Brown, C., 2001, 145–69; Crockett and Voas, 2006.
11 Brown, C., 2001, 187–92.
12 Waite, 2022.
13 See, on this point, Davie, 1994; Woodhead, 2016.
14 See Brown, C., 2001, chs 4–6.
15 Quoted in ibid., 80.
16 Brown, C., 2001, 63.
17 ibid., 35–57; Bebbington, 2011, 26.
18 I am indebted to Andrew Heavens for this observation.
19 Quoted in Brown, C., 2001, 132.
20 Brown, C., 2001, 131.
21 ibid., 129.
22 McLeod, 2005, 215.
23 Brown, C., 2001, 175–80; McLeod, 2005, 215–18; Brown, C., 2010; Tombs, 2014, 783–91.
24 McLeod, 2005, 210.
25 Quoted in Berner, 2007, 223.
26 Tennyson, 'Ode on the Death of the Duke of Wellington', VIII.
27 Quoted in Berner, 2007, 224.
28 Berner, 2007.
29 Hastings, 1986, 536–42; MacCulloch, 2009, 988; Milbank, 2023, 22–5.
30 Smith, R., 1957, 357–9.
31 Wolffe, 1994, 255.
32 Quoted in Spencer, 2011, 275.
33 Brown, C., 2010, 475.
34 Bruce, 2002.

14 IDENTITY

1 See, for example, Kumar, 2006, 430–34.
2 From 'Britishness in the Twenty-First Century', a lecture delivered by Colley at 10 Downing Street, quoted in Bryant, 2009, 6–7.
3 See Anderson, 1983.
4 Education Act 2002, section 78.
5 Department for Education, Press Release, 27 November 2014.
6 Carlile, 2011, paras 5, 67.
7 Durkheim, 1972, 203.
8 Shakespeare, *The Merchant of Venice*, 1.1.3–5.
9 Virgil, *Aeneid*, VI.853.
10 Cannadine, 1993, 4.
11 Weight, 2002.
12 Quoted in McLeod, 2005, 220.
13 Text available at http://news.bbc.co.uk/1/hi/uk_politics/1959753.stm (accessed 18 November 2024).
14 Hillman, 2022.
15 See NCVO, 2023.
16 See Royal Holloway, 4 July 2024.
17 See YouGov, 18 June 2018.
18 Grimley, 2007, 905–6.

15 SPIRITUAL SPACE

1 Donne, 'Holy Sonnet V'.
2 Muller, 2019: McGilchrist, 2019.
3 For a discussion of the importance of place and, in particular, the Anglican Parish, see Rumsey, 2017, and Partridge, 2024
4 See Bagehot, 1867, 'The Cabinet'.
5 See Christians in Parliament, n.d.
6 See Daly, 23 December 2023.
7 Quoted in Hatcher, 2024, 176.
8 Hatcher, 2024, 175, 174.

16 MORAL SPACE

1 Anglican Church, October 2020, vi.
2 See Church of England, 10 October 2024; see also Eastham, 17 November 2024.
3 See Roman Catholic Church, November 2020, Executive Summary.
4 Flinders, 4 June 2020.
5 See Anglican Futures, 19 April 2024.
6 Summary available at Global Connections, 3 July 2024.
7 See report in *The Times*, 24 January 2024.
8 Available at Department for Digital, Culture, Media & Sport, 25 July 2017.
9 See https://www.trussell.org.uk/our-work (accessed 16 October 2024).
10 See Church of England, Press Release, 22 December 2022.
11 See Church of England, Press Release, 7 December 2018.
12 See discussion in Williams, 2012, 149–50.
13 See Wolterstorff, 2011; Williams, 2012, 157.
14 See discussion in Brown, 2019, 338–9.

17 SPACE BETWEEN FAITHS

1 See Chivers, 23 December 2010.
2 See National Secular Society, 15 January 2020.
3 For their latest position, see Humanists UK, n.d.
4 See University of Brighton, March

2022.
5 See Vetch, 13 October 2024.
6 Quoted in Modood, 2010, 12.
7 See Elgot, 17 December 2013.
8 Prime Minister's Office, Press Release, 9 April 2023.
9 Prime Minister's Office, Press Release, 1 March 2024.
10 In conversation with the author.
11 See Modood, 2010, 12.
12 In conversation with the author.
13 In conversation with the author. On the development of the Church of England's role in this field, see Loss, 2020.
14 Queen Elizabeth II, 15 February 2012.

18 SPIRITUAL WORTH
1 Hay and Hunt, 2000.
2 Waite, 2022.
3 Quoted in Hunt, 2003, 161–6.
4 Hunt, 2003, 164–5.
5 ibid., 162.
6 ibid., 161.
7 ibid., 166–8.
8 See George Herbert, 'The Search'; John Donne, 'Holy Sonnet XIV'.
9 Traherne, *Meditations*, III.3.

Bibliography

References in the notes are given by surname and year. Earlier texts in modern editions are given by surname and short title; for clarity this title is shown in square brackets in the bibliography below.

Ackroyd, Peter, 2024, *The English Soul: The Faith of a Nation*, Reaktion Books, London

Adams, Claire, 2021, 'Economic Collapse? A Historical and Archaeological Perspective on the Anglo-Saxon Emporium', *Primary Source*, 2:2, 1–8

Aeddi, 1985, *The Life of Bishop Wilfrid*, Colegrave, Bertram (ed. and trans.), Cambridge University Press, Cambridge

Aethelbert, [Law Code] 'The Laws of Aethelbert', 1922, in *The Laws of the Earliest English Kings*, 4–17, Attenborough, Frederick Levi (ed. and trans.), Cambridge University Press, Cambridge

Aldhelm, [*Riddles*] 1925, *Riddles of Aldhelm*, Pitman, J.H. (trans.), Yale University Press, New Haven, CT

Alfred, [*Pastoral Care*] 'Preface to St Gregory's Pastoral Care', 1975, in *Anglo-Saxon Prose*, 30–2, Swanton, Michael (ed. and trans.), J.M. Dent & Sons, London

Anderson, Benedict, 1983, *Imagined Communities: Reflections on the Origin and Spread of Nationalism*, Verso, London

Anglican Church, October 2020, *Safeguarding in the Church of England and the Church in Wales Investigation Report*, at https://webarchive.nationalarchives.gov.uk/ukgwa/20221215023918/https:/www.iicsa.org.uk/key-documents/22519/view/anglican-church-investigation-report-6-october-2020.pdf (accessed 18 November 2024)

Anglican Futures, 19 April 2024, 'Clergy Mental Health is at Breaking Point', at https://www.anglicanfutures.org/post/clergy-mental-health-is-at-breaking-point (accessed 16 October 2024)

Aston, Margaret, 1983, *Lollards and Reformers: Images and Literacy in Late Medieval Religion*, Hambledon Press, London

—, 2015, *Broken Idols of the English Reformation*, Cambridge University Press, Cambridge

Atkin, James Richard, Baron Atkin, 1932, 'Law as an Educational Subject', *Journal of the Society of Public Teachers of Law*, 27–31

Atkins, Gareth, 2019, *Converting Britannia: Evangelicals and British Public Life 1770–1840*, Boydell & Brewer, Woodbridge, Suffolk

Attenborough, Frederick Levi (ed. and trans.), 1922, *The Laws of the Earliest English Kings*, Cambridge University Press, Cambridge

Augustine, Saint, 1845, *The Confessions of S. Augustine*, translation by E.B. Pusey, John Henry Parker, Oxford

Avis, Paul, 2001, *Church, State, and Establishment*, SPCK, London

Bagehot, Walter, 1867, *The English Constitution*, Chapman & Hall, London

Bailey, Merridee L., 2012, *Socialising the Child in Late Medieval England, c.1400–1600*, Boydell & Brewer, Woodbridge, Suffolk

Baldwin, John W., 2015, 'Due Process in Magna Carta: Its Sources in English Law, Canon Law and Stephen Langton', ch.3, 31–52, in *Magna Carta, Religion and the Rule of Law*, Griffith-Jones, Robin, and Hill, Mark (eds), Cambridge University Press, Cambridge

Baring-Gould, Sabine, 1949, *The Vicar of Morwenstow, being a Life of Robert Stephen Hawker, M.A.*, Methuen & Co., London

Barnardo, Syrie Louise Elmsie, and Marchant, James, 1907, *Memoirs of the Late Dr Barnardo*, Hodder & Stoughton, London

Bassard, Katherine Clay, 2010, 'The King James Bible and African American Literature', ch.14, 294–317, in *The King James Bible after Four Hundred Years: Literary, Linguistic, and Cultural Influences*, Hamlin, Hannibal, and Jones, Norman W. (eds), Cambridge University Press, Cambridge

Bassett, Steven, 1989, 'In Search of the Origins of Anglo-Saxon Kingship', ch.1, 3–27, in *The Origins of Anglo-Saxon Kingdoms*, Bassett, S. (ed.), Leicester University Press, Leicester

Bayle, Pierre, [*Philosophical Commentary*] 2005, *A Philosophical Commentary on These Words of the Gospel, Luke 14.23, 'Compel Them to Come In, That My House May Be Full'*, Kilcullen, John, and Kukathas, Chandran (eds), Liberty Fund, Indianapolis, IN

Beaumont, Sheona, and Thiele, Madeleine Emerald, 2023, 'Introduction: "All Great Art Is Praise": John Ruskin' in *John Ruskin, the Pre-Raphaelites, and Religious Imagination*, Beaumont, Sheona, and Thiele, Madeleine Emerald (eds), Palgrave Macmillan, Basingstoke

Bebbington, David W., 2003, *Evangelicalism in Modern Britain: A History from the 1730s to the 1980s*, Routledge, Abingdon

—, 2011, *Victorian Nonconformity*, Lutterworth Press, Cambridge

Bede, The Venerable Bede, [*Lives of the Abbots*] 1910, *Lives of the First Five Abbots of Wearmouth and Jarrow: Benedict, Ceolfrid, Eosterwine, Sigfrid, and Huetbert*, Wilcock, P. (trans.), Hills & Company, Sunderland

—, [*Life of Cuthbert*] 1965, *Life of Cuthbert*, Webb, J.F. (trans.), Penguin Books, Harmondsworth

—, [*EH*] 1989, *Ecclesiastical History of the English People*, Loeb Classical Library, Harvard University Press, Cambridge, MA

—, 1989a, *Epistle to Egbert*, vol.2, in *Ecclesiastical History of the English People*, Loeb Classical Library, Harvard University Press, Cambridge, MA

Beeson, Trevor, 2003, *The Bishops*, SCM Press, London

Behr, Charlotte, 2000, 'The Origins of Kingship in Early Medieval Kent', *Early Medieval Europe*, 9:1, 25–52

Bennett, Joshua, 2019, *God and Progress: Religion and History in British Intellectual Culture, 1845–1914*, Oxford University Press, Oxford

Bequette, John P., 2022, *Bede the Theologian: History, Rhetoric, and Spirituality*, Catholic University of America Press, Washington, DC

Berman, Harold J., 1983, *Law and Revolution: The Formation of the English Legal Tradition*, Harvard University Press, Cambridge, MA

—, 2009, *Law and Revolution II: The Impact of the Protestant Reformations on the Western Legal Tradition*, Harvard University Press, Cambridge, MA

Berner, Ashley Rogers, 2007, 'Is English Education Secular?', 222–32, in *Redefining Christian Britain: Post-1945 Perspectives*, Garnett, J., et al. (eds), SCM Press, London

Betjeman, John, 2007, *Sweet Songs of Zion: Selected Radio Talks*, Games, Stephen (ed.), Hodder & Stoughton, London

Binski, Paul, 2019, *Gothic Sculpture*, Yale University Press, London

Bischoff, B., and Lapidge, M. (eds), 1995, *Biblical Commentaries from the Canterbury School of Theodore and Hadrian*, Cambridge Studies in Anglo-Saxon England, Cambridge University Press, Cambridge

Blair, John, 2005, *The Church in Anglo-Saxon Society*, Oxford University Press, Oxford

Blair, Peter Hunter, 1970, *The World of Bede*, Cambridge University Press, Cambridge

Bolton, W.F., 1967, *A History of Anglo-Latin Literature, 597–1066*, vol.1, Princeton University Press, Princeton, NJ

Boniface, [Letters] 1919, in *Die Briefe des heiligen Bonifatius*, Tangl, M. (ed.), Berlin; English version available at https://origin-rh.web.fordham.edu/halsall/basis/boniface-letters.asp

Bradley, Ian C., 1976, *The Call to Seriousness: The Evangelical Impact on the Victorians*, J. Cape, London

—, 1997, *Abide with Me: The World of Victorian Hymns*, SCM Press, London

Bradley, S.A.J. (ed.), 1982, *Anglo-Saxon Poetry: An Anthology of Old English Poems in Prose Translation*, Dent, London

Bragg, Melvyn, 2012, *The Book of Books: The Radical Impact of the King James Bible 1611–2011*, Counterpoint, Berkeley, CA

Brendon, Piers, 1975, *Hawker of Morwenstow: Portrait of a Victorian Eccentric*, J. Cape, London

Brierley, Peter, 1998, 'Religion', ch.13, 518–60, in *British Social Trends since 1900: A Guide to the Changing Social Structure of Britain*, Halsey, A.H. (ed.), Macmillan, London

British Social Attitudes Survey, 2017, National Centre for Social Research, table of figures available at https://web.archive.org/web/20170927052351/http://www.natcen.ac.uk/media/1469605/BSA-religion.pdf

Brooks, Nicholas, 2000, 'Canterbury, Rome and the Construction of English Identity', 221–47, in *Early Medieval Rome and the Christian West: Essays in Honour of Donald A. Bullough*, Smith, Julia (ed.), Brill, Leiden

—, 2005, 'The Henry Loyn Memorial Lecture: English Identity from Bede to the Millennium', *The Haskins Society Journal 14:2003. Studies in Medieval History*, 33–52

Browett, Rebecca, 2017, 'Touching the Holy: The Rise of Contact Relics in Medieval England', *Journal of Ecclesiastical History*, 68:3, 493–509

Brown, Callum G., 2001, *The Death of Christian Britain*, Routledge, Abingdon

—, 2010, 'What was the Religious Crisis of the 1960s?', *Journal of Religious History*, 34:4, 468–79

Brown, Frances, 2002, *Joanna Southcott: The Woman Clothed with the Sun*, Lutterworth Press, Cambridge

Brown, Malcolm, 2019, 'Establishment: Some Theological Considerations', *Ecclesiastical Law Journal*, 21:3, 329–41

Brown, Michelle P., 2017, 'Strategies of Visual Literacy in Insular and Anglo-Saxon Book Culture', ch.4, 71–104, in *Transformation in Anglo-Saxon Culture: Toller Lectures on Art, Archaeology and Text*, Insley, Charles, and Owen-Crocker, Gale R. (eds), Oxbow Books, Oxford

Brown, Peter, 2013, *The Rise of Western Christendom: Triumph and Diversity, A.D. 200–1000*, Wiley-Blackwell, Chichester

Bruce, Steve, 2002, 'Praying Alone? Church-Going in Britain and the Putnam Thesis', *Journal of Contemporary Religion*, 17:3, 317–28

—, 2003, 'The Demise of Christianity in Britain', ch.4, 53–63, in *Predicting Religion: Christian, Secular and Alternative Futures*, Davie, Grace, Heelas, Paul, and Woodhead, Linda (eds), Ashgate, Aldershot

Bruce-Mitford, R.L.S., 1967, 'The Art of the Codex Amiatinus', Jarrow Lecture 1967, *Journal of the British Archaeological Association*, 32:1, 1–25

Bryant, Christopher, 2009, 'The British Question', *British Politics Review*, 4:3, 6–7

Bunyan, John, [*Pilgrim's Progress*] 1928, *The Pilgrim's Progress*, Wharey, James Blanton (ed.), Clarendon Press, Oxford

Butcher, Ben, and Swerling, Gabriella, 17 February 2024, 'Clergy Warn of "Doom Spiral" as Church Attendance Drops Off at Record Rate', *The Telegraph*, at https://www.telegraph.co.uk/news/2024/02/17/clergy-warn-doom-spiral-church-attendance-drops-record-rate/

Butler-Gallie, Fergus, 2021, *A Field Guide to the English Clergy*, Oneworld, London

Byrne, Philippa, 2019, *Justice and Mercy: Moral Theology and the Exercise of Law in Twelfth-Century England*, Manchester University Press, Manchester

Byron, George Gordon, Lord Byron, [*English Bards and Scotch Reviewers*] 1903, in *The Works of Lord Byron*, vol.1, John Murray, London

Calvin, Jean, [*Institutes*] 1845, *Institutes of the Christian Religion*, Beveridge, Henry (trans.), Calvin Translation Society, Edinburgh

Camille, Michael, 1985, 'Seeing and Reading: Some Visual Implications of Medieval Literacy and Illiteracy', *Art History*, 8:1, 26–49

—, 1987, 'The Language of Images in Medieval England, 1200–1400', 33–40, in *Age of Chivalry: Art in Plantagenet England 1200–1400*, Alexander, J., and Binski, P. (eds), Royal Academy of Arts, London

Cannadine, David, 12 March 1993, 'Penguin Island Story', *Times Literary Supplement*, 4693

Carlile, Alex, Lord Carlile, 2011, *Report to the Home Secretary of Independent Oversight of Prevent Review and Strategy*, Home Office, London

Castle, Richard, 2003, 'Lord Atkin and the Neighbour Test: Origins of the Principles of Negligence in Donoghue v Stevenson', *Ecclesiastical Law Journal*, 7:33, 210–14

Catto, J.I., and Evans, T.A.R. (eds), 1992, *The History of the University of Oxford*, vol.2: *Late Medieval Oxford*, Oxford University Press, Oxford

Chadwick, Owen, 1966, *The Victorian Church*, 2 vols, A. & C. Black, London

Chapman, Matthew, 2010, *The Snail and the Ginger Beer: The Story of Donoghue v Stevenson*, Wildy, Simmonds & Hill, London

Cheshire, Jim, 2020, 'Victorian Medievalism and Secular Design', ch.27, 447–62, in *The Oxford Handbook of Victorian Medievalism*, Parker, J., and Wagner, C. (eds), Oxford University Press, Oxford

Chivers, Tom, 23 December 2010, 'The Biggest "War on Christmas" Myths', *The Telegraph*, at https://www.telegraph.co.uk/topics/christmas/8220780/The-biggest-war-on-Christmas-myths.html (accessed 16 October 2024)

Christians in Parliament, n.d., 'Prayers have been Said in Parliament for Centuries. My Colleagues Should Not Abolish It', at https://www.christiansinparliament.org.uk/latest/blog-parliamentary-prayers/ (accessed 16 October 2024)

Chula, Alexander, 2023, *Goodbye Dr Banda: Lessons for the West from a Small African Country*, Polygon, Edinburgh

Church of England, Press Release, 7 December 2018, 'Church of England Parishes Set to Support Winter Shelters', at https://www.churchofengland.org/media/press-releases/church-england-parishes-set-support-winter-shelters (accessed 16 October 2024)

—, 22 December 2022, 'Cost of Living Crisis: 2.6 Million Seek Help from Churches and Faith Groups', at https://www.churchofengland.org/media/press-releases/cost-living-crisis-26-million-seek-help-churches-and-faith-groups (accessed 16 October 2024)

—, 20 May 2024, 'Weekly Church Attendance Up Five Per Cent in Third Year of Consecutive Growth', at https://www.churchofengland.org/media/press-releases/weekly-church-attendance-five-cent-third-year-consecutive-growth (accessed 18 November 2024)

—, 10 October 2024, 'Independent Learning Lessons Review: John Smyth QC, by Keith Makin, Independent Reviewer', at https://www.churchofengland.org/sites/default/files/2024-11/independent-learning-lessons-review-john-smyth-qc-november-2024.pdf (accessed 18 November 2024)

Clark, James G., 2008, 'Monasteries and Secular Education in Late Medieval England', ch.10, 145–67, in *Monasteries and Society in the British Isles in the Later Middle Ages*, Burton, Janet, and Stober, Karen (eds), Boydell Press, Woodbridge, Suffolk

Cochran, Robert Jr, and Moreland, Michael (eds), 2021, *Christianity and Private Law*, Routledge, Abingdon

Coffey, John, 1998, 'Puritanism and Liberty Revisited: The Case for Toleration in the English Revolution', *The Historical Journal*, 41:4, 961–85

Colegrave, Bertram (ed. and trans.), 1968, *The Earliest Life of Gregory the Great by an Anonymous Monk of Whitby*, Cambridge University Press, Cambridge

Committee on Government Reform and Oversight, 1998, *The Year 2000 Problem: Fourth Report by the Committee on Government Reform and Oversight, Together with Additional Views*, Washington, DC

Comper, Frances, 1933, *The Life of Richard Rolle Together with an Edition of his English Lyrics*, Dent & Sons, London and Toronto

Cox, Michael, 1983, *Mysticism: The Direct Experience of God*, Aquarian Press, Wellingborough

Craig, Hardin, 1938, 'The Geneva Bible as a Political Document', *Pacific Historical Review*, 7:1, 40–49

Cressy, David, 2004, *Bonfires and Bells: National Memory and the Protestant Calendar in Elizabethan and Stuart England*, Sutton Publishing, Stroud

Crockett, Alasdair, and Voas, David, 2006, 'Generations of Decline: Religious

Change in 20th-Century Britain', *Journal for the Scientific Study of Religion*, 45:4, 567–84

Crystal, David, 2010, *Begat: The King James Bible and the English Language*, Oxford University Press, Oxford

Cummings, Brian, 2016, 'Print, Popularity, and the Book of Common Prayer', ch.6, 135–44, in *The Elizabethan Top Ten*, Kesson, Andy, and Smith, Emma (eds), Routledge, London

Cynewulf, *Christ I*, in Krapp, George Philip and Dobbie, Elliott van Kirk (eds) 1936, *The Exeter Book*, The Anglo-Saxon Poetic Records: A Collective Edition, vol.3, New York: Columbia University Press

Dales, Douglas, 2012, *Alcuin: His Life and Legacy*, James Clarke & Co., Cambridge

Daly, Patrick, 23 December 2023, 'The Commons Would Be Lessened without its Daily Prayers, Says Speaker's Chaplain', *Independent*, at https://www.independent.co.uk/news/uk/uk-parliament-lindsay-hoyle-national-secular-society-mps-commons-b2468669.html (accessed 16 October 2024)

Daniell, David, 1994, *William Tyndale: A Biography*, Yale University Press, New Haven, CT, and London

—, 2003, *The Bible in English: Its History and Influence*, Yale University Press, New Haven, CT, and London

Darby, Peter, 2013, 'Bede, Iconoclasm and the Temple of Solomon', *Early Medieval Europe*, 21:4, 390–421

Davidson, Clifford, 2016, 'The Coventry Mysteries and Shakespeare's Histories', *Early Drama, Art, and Music*, 6, n.p.

Davie, Grace, 1994, *Religion in Britain since 1945: Believing without Belonging*, Blackwell, Oxford

Davie, Grace, Heelas, Paul, and Woodhead, Linda (eds), 2003, *Predicting Religion: Christian, Secular and Alternative Futures*, Ashgate, Aldershot

Davis, David J., 2013, *Seeing Faith, Printing Pictures: Religious Identity during the English Reformation*, Brill, Leiden

Dawkins, Richard, 2006, *The God Delusion*, Houghton Mifflin Company, New York

Denning, Alfred Thompson, Baron Denning, 1989, *The Influence of Religion on Law*, Canadian Institute for Law, Edmonton

Dent, Chris, 2017, 'Religion and the Early Modern Patent System, 1560–1660', *Oxford Journal of Law and Religion*, 6, 580–99

Denton, Jeffrey, 1987, 'Image and History', ch.1, 20–26, in *Age of Chivalry: Art in Plantagenet England 1200–1400*, Alexander, J., and Binski, P. (eds), Royal Academy of Arts, London

Department for Digital, Culture, Media & Sport, 25 July 2017, 'Community Life Survey 2016–2017', at https://assets.publishing.service.gov.uk/media/5a81beeae5274a2e87dbf414/Community_Life_Survey_-_Statistical_

Release_2016-17_FINAL_v.2.pdf (accessed 16 October 2024)

Department for Education, Press Release, 27 November 2014, 'Guidance on Promoting British Values in Schools Published', at https://www.gov.uk/government/news/guidance-on-promoting-british-values-in-schools-published (accessed 16 October 2024)

Devlin, Patrick Arthur, Baron Devlin, 1965, *The Enforcement of Morals*, Oxford University Press, Oxford

DiMaggio, Kenneth, 2013, 'The Unknown Cloud behind the Yellow Fog: The Medieval Religious Journey in T.S. Eliot's "The Love Song of J. Alfred Prufrock"', *The International Journal of Religion and Spirituality in Society*, 2:2, 35–42

Doan, James E., 1982, 'Mediterranean Influences on Insular Manuscript Illumination', *Proceedings of the Harvard Celtic Colloquium*, 2, 31–8

Doe, Norman, 1990, *Fundamental Authority in Late Medieval English Law*, Cambridge University Press, Cambridge

—, 2017, 'Richard Hooker: Priest and Jurist', ch.6, 115–38, in *Great Christian Jurists in English History*, Hill, Mark, and Helmholz, R.H. (eds), Cambridge University Press, Cambridge

Douie, Decima L., and Farmer, Hugh (eds), 1985, *Magna vita Sancti Hugonis: The Life of St. Hugh of Lincoln*, vol.2, Clarendon Press, Oxford

Drury, John, 2013, *Music at Midnight: The Life and Poetry of George Herbert*, Penguin Books, London

Duffy, Eamon, 2005, *The Stripping of the Altars: Traditional Religion in England, 1400–1580*, Yale University Press, New Haven, CT, and London

Dumitrescu, Irina, 2018, 'Violence: Ælfric Bata's Colloquies', ch.3, 60–89, in *The Experience of Education in Anglo-Saxon Literature*, Dumitrescu, Irina, Cambridge University Press, Cambridge

Durkheim, É., 1972, *Emile Durkheim: Selected Writings*, Giddens A. (ed.), Cambridge University Press, Cambridge

Eastham, Janet, 17 November 2024, 'Calls for Archbishop of York to Step Down following Justin Welby Scandal', *The Telegraph*, at https://www.telegraph.co.uk/news/2024/11/17/archbishop-york-justin-welby-sex-abuse-scandal/ (accessed 18 November 2024)

Edwards, David, 2002, *John Donne: Man of Flesh and Spirit*, Bloomsbury Publishing, London

Edwards, Katie, 29 November 2022, 'Christianity in the UK is in Decline but its Influence is Not – and That's a Real Problem', *The i Paper*, at https://inews.co.uk/opinion/christianity-in-the-uk-is-in-decline-but-its-influence-is-not-and-thats-a-real-problem-2000872

Ehsan, Rakib, 2023, *Beyond Grievance: What the Left Gets Wrong about Ethnic Minorities*, Forum, London

Elgot, Jessica, 17 December 2013, '"We Really Don't Want to Ban Christmas", Muslims Insist', *The Huffington Post*, at https://www.huffingtonpost.co.uk/2013/12/17/ban-christmas-muslims_n_4460151.html (accessed 18 November 2024)

Eliot, T.S., 1939, *The Idea of a Christian Society*, Faber & Faber, London

Elizabeth II, Queen, 15 February 2012, 'A Speech by The Queen at Lambeth Palace, 2012', at https://www.royal.uk/queens-speech-lambeth-palace-15-february-2012 (accessed 17 October 2020)

Everett, Edward John, 2021, 'Sanctuary in Sixteenth-Century England', PhD Thesis, University of Cambridge, Cambridge

Fincham, Kenneth, and Tyacke, Nicholas, 2007, *Altars Restored: The Changing Face of English Religious Worship, 1547–c.1700*, Oxford University Press, Oxford

Fisch, Harold, 1999, *The Biblical Presence in Shakespeare, Milton, and Blake: A Comparative Study*, Clarendon Press, Oxford

Flanigan, C. Clifford, 1996, 'Medieval Liturgy and the Arts: Visitatio Sephulcri as Paradigm', ch.1, 9–35, in *Liturgy and the Arts in the Middle Ages: Studies in Honour of C. Clifford Flanigan*, Lille, E.L., et al. (eds), Museum Tusculanum Press, Copenhagen

Flinders, Karl, 4 June 2020, 'MPs' Investigation into Post Office Horizon IT Scandal Bares Teeth', *Computer Weekly*, at https://www.computerweekly.com/news/252484163/Government-investigation-into-Horizon-scandal-bares-teeth (accessed 18 November 2024)

Foot, Sarah, 1996, 'The Making of Angelcynn: English Identity before the Norman Conquest', *Transactions of the Royal Historical Society*, 6, 25–49

—, 2011, *Æthelstan: The First King of England*, Yale University Press, New Haven, CT

—, 2017, 'Bede's Kings', ch.3, 25–51, in *Writing, Kingship and Power in Anglo-Saxon England*, Naismith, Rory, and Woodman, David (eds), Cambridge University Press, Cambridge

Forbes, Helen Foxhall, 2013, *Heaven and Earth in Anglo-Saxon England: Theology and Society in an Age of Faith*, Routledge, Abingdon

Frassetto, Michael (ed.), 2016, *The Year 1000: Religious and Social Response to the Turning of the First Millennium*, Palgrave Macmillan, New York

Frazer, William, and Tyrrell, Andrew (eds), 2001, *Social Identity in Early Medieval Britain*, Bloomsbury, London

Froissart, Sir John, [*Chronicles*] 1848, *Chronicles of England, France and Spain and the Surrounding Countries*, Johnes, Thomas (trans.), William Smith, London

Gant, Andrew, 2017, *O Sing unto the Lord: A History of English Church Music*, University of Chicago Press, Chicago, IL

Geary, Ian, 2024, *Faith, Politics and Belonging: A Reflection on Identity, Complexity, Simplicity and Obsession*, Resource Publications, Eugene, OR

Giebelhausen, Michaela, 2016, *Painting the Bible: Representation and Belief in Mid-Victorian Britain*, Routledge, Abingdon

Gildas, [*Works*] 1841, in *The Works of Gildas and Nennius*, Giles, J.R. (trans.), James Bohn, London

Gittos, Helen, 2015, *Liturgy, Architecture, and Sacred Places in Anglo-Saxon England*, Oxford University Press, Oxford

Global Connections, 3 July 2024, 'The Generosity Report', at https://globalconnections.org.uk/news/the-generosity-report (accessed 16 October 2024)

Gregorii I Papae registrum epistolarum, 1887–91, Ewald, Paulus, and Hartmann, Ludovicus (eds), Weidmann, Berlin

Griffith-Jones, Robin, and Hill, Mark (eds), 2015, *Magna Carta, Religion and the Rule of Law*, Cambridge University Press, Cambridge

Grimley, Matthew, 2007, 'The Religion of Englishness: Puritanism, Providentialism, and "National Character" 1918–1945', *Journal of British Studies*, 46:4, 884–906

Groves, James, 1907, 'Crabbe as a Botanist', *Proceedings of the Suffolk Institute of Archaeology and Natural History*, 12:2, 223–32

Gwara, Scott, and Porter, David W., 1997, *Anglo-Saxon Conversations: The Colloquies of Aelfric Bata*, Boydell Press, Woodbridge, Suffolk

Hamlin, Hannibal, 2000, '"Very Mete to be Used of All Sortes of People": The Remarkable Popularity of the "Sternhold and Hopkins" Psalter', *The Yale University Library Gazette*, 75:1/2, 37–51

—, 2010, 'Bunyan's Biblical Progresses', ch.9, 202–18, in *The King James Bible after Four Hundred Years: Literary, Linguistic, and Cultural Influences*, Hamlin, Hannibal, and Jones, Norman W. (eds), Cambridge University Press, Cambridge

—, 2013, *The Bible in Shakespeare*, Oxford University Press, Oxford

Hamlin, Hannibal, and Jones, Norman W. (eds), 2010, *The King James Bible after Four Hundred Years: Literary, Linguistic, and Cultural Influences*, Cambridge University Press, Cambridge

Hamling, Tara, 2007, 'To See or Not to See? The Presence of Religious Imagery in the Protestant Household', *Art History*, 30:2, 170–97

—, 2011, *Decorating the 'Godly' Household: Religious Art in Post-Reformation Britain*, Yale University Press, London

Hamling, Tara, and Willis, Jonathan, 2023, 'From Rejection to Reconciliation: Protestantism and the Image in Early Modern England', *Journal of British Studies*, 62, 932–63

Hare, Kent Gregory, 2004, 'Christian Heroism and the West Saxon Achievement: The Old English Poetic Evidence', *Medieval Forum*, 4, n.p.

Harries, Richard, 2013, *The Image of Christ in Modern Art*, Ashgate, Farnham

Harvey, Margaret, 2006, *Lay Religious Life in Late Medieval Durham*, Boydell & Brewer, Woodbridge, Suffolk

Hastings, Adrian, 1986, *A History of English Christianity 1920–1985*, Collins, London

Hatcher, Mark, 2024, 'Bishops in the House of Lords: Fit for the Future?', *Ecclesiastical Law Journal*, 26:2, 147–80

Hay, David, and Hunt, Kate, 2000, *Understanding the Spirituality of People Who Don't Go to Church: A Report on the Findings of the Adults' Spirituality Project at the University of Nottingham*, Mission Theological Advisory Group, at https://www.spiritualjourneys.org.uk/pdf/look_understanding_the_spirituality_of_people.pdf (accessed 17 October 2024)

Haynes, Clare, 2006, *Pictures and Popery: Art and Religion in England, 1660–1760*, Ashgate, Aldershot

Heasman, Kathleen, 1962, *Evangelicals in Action: An Appraisal of their Social Work in the Victorian Era*, Geoffrey Bles, London

Hedlund, Richard, 2015, 'The Theological Foundations of Equity's Conscience', *Oxford Journal of Law and Religion*, 4, 119–40

Helmholz, Richard H., 1990, *Roman Canon Law in Reformation England*, Cambridge University Press, Cambridge

—, 2009, 'Bonham's Case, Judicial Review, and the Law of Nature', *Journal of Legal Analysis*, 1:1, 325–54

—, 2021, 'English Property Law and Christianity, 1500–1700', ch.6, 94–108, in *Christianity and Private Law*, Cochran, Robert Jr, and Moreland, Michael (eds), Routledge, Abingdon

Helmholz, Richard H., et al., 1997, *The Privilege against Self-Incrimination: Its Origins and Development*, University of Chicago Press, Chicago, IL, and London

Henderson, George, 1999, *Vision and Image in Early Christian England*, Cambridge University Press, Cambridge

Herbert, George, 1652, *A Priest to the Temple*, T. Garthwait, London

Heslop, T.A., 1987, 'Attitudes to the Visual Arts: The Evidence from Written Sources', 26–32, in *Age of Chivalry: Art in Plantagenet England 1200–1400*, Alexander, J., and Binski, P. (eds), Royal Academy of Arts, London

Heyck, Thomas William, 1996, 'The Decline of Christianity in Twentieth-Century Britain', *Albion: A Quarterly Journal Concerned with British Studies*, 28:3, 437–53

Higham, Nicholas John, 1997, *The Convert Kings: Power and Religious Affiliation in Early Anglo-Saxon England*, Manchester University Press, Manchester

Hill, Christopher, 1991, *The World Turned Upside Down: Radical Ideas during the English Revolution*, Penguin Books, London

—, 1993, *The English Bible and the Seventeenth-Century Revolution*, Allen Lane, London

—, 2014, *The Century of Revolution, 1603–1714*, Routledge, London

—, 2018, *Society and Puritanism*, Verso, London

Hill, Mark, and Helmholz, R.H. (eds), 2017, *Great Christian Jurists in English History*, Cambridge University Press, Cambridge

Hill, Rosemary, 1999, 'Reformation to Millennium: Pugin's Contrasts in the History of English Thought', *Journal of the Society of Architectural Historians*, 58:1, 26–41

Hillman, Nick, 2022, '"You Can't Say That!" What Students Really Think of Free Speech on Campus', *HEPI Policy Note*, 35, at https://www.hepi.ac.uk/wp-content/uploads/2022/06/You-cant-say-that-What-students-really-think-of-free-speech-on-campus.pdf (accessed 16 October 2024)

Holland, Tom, 2016, *Athelstan: The Making of England*, Penguin Monarchs, Penguin Books, London

—, 2019, *Dominion: The Making of the Western Mind*, Little, Brown, London

Hooton, William R., III, 1997, 'Herbert, Keats, and the Romantic Revival of Metaphysical Poetry', *George Herbert Journal*, 21:1, 33–57

Howse, Ernest Marshall, 1952, *Saints in Politics: The 'Clapham Sect' and the Growth of Freedom*, Allen & Unwin, London

Humanists UK, n.d., 'Collective Worship and School Assemblies: Your Rights', at https://humanists.uk/education/parents/collective-worship-and-school-assemblies-your-rights (accessed 16 October 2024)

Hunt, Kate, 2003, 'Understanding the Spirituality of People Who Do Not Go to Church', ch.13, 159–69, in *Predicting Religion: Christian, Secular, and Alternative Futures*, Davie, Grace, Heelas, Paul, and Woodhead, Linda (eds), Ashgate, Aldershot

Hunt, R.W., 1936, 'English Learning in the Late Twelfth Century', *Transactions of the Royal Historical Society*, 19, 19–42

Hutton, Ronald, 1996, *Stations of the Sun: A History of the Ritual Year in Britain*, Oxford University Press, Oxford

—, 1996a, *The Rise and Fall of Merry England: The Ritual Year, 1400–1700*, Oxford University Press, Oxford

—, 2013, *Pagan Britain*, Yale University Press, New Haven, CT, and London

Innes, Matthew, 2007, *Introduction to Early Medieval Europe, 300–900: The Sword, the Plough and the Book*, Routledge, Abingdon

Johnson, Samuel, [*Lives of the English Poets*] 1911, *Lives of the English Poets*, Meynell, Alice, and Chesterton, G.K. (eds), Herbert & Daniel, London

Jones, Anthea, 2000, *A Thousand Years of the English Parish: Medieval Patterns and Modern Interpretations*, Windrush Press, Moreton-in-Marsh

Julian of Norwich, [*Revelations*] 1966, *Revelations of Divine Love*, Wolters, Clifton (ed.), Penguin, London

Jurasinski, Stefan, and Oliver, Lisi, 2021, *The Laws of Alfred: The Domboc and the Making of Anglo-Saxon Law*, Studies in Legal History, Cambridge University Press, Cambridge

Kamali, Elizabeth Papp, 2019, *Felony and the Guilty Mind in Medieval England*, Cambridge University Press, Cambridge

Kaske, Carol V., 2000, 'Neoplatonism in Spenser Once More', *Religion and Literature*, 32:2, 157–69

Keeble, N.H., 2002, *The Restoration: England in the 1660s*, Blackwell, Oxford

Kelly, Stuart, 2018, *The Minister and the Murderer: A Book of Aftermaths*, Granta Books, London

King, John N., and Pratt, Aaron T., 2010, 'The Materiality of English Printed Bibles from the Tyndale New Testament to the King James Bible', ch.3, 61–99, in *The King James Bible after Four Hundred Years: Literary, Linguistic, and Cultural Influences*, Hamlin, Hannibal, and Jones, Norman W. (eds), Cambridge University Press, Cambridge

Kingsley, Charles, [*The Water Babies*] 2013, *The Water Babies*, Oxford World's Classics, Oxford University Press, Oxford

Kirkland, J.S., 2013, 'From Rite to Right: How Holy Days Became a Natural Right in Medieval England', MA Thesis, Texas Tech University, Lubbock, TX

Knights, Samantha, 2021, *Law, Rights, and Religion*, Oxford University Press, Oxford

Knowles, David, 1934, 'The Excellence of *The Cloud*', *The Downside Review*, 52, 92

—, 1955, *The Religious Orders in England*, vol.2, Cambridge University Press, Cambridge

—, 1961, *The English Mystical Tradition*, Harper & Row, New York

Kumar, Krishan, 2006, 'English and British National Identity', *History Compass*, 4:3, 428–47

Lambert, Tom, 2017, *Law and Order in Anglo-Saxon England*, Oxford University Press, Oxford

Lang, S., 1966, 'The Principles of the Gothic Revival in England', *Journal of the Society of Architectural Historians*, 25:4, 240–67

Lawson, Penelope (trans.), 1953, 'The Letter of St. Athanasius to Marcellinus on the Interpretation of the Psalms', in *St. Athanasius on the Incarnation: The Treatise De incarnatione Verbi Dei*, St Vladimir's Orthodox Theological Seminary, Crestwood, NY

Lemon, Rebecca, et al. (eds), 2009, *The Blackwell Companion to the Bible in English Literature*, Wiley-Blackwell, Chichester

Lewalski, Barbara Kiefer, 1979, *Protestant Poetics and the Seventeenth-Century Religious Lyric*, Princeton University Press, Princeton, NJ

—, 2013, 'The KJV and the Seventeenth-Century Religious Lyric', 385–400, in *The King James Version at 400: Assessing its Genius as Bible Translation and its Literary Influence*, Burke, D.G., et al. (eds), Society of Biblical Literature, Atlanta, GA

Lewis, Barry, Gray, Madeleine, Ceri Jones, David, and Morgan, D. Densil, 2022, *A History of Christianity in Wales*, University of Wales Press, Cardiff

Lindberg, David C., 1987, 'Science as Handmaiden: Roger Bacon and the Patristic Tradition', *Isis*, 78:4, 518–36

Lister, Raymond, 1984, *Samuel Palmer and 'The Ancients': Selected and Catalogued*, exh.cat., Fitzwilliam Museum, Cambridge, 9 October–16 December 1984, Cambridge University Press, Cambridge

Liuzza, R.M., 2013, 'The Sense of Time in Anglo-Saxon England', *Bulletin of the John Rylands University Library*, 89:2, 131–53

Lloyd, Roger Bradshaigh, 1966, *The Church of England, 1900–1966*, SCM Press, London

Loss, Daniel S., 2020, 'The Church of England, Minority Religions and the Making of Communal Pluralism', ch.14, 298–316, in *The Church of England and British Politics since 1900*, Rodger, T., et al. (eds), Boydell & Brewer, Woodbridge, Suffolk

Love, Rosalind, 2011, 'The Library of the Venerable Bede', ch.31, 606–32, in *The Cambridge History of the Book in Britain*, Gameson, Richard (ed.), Cambridge University Press, Cambridge

Marsh, Christopher W., 1994, *The Family of Love in English Society, 1550–1630*, Cambridge University Press, Cambridge

Martz, Louis, 1954, *The Poetry of Meditation*, Yale University Press, London and New Haven, CT

Mason, Emma, 2010, 'The Victorians and Bunyan's Legacy', ch.11, 150–61, in *The Cambridge Companion to Bunyan*, Dunan-Page, Anne (ed.), Cambridge Companions to Literature, Cambridge University Press, Cambridge

Mayhew, Robert J., 2004, *Landscape, Literature and English Religious Culture, 1660–1800: Samuel Johnson and Languages of Natural Description*, Palgrave Macmillan, London

Mayr-Harting, Henry, 1972, *The Coming of Christianity to Anglo-Saxon England*, B.T. Batsford, London

McCann, Justin (ed.), 1924, *The Cloud of Unknowing and Other Treatises by an English Mystic of the Fourteenth Century*, Benzinger Brothers, New York

MacCarron, Máirín, 2019, *Bede and Time: Computus, Theology and History in the Early Medieval World*, Routledge, Abingdon

MacCarthy, Fiona, 1989, *Eric Gill: A Lover's Quest for Art and God*, Dutton, New York

McClure, Judith, 1983, 'Bede's Old Testamant Kings', ch.5, 76–98, in *Ideal and Reality in Frankish and Anglo-Saxon Society: Studies Presented to J.M. Wallace-Hadrill*, Wormald, Patrick, Bullough, David, and Collins, Roger (eds), Basil Blackwell, Oxford

MacCulloch, Diarmaid, 2009, *A History of Christianity*, Allen Lane, London
McGilchrist, Iain, 2019, *The Master and His Emissary: The Divided Brain and the Making of the Western World*, Yale University Press, Germany
McKinney, Windy A., 2013, 'Creating a Gens Anglorum: Social and Ethnic Identity in Anglo-Saxon England through the Lens of Bede's Historia Ecclesiastica', PhD Thesis, York University, York
McLeod, Hugh, 2005, 'The Religious Crisis of the 1960s', *Journal of Modern European History / Zeitschrift für moderne europäische Geschichte / Revue d'histoire européenne contemporaine*, 3:2, 205–30
Milbank, Alison, 2023, *The Once and Future Parish*, SCM Press, London
Mill, J.S., 1865, *On Liberty*, Longman's, Green & Co., London
Modood, T., 2010, 'Moderate Secularism, Religion as Identity and Respect for Religion', *The Political Quarterly*, 81:1, 4–14
More, Hannah, 1791, *An Estimate of the Religion of the Fashionable World*, P. Wogan et al., Dublin
—, 1833, *The Works of Hannah More*, 6 vols, Fisher, Fisher & Jackson, London
Morris, Marc, 2021, *The Anglo-Saxons: A History of the Beginnings of England*, Hutchinson, London
Muller, Jerry Z., 2019, *The Tyranny of Metrics*, Princeton University Press, Germany
Naismith, Rory, and Woodman, David (eds), 2017, *Writing, Kingship and Power in Anglo-Saxon England*, Cambridge University Press, Cambridge
National Secular Society, 15 January 2020, 'Calls for Parliamentary Prayers Review after MP Compelled to Attend', at https://www.secularism.org.uk/news/2020/01/calls-for-parliamentary-prayers-review-after-mp-compelled-to-attend (accessed 16 October 2024)
NCVO, 2023, 'Volunteer Participation – Signs of Decline?', at https://www.ncvo.org.uk/news-and-insights/news-index/key-findings-from-time-well-spent-2023/#volunteer-participation-signs-of-decline (accessed 16 October 2024)
Nicholson, Adam, 2003, *Power and Glory: Jacobean England and the Making of the King James Bible*, HarperCollins, London
North, John, 2013, 'Medieval Oxford', ch.1, 37–50, in *Oxford Figures: Eight Centuries of the Mathematical Sciences*, Fauvel, John, Flood, Raymond, and Wilson, Robin (eds), Oxford University Press, Oxford
Norton, David, 2000, *A History of the English Bible as Literature*, Cambridge University Press, Cambridge
—, 2013, 'The KJV at 400: Assessing Its Genius as Bible Translation and Its Literary Influence', 3–28, in *The King James Version at 400: Assessing its Genius as Bible Translation and its Literary Influence*, Burke, D.G., et al. (eds), Society of Biblical Literature, Atlanta, GA

Office for National Statistics (ONS), 29 November 2022, 'Religion, England and Wales: Census 2021', ONS website, statistical bulletin, at https://www.ons.gov.uk/peoplepopulationandcommunity/culturalidentity/religion/bulletins/religionenglandandwales/census2021

Oliver, Simon, 2004, 'Robert Grosseteste on Light, Truth and "Experimentum"', *Vivarium*, 42:2, 151–80

Omrani, Bijan, 2017, *Caesar's Footprints: Journeys to Roman Gaul*, Head of Zeus, London

Orme, Nicholas, 2006, *Medieval Schools: From Roman Britain to Renaissance England*, Yale University Press, New Haven, CT, and London

—, 2022, *Going to Church in Medieval England*, Yale University Press, New Haven, CT, and London

Owen, Alex, 2006, 'The "Religious Sense" in a Post-War Secular Age', *Past and Present*, 1, supplement 1, 159–77

Owens, Susan, 2020, *Spirit of Place: Artists, Writers and the British Landscape*, Thames & Hudson, London

Paley, Morton D., 1989, 'The Art of "The Ancients"', *Huntington Library Quarterly*, 52:1, 97–124

Pantin, W.A., 1930, 'A Medieval Collection of Latin and English Proverbs and Riddles from the Rylands Latin MS 394', *Bulletin of the John Rylands Library*, 14:1, 81–114

Parker, Eleanor, 2023, *Winters in the World: A Journey through the Anglo-Saxon Year*, Reaktion Books, London

Partlett, David F., 2021, 'Tort Law and its Three Christian Pillars', ch.15, 254–74, in *Christianity and Private Law*, Cochran, Robert Jr, and Moreland, Michael (eds), Routledge, Abingdon

Partridge, Esmé, 2024, *Restoring the Value of Parishes: The Foundations of Welfare, Community and Spiritual Belonging in England*, Civitas, London

Pedersen, Olaf, 1998, *The First Universities: Studium Generale and the Origins of University Education in Europe*, Cambridge University Press, Cambridge

Pennington, Kenneth, 1998, 'Due Process, Community, and the Prince in the Evolution of the Ordo Iudiciarius', *Rivista internazionale di diritto comune*, 9, 9–47

—, 2003, 'Innocent until Proven Guilty: The Origins of a Legal Maxim', *The Jurist*, 63, 106–24

Pepinster, Catherine, 2022, *Defenders of the Faith: The British Monarchy, Religion and the Coronation*, John Murray Press, London

Perkin, Harold, 1969, *The Origins of Modern English Society*, Routledge & Kegan Paul, London

Perks, Stephen, 2013, *Christianity and Law: The Influence of the Development of Christianity on English Common Law*, Kuyper, Taunton

Petersen, Nils Holger, 2000, 'Les textes polyvalents du Quem quaeritis à Winchester au Xe siècle', *Revue de musicologie*, 86:1, 105–18

Plucknett, Theodore F.T., 1926, 'Bonham's Case and Judicial Review', *Harvard Law Review*, 40:1, 30–70

Pope, Alexander, 1996, 'The First Epistle of the Second Book of Horace Imitated' in Butt, J., *The Poems of Alexander Pope: A One Volume Edition of the Twickenham Pope*, Routledge, London

Poole, William, 2005, *Milton and the Idea of the Fall*, Cambridge University Press, Cambridge

Power, Amanda, 2006, 'A Mirror for Every Age: The Reputation of Roger Bacon', *The English Historical Review*, 121:492, 657–92

Power, E., 1922, *Medieval English Nunneries*, Cambridge University Press, Cambridge

Powers, Alan, 2019, 'Art, Faith and Modernity', Introductory essay, 11–28, in *Art, Faith and Modernity*, Llewellyn, S., and Liss, P. (eds), Liss Llewellyn, London

Prime Minister's Office, Press Release, 9 April 2023, 'The Prime Minister Rishi Sunak's Easter Message', at https://www.gov.uk/government/news/prime-minister-rishi-sunaks-easter-message-9-april-2023 (accessed 16 October 2024)

—, 1 March 2024, 'PM Address on Extremism', at https://www.gov.uk/government/speeches/pm-address-on-extremism-1-march-2024 (accessed 16 October 2024)

Prochaska, Frank, 2008, *Christianity and Social Service in Modern Britain: The Disinherited Spirit*, Oxford University Press, Oxford

Procopius, [*Vandalic War*] 1916, in *History of the Wars*, vol.2, Dewing, H.B. (trans.), Loeb Classical Library 81, Harvard University Press, Cambridge, MA

Pugin, Augustus, 1843, *An Apology for the Revival of Christian Architecture in England*, John Weale, London

Puttenham, George, [*Art of English Poesy*] 2007, *The Art of English Poesy*, Whigham, Frank, and Rebhorn, Wayne (eds), Cornell University Press, Ithaca, NY

Ramsay, James, 1784, *An Essay on the Treatment and Conversion of African Slaves in the British Sugar Colonies*, J. Phillips, London

Redgate, Anne Elizabeth, 2014, *Religion, Politics and Society in Britain, 800–1066*, Routledge, Abingdon

Reiss, Athene, 2008, 'Beyond "Books for the Illiterate": Understanding English Medieval Wall Paintings', *The British Art Journal*, Spring, 9:1, 4–14

Richter, Michael, 1984, 'Bede's Angli: Angles or English?', *Peritia*, 3, 99–114

Riehle, Wolfgang, 2014, *The Secret Within: Hermits, Recluses, and Spiritual Outsiders in Medieval England*, Scott Stokes, Charity (trans.), Cornell University Press, Ithaca, NY

Ripperger, M. Aloysia, 1934, 'George Crabbe as Social Critic of His Times', MA Thesis, Loyola University Chicago, Chicago, IL

Rogers, Pat, 2014, 'God's Judgment upon Hereticks: A "Lost" Satire on Thomas Woolston and Edmund Gibson', *The Review of English Studies*, 65:268, 78–98

Rollason, David, 2012, *Early Medieval Europe 300–1000: The Birth of Western Society*, Pearson, Edinburgh

Rolle, Richard, [*Fire of Love*] 1920, *The Fire of Love or Melody of Love and the Mending of Life or Rule of Living*, Misyn, Richard (trans.), and Comper, Francis (ed.), Methuen, London

Roman Catholic Church, November 2020, 'Investigation Report: Independent Inquiry on Child Sexual Abuse', at https://www.iicsa.org.uk/reports-recommendations/publications/investigation/roman-catholic-church.html (accessed 18 November 2024)

Routley, Erik, 1959, *The English Carol*, Oxford University Press, Oxford

Royal Holloway, 4 July 2024, 'Survey Finds that Nearly Half of Young People are Unhappy with UK Democracy', at https://www.royalholloway.ac.uk/about-us/news/survey-finds-that-nearly-half-of-young-people-are-unhappy-with-uk-democracy/ (accessed 16 October 2024)

Rumsey, Andrew, 2017, *Parish: An Anglican Theology of Place*, SCM Press, London

Ruskin, John, [*Modern Painters*] 1907, *Modern Painters*, vol.3, George Routledge & Sons, London

Russell, Josiah Cox, 1944, 'The Clerical Population of Medieval England', *Traditio*, 2, 177–212

Ryan, Robert, 2003, 'Blake and Religion', ch.8, 150–68, in *The Cambridge Companion to William Blake*, Eaves, M. (ed.), Cambridge Companions to Literature, Cambridge University Press, Cambridge

Scott, George Gilbert, 1858, *Remarks on Secular and Domestic Architecture Present and Future*, John Murray, London

Sheils, W.J., 2013, *The English Reformation 1530–1570*, Routledge, Abingdon

Sherlock, Peter, 2020, 'Monuments and the Reformation', ch.8, 168–84, in *Memory and the English Reformation*, Walsham, Alexandra, Wallace, Bronwyn, Law, Ceri, and Cummings, Brian (eds), Cambridge University Press, Cambridge

Sherwood, Harriet, 4 September 2017, 'More than Half UK Population has No Religion, Finds Survey', *The Guardian*, at https://www.theguardian.com/world/2017/sep/04/half-uk-population-has-no-religion-british-social-attitudes-survey

Shortt, Rupert, 2024, *The Eclipse of Christianity: And Why it Matters*, Hodder & Stoughton, London

Shyllon, F.O., 1977, *James Ramsay: The Unknown Abolitionist*, Canongate, Edinburgh

Sidney, Sir Philip, [*Selected Writings*] 2002, *Selected Writings*, Dutton, Richard (ed.), Routledge, New York

Skinner, Quentin, 1978, *The Foundations of Modern Political Thought*, vol.2: *The Age of Reformation*, Cambridge University Press, Cambridge

Slow, Oliver, 18 September 2023, 'Two Pubs a Day Disappearing in England and Wales', BBC News, at https://www.bbc.co.uk/news/uk-66839984 (accessed 18 November 2024)

Smith, Alan, 1967, 'The Cultivation of Music in English Cathedrals in the Reign of Elizabeth I', *Proceedings of the Royal Musical Association*, 94, 37–49

Smith, David Chan, 2017, 'Sir Edward Coke: Faith, Law and the Search for Stability in Reformation England', ch.5, 93–114, in *Great Christian Jurists in English History*, Hill, Mark, and Helmholz, R.H. (eds), Cambridge University Press, Cambridge

Smith, George, 1864, *History of Wesleyan Methodism*, Longman, Green, Longman & Roberts, London

Smith, Julia (ed.), 2000, *Early Medieval Rome and the Christian West: Essays in Honour of Donald A. Bullough*, Brill, Leiden

Smith, R.W., 1957, 'Religious Influences in the Background of the British Labour Party', *The Southwestern Social Science Quarterly*, 37:4, 355–69

Smith, Sydney, 1957, *Selected Writings of Sydney Smith*, Auden, W.H. (ed. and intro.), Faber & Faber, London

Smyth, Alfred, 1998, 'The Emergence of English Identity, 700–1000', ch.2, 24–52, in *Medieval Europeans*, Smyth, Alfred (ed.), Palgrave Macmillan, London

Snobelen, Stephen D., 2003, '"A Time and Times and the Dividing of Time": Isaac Newton, the Apocalypse, and 2060 AD', *Canadian Journal of History*, 38:3, 537–52

Sommerville, C. John, 1992, *The Secularization of Early Modern England: From Religious Culture to Religious Faith*, Oxford University Press, New York

Spencer, N., 2011, *Freedom and Order: History, Politics and the English Bible*, Hodder & Stoughton, London

—, 2024, *Magisteria: The Entangled Histories of Science and Religion*, Oneworld, London

Spiegel, Jayson L., 1984, 'Christianity as Part of the Common Law', *North Carolina Central Law Review*, 14:2, 494–516

Stanbury, Sarah, 2008, *The Visual Object of Desire in Late Medieval England*, University of Pennsylvania Press, Philadelphia, PA

Stark, Rodney, 1999, 'Secularization, R.I.P.', *Sociology of Religion*, 60:3, 249–73

Strong, Roy, 2007, *A Little History of the English Country Church*, Jonathan Cape, London

—, 2011, *Visions of England*, Bodley Head, London

Sytsma, David S., 2017, 'Matthew Hale as Theologian and Natural Law Theorist', ch.8, 163–86, in *Great Christian Jurists in English History*, Hill, Mark, and Helmholz, R.H. (eds), Cambridge University Press, Cambridge

Taylor, Jeremy, 1667, ΔΕΚΑΣ ΕΜΒΟΛΙΜΑΙΟΣ. *A Supplement to the* ΕΝΙΑΥΤΟΣ . . . *Sermons for . . . Explaining the Nature of Faith, and Obedience, in Relation to God, and the Ecclesiastical and Secular Powers Respectively*, R. Royston, London

Taylor, Martin, 1991, 'Mrs Donoghue's Journey', in *Donoghue v. Stevenson and the Modern Law of Negligence: The Paisley Papers: The Proceedings of the Paisley Conference on the Law of Negligence*, Burns, Peter T., Lyons, Susan J., and Continuing Legal Education Society of British Columbia (eds), Continuing Legal Education Society of British Columbia, Vancouver

Temperley, Nicholas, 1979, *The Music of the English Parish Church*, vol.1, Cambridge University Press, Cambridge

Thacker, Alan, 2000, 'In Search of Saints: The English Church and the Cult of Roman Apostles and Martyrs in the Seventh and Eighth Centuries', 247–78, in *Early Medieval Rome and the Christian West: Essays in Honour of Donald A. Bullough*, Smith, Julia (ed.), Brill, Leiden

Thomas, Keith, and Hessayon, Ariel, 2009, 'The Perception of the Past in Early Modern England', 181–218, in *The Creighton Century, 1907–2007*, Bates, D., et al. (eds), University of London Press, London

Thompson, Elbert N.S., 1921, 'Mysticism in Seventeenth-Century English Literature', *Studies in Philology*, 18:2, 170–231

Thuillier, Rosalind, 2015, 'Religious Subjects', ch.6, 81–106, in *Graham Sutherland: Life, Work and Ideas*, Thuillier, Rosalind, Lutterworth Press, Cambridge

Times, The, 24 January 2024, 'Rich are Getting Meaner with Charitable Donations', *The Times*, at https://www.thetimes.com/uk/article/rich-are-getting-meaner-with-charitable-donations-okfz9wzno (accessed 16 October 2024)

Tindal Hart, Arthur, 1959, *The Country Priest in English History*, Phoenix House, London

—, 1970, *The Curate's Lot: The Story of the Unbeneficed English Clergy*, J. Baker, London

—, 1980, *Some Clerical Oddities in the Church of England from Medieval to Modern Times*, New Horizon, Bognor Regis

Tombs, Robert, 2014, *The English and Their History*, Allen Lane, London

Tottel, Richard, 1557, *Songes and Sonettes* [also known as *Tottel's Miscellany*], Richard Tottel, London

Traherne, Thomas, [*Meditations*] 1948, *Centuries of Meditations*, Dobell, Bertram (ed.), P.J. and A.E. Dobell, London

University of Brighton, March 2022, 'Inclusive Language Guidance', at https://

cpb-eu-w2.wpmucdn.com/blogs.brighton.ac.uk/dist/e/8027/files/2022/07/Inclusive-Language-Guidance-1.pdf (accessed 16 October 2024)

Vaughan, William, 2015, *Samuel Palmer: Shadows on the Wall*, Yale University Press, London

Vetch, Frankie, 13 October 2024, 'The Canterbury Tales Given Trigger Warning over "Expressions of Christian Faith"', *The Telegraph*, at https://www.telegraph.co.uk/news/2024/10/13/canterbury-tales-trigger-warning-christian-faith-chaucer/ (accessed 16 October 2024)

Villers Committee, July 1854, *Report from the Select Committee on Public-Houses*, London

Vincent, Nicholas, 2017, 'Henry of Bratton (Alias Bracton)', ch.2, 19–44, in *Great Christian Jurists in English History*, Hill, Mark, and Helmholz, R.H. (eds), Cambridge University Press, Cambridge

Volokh, Alexander, 1997, '*n* Guilty Men', *University of Pennsylvania Law Review*, 146, 173–216

Wagner, Donald Owen, and Hunt, Erling Messer, 1930, *The Church of England and Social Reform since 1854*, Columbia University Press, New York

Wagner, Peter, 1907, *Introduction to the Gregorian Melodies: A Handbook of Plainsong*, part 1, The Plainsong and Medieval Music Society, London

Waite, Hannah, 2022, *The Nones: Who Are They, and What Do They Believe?*, Theos, London

Wallace-Hadrill, John Michael, 1971, *Early Germanic Kingship in England and on the Continent*, Clarendon Press, Oxford

Wallis, Faith, 2004, Introduction, in *Bede: The Reckoning of Time*, Wallis, Faith (ed. and trans.), Liverpool University Press, Liverpool

Walsham, Alexandra, 2011, *The Reformation of the Landscape: Religion, Identity, and Memory in Early Modern Britain and Ireland*, Oxford University Press, Oxford

—, 2020, 'Eating the Forbidden Fruit: Pottery and Protestant Theology in Early Modern England', *Journal of Early Modern History*, 24, 63–83

Ward-Perkins, Bryan, 2000, 'Why Did the Anglo-Saxons Not Become More British?', *The English Historical Review*, 115:462, 513–33

Watson, J.R., 1999, *The English Hymn: A Critical and Historical Study*, Oxford University Press, Oxford

Watts, Isaac, 1799, *Horæ Lyricæ: Poems, Chiefly of the Lyric Kind: in Three Books*, London

Waugh, Benjamin, 1873, *The Gaol Cradle: Who Rocks It?*, Stahan & Co., London

Weber, Benjamin, 2019, 'A Brief History of Anglo-Saxon Education', *History Compass*, 17:2, 1–13

Webster, Leslie, 2017, 'Anglo-Saxon Art: Tradition and Transformation', ch.2, 23–46, in *Transformation in Anglo-Saxon Culture: Toller Lectures on Art,*

Archaeology and Text, Insley, Charles, and Owen-Crocker, Gale R. (eds), Oxbow Books, Oxford

Weight, Richard, 2002, *Patriots: National Identity in Britain, 1940–2000*, Macmillan, London

Wesley, John, 1778, *Thoughts upon Slavery*, Joseph Crukshank, Philadelphia, PA

—, [*Journal*] 1909–16, *The Journal of the Rev. John Wesley*, Curnock, N. (ed.), Culley, London

Wigley, John, 1980, *The Rise and Fall of the Victorian Sunday*, Manchester University Press, Manchester

Will, Frederic, 1957, 'Blake's Quarrel with Reynolds', *The Journal of Aesthetics and Art Criticism*, 15:3, 340–49

Williams, Rowan, 2012, *Faith in the Public Square*, Bloomsbury, London

Winskill, R.T., 1892, *The Temperance Movement and Its Workers: A Record of Social, Moral, Religious, and Political Progress*, vol.3, Blackie, London

Witte, John Jr, 1987, 'Blest Be the Ties that Bind: Covenant and Community in Puritan Thought', *Emory Law Journal*, 36, 579–601

—, 2008, *The Reformation of Rights: Law, Religion and Human Rights in Early Modern Calvinism*, Cambridge University Press, Cambridge

Witte, John Jr, and Berman, Harold, 2017, 'The Integrative Christian Jurisprudence of John Selden', ch.7, 139–62, in *Great Christian Jurists in English History*, Hill, Mark, and Helmholz, R.H. (eds), Cambridge University Press, Cambridge

Witte, John Jr, and Hauk, Gary S. (eds), 2017, *Christianity and Family Law: An Introduction*, Routledge, Abingdon

Wolffe, John, 1994, *God and Greater Britain: Religion and National Life in Britain and Ireland, 1843–1945*, Routledge, Abingdon

Wolters, Clifton (trans.), 2018, *The Cloud of Unknowing*, Ixia Press, Mineola, NY

Wolterstorff, Nicholas P., 2011, 'Christianity and Human Rights', ch.2, 42–55, in *Religion and Human Rights: An Introduction*, Witte, J., and Green, M. Christian (eds), Oxford University Press, Oxford

Woodhead, Linda, 2016, 'The Rise of "No Religion" in Britain: The Emergence of a New Cultural Majority', *Journal of the British Academy*, 4, 245–61

Woodhead, L., and Catto, R. (eds), 2012, *Religion and Change in Modern Britain*, Routledge, Abingdon

Woolston, Thomas, 1729, *A Sixth Discourse on the Miracles of our Saviour*, Thomas Woolston, London

Worden, Blair, 2012, *God's Instruments: Political Conduct in the England of Oliver Cromwell*, Oxford University Press, Oxford

Wormald, Patrick, 1977, 'The Uses of Literacy in Anglo-Saxon England and its Neighbours', *Transactions of the Royal Historical Society*, 27, 95–114

—, 1983, 'Bede, Bretwaldas and the Origins of Gens Anglorum', ch.5, 99–129, in *Ideal and Reality in Frankish and Anglo-Saxon Society: Studies Presented to J.M. Wallace-Hadrill*, Wormald, Patrick, Bullough, David, and Collins, Roger (eds), Basil Blackwell, Oxford

—, 1999, *Legal Culture in the Early Medieval West: Law as Text, Image and Experience*, Hambledon Press, London

—, 1999a, *The Making of English Law: King Alfred to the Twelfth Century*, vol.1: *Legislation and its Limits*, Blackwell, Oxford

—, 2009, 'The Venerable Bede and the "Church of the English"', ch.1, 13–32, in *The English Religious Tradition and the Genius of Anglicanism*, Rowell, Geoffrey (ed.), Wipf & Stock Publishers, Eugene, OR

—, 2014, *Papers Preparatory to the Making of English Law: King Alfred to the Twelfth Century*, vol.2: *From God's Law to Common Law*, Baxter, Stephen, and Hudson, John (eds, posthumous publication), University of London, London

Wormald, Patrick, Bullough, David, and Collins, Roger (eds), 1983, *Ideal and Reality in Frankish and Anglo-Saxon Society: Studies Presented to J.M. Wallace-Hadrill*, Basil Blackwell, Oxford

Wulfstan, 1972, *Canons of Edgar*, Fowler, R. (ed.), Early English Text Society, Oxford University Press, London

Wymer, Norman, 1954, *Father of Nobody's Children: A Portrait of Dr. Barnardo*, Hutchinson, London

Yorke, Barbara, 2001, 'Political and Ethnic Identity: A Case of Anglo-Saxon Practice', ch.4, 69–89, in *Social Identity in Early Medieval Britain*, Frazer, William, and Tyrrell, Andrew (eds), Bloomsbury, London

—, 2003, *Kings and Kingdoms of Early Anglo-Saxon England*, Routledge, London and New York

YouGov, 18 June 2018, 'Young People are Less Proud of Being English than their Elders', at https://yougov.co.uk/politics/articles/20993-young-people-are-less-proud-being-english-their-el (accessed 16 October 2024)

Zimmermann, Augusto, 2014, 'Christianity and the Common Law: Rediscovering the Christian Roots of the English Legal System', *University of Notre Dame Australia Law Review*, 16, 145–77

Zosimus, [*New History*] 1982, *New History: A Translation with Commentary*, Ridley, R.T. (ed.), Australian Association for Byzantine Studies, Canberra

Index